Truth in Lending

FINANCIAL MANAGEMENT ASSOCIATION
Survey and Synthesis Series

Real Options: Managing Strategic Investment in an Uncertain World
Martha Amram and Nalin Kulatilaka

Beyond Greed and Fear: Understanding Behavioral Finance and the Psychology of Investing
Hersh Shefrin

Dividend Policy: Its Impact on Firm Value
Ronald C. Lease, Kose John, Avner Kalay, Uri Loewenstein, and Oded H. Sarig

Value Based Management: The Corporate Response to Shareholder Revolution
John D. Martin and J. William Petty

Debt Management: A Practitioner's Guide
John D. Finnerty and Douglas R. Emery

Real Estate Investment Trusts: Structure, Performance, and Investment Opportunities
Su Han Chan, John Erickson, and Ko Wang

Trading and Exchanges: Market Microstructure for Practitioners
Larry Harris

Valuing the Closely Held Firm
Michael S. Long and Thomas A. Bryant

Last Rights: Liquidating a Company
Dr. Ben S. Branch, Hugh M. Ray, Robin Russell

Efficient Asset Management: A Practical Guide to Stock Portfolio Optimization and Asset Allocation, Second Edition
Richard O. Michaud and Robert O. Michaud

Real Options in Theory and Practice
Graeme Guthrie

Slapped by the Invisible Hand: The Panic of 2007
Gary B. Gorton

Working Capital Management
Lorenzo A. Preve and Virginia Sarria-Allende

Asset Pricing and Portfolio Choice Theory
Kerry E. Back

Truth in Lending

Theory, History, and a Way Forward

THOMAS A. DURKIN
GREGORY ELLIEHAUSEN

OXFORD
UNIVERSITY PRESS

OXFORD
UNIVERSITY PRESS

Oxford University Press, Inc., publishes works that further Oxford University's objective of excellence in research, scholarship, and education.

Oxford   New York
Auckland   Cape Town   Dar es Salaam   Hong Kong   Karachi   Kuala Lumpur   Madrid
Melbourne   Mexico City   Nairobi   New Delhi   Shanghai   Taipei   Toronto

With offices in
Argentina   Austria   Brazil   Chile   Czech Republic   France   Greece   Guatemala   Hungary
Italy   Japan   Poland   Portugal   Singapore   South Korea   Switzerland   Thailand   Turkey
Ukraine   Vietnam

Library of Congress Cataloging-in-Publication Data

Durkin, Thomas A.
  Truth in lending: theory, history, and a way
  forward/Thomas A. Durkin, Gregory Elliehausen.
    p. cm.
  ISBN 978-0-19-517295-9 (hbk.: alk. paper)
1. Consumer credit—Law and legislation—United States.
2. Interest—Law and legislation—United States.
3. Disclosure of information—Law and legislation—United States.
I. Elliehausen, Gregory E. II. Title.
  KF1040.D87 2010
  346.7307'3--dc22   2010011240

1 2 3 4 5 6 7 8 9
Printed in the United States of America on acid-free paper.

Note to Readers
This publication is designed to provide accurate and authoritative information in regard to the subject matter covered. It is based upon sources believed to be accurate and reliable and is intended to be current as of the time it was written. It is sold with the understanding that the publisher is not engaged in rendering legal, accounting, or other professional services. If legal advice or other expert assistance is required, the services of a competent professional person should be sought. Also, to confirm that the information has not been affected or changed by recent developments, traditional legal research techniques should be used, including checking primary sources where appropriate.

(Based on the Declaration of Principles jointly adopted by a Committee of the American Bar Association and a Committee of Publishers and Associations.)

For Carolyn, Sarah, Catherine, and Molly
and
for Laurie and Lieselotte

Contents

Preface

In a January 2005 speech, Julie L. Williams, then Acting Comptroller of the Currency and chief regulator of national banks in the United States, warned of a looming failure of federal financial disclosure policy as a consumer protection (Williams 2005):

> Despite good intentions and enormous resources expended, it is not working as well as it should for consumers, and it is imposing unnecessary burdens on bankers.... And it's reached that point not because consumers are getting too little information, but because they are getting too much information that's not what they're really after; and because the volume of information presented may not be informing consumers, but rather obscuring what's most helpful to their understanding of financial choices.

Speaking further of the need for reforms, she spared no one from her finger-pointing:

> I respectfully suggest that just about every major participant in the process of developing, designing, implementing, overseeing, and evaluating consumer disclosures for financial products and services needs to rethink the approach to those tasks. This includes Congress, the regulators, the financial industry, and consumer advocates.

Williams' speech was not notable for any novelty of substance. Worries about the costs, and concerns that the benefits could become smothered by excessive requirements, are as old as the initial regulatory proposals. Rather, the significance of Williams's speech came from her willingness as a top regulator publicly to assign responsibility across the full spectrum of participants for the dire condition of consumer disclosures.

Was this mere bureaucratic blame shifting? About an hour and a half before listening to Williams' speech, one of the authors had just finished a draft of a paper that subsequently evolved into this book. At the time, it seemed to him that she was right about the substance as well as the blame. And her contentions still resonate years after her remarks: There *is* much that is valuable with disclosure as a consumer protection in the financial area, but there is much that has gone wrong as well. The degree to which such disclosures can protect consumers is still a matter of debate, and it deserves careful consideration. Indeed, the failure to produce a comprehensive and workable disclosure regime has caused many to question whether disclosure as a consumer protection is useful at all.

We strongly believe that the disclosure of information to consumers in the financial area — truth in finance — provides clear benefits. But the disclosure regime that has developed over the decades suffers from the burdens listed by Williams. And the fact that its problematic condition stems from a long history of efforts to improve it suggests that further attempts at reform can easily add to rather than reduce the problem.

Review, let alone reform, of financial disclosures as a consumer protection is a big job, and so this book necessarily concentrates on only a part of it, albeit, we think, the key part: the federal Truth in Lending Act (TILA), its associated regulations (Regulation Z, promulgated 1968–2010 by the designated rulewriting agency for TILA, the Federal Reserve Board [the FRB or the Board]), its goals, and its problems. This extensive and ever-controversial law is the centerpiece of federal financial consumer protection. Consideration of any needed reforms must start somewhere, and the TILA is a good choice. Experience with this law also has an important bearing on other areas of consumer finance, which we also discuss.

Importantly, the TILA has entered a new reform phase. The process began with an Advance Notice of Proposed Rulemaking from the FRB in late 2004, kicking off an effort that undoubtedly will last many years and may yield legislative recommendations. In 2008, the FRB enacted the first fruit of its effort — a massive rewrite of its TILA rules governing open-end (primarily credit card) credit, to become effective in 2010. Going forward, the new Bureau of Financial Consumer Protection that replaces the FRB as the TILA rule-writing agency in 2011 may propose many new rules. Unfortunately, despite some improvements, the 2008-2010 effort contains much that disappoints. And even this initial phase has taken half a decade and prompted congressional entry into the process with more legislation in 2009. So the legislative and regulatory review of disclosures to consumer and mortgage credit promises to stretch far into the future.

This book reviews the theory and history of truth in lending and arrives at principles that we think will allow us to avoid repeating the history of dysfunctional reform in this area. Despite the inevitable need to devote considerable space to the problems that have developed with disclosures, we think this book is optimistic: Disclosures are useful; improvements are possible; and so, in our view, it is time to get on with them.

Acknowledgments

In developing our viewpoint over the years, we have accrued large intellectual debts to many people. It is not possible to establish true *truth in borrowing* of the ideas here, but a few people deserve special mention. We have benefited greatly from many discussions about consumer credit matters with the late Robert Shay of Columbia University and Robert Johnson of Purdue University and in the consumer disclosure area with Ralph Rohner, former Dean of Catholic University Law School and the ongoing "dean" of the truth in lending field. We also thank J. Russell Ezzell, Pennsylvania State University; Michael Staten, University of Arizona; David Walker, Georgetown University; and Todd Zywicki of George Mason University School of Law.

Many of our current and former colleagues at the Federal Reserve Board, especially from the Division of Consumer and Community Affairs, cheerfully and generously gave their time to discuss these matters with us: Jane Ahrens, Krista Ayoub, Neil Butler, Glenn Canner, Leonard Chanin, Joseph Crouse, Griffith Garwood, Winthrop Hambley, Glenn Loney, Barbara Lowrey, Ellen Maland, James Michaels, Neal Peterson, Daniel Sokolov, John Wood, and Steven Zeisel. The same thanks extend to James Lacko and Janis Pappalardo of the Federal Trade Commission staff. Also from the Federal Reserve, we thank Gregg Forte and Christy Thomas for important help with both content and organization of the text and tables.

We also thank many other individuals in the lending and legal professions for helpful discussions and answers to questions over the years, including Dennis Young, formerly of Wells Fargo Financial; Robert McKew and Randy Lively, formerly of the American Financial Services Association; and many legal and operating personnel too numerous to mention individually. We thank all of you.

We heartily thank all of these individuals and state emphatically that none bears any responsibility for any errors of judgment or interpretation we have made here.

Foreword

The pendulum of American public policy for protecting consumer borrowers from abuse swings to and fro. In some decades, it is aggressively solicitous; in others, the direction is more *laissez faire*. At yet other times, the focus is on pricing, and at still other times it stresses restrictions on contract terms. The pattern of to and fro is irregular and variant, but it is relentlessly repetitive. If you want to see consumer protection policy standing on its head, wait a generation. Until the 1960s, consumers were protected mostly by price controls–usury laws. The federal Truth in Lending Act (TILA) of 1968 stressed protecting consumers by disclosure, and the 1970s became the decade of disclosure litigation gone wild. Over the next twenty years, the market was dramatically deregulated, and creditors were free to introduce almost any kind of consumer financial product, at any price, so long as it was disclosed according to regulatory specifications. Now, in the early decades of the twenty-first century, there are cries for tougher rules and more powerful enforcement of them, and it appears that freedom of contract will retreat somewhat in favor of more prescriptive regulation of consumer financial products. This recent shift in equilibrium traces directly to competitive credit card marketing and pricing practices, and to the vast production of toxic subprime mortgage loans that threatened to topple our financial system

Yet in almost any regime of consumer financial protection laws, the centerpiece remains, more or less, disclosure. In 1980, barely ten years

after TILA was enacted, Congress simplified and reformed the statute to
streamline the disclosure rules and curtail litigation over them. "More
disclosure is not necessarily better disclosure," said the United States
Supreme Court at the time (*Milhollin v. FMCC*). A few years later, though,
Congress was busy layering on new disclosure details, for credit card
solicitations, home equity lines of credit, high-priced residential mortgages, and more. Disclosure readily became the ground for political
compromise when the proponents of more restrictive or more relaxed
rules could not otherwise agree. A Treasury Department report from
2009 (*Financial Regulatory Reform, A New Foundation*) acknowledges the
current pro consumer strategy:

> Where efforts to improve transparency and simplicity prove
> inadequate to prevent unfair treatment and abuse, [a new fed-
> eral agency should] be authorized to place tailored restrictions
> on product terms and provider practices, if the benefits outweigh
> the cost.

A perfect economic paradigm: try disclosure, but when it does not
work, do not hesitate to regulate market practices directly under a financial efficiency test. This tug of war between disclosure and prescriptive
rules remains in play up to and including the current catharsis.

But what about disclosure? What can we expect in the way of consumer guidance from credit cost information presented in some fashion,
in some format, at some point or points in the negotiating and perform-
ing of often complicated financial transactions? The same 2009 Treasury
Department report begins optimistically:

> We propose a new proactive approach to disclosure. The [new
> federal regulatory agency] will be authorized to require that all
> disclosures and other communications with consumers be rea-
> sonable: balanced in their presentation of benefits, and clear and
> conspicuous in their identification of costs, penalties, and risks.

An admirable perspective, one might say — Out with the bad
disclosures, and in with the good ones. But what, pray tell, are we to
make of the forty years of TILA disclosure experience? Are we to junk it
all, and start over from scratch? TILA disclosures have been required to
be "clear and conspicuous" since 1969, so the new use of that phrase
must contemplate some new approach to disclosure *content* as well as
format; reasonable and balanced communication of information seems
to be called for. If reasonable disclosures are to be retained or created,

presumably we can identify *unreasonable* ones, and discard or avoid them. The problem, of course, is that it begs the question to posit proactive rules for customer communications that are reasonable, balanced, clear, and conspicuous, all at one time, for all the consumers affected by them. How do we decide which version of a disclosure will register or resonate across the spectrum of consumer sophistication and financial savvy? There are many obstacles to creating effective credit cost disclosures: from consumer financial illiteracy at one end, to abject customer disinterest, or merchant fraud, at the other. We have never quite settled whether and when TILA disclosures are passive sources of information, or some sharper form of warning. We are just beginning to appreciate that disclosures drafted by lawyers may not communicate as well as those tested with focus groups and behavioralists.

Above all, it seems to me, we need to ponder the conceivable purposes and goals of credit disclosure requirements, and decide how can we design — and measure the effectiveness of — disclosure rules likely to advance those goals without inconsistency, dense complexity, redundancy, and undue litigation exposure. Disclosure rules created even a few years ago, much less back in the 1970s, cannot possibly have optimum impact on a citizenry that communicates anywhere in the world, electronically and in real time.

I have admired the work of Drs. Durkin and Elliehausen for many years, and am delighted they have completed this enlightening book as a primer for anyone embarking onto the seas of truth in lending policy and implementation. The book is an elegantly written, stimulating compendium of thinking from an economist's perspective about the role of credit cost disclosure as a healthy market constraint. There is no comparable work in the field.

Ralph J. Rohner
Catholic University of America

Truth in Lending

1

The Evolution of the Truth in Lending Act: The Truth Can Be Hard to Handle

Before 1968, the regulation of consumer credit in the United States was primarily in the hands of the individual states, and they were less concerned with disclosing the cost of credit in a consistent way than with controlling the pricing and quality of credit services. Price controls came in the form of interest-rate ceilings—usury laws that still exist for some types of credit but are less restrictive than they once were. The states controlled the quality of credit services then, as now, through licensing and performance requirements for lenders. As for expressing and comparing credit costs, the states sanctioned various methods, and each method had its adherents and advocates. The federal government mostly did not consider credit regulation to be its responsibility, except during World War II and again in the late 1940s and during the Korean War, periods when Washington believed that curbs on consumer credit could help stabilize inflation (see Shay 1953).

By the early 1960s, disclosure methods in place usually permitted comparisons of credit costs within lender groups (that is, for example, among banks, or among credit unions, or among retail outlets), but not across lender group boundaries. According to one careful observer at the time, "The result of the varying disclosure practices is that consumers do not obtain easily comparable information from alternative suppliers of credit" (Mors 1965, p. 4). Likewise, a retrospective look at those years noted that "shopping for credit across industry lines was almost impossible" and this "helped create a climate favorable for legislation requiring uniform quoting of rates of charge" (National Commission on Consumer Finance 1972, p. 170).

On May 29, 1968, that climate brought to an end the mostly hands-off stance of the federal government — and the variety of legally sanctioned methods for expressing the cost of consumer borrowing — when President Johnson signed the Consumer Credit Protection Act of 1968. This act included the Truth in Lending Act (TILA) as its most important component; this provision became effective on July 1, 1969. TILA sought something new for the regulatory landscape: a nationwide mandate for disclosure of one mathematical conception of credit pricing that would be calculated similarly for all kinds of credit — the now ubiquitous annual percentage rate (APR).[1]

TILA and its innovation, the APR, had many advocates, but the 1968 legislation reflected the wisdom and stubbornness of one man: economist and three term United States Senator from Illinois, Paul H. Douglas (1892–1976). Before entering the Senate, Douglas had been a professor of economics at the University of Chicago and, in the year before his successful 1948 Senate campaign, president of the American Economic Association. By his own account, Douglas first came to form his thinking about truth in lending and an APR as early as the World War I period, well before the long-standing interest of economists in the importance of information became established in the branch of microeconomic theory now known as the economics of information.[2]

The Road to TILA: Calculating and Disclosing the Finance Charge

In the years before passage of TILA, the method of calculating the dollar amount of credit charges varied across industries and resulted in varying state disclosure requirements. In the automobile, furniture, and home repair industries, retail outlets preferred the simplicity of expressing the finance cost in terms of dollars and cents per hundred dollars of initial balance per year. Eventually, in many states, the legal ceilings for credit charges (usury laws) were stated in the same manner.[3] Creditors in states with such laws then had an incentive to continue using that method since, by doing so and by not using a rate above the allowed numerical limit, they would not violate the usury law.

If expressed in percentage terms, the measure of dollars and cents per hundred dollars of initial balance per year was known as an *add-on rate* because the result of that formula — the total finance charge — was added onto the loan principal to derive the total amount that would be paid over the life of the loan.

The only key piece of information missing from an add-on calculation was the actuarial annuity equivalent rate that applied to the declining unpaid balance over time, known then and now as the *effective rate*. A precise and detailed version of the effective rate became the APR later mandated under TILA. The effective rate on a loan allowed comparisons with interest rates on asset accounts like deposit accounts (although that comparison was not crucial for those who were not considering paying cash instead of borrowing). The add-on rate was approximately half the effective rate, because add-on rates apply to the original balance while the effective rates apply to the declining outstanding balance. Because of its simplicity as well as its placement in usury laws and in many state disclosure laws, the add-on rate survived as a *calculating rate* long after TILA replaced it for legal purposes of disclosure.

In fact, many retail managers and other observers argued that the add-on method was better than the effective rate for those legal purposes. The add-on formula was popular with creditors because the calculations they entailed were easy for employees to learn and use, and thousands of retail establishments used the formula daily. Many other adherents preferred add-on rates because even financially unsophisticated individuals with scant mathematical skills could use them in mental arithmetic to compute quickly the total finance charge and monthly payment on a proposed credit contract. A pencil and the back of an envelope were more than adequate for add-on calculations.

At an auto dealership, for instance, a consumer armed with the add-on rate could mentally calculate total cost and rough monthly payments while still outside in the car lot. To illustrate, someone looking at a three-thousand-dollar automobile purchase after down payment (a reasonable amount due on a substantial auto in the early 1960s) on a three-year contract at five dollars per hundred per year add-on rate (that is, a calculating rate of 5 percent per year of initial balance add-on) could easily and rapidly estimate the finance charge and monthly payment:

1. $3,000 × 5 percent = $150 per year for 3 years = $450 finance charge.
2. Then, $3000 + $450 = about $3,500. When divided by 36 = a bit under $100 per month for the payments. Using a pencil and envelope, actual monthly payments = $95.83.

Thus, with no mathematical heavy lifting, the consumer who knew the add-on dollars per hundred dollars financed per unit of time, very quickly had available all the key numbers for a credit use decision: the finance charge (credit cost), a rough estimate of the monthly payment, and a means of comparing credit costs across dealers (the add-on rate itself). Additional fees might complicate the transaction, but the math was still simple, never rising above the pencil and envelope level. After TILA, some observers even viewed add-on disclosures with nostalgic hindsight as a golden age of workable simplicity.

Another sort of calculating rate commonly quoted for disclosure purposes in the years before TILA was a monthly finance rate applied to a *current* balance, declining or not, and not to the original balance. A monthly rate could be multiplied by twelve to produce the annualized equivalent, which was sometimes also required to be stated. This calculating method typically was called the *"percent per month"* method.

This approach— annualizing a periodic rate applied to a current balance—is exactly the method used today to produce an APR for disclosure on an open-end account (such as credit card accounts) under TILA rules, although a daily rather than monthly rate has become more common in recent years. It is also the method used under some state laws to calculate the finance charge on so-called payday loans, a type of single payment loan in which the period to maturity varies according to the time of the borrower's next payday. The dollar amount obtained by multiplying the periodic rate by the credit balance is added to the credit balance, as with add-on calculations. Because the calculating rate is applied each period to the current balance, annualizing it is equivalent to the annual effective rate. But the periodic calculating rate cannot easily be used to calculate total finance charges or periodic payments on balances that decline under installment payments, especially if the payments are constant in size.

Before TILA, stating the periodic calculating rate on unsecured loans was common for finance companies and credit unions. In the early decades of the twentieth century, when finance companies were the most important source of consumer cash loans, the requirement appeared in the law of many states governing those firms. Credit unions became obliged to use the periodic calculating rate by the Federal Credit Union Act of 1934. Annualizing the calculating rate made it conceptually analogous to the effective rates applied to deposit accounts and compounded monthly, but neither the monthly rate nor its annual multiple was even roughly comparable to the add-on rates, which, at that time were common or required for goods financing.

To complicate matters still further, many state laws specified interest-rate ceilings on loans at consumer finance companies in a step-wise manner. The charge on the first $200 of loan might, for example, be calculated at a three percent monthly calculating rate, the next $300 at two percent, and any remaining amount at one percent per month. Calculating the finance charge and an effective rate on a $2,000 loan for two years with constant payment size became very complicated very quickly. Even experts had to use a multistage iterative process to determine the finance charges and payments on split-rate loans, which in some states involved up to four different rates. In addition, unlike with add-on rates, most consumers were unable to use percentage rates on a current balance to calculate total finance charges or periodic payments on balance that declined due to installment repayment, especially if the payments were constant in size. The calculation of such rates on the back of the envelope in the add-on manner would produce total finance charges roughly twice the correct calculation and bias calculated payment size upward. Required disclosure under such state laws typically consisted of stating the various monthly calculating rates on the components of the original balance.

The third basic calculating method for producing finance charges and making disclosures in the years before TILA involved a concept known as the *bank discount rate*. To determine the finance cost of a loan at this rate, a lender applied a percentage to an initial balance and multiplied the result by the number of years of the loan, as would be done with an add-on rate. But instead of adding the result to the borrowed amount, as would be done with the add-on method, the lender subtracted the resulting finance charge from the amount borrowed. This approach, which had been the familiar calculating method in the banking industry for commercial loans for centuries, produced an effective rate slightly higher than that of the add-on method for the same initial balance. (Because of the subtractions, the bank discount rate also has somewhat different mathematical properties than add-on rates as maturities lengthen.) When banks began to move more aggressively into consumer credit beginning in the 1930s, they applied the bank discount method of calculation to consumer lending.[4]

As with add-on rates, the bank discount rate attracted criticism as a disclosure term because, for installment payments, it was about one-half the effective rate. The calculations also were considerably more complicated than for the add-on method because of the subtraction of the interest from the principle at the outset. This meant the discount method had the same disadvantages for comparisons with deposit rates as the add-on method but without its consumer-friendly calculating simplicity. Nevertheless, many states enacting a rate ceiling adopted the bank discount method in bank cash lending.

Before TILA, no one used the measure that became the APR either as a calculating device or for disclosures — the math was widely considered to be too complicated. The mathematical difficulties prompted extensive academic and public discussions about what simpler algebraic formulas might produce acceptably close estimates (see, for example, Ayers 1946, Neifeld 1951, Johnson 1961, and Mors 1965 for discussions of the algebra of formulas such as the constant ratio method, the direct ratio method, and the minimum yield method). Today, computer power allows the practical use of APRs for both calculations and disclosures, but of course such computing power did not become widely available until decades after the passage of TILA.[5] Even so, the APR is very often produced today only for regulatory purposes after applying a calculating rate or other method of producing a finance charge and payment amount.

TILA Enters and Expands

Thus, the environment of consumer disclosure in the first half of the 1960s was one of multiple standards and a resistance to the APR as the most widely considered replacement. In 1960, Senator Douglas introduced the Consumer Credit Labeling Bill, which required a single percentage disclosure for the cost of credit, a percentage not well defined in the earliest version of the bill. Congressional committees held hearings on credit cost disclosure every year from 1960 to 1964 to explore these issues, but Douglas did not see enactment of the concept behind his bill before losing his 1966 bid for re-election.[6] On January 11, 1967, Senator William Proxmire of Wisconsin, Douglas' successor as chairman of the Senate Banking Committee, introduced Douglas' bill in a new form as the Consumer Credit Protection Act, with the Truth in Lending Act as Title I. In his introductory remarks, Senator Proxmire outlined his intention for credit price disclosure, focusing on full disclosure of the comprehensive unit price (Proxmire 1967, p. S1202).

> The first principle of the bill is to insure that the American consumer is given the whole truth about the price he is asked to pay for credit. The bill would aim at full disclosure of the cost of

credit so that the consumer can make intelligent choices in the marketplace.

The second principle is that the whole truth about the cost of credit really is not meaningfully available unless it is stated in terms that consumers in our society can understand. Without easy knowledge of this unit price for credit, it is virtually impossible for the ordinary person to shop for the best credit buy.

A third principle is that the definition of finance charge, upon which an Annual Percentage Rate is calculated, needs to be comprehensive and uniform. It needs to be uniform to permit a meaningful comparison between alternative sources of credit. The definition of finance charge also needs to be comprehensive in order to convey the true cost of credit.

Ultimately, the Truth in Lending Act achieved what Proxmire said he wanted: an extensive disclosure law that focuses on a comprehensive finance charge and a corresponding unit price – the annual percentage rate.

As the Congressional committees moved the legislation forward, the House, Senate, and Conference committees produced reports to explain the legislation and express the intentions of Congress. These reports exhibited both the simplicity of Proxmire's ideas for the bill and the underlying reason for their operational complexity.[7] According to the Senate report (United States Senate Committee on Banking and Currency 1967, P.1.):

> The basic purpose of the Truth in Lending bill is to provide a full disclosure of credit charges to the American consumer. The bill does not in any way regulate the credit industry nor does it prescribe ceilings on credit charges. Instead it requires that full disclosure of credit charges be made so that the consumer can deduce for himself whether the charge is reasonable.

This statement, and many others in the Congressional reports, makes it abundantly clear that, first, after full consideration over the better part of a decade, Congress intended the Truth in Lending Act to be a disclosure law and an information-based protection rather than a market-based protection that would regulate contracts and practices. It also shows that credit charges were the disclosures intended.

Second, it reveals the genesis of many later problems with TILA: the concept of full disclosure. Rather than concentrating on a few fundamental pricing disclosures that might be provided for a given purpose, the

Truth in Lending Act has always required much more. With that underlying conception, a potentially limited law quickly became very big and very complicated.

The Evolution of Disclosures Under TILA

The breadth of TILA's reach under *full disclosure* has meant that defining the credit costs to be disclosed — challenging enough — was only the start. From the outset, the law and its implementing regulations mandated wide range, scope, and detail in disclosure, all of which were specified by type of transaction. For example, the law and regulations require the disclosure of certain contract terms that do not directly involve credit pricing, such as security interests (collateral) and repayment terms. The law was apparently drafted under the assumption that more disclosure is necessarily better than less, and it and the relevant regulations sometimes seem to confuse pricing disclosures with broad consumer education efforts for consumer credit. In effect, the Truth in Lending Act has come to require consistency of disclosure for all information items that might conceivably be useful to someone, sometime. In conjunction with the diversity of consumer credit transactions and the penalties for violating the law or its regulations, the guiding principle of full disclosure undoubtedly has contributed substantially to TILA's operational complexity.

Douglas' original Consumer Credit Labeling Bill (S2755, January 7, 1960) required only two federal disclosures, namely, the total finance charge and the *simple annual interest*, not well defined in the original draft but apparently referring to an annual actuarial interest rate. The whole bill, including definitions and penalties, consisted of only three and one-half pages of large type. Congress's process of developing the 1967 bill introduced by Proxmire from the slim beginnings introduced by Douglas was called "accretive" by one researcher who has read the thousands of pages of hearings transcripts (Rubin 1991, p. 279):

> ...[T]he Subcommittee members tended to interpret any available information according to the internal dictates of their own [Subcommittee] debate, rather than the effects that the statute might ultimately generate. Consequently, they adopted an essentially reactive and accretive approach to statutory design; each argument had to be answered, and the easiest way to answer it was to add a new provision.

The accretive approach has continued in the years since then. As passed in 1968, the Truth in Lending Act filled more than thirteen printed pages in the Conference Committee report and included thirty separate sections. As the rule-writing agency designated to implement TILA, the Federal Reserve Board (FRB or the Board) promulgated Regulation Z. The original Regulation Z filled 30 pages in 98 separate sections plus a substantial supplemental booklet dealing with the calculation of annual percentage rates (APRs). Congress amended TILA in 1970, 1974, 1975, 1976 (twice), 1978, 1980 (major revision), 1981 (twice), 1982, 1984, 1987, 1988 (twice), 1992, 1993, 1994, 1995 (twice), 1996, 1997, and 1998. Congress then debated changes for the three Congresses from 1999 to 2004 before resuming amendments in 2005, 2008, and 2009. In 2007, even a Department of Defense appropriation act contained a provision that raised Truth in Lending issues concerning military service personnel (for review of this episode, known as the "Talent Amendment," see Edelman, Aitken, and Yballe 2008). At year-end 2008, TILA filled 55 double-column pages of small type (including the four pages on consumer leasing).

Further, the FRB has amended its Regulation Z more than fifty times, sometimes because of legislative action and other times at its own initiative.[8] In the *Code of Federal Regulations* (CFR) for January 1, 2009, the regulation measured almost 300 double-column pages of small type including twelve appendices, a lengthy official interpretation of the regulation by the Federal Reserve Board staff known as the *Commentary* (updated at least yearly), and a four-page *Joint Policy Statement* concerning restitution in cases of inaccurately disclosed annual percentage rates. In all, Regulation Z contains well over 125,000 words of complicated legalese, enough to fill a sizable book. In 1976, the Federal Reserve Board assigned a separate rule to consumer leasing, Regulation M, which by year end 2010 consisted of another fourteen pages in the CFR, plus its own *Commentary* of twelve more pages. The sheer mass of the Truth in Lending Act and its associated regulations, together with its technical nature and frequent changes, has generated an industry of lawyers, consultants, trade associations, and printing and software companies dedicated to aiding creditors in complying with TILA.

Probably most indicative of the early difficulties surrounding implementation of TILA was the number of times that Regulation Z was interpreted, both by the FRB itself and by the courts. In 1969, thirty-four official interpretations of the regulation were already in place a week before its effective date. A decade later, in June 1979, more than 13,000 TILA lawsuits had been filed in federal courts, about two percent of the federal civil caseload but up to 50 percent of the cases in some districts (see US Courts Administrative Office, 1979). The large flow of legal actions produced a seemingly unending and often inconsistent set of judicial decisions, interpretations, and reinterpretations, each of which could mandate costly new paperwork, procedures, and employee training. To settle arguments and reduce the uncertainty created by frequent litigation, by early 1980, the FRB and its staff had published more than 1,500 interpretations with varying degrees of legal authority. Even then, the agency could not prevent further judicial action or the resulting new legal directives, in large part because of the uncertain legal authority of the interpretations (Landers 1976, p. 567):

> As an interpretation of the statute the opinions have serious shortcomings that should preclude undue reliance on them. For example, the authors may range from the highest officers to low level staff personnel; it is unclear whether and to what extent the opinions are subject to intra agency review; they frequently state the facts sparsely or with great generality; the opinions are in response to a specific factual situation presented in the best possible light by the correspondent; their application to different factual situations may be unclear; and the opinions frequently state broad principles with little or no reasoning or support. The novelty and complexity of the Truth in Lending Act and the automatic penalties that accompany a violation have led many of those engaging in consumer transactions to place great weight on such staff opinions. In fact, staff opinions may have acquired an appearance of legitimacy that they might not otherwise possess.[9]

Total compliance with the law was difficult at best, given the almost continuous stream of amendments, interpretations, and court decisions in the decade after TILA's July 1, 1969, effective date, along with interacting changes in state laws affecting, for instance, interest-rate ceilings and security interests.[10] In 1979, the federal bank regulatory agencies reported that more than 80 percent of banks were not wholly in compliance, although most violations were judged "non substantive" or "technical" (Board of Governors of the Federal Reserve System 1979, pp. 10-11).[11] Ironically, much of the litigation over TILA in the late 1970s did not concern the disclosure of credit costs (that is, the total finance charge and the APR), which, according to Congress, were the original critical elements of the act. Notable among disputed areas in the late 1970s were the identity of the creditor (believe it or not!), security interest, disclosure of the allocation of loan proceeds, the acceleration clause, and rescission.[12]

The 1980 Simplification Act

As a result of the difficult legal conditions, a movement to simplify truth in lending gained support in the second half of the 1970s, with the hope of easing compliance burdens on creditors and reducing information overload for consumers. *Simplification* is, of course, a concept that is easy to support in principle, but strong differences of view may develop if the concept is defined more closely. Would simplifying mean, for example, a shorter regulation, a more complete regulation, a clearer regulation? Fewer, more, clearer, or better focused interpretations? In any case, by mid 1977, the idea of simplifying truth in lending had gained a measure of bipartisan support in the US Senate, even if not complete agreement on details. Simplification of TILA was also strongly urged in 1977 in the report of the Commission on Federal Paperwork (1977).

Encouraged as well by Proxmire and the FRB, and after four simplification bills were introduced in 1977, the Congress in 1980 adopted the Truth in Lending Simplification and Reform Act as part of the Depository Institutions Deregulation and Monetary Control Act of 1980 (Public Law 96–221). After a period of public comment, the FRB issued a completely revised Regulation Z, which became effective on April 1, 1982.

Many observers have questioned whether the 1980 amendments made meaningful improvements or even significant alterations to the disclosure scheme under TILA, but there is little doubt that the changes clarified many disputed legal issues. Among other things, the amendments provided for optional model forms to be issued by the FRB that would provide a legal safe harbor for creditors who used them correctly. The amendments also provided that civil liability would extend only to material disclosures that affected consumer shopping needs.[13]

Simplification did not dramatically slow the pace of change, however, or eliminate all the complexity of the Truth in Lending Act.[14] As already noted, Congress amended the act eighteen more times by 2009, and the regulation implementing it has changed many times as well. The FRB staff has replaced the 1,500 earlier interpretations with the Regulation Z official staff *Commentary*, which is more helpful to creditors but must be revised yearly.

The 2008–2010 Revisions

In late 2004, the Federal Reserve Board began a massive review and updating of Regulation Z. The first stage was a request for public comment on the need for reforms in the area of open-end unsecured credit (mostly credit card credit). A second request for public comment issued in October 2005 concerned TILA changes required under the Bankruptcy Abuse Prevention and Consumer Protection Act of 2005 (Public Law 109-8, April 2005).

In June 2007, after considering the responses to those two requests, the Board issued a reform proposal comprising the most extensive set of changes to Regulation Z since the revisions in response to the 1980 Truth in Lending Simplification and Reform Act. Moreover, leaving aside the revisions required by the 2005 bankruptcy act, it was also the most extensive revision without specific legislative requirement since the effective date of the original Regulation Z on July 1, 1969. The Board issued the final rules in December 2008, with an effective date of July 1, 2010.[15]

The amount of material associated with the 2008 disclosure changes — which, again, concerned only open-end credit — was almost overwhelming. As released at the Federal Reserve Board meeting at which the changes were approved, new text to Regulation Z occupied 159 typed pages plus 266 pages of official *Commentary* (interpretations), 16 new model forms for open-end creditors, and 611 pages of *Supplementary Information* (explanations), for a total of well over 1,000 pages of new legal material. In addition, the Board approved, at the same time, 121 pages of new text and three model forms involving changes to Regulation E (Electronic Fund Transfers), 369 pages regarding credit card operations under Regulation AA (Unfair or Deceptive Acts or Practices), and 43 pages and a model form for Regulation DD (Truth in Savings).

Despite the vast quantity of material for creditor attorneys to digest (or choke upon), the issues were not even settled. Congress apparently was still not satisfied and in May 2009 passed further revisions to TILA requirements in precisely the same areas, necessitating additional regulatory effort, public comment periods and regulatory revisions.

Under the revisions to Regulation Z promulgated in 2008 and 2009, credit card issuers had to alter virtually every aspect of their credit card programs in significant ways to implement the required changes in disclosures for solicitations, account opening statements, periodic statements, change in terms notices, and advertisements. Timing rules for many disclosures also changed. Every computer system required major reprogramming, and every contact with consumers was influenced, necessitating retraining of every customer contact employee. The complexity required large amounts of legal and management time to understand, evaluate, and implement. (There is a bit more discussion of required changes in Chapter 6, "The Outlay and Unknown Future Events Issues: Open-End Credit.")

The 2008–2009 revisions raised with renewed force the question of whether the information- based approach to consumer protection in the area of finance is still viable. Can a way forward be mapped that would narrow rather than expand the vast scope of the law that now seems so burdensome, while at the same time improving its outcomes? In the remainder of the book, we will look in detail at the justification for the information-based approach, consider the evidence regarding the effectiveness of TILA in bringing that approach to the marketplace, and propose some guiding principles for reform that may lead to a more effective law.

Overview of Book

With these objectives in mind, the book explores the theory, goals, potential benefits, outcomes, and difficulties of consumer finance disclosure programs, focusing especially but not exclusively on the federal Truth in Lending Act.[16] Aimed at informed lay readers and other interested observers, this book also gives a nontechnical summary of the research on these questions, reports some previously unpublished empirical findings, and recommends areas for additional research and study. At the end, the book offers some suggestions for improvements to the process of establishing disclosure requirements and to the requirements themselves.

Chapter 2, "Disclosures in the Regulatory Scheme," suggests some reasons why disclosure has been a popular means of consumer protection, and Chapter 3, "Why Disclosures?" reviews theories of information that underlie the use of information-based protections. The latter chapter looks at the economics of information as well as theories from the provinces of psychology and consumer behavioral science. These theories from economics and psychology form the intellectual basis for approaching consumer protection through disclosures, so they have a key role in this story.

Chapters 4 to 7 examine the federal Truth in Lending Act. In many ways, this law is the centerpiece of federal financial disclosure requirements, and much of the evidence about financial disclosures concerns this rule. Chapter 4, "What is Truth in Lending? Key Conceptual Problems Facing the Truth in Lending Act," looks at a central problem in drafting disclosure requirements: both the components and outcome of a transaction, and consumers' individual needs for further information are difficult to know at the time that disclosures must be given. The attempts to overcome that problem underlie much of the extensive, highly legalistic, and complicated consumer disclosures in the financial area, including in the Truth in Lending Act.

Chapters 5, "The Outlay and Unknown Future Events Issues: Closed-End Credit," and 6, The Outlay and Unknown Future Events Issues: Open-End Credit," present examples of anomalies and legal controversies that have arisen with the Truth in Lending Act on account of the problems laid out in Chapter 4. In some cases, the examples lead to the conclusion that another disclosure approach might be better, more effective, or less expensive; or even all three. In other instances, the examples merely illustrate the difficulties that arise from continuous, undisciplined tinkering with the requirements.[17]

Chapter 7, "The Rubber Meets the Road: Evaluating the Effectiveness of the Truth in Lending Act," looks at the empirical evidence, albeit limited, that researchers have assembled over the years on the impact of the law relative to the underlying goals that have been suggested for it. The findings are interesting and also suggest the possibility of substantial further research.

Finally, Chapter 8, "Suggestions for a Way Forward," offers some suggestions for reforming and modernizing TILA and, by implication, other consumer financial regulatory laws as well.

2

Disclosures in the Regulatory Scheme

Credit for individuals has been in use — and regulated — since the earliest days of recorded antiquity, and probably well before that. Credit regulation began at least with the laws of ancient India and Babylon, but it probably started much earlier with nomadic hunter-gatherer chieftains who desired to straighten out borrowing and lending misunderstandings and abuses among clan and tribe members. In the United States, credit regulation began in the colonial period with the adoption of England's legal system, and it continued after the American Revolution, expanding its geographic reach with the westward migration of settlers.

Throughout American financial history through World War II, mortgage and consumer credit was often hard to obtain, but since 1945, the amount of outstanding credit subject to regulation has taken on massive proportions. Interestingly, however, the postwar growth of credit has not been nearly as large as is often believed when measured in real (inflation-adjusted) terms. It is reasonable to assume that a complete return to a peacetime economy, occurred by 1955 following the Korean War. Calculating real compound annual growth rates from that year to 2008, mortgage credit grew 5.2 percent annually and consumer credit 3.9 percent. Both amounts actually declined in 2009.

But it is the sheer size of credit outstanding and its pervasiveness in modern life that keeps issues of government oversight near the center of the political agenda. In current dollars, mortgage debt outstanding at the end of 2009 amounted to $10.3 trillion, and that of consumer credit (including credit card loans and loans for education, vehicles, and mobile homes) stood at $2.5 trillion (Table 2.1). Virtually all domestic households use some variety of mortgage or consumer credit at one or more important points in their financial lifetimes.

Table 2.1 Selected Measures of Assets, Debts, and Income of American Consumers, Selected Years, 1945–2009

	1945	1955	1965	1975	1985	1995	2005	2009
	Current dollars (billions)							
Disposable personal income[a]	152	283	498	1,187	3,079	5,457	9,277	11,050
Total assets	678	1,531	2,787	5,656	16,040	32,106	69,510	66,326
Financial assets	516	1,015	1,954	3,664	9,964	21,520	43,848	45,115
Deposits	104	172	373	908	2,526	3,357	6,155	7,750
Other financial	411	843	1,580	2,756	7,438	18,163	37,193	37,365
Total liabilities	30	144	352	761	2,368	5,038	12,157	14,001
Home mortgages	19	88	219	459	1,450	3,319	8848	10,262
Consumer credit	7	43	98	207	611	1,168	2,321	2,481
Other liabilities	5	13	35	95	308	551	989	1,258
Net worth	647	1,390	2,436	4,595	13,762	27,067	57,353	52,325
	2009 dollars (billions)							
Disposable personal income[a]	1,814	2,266	3,390	4,734	6,139	7,681	10,189	11,050
Total assets	8,076	12,252	18,980	22,550	31,976	45,188	76,344	66,326
Financial assets	6,143	8,126	13,304	14,610	19,862	30,289	47,610	45,115
Deposits	1,241	1,380	2,542	3,621	5,035	4,725	6,760	7,750
Other financial	4,901	6,746	10,762	10,988	14,827	25,564	40,850	37,365
Total liabilities	361	1,152	2,394	3,034	4,721	7,091	13,353	14,001
Home mortgages	222	704	1,494	1,830	2,890	4,671	9,717	10,262
Consumer credit	81	343	664	825	1,217	1,644	2,549	2,481
Other liabilities	58	105	236	378	614	776	1,086	1,258
Net worth	7,715	11,100	16,586	19,517	27,256	38,097	62,991	52,325

Source: Federal Reserve Board Statistical Release Z1, "Flow of Funds Accounts of the United States," various issues. Figures shown are year-end, not seasonally adjusted. Table excludes assets but not liabilities of nonprofit organizations, thereby somewhat understating consumer sector net worth.
[a]Measured at annual rate. All other amounts are year-end, not seasonally adjusted.
Adjustments to 2009 dollars are made using the Consumer Price Index for All Urban Consumers (CPI-U). Components may not add exactly to totals due to rounding.

The Federal Reserve Board's (FRB's or the Board's) periodic *Survey of Consumer Finances* shows that three-fourths of households had some kind of credit outstanding at the time of the most recent survey, in 2007 (Table 2.2). Almost half of domestic households had housing-related credit outstanding, and almost two-thirds of households owed on consumer credit. Survey results show that the bulk of consumer credit supports the purchase of important consumer durable investment goods and services like automobiles, appliances, home repairs, and education (Table 2.3).[1]

Types of Consumer Protections

Governments, over the years, have tried various approaches to protecting consumers in their financial and other transactions. One approach with a long history is *direct regulation of product content*. To a large extent, this is the approach of the Food and Drug Administration (FDA) and the Consumer Product Safety Commission, among others. In the financial area, content regulation involves any governmental intervention in financial services contracts, such as the imposition of interest-rate ceilings or maximum maturities on loans. Maturity limits and rate ceilings have long been used at the state level. A well-known example of content regulation at the federal level is the Federal Trade Commission (FTC) Credit Practices Rule, which limits a variety of credit contract provisions involving creditors' remedies to consumers' defaults.

A second approach to consumer protection is the *direct regulation of the market conduct of firms* offering products or services. For consumer financial services, this approach includes limiting the pressures imposed on consumers both by salespersons and operating personnel, and debt collectors. Much of the credit law at the state level adopts the conduct approach, as does the federal Fair Debt Collection Practices Act. In addition, many of the other federal financial regulatory statutes put in place since 1968 include such regulation. For example, the Equal Credit Opportunity Act regulates the conduct of financial service providers by prohibiting them from discriminating against credit applicants on the basis of the applicant's sex, marital status, race, and a number of other factors. Likewise, the Fair Credit Reporting Act carefully regulates the record keeping of credit-reporting agencies, typically known as credit bureaus.

Table 2.2 Proportions of Households Using Credit, 1951–2007 (in Percent)

Type of credit	1951	1956	1963	1970	1977	1983	1989	1995	2001	2004	2007
Closed-end installment credit	32	45	50	49	49	41	44	45	44	46	46
Note:											
Have auto credit (part of closed-end installment credit)	26	21	26	29	34	28	33	31	34	35	34
Credit card with revolving balance[a]				22	34	37	40	47	44	46	46
Notes:											
Have any credit card[a]				51	63	65	70	74	76	75	73
Have bank-type credit card				16	38	43	56	66	73	71	70
Have revolving balance on bank-type credit card				6	16	22	29	37	39	40	41
Consumer credit[b]	46	53	59	54	61	61	62	64	63	64	66
Mortgage credit[c]	20	24	32	35	40	39	38	39	42	45	46
Consumer credit or mortgage credit	53	62	67	64	70	69	70	72	73	75	75

Source: Data from the Surveys of Consumer Finances.

[a]In 1995–2007 includes a few respondents with open-end retail revolving credit accounts not necessarily evidenced by a plastic credit card.

[b]Closed-end installment credit, open-end installment credit (including credit card accounts and unsecured lines of credit), and noninstallment credit (excluding credit for business or investment purposes).

[c]Includes home equity credit and home equity lines of credit with a balance outstanding.

Table 2.3 Consumer Installment Credit by Purpose of Credit Use, 1951–2007

Type of Credit	1951[a]	1956[b]	1963[b]	1970[c]	1977	1983	1989	1995	2001	2004	2007
Percent of households using consumer installment credit											
Closed-end installment credit											
Automobiles	26	21	26	29	34	28	33	31	34	35	34
Nonauto durables		30	22		14	10	9	7	5	3	5
Home improvement	3	6	6		6	5	3	2	1	1	1
Education					2	2	5	12	11	13	15
Mobile homes					2	2	2	2	2	2	2
Other	7	7	25	37	12	7	7	6	4	4	5
Any closed-end installment	32	45	50	49	49	41	44	45	44	46	46
Revolving credit account with balance				22	34	37	40	47	44	46	46
Closed-end or revolving installment credit	32	45	50	54	59	58	59	64	62	64	65
Shares of outstanding balances on consumer installment credit by purpose (percent of total)											
Closed-end installment credit											
Automobiles	67	60	57	53	60	47	55	43	45	41	35
Nonauto durables		23	13		5	6	7	4	3	3	5
Home improvement	8	8	7		6	8	3	3	1	1	1
Education					1	3	5	16	19	21	25
Mobile homes					8	9	5	6	7	6	5
Other	25	9	23	42	9	5	5	3	2	6	3
Revolving credit account with balance				6	11	23	20	26	23	22	27
Closed-end or revolving installment credit	100	100	100	100	100	100	100	100	100	100	100

Source: Data from the Surveys of Consumer Finances.

[a]In 1951, category *automobiles* also includes nonauto durable goods; category *other* also includes education and mobile homes.

[b]In 1956 and 1963, category *other* also includes education and mobile homes.

[c]In 1970, category *other* also includes nonauto durable goods, home improvements, education, and mobile homes.

Improving the flow of information is a third approach to consumer protection. The approach ranges from passive efforts — such as the removal of constraints on advertising by professionals such as accountants, doctors, and lawyers — to specific, direct attempts to improve the availability of information. Examples are publishing comparative price information in the newspaper or on the Internet and requiring specific, detailed disclosures about certain goods or services. Affirmatively suppressing information regarded as misleading or otherwise harmful, including attacking false advertising, is another active approach. The Truth in Lending Act (TILA) and some other important federal initiatives go beyond general information approaches and instead mandate specific information disclosures for particular transactions.

In the financial area, the problem of incomplete information underlies much of the demand for consumer finance protections. If consumers were always aware of and fully understood the implications and consequences of what they were doing in their marketplace transactions, presumably they would always make the right choices and need little further protection of any sort. But some consumers do not always fully understand all transactions, future outcomes are unknown, and consumers sometimes make mistakes, even getting themselves into serious difficulties. Even small misunderstandings and mistakes often generate calls for consumer protection.

In fact, mandatory information disclosure has become the core approach to consumer finance protection in the United States at the federal level. In broad outline, federal statutes specify disclosures for the following:

- Consumer credit prices and terms
- Mortgage lending
- Credit denials and restrictions
- Credit reporting
- Consumer leasing
- Deposits
- Electronic funds transfers
- Securities and mutual fund purchases
- Institutional privacy policies
- Geographical lending patterns of financial institutions

In most areas, the requirements are extensive and often complicated, sometimes involving multiple laws and rules. Taken together, the disclosure requirements involve hundreds of pages of detailed regulations, enforced by a slew of federal agencies. The Truth in Lending Act alone has assigned enforcement responsibilities to nine separate federal agencies (Section 108).

Advantages of Disclosures

The dominance of information-based protections for consumers at the federal level can be attributed to the advantages they bring in four areas: the support of market forces, alignment with the problem of weak information in the marketplace, avoidance of conflict with state approaches, and relatively low cost. Individually and together, these perceived advantages have influenced the spread of the disclosure method.

First, disclosure requirements are compatible with existing market forces already at work to protect consumers. Consequently, supporters of these disclosures argue that the requirements enhance the benefits of market processes rather than change or undermine them. The marketplace already provides incentives for institutions to make their products known, disclose favorable pricing and product features, and treat consumers fairly so as to acquire a good reputation and generate referrals and repeat business. Freely providing useful pricing and product information is one way firms respond to such incentives, often through advertising.

To assist the process, required disclosures can mandate standardized product measures such as the finance charge and annual percentage rate (APR) under the Truth in Lending Act, that make financial comparisons easier for consumers. Mandatory standards can enhance the power of existing market incentives to provide information, thereby advancing consumers' learning process by lowering its cost and making it more efficient. Required disclosures in a standard format help highlight the performance of the best institutions and expose the inadequacies of the poorer ones.

Second, if the consumer's problem in the marketplace for credit is a lack of information about pricing or terms of consumer credit contracts, for example, then it seems more reasonable to require the disclosure of the information than to regulate prices or contract terms directly. Providing information rather than directly intervening does not require that government agencies know or presume to know the product feature preferences of all consumers. Providing information thus avoids the market disruptions that arise from direct interventions such as the regulation of interest rates and other contract terms. In contrast, direct interventions can reduce consumers' choices, create shortages in the marketplace, stifle innovation and competition, and cause other disruptions (for further discussion, see, for example, Durkin 1993). With disclosures, consumers can decide for themselves what their own preferences are in the tradeoff between price and product features, and the success of the disclosure approach does not depend on consumers' preferences being the same.

A third advantage is that it is relatively easy to layer federally mandated disclosures on top of state consumer protection laws without forcing widespread changes to the long-standing legal approaches of the individual states. Federal legal theories that force the rewriting of state statutes, if put into action, are likely to engender more political opposition than the layering approach.

Fourth, in principle, the required disclosures carry a relatively low cost, both in terms of market disruption and expenditures for implementation and enforcement. Granted that the plethora of laws and regulations that now exist seems to cast doubt on this advantage, the anticipation of lower costs from disruption has undoubtedly been instrumental in encouraging the adoption of disclosures. Frequently, disclosure has been the political compromise between the supporters and opponents of consumer protection. The latter insist that such protection is either an unnecessary or harmful intrusion upon the operation of a market-based system.

Both arguments have been influential, regardless of which is stronger, or by whom and how they are supported. Chapter 3, "Why Disclosures?" examines at greater length some more specific theoretical reasons why financial disclosures have attracted so much attention and intellectual support.

3

Why Disclosures?

Fundamentally, the theoretical underpinnings for requiring disclosures as consumer protections arise from the economics of information. This is the branch of economic analysis that explores whether free markets left to themselves will provide market participants with enough information to ensure optimal outcomes. For consumer protection policy, the concern is especially with unequal information available to market participants, a situation known as *asymmetric information*. Asymmetric information could lead to market failures for consumers in that, even in an otherwise competitive marketplace, they might not always obtain the lowest possible price for a given set of product characteristics. Enter mandatory disclosures.

However, researchers, including economic theoreticians, have long understood that consumers do not base purchase decisions only on the optimization metrics central to traditional economic theory. Other factors clearly also exercise significant influence on consumers' choices of products and brands, including idiosyncratic internal motivations and environmental, cultural, and other external influences. For analytical and model building purposes, however, economic theory usually subsumes such considerations into discussions of preferences, tastes, and utility functions whose distributions and properties are assumed to be given and largely constant. But focusing solely on price and quality and downplaying the rest of the range of motivations for economic behavior seems unsatisfying. There certainly is more to the buying process, as marketers are well aware.[1]

This chapter will review both the economic optimization theories that point to a need for information disclosures and the newer behavioral analyses that portray that need in the context of a richer account of consumer decision-making.

The Economics of Information

Presumably, disclosures should improve the problem of asymmetric information. Disclosures should enhance *market transparency*, defined by Maynes (1986, p. 61) as "a condition in which consumers 'see through' markets and accurately discern *all* the relevant magnitudes—the existence of products, product varieties (brand-model combinations), retailers, prices, qualities."

This definition illustrates the reason for widespread concern over asymmetric information in the area of consumer protection: Consumers without sufficient information might make the wrong choices, and markets might not provide the most desirable products and features. If individuals cannot see through markets, that is, if information on market conditions is not available or is not used, then consumers might not make the best possible purchase decisions, and markets themselves might not function well. Thus, lack of knowledge of products, varieties, retailers, market prices, or qualities clearly could easily lead to unsatisfactory outcomes. Consumers may pay prices that are too high for the quality of the chosen product or may choose products with characteristics that do not best address their needs. Because of its obvious significance, market transparency has become an important issue for consumer protection policy in the United States and in many other countries over the past few decades.

Perfect Information

Careful exploration of the implications of incomplete information is relatively new in the long history of economics, with its real beginnings only in the 1960s, the decade in which the Truth in Lending Act (TILA) was born. Although economists recognized that consumers' and producers' information was limited, the theoretical discussions and models economists developed typically assumed that both consumers and producers possessed complete knowledge of market prices, retailers, and product characteristics, a condition that economists call perfect information. In this environment, consumers could choose their purchases to maximize utility subject to existing prices and their budget constraint. Producers would price their output depending upon their costs and the competitiveness of the market structure.

Within this framework, economists' explorations included the important issue of market structure and its effect on pricing and the functioning of markets. In an outcome important for consumer protection, theorists concluded that competitive markets maximized consumer welfare because they produced the lowest possible price for a product. Economists did not explicitly contend that information was perfect in the real world, but they did not explore in detail how violation of this information assumption might invalidate the conclusions of their theoretical models of the operations and outcomes of market processes.

Homogeneous Products

Significantly, traditional economic theory further concluded that, under most conditions, a given market structure would offer consumers a *single* price for any *homogeneous product* (that is, a product with the same characteristics regardless of seller). This would be true whether the market structure was competitive (many sellers), or under monopoly (one source) or oligopoly (a few). Such a conclusion offers an immediate and obvious corollary for consumer protection policy: If there is only one price (whether known to all or not), there is no need for costly government-mandated disclosure requirements for prices. But, how would a single price come about, especially if there are many independent sellers, each of which sets its own price?

The answer followed directly from the information assumption of the theory: If consumers have perfect information, they will know when firms try to price above the marginal cost of a product because they will know about other sellers charging less. Industry dynamics then follow the route mapped in the basic textbook: Firms with prices above the equilibrium market price soon will have no customers and be forced either to lower prices or leave the industry. If all firms try to raise prices above the equilibrium price determined by supply and demand, even through collusion, they will still not be able to make the higher price stick. If necessary, new producers will enter the industry to take away business from those charging noncompetitive prices (and earning abnormal profits), unless all potential new producers can be convinced to join and stick with the cartel, an unlikely outcome, especially in the long run.

Consequently, in the long run, if everything is variable, including entry and exit from the industry, no seller of a homogeneous product or service can charge a price above the market equilibrium price; entry and reactions in the marketplace drive prices back down. On the opposite side, pricing below the market equilibrium price would be unprofitable and would cause any firms doing so to go out of business, eliminating the lower price. The competitive market with full information produces a single price known to all.

In monopolistic (one seller) or oligopolistic (few sellers) market situations, there still would not be any need for disclosure policies. In both cases, barriers to new entry, including the cost structures of existing sellers, regulation, or other market features, prevent the arrival of new sellers. Protected in this way, monopolists and oligopolists could raise prices above production costs and restrict output, enabling them to earn a higher return than under competitive conditions. Under conditions that characterize markets for consumer financial products, however, there still would be only one price, as long as there is still perfect information. The monopolistic situation would involve one price since there is only one seller and, in most cases, no reason to charge more than one price.[2] Describing the oligopolistic case is somewhat more complicated, but under reasonable assumptions about market conditions for consumer financial services, oligopoly would also normally involve a single price.[3] Consequently, in competitive, monopolistic, or oligopolistic situations with perfect information and a homogeneous product, it seems that there is little room for price disclosure policy to enhance consumer well-being.

Heterogeneous Products

Analyzing consumer protection in a market for a homogeneous product with perfect information is a trivial issue, however, since it is not realistic. Leaving aside the matter of the perfect information assumption, most goods and services are not homogeneous, that is, existing in only one form without varieties. Rather, most goods and services come in an array of related varieties, each with its own characteristics and price. It is obvious, in the marketplace, that there is really not a single market for most products, but rather a corresponding array of submarkets, one for each variety.

Related products, but with different features or combinations of characteristics, are called *differentiated* or *heterogeneous* products, and a moment's reflection shows why they do not have to sell for the same price. Heterogeneous characteristics mean that the varieties will appeal differentially to the potential range of customers. They may also have different production costs. In effect, the multiple prices reflect different demands for product characteristics as well as different production technologies and costs (such as, for financial products, variations arising from different risks).

Thus, even with perfect information, varieties do not have to sell for the same price because demand, supply, and market conditions for the different varieties are not the same. Some people may prefer Cadillacs, for example, or cars with Cadillac characteristics may be more costly to produce than Chevrolets, or both. This allows multiple prices in the markets for (heterogeneous) cars, however, as Cadillacs and Chevrolets sell for different prices.

Likewise, interest rates on loans also can vary as either demand or supply (or both) differs for loans with different characteristics; for example, alternate degrees of riskiness or different amounts of necessary processing. Consequently, the range of demands, costs, and market power of sellers can produce an assortment of prices from a grouping of related but differentiated products. Even if the submarket for each is competitive, which means it is characterized by many sellers, each of whom is too small to influence the market by itself, a variety of prices can arise because production costs differ, reflecting products with different features or different quality dimensions.

In a competitive market with perfect information, however, attempts by a seller to raise prices for a given combination of characteristics will result in customer loss for that seller as customers move to competitors or refuse to purchase from the high-price sellers and new-market entrants take buyers away from them. This process drives prices back down until they reflect the quality of the given variety. The equilibrium outcome is that the market prices for each quality of good must reflect its worth if markets are competitive, an outcome known as the "*efficient market*. As long as full information and other competitive conditions exist in the markets for differentiated products, different prices indicate different characteristics and higher prices indicate higher quality. As a result, the current set of market prices, which is fully known to everyone, is a perfect reflection of the value of heterogeneous products. This possibility, though it may or may not ever be completely true, is clearly reflected in the familiar old declaration, "You get what you pay for."

Significantly, this very brief summary of traditional theory suggests little role for disclosure policy as a consumer protection in markets, even for differentiated products, as long as consumers are assumed to have full information about prices, products, and alternatives. Instead, competition decides whether consumers receive the lowest possible price for their chosen purchases. Competitive, monopolistic, and oligopolistic market structures each would produce a single price, albeit not the same price, for homogeneous products. For heterogeneous products under competitive conditions, prices, known to all, perfectly reflect product quality. Under the circumstances, rather than worrying about market transparency, consumer protection logically becomes a policy of preserving and enhancing competition. Not surprisingly, preserving and enhancing competition has long been a cornerstone of economic policy in the United States, through the anti-monopoly and antitrust traditions that date to the nineteenth century.

Imperfect Information

Thus, apart from issues of competition policy, the need for consumer protection arises from imperfect information. Advocates for disclosure policies in the financial area argue, in effect, that information in these markets is not good enough to produce a single price market outcome for homogeneous products or the efficient market for differentiated ones. They contend that, although it is possible to imagine a market with perfectly available information (a small market with few participants and in which nothing ever changes, for example), common sense, as well as normal experience, suggests that it does not happen very often. Importantly, it does not occur in the large markets for differentiated financial products with thousands of producers and millions of consumers. To these disclosure advocates, *perfect* information and *perfect* competition are only theoretical constructs, useful mostly as reference points for comparison to actual market conditions. Since information actually is only *imperfectly* available to consumers, in this view, governmental policies to produce disclosures are warranted.

Consumers and Information

Consumers' stock of information about potential purchases clearly may be incomplete for a variety of reasons. First, at the personal level, consumers differ in their abilities to assimilate, evaluate, process, and retain the new information that swirls around them daily in a modern economy. Also, information they have obtained through prior experience may be incomplete, misleading, biased, or forgotten. Even personal experience with a particular product or seller may provide biased information because the experience may have been especially lucky or unlucky. This may also be the case with the experiences of relatives and acquaintances from whom consumers seek advice. In addition, there may be product changes over time, including unseen ones, that can affect conclusions even from unbiased personal experience or advice.

Beyond the personal level, there are also environmental factors that affect information availability and processing. A modern, affluent, capitalistic economy provides a wide variety of choices in many areas. Innumerable products are available in today's marketplace, and many of them have closely related varieties and substitutes. Identifying sellers and questioning them about prices and product varieties is a time-consuming process. Many products, including financial services, are technologically or legally complex and may have numerous complicated components. In such cases, assembling reasonably complete information may be very difficult (in other words, costly) for consumers.

In addition, the retail outlets that provide products and services to consumers are widely diverse. Often, there simply may be too many outlets for consumers to be fully aware of the range of prices, products, and sales practices. In these situations, sellers may sometimes actively limit the availability of complete information. In some cases, insiders, have better information than that which is generally available in the marketplace.

Another set of difficulties arises because much information about product or service quality comes from interested parties (including both product producers and sellers) who may provide incomplete, biased, or otherwise self-serving and unreliable information or with-hold damaging information. In these cases, even competitors may have little incentive to expose possible defects in the products or claims of others; their own products may exhibit the same potential difficulties. Furthermore, even if some producers might benefit from making more disclosures (because their products do not exhibit the problematic characteristics), they might not do so in an attempt to avoid free-riders. *Free-riders* are nonpaying producers who benefit from costly disclosing, which cannot be confined to information about a specific source. The outcome of all these situations can be a shortage of useful information.

Economists and others long recognized the unreality of the information assumption of historical economic theory, but a full exploration of the implications of imperfect information, and especially asymmetric information, began to receive broader discussion in the professional economic literature in the 1960s and 1970s. This work focused more explicitly on the role and value of information in economic decisions, the importance of information for the efficient functioning of markets, and particularly how markets and market outcomes themselves transmit information.[4]

The Market for Information

The new theory postulated that obtaining information, like obtaining virtually everything else, is not free. Rather, consumers must assemble information, which is costly to do, and rational consumers will incur the costs of collecting information only as long as their anticipated personal gain exceeds those costs. In effect, the economics of information suggests that the market for information operates like other markets: There is a demand, a supply, and an equilibrium price and quantity exchanged. The amount of information any individual has about a particular product depends on the functioning of the information market. Obviously, if a given individual or the market as a whole assembles or has available less-than-perfect information, this has implications for the functioning of product markets.

Demand for information arises from product demand. Since information is not perfect, fuller information suggests a higher likelihood of satisfaction with purchases. Therefore, there is an incentive to gather information about prices, characteristics, and quality of products, as long as there is an expectation of an improved outcome. In other words, shopping is useful as long as there is the likelihood of a gain. The demand curve for information is downward sloping like any normal demand curve: At a lower price, more information will be gathered.

Information supply comes from a variety of sources. One is consumers themselves, through their shopping, inspecting, and personal experience. Producers and sellers of products are another source (for example, through advertising). There are also various third-party providers like acquaintances, product reviewers, and the public information media (including print and electronic sources such as radio, television, and, more recently, the Internet). The product market itself also provides information including market shares (the ubiquity and popularity of certain brands) and the reputations of various producers.

A rigorous investigation of information economics essentially began with Stigler's (1961) exploration of the consequences of incomplete price information. He argued that multiple prices could arise, even for homogeneous products in a competitive market, because knowledge becomes obsolete. Supply and demand conditions change for individual sellers over time, potentially leading to price changes. In this environment, sellers have difficulty ascertaining and keeping up with their rivals' pricing on all products.

Importantly, potential buyers also typically are unaware of the marketplace prices of all products, especially those of infrequent purchases.

Consequently, neither sellers nor buyers can fully determine or keep up with changing prices without costly search. Consumers will not search forever for the best price, however. Stigler contended that they will search only as along as the marginal expected gain from further search exceeds the marginal cost. This can cause changes in the competitive market outcome; let us examine this possibility.

The benefit from price search is the expected reduction in price of the product or the improvement in quality for the same price. The cost of search depends on (1) the technology of information production and diffusion; (2) the complexity of the product; and (3) the buyer's prior experience, preferences, and ability to gather and use information effectively. Similarly, sellers' information is imperfect. Sellers generally do not know all their rivals' prices and products, and must incur search costs to obtain such information. They risk losing sales if they quote a price that is too high or too low (and their returns are below market). These possibilities provide an incentive for sellers to price competitively, but the cost for sellers of becoming perfectly informed may also be greater than the expected gain. In this environment, it generally will not be optimal for either buyers or sellers to become perfectly informed; doing so is just too costly relative to the expected gain (see also Grossman and Stiglitz 1976). Thus, as long as search costs are positive, sellers may charge a price that exceeds the competitive price by up to the amount of search costs without losing customers. Positive search costs permit price dispersion, even in a market for a homogenous product that is otherwise competitive.

Stigler suggested that advertising can supply the economic service of providing information, even though often it is often considered merely wasteful (or, worse, a barrier to entry). Sellers have an incentive to lower prices and advertise as a means of gaining customers. In effect, price advertising is equivalent to the introduction of a large amount of relatively low-cost search (shopping) by a large portion of potential buyers. Advertising can lower search costs for consumers and, in Stigler's view, price advertising can decisively influence the level and dispersion of prices, lowering price levels and diminishing dispersion. Advertising is especially prevalent for products with high marginal values of search, and tends to reduce price dispersion most for commodities with large aggregate expenditures.

Following Stigler's article, other analysts explored and extended his ideas about costly information. Within a few years, they had developed a variety of theoretical economic models analyzing the market implications of incomplete price information and costly search.[5] A number of models detail the conditions under which costly information and search could allow sellers to raise prices by an amount up to the search costs without losing customers, even in a competitive market for a homogeneous product in which entry is free. Depending on the distribution of search costs, some theoretical models show that there could be multiple prices in the market for the same product.[6] There might not even be an equilibrium price (see Salop 1976 and Stiglitz 1979, 1985).

Other theoreticians investigated the conditions under which it would not be necessary for all consumers to search for the market in order to behave competitively. Theoretical work by Schwartz and Wilde (1979), and Wilde and Schwartz (1979) demonstrated that a competitive equilibrium can occur even if only a proportion of consumers search. This means that imperfect price information or the presence of uninformed consumers by itself does not necessarily imply the existence of noncompetitive pricing. Rather, it suggests that a competitive outcome is still possible since a portion of consumers can police the market. Such an outcome is of obvious significance for consumer protection.

Because these economic models demonstrate that information is very significant for the efficient functioning of markets, they have stimulated government policy makers to seek ways to make the technology of information production and diffusion more efficient. They were important in encouraging government policy makers to remove barriers to information flows, such as by ending bans on advertising by professionals like physicians and attorneys. Advertising, as a whole, became more favorably regarded as a way to encourage information flows and reduce the possibility of price dispersion for homogeneous products. As a matter of governmental consumer protection, it seems that policy should attempt to encourage truthful advertising, especially price advertising, and not do anything to discourage it.[7] The conclusions of the theoretical economic models also suggested to some observers the usefulness of requiring disclosures as another way to reduce consumers' search costs. Consequently, as concern for information availability increased, so did calls for required disclosures as a central element of government consumer protection policy.

Information about Product Quality

When shopping for many products, including many consumer financial services, it seems that price is the key variable for many consumers, perhaps the only one of real significance in many cases. Many such products have few, if any, important differentiating features in the eyes of consumers. Suppliers offer deposit accounts and payment services in local and national markets, for example, and the main shopping variable for most consumers is pricing, even though some consumers may be attracted to other characteristics of the services, on occasion, and may even search for them.[8] Using previous terminology, these products are largely homogeneous across suppliers.

In contrast, other financial services, such as consumer credit, life insurance, or mutual funds, are more complicated; obtaining reasonably full information about them entails more dimensions. For these products, consumers may not be fully aware either of price or product features, and more or different shopping skills and effort may be needed to obtain workably full knowledge. Theory promises, given full information and competitive markets, that price is a full reflection and perfect indicator of the quality and value of heterogeneous goods. Nevertheless, the absence of perfect information about either the price or quality dimension allows the chance of significantly less favorable outcomes.

Akerlof's (1970) famous *lemons model* is undoubtedly the best-known theoretical discussion of the complete absence of information on the quality of products. In the Akerlof situation, imperfect information permits an extreme outcome in which only low-quality goods are sold because, otherwise, the value of the good to the seller exceeds the price available in the marketplace, compromising the willingness to sell.

Suppose, using Akerlof's example of used cars, that there is a range of quality among the cars possibly for sale, but there is asymmetric information: Only the sellers know which cars are high quality or low quality, and buyers have no quality information. Thus, the only certainty for *buyers* is that the goods on the market are not worth more (better value) than their price. Asymmetric information places a ceiling on the quality of the cars for sale; the higher quality cars are withdrawn from sale, since *sellers* know they are worth more than the market price. In such a market, in which sellers but not buyers have information about quality, only low-quality goods (lemons) are for sale, a situation known as *adverse selection*. In this case, if sellers of high-quality products know that the opportunity cost of parting with their merchandise is greater than the average market price, they will not enter the market; they will not sell.

The lemons case clearly is an extreme. It is rare that buyers have *no* information about quality, if only because typically it is in the best interest of at least some sellers to provide information about quality to potential buyers.[9] The sellers who want to provide information about quality include those selling high-quality goods that could command higher prices, but also sellers who do not want to cheat customers because they are interested in repeat sales. In the case of used cars, for example, it is important for potential sellers of higher quality, higher value used cars to communicate that their merchandise is higher quality and, therefore, it should command the higher price that reflects its worth.

The usefulness of providing information on quality gives rise to the likelihood of attempts by sellers to disclose quality information, even in the absence of any government-sponsored or required disclosure policies. In general, sellers with positive information about their own products have an incentive to disclose this fact. Naturally, simple assertions by sellers about the high quality of their products are not going to be sufficient to convince possible purchasers. Anyone can say that the products for sale are high quality, or good value for the price, even if they are not. (Colloquially, for instance, *used-car salesman* has come to mean an individual who exaggerates claims of quality.) The challenge for both sellers and purchasers is to find an observable product characteristic that is economically related to quality but not easily falsified.

Information and the Search for Quality

Information economists use the term *signals* to describe the observable characteristics of products that are related to unobservable dimensions, as well as the observable indicators of hidden characteristics. In particular, signals are the observable characteristics of products for sale that improve the predictability of product quality. Sellers of either used cars or loan contracts, for example, can attach signals to their merchandise offerings. In either case, the intent is to improve the available information about the quality of the product. From the point of view of the purchaser of the product, the signalling characteristic is known as a *screening device*. Buyers can use the presence or absence of the signal as a quality screen (see Spence 1973, 1974).

For a characteristic to be useful as a signal of quality, it must be easier (less costly) for producers of higher quality products to attach the signal to their product than for producers of lower quality output. For example, in the labor market, in which workers sell labor services, it should be easier (less costly) for more intelligent or more dedicated potential workers than for less intelligent or lazier potential employees to graduate from top schools. If so, then education can serve as the signal of a potentially productive worker.

Similarly, for other products, guarantees or warranties can function as signals of quality if attaching a money-back guarantee or repair warranty is less costly to a producer of high-quality products than to a producer of low-quality products. It is reasonable to believe that it would be easier (less costly) for used-car dealers to provide such a guarantee on high quality used cars than on lemons. As long as the benefits to the producer from adding and disclosing the characteristic exceed the costs involved, the producer will attach the signal.

There are many theoretical models of signaling, market dynamics with signals of quality, and market equilibrium with incomplete quality information. Analyses of these issues in the economics literature is so extensive and diverse that only the flavor of the discussion will be mentioned here.[10]

The economic literature on signaling begins with an explanation of a variety of types of signals. *Bonding signals*, for example, are capital assets like a sum of money or an insurance policy that guarantee performance. A municipality, for example, may require that a contractor post a performance bond to guarantee satisfactory completion before the firm can begin constructing houses in the town. Presumably, it is easier for a high-quality builder to risk posting a bond than it is for a fly-by-night builder. *Reputation* is another kind of signal, consisting of a particular kind of bond. Attaining a good reputation requires a costly investment of time and resources. Once formed, a reputation is a capital asset. Again, acquiring a good reputation will be more difficult for fly-by-night sellers than for legitimate vendors. Thus, both bonds and good reputations are easier for producers of high-quality products to supply and, therefore, they can serve as useful signals of quality. Either exhibits lower marginal cost per unit of sales for the high-quality producer.[11]

In the context of signaling, economists have also analyzed issues such as reasons for choosing one signaling device or another, whether signals are sufficient to discipline sellers and the marketplace, and even whether they improve society's overall allocation of resources.[12] An important question for formal economic analysis of these issues is how readily information about cheaters spreads in the marketplace. Producers may use bonds and reputations as signals most easily if information about potential cheating circulates freely. If word spreads rapidly and completely, the penalties for cheating (loss of money, reputation, and customers) will bite quickly, and the cost to the bond or reputation has some meaning.[13]

Economists have also modeled how individuals can search for information about product characteristics other than price. In exploring information search by consumers if products are heterogeneous, economists typically have adopted the distinction proposed by Nelson (1970) between *search goods* and *experience goods*, a distinction derived from the search characteristics and experience characteristics that form the basis of the classification.[14] *Search* or *inspection characteristics* are those that can be examined before purchase. *Experience characteristics* are those that can only be experienced after the fact (characteristics of restaurant meals or health care, for example). Some goods and services, such as automobiles or vacation tour packages, exhibit both kinds of characteristics, but for many other goods and services, one form or the other rather clearly predominates. Analyzing consumers' search for search characteristics, as the name suggests, is much easier than examining their study of experience characteristics. Economists have found that providing a rigorous analysis of the market outcomes for the quality of experience goods is very complicated.[15]

Pricing as a Search Characteristic

Fortunately, the difficulties of analyzing or undertaking the search for experience characteristics are not important for financial products, which are largely pure search products. If all the important characteristics of pure search goods are observable, many of the difficulties of understanding search in the case of heterogeneous products fall away. More important for consumers, many of the practical difficulties of obtaining information about characteristics do not arise if the unknown aspects of a transaction largely involve search features.

Prices are certainly search characteristics for financial services like deposits or credit, as already discussed, but so are other contract provisions. All contract terms are accessible by asking the provider or by reading the contract (or both). Consequently, as search characteristics these features of financial contracts are also amenable to disclosure by providers, either in person or through media advertising (or both). Moreover, they are also available to become the subject of legally mandated disclosures, as legislatures, regulatory bodies, and regulated industries have become well aware.

Either voluntary or mandatory disclosures, as well as advertising of search characteristics (including price but also other terms) can reduce for consumers the costs of acquiring information by reducing the complexities of information search. The reduced cost of information acquisition should then make the product market function better for consumers. In this context, economic models of the sort advanced by Wilde and Schwartz (1979) become especially relevant. Their work suggests that not all consumers need be fully informed about either price or contract terms, since shopping by some of them can influence the market to the benefit of everyone. As long as a sufficient portion of consumers police the market, the market can behave competitively with respect to combinations of prices and contract terms. A lower cost for information search enabled by disclosures should enhance the portion of consumers willing to search and the effectiveness of their efforts.

Ultimately, the goal of lowering the cost to consumers of acquiring price and contract information is the theoretical foundation for why the disclosure of prices and terms in a consistent manner has become a ubiquitous requirement of governmental policy for financial services in the United States. If required disclosures can and have lowered information acquisition costs for both price and quality information, as seems probable for at least some consumers, this feature of policy suggests that markets for these products probably have become more competitive over time as sellers are forced to struggle more for their customers' attention. If so, based upon the models of Wilde and Schwartz, the consumer benefits of better information extend beyond increasing the awareness of those who search for information. It is competitive markets that produce the lowest prices for homogeneous products, and efficient combinations of price and quality for heterogeneous ones. If better information flows or more efficient (less costly) information search improves the competitiveness of markets, then all consumers can benefit, the uninformed as well as the informed. Reputations and other signaling devices of service providers can enhance the confidence of even the most uninformed consumers.[16]

Some Special Features of Markets for Consumer Financial Products

Typically, consumer financial services are provided by financial intermediaries like banks and other depository institutions, insurance companies, mutual funds, pension funds, and finance companies. As a result of bringing together the providers and users of these services, the markets for many consumer financial products are characterized by the interesting condition that both the consumer and institutional sides of the market are subject to problems of asymmetric information. Consumers may not be fully informed about prices and other features of financial products, but the providers of services like loans and insurance also are unaware of important characteristics of the purchasers of the contracts they sell, especially riskiness.

This two-sided information problem is easy enough to see for either consumer credit or insurance. From the viewpoint of the consumer, prior information on both prices and quality of contracts often is inexact, as discussed previously. Both creditors and insurance providers offer contracts with different features and charge different prices, and it is not likely that any consumer would be aware of all the possibilities. Ultimately, this is why TILA requires the disclosure of prices, but also of some other specific contract terms in addition to pricing measures.

From the viewpoint of the institutions, however, there is also incomplete information. Focusing on the credit market is instructive. In credit markets, lenders are buyers; from their standpoint, individuals are producers. Consumers generate credit contracts (promises to pay or IOUs) that creditors purchase, discounted from their maturity value, by giving consumers current resources in the form of merchandise or cash today. Creditors are willing to purchase higher quality credit contracts by paying more in current resources (higher price). In financial terms, this means they reduce the discount factor, the interest rate, for the higher quality contracts.

The difficulty for creditors is judging the contract quality, a problem in an environment of incomplete and asymmetric information. Information about consumers is imperfect because there is an unknown group of consumers who will not fully honor their obligation to provide the agreed-upon stream of payments; they will default. Simply stated, the agreements of consumers are subject to default risk.

In the absence of any information about the quality of the contracts offered by consumers, all that a financial institution knows for sure is that any unscreened selection pool of potential credit applicants is likely to contain a proportion of potential borrowers who will not live up to their contracts. This comes about because, at any interest rate, only those whose personal discount rate for the future payments is *higher* than the market rate (*i.e.,* the present value of the resources repayable over time is *less* than the current resources received) will be willing to apply for credit. Since this always includes those who will be unwilling or unable to repay, the unscreened risk pool is never favorable to the creditor.

As a result, the issue for creditors involves more than just raising the interest rate to cover the average risk. In the absence of information on the quality of consumer promises, the creditors know only that the higher the interest rate, the higher the proportion of consumer contract sellers who will default, because the better risks leave the market as the price to them rises. This sets up a lemon dynamic for the quality of borrowers;

the higher the interest rate, the worse the credit risks still in the pool of applicants and the lower the enthusiasm of the lenders. If lenders have no information at all about the quality (creditworthiness) of potential borrowers, little or no lending takes place. Modern analyses of credit rationing have suggested that rationing arises because of imperfect information (see, for example, Stiglitz and Weiss 1981 and Durkin, Elliehausen, Staten, and Zywicki 2011, forthcoming, Chapter 5). The idea is that rather than just increasing the interest rate charged to compensate for risk, lenders will instead limit the amounts they will lend. They do this because there are costs associated with credit-screening activities, and creditors will not expend unlimited resources on screening.

In this environment of substantially less-than-perfect information on both sides, there will be an incentive for market participants to find or provide more information: Both creditors and consumers will attempt to improve the information situation. Consumers can find information from a variety of sources, including advertising, publications, and required disclosures. They may also turn to the views of advisers, ranging from acquaintances and relatives to professionals such as accountants and lawyers.

For their part, creditors will, as noted, attempt to obtain information through the process of screening out bad risks. They will take and examine applications, peruse credit reports, and look at their previous experience with applicants and with similar customers. Credit bureaus and other mechanisms for creditors to exchange information respond to risk and the costs of credit screening. Whenever possible, creditors will employ technology to reduce the costs of the process of screening, which today includes mathematical methods like credit scoring. Lenders will attempt to acquire information about consumers as long as benefits exceed costs.

Moreover, just as it is reasonable to expect that low-cost and reputable creditors will want to make these facts known, it is also reasonable to presume that high-quality (low-risk) borrowers will want to make their creditworthiness known to creditors, both in order to receive the loan and qualify for a favorable interest rate. Thus, consumers with favorable information about their creditworthiness will want to disclose it, and creditors will look for signals (screening devices) from potential borrowers. Self-selection or screening devices could even involve decisions such as the choice of class of creditor. Only better (lower) risk consumers might apply to a bank, for instance, if consumers believe that banks are more likely to reject applications with any hint of past credit troubles.[17]

For the same reason, consumers might be willing to reduce risk by offering a bond in the form of collateral on their loan or seeking only secured credit as a signal of the quality of their accounts. Sellers of high-quality promises to pay (that is, consumers who are good credit risks) should find it easier to offer collateral on their loans since they are less likely to default.[18] Signals of this sort are analogous to offers of a willingness to assume deductibles and copayments in insurance markets. Insurers are able to use such self-selection devices to help segment insurance risks into risk pools for insurance underwriting purposes, and lenders can do likewise for credit contracts.

Implications for Consumer Protection Policy

Although information imperfections may exist on both sides of the market for many consumer financial services, government policy actions have focused almost exclusively on improving information for consumers, especially price information. The federal disclosure laws provide only for disclosures to consumers, not generally to lenders by consumers. Indeed, it is possible to argue that the restrictions contained in the Fair Credit Reporting Act or privacy requirements of the Gramm, Leach, Bliley Act of 1999 have actually reduced the availability of information for creditors by restricting the kinds and amount of information about consumers they can retain and exchange. Furthermore, regulatory zeal to protect personal privacy presents a risk of the future enactment of laws that significantly interfere with signalling by consumers. This outcome would raise the price and limit availability of credit, other things being equal, by interfering with both creditors' ability to obtain information about contract quality and the ability of consumers to disclose their own favorable standing, thus raising creditors' costs.

For the consumer side of the market, it is clear from theory that consumers benefit if they have sufficient information on price and contract features. Ultimately, three contentions serve as the economic rationale for government intervention to require disclosures:

- Potential buyers of goods and services have only imperfect information about prices and products;
- Imperfect information can reduce consumer welfare; and
- Useful and beneficial information can be provided at reasonable cost.

The argument is that if the costly nature of information can enable sellers to raise prices or cut corners on quality, then insufficient information can interfere with the efficient market that relates price directly to production cost and value. Therefore, government efforts to require disclosures that reduce the costliness of information acquisition for consumers can improve the efficiency of the private marketplace and overall consumer welfare.

Obviously, the ratio of benefits to costs of disclosure programs is important; all interventions to improve information flows are not automatically justified or justifiable. Instead, it seems that government policy decisions should depend on the seriousness of the information deficiency, its market impact, the likelihood of a favorable outcome of the policy, and some measurement of the costs of the policy in relation to the favorable impact that the disclosure policy can achieve. The review and comparison of competing approaches also is important, if the policy initiative is to achieve a high ratio of benefits to costs. Bloom (1989) provides a taxonomy of these concerns and a useful road map for addressing them.

The larger the improvement in market efficiency following the implementation of the disclosure program and the smaller the costs of government intervention, the more likely a favorable outcome for consumer welfare. In contrast, if the government requires the disclosure of information that is not very useful to consumers, or if the government program is very expensive, then there may not be much or any improvement in consumer welfare. There even could be a decrease. With the range of theoretical possibilities suggested by the search models, the questions of which conditions exist in which markets and whether the models accurately reflect true market conditions at all become important issues for empirical study.

In sum, information theory has changed the way that the economics profession views consumer protection. In many ways, the economics of information became, over time, the essence of the economics of consumer protection, at least at the federal level. Before the economics of information arose, the economics of consumer protection had focused largely on the structure of markets. The reasoning was that, if markets exhibit competitive structure, the optimal set of goods and services become available, and the chief concerns for consumer protection are monopoly and fraud. With the development of information economics, however, consumer protection also depends on the state of information in consumer markets, and the benefits and costs of government interventions. Not surprisingly, therefore, the professional literature on the economics of consumer protection developed along two lines: "identification of the variety of ways in which asymmetric information can affect market performance and . . . the detailing of the many mechanisms that the market or government can use to reduce these information problems" (Ippolito 1984, p. 3).

Frequently, however, it seems that proponents of mandatory disclosures have tended to focus on more than just market outcomes, preferring to look instead at the level of individual consumers. Information theory argues that the proper goal should be the efficient market in which price and value are directly related, and all market participants benefit whether they have or search for information or not. Indeed, economists would argue that you cannot judge the effectiveness of an information program by examining only the impact of the program on individual consumers. In their view, the test is whether the market has produced competitive prices and terms, not whether specific individual consumers are informed or not.

In contrast, many of those favoring disclosures, more often than not, have tended to frame the debate in terms of the direct behavioral impact of disclosures on individuals.[19] Looking at disclosures this way, a program may be judged a failure or inadequate if some individuals do not change their own individual behavior (for example, do not search or shop) as a result of required disclosures, even if the overall market impact of disclosures and information is favorable. Furthermore, much of the research on disclosures as a consumer protection in the financial area (discussed later in Chapter 7, "The Rubber Meets the Road: Evaluating the Effectiveness of the Truth in Lending Act") has focused on the impact of policy on the knowledge and behavior of individual consumers rather than on market impact as a whole.[20]

Contributing to the imprecision of political debate in this area are the different approaches of economists and other behavioral scientists to studying information issues. Economists typically focus on market outcomes and market equilibrium, using deductive theory as a guide. Other behavioral scientists tend to concentrate more on individual choice, using experiments and surveys as guides. Thus, economic researchers theorizing about market outcomes often do not explore individual behavioral results, while those observers who concentrate on the behavioral results visible through surveys or experimental designs typically do not explore market outcomes.[21]

Consequently, even though the economics of information may well be the foundation of the *economics* of consumer protection, there has been more to the consumer protection debate than the theory of market outcomes. Certainly in the United States, the proponents of required disclosures as consumer protections have tended to focus, for the most part, on the impact on the behavior of individuals. For this reason, the remainder of this chapter looks at some theories and experiments in behavioral science regarding the usefulness of information to individuals.

Before turning to the behavioral issues, however, it is worth noting some fundamental empirical questions about consumer financial services that clearly arise from the economics of information. To a large extent they remain unexplored:

1. What is the competitive condition of markets for consumer financial services? Do they differ across products or subproducts?
2. In a given market, what is the proportion of potential purchasers who must be informed or must search in order for the market to function well?
3. Are there cultural or other differences in search behavior among population subgroups that could lead to variable competitive conditions across submarkets? For example, are there differences between lower income and upper income, or younger and older consumers?
4. Does insufficiency of information about consumers cause creditors to segment markets to the detriment of consumers?
5. Would better information about consumers enable the creditors to screen risks better, leading to more favorable pricing? What would this better information be?
6. What are the costs of implementing required disclosure programs, and do the disclosure regimes require distribution of new information at the margin? Information, after all, is costly to disseminate; where is the point at which the provision of additional information is no longer socially optimal?

Development and Growth of Behavioral Theories of Information

Purchasing is very individualistic. People buy things on their own schedules, and they approach the purchasing process in personal ways. Consumers also use information differently, and they respond differently to its presence or absence. Ultimately, individual variations in information use should influence the structure and conclusions of economic search models through the economic benefits and costs of information availability and search. Economists long have understood this. They also have realized the scope of the factors that affect information seeking, but a host of technical difficulties stands in the way of formally including the range of individual behavior in structural economic equilibrium models.[22] Simply put, a full and formal accounting for all potential influences on buying would make the economic models intractable.

Ultimately underlying the problems of economic modeling of information use is the inherent variability of human nature. As the old saying goes, no two people are alike. They do not live in precisely the same environment either, and both individual and environmental differences have implications for the importance of any specific information (including disclosures) on behavior. Some people can use information more effectively than others, and some can collect it less expensively. Different people want and use different information. This means, of course, that the impact and effectiveness of governmental disclosure programs likely will vary across individuals. Some consumers will carefully peruse available information, including disclosures but also other information, and adjust their purchasing behavior as needed, while others will largely ignore the information. Thus, if behavioral researchers are able to shed any light on how such diversity might influence information use, it should enrich the understanding of consumer behavior for the benefit of both economists and policy makers who propose disclosures.

Early Behavioral Research

Researchers conducted a considerable amount of empirical behavioral research on consumers' economic decisions in the decades following World War II, much of it at the Survey Research Center of the University of Michigan.[23] Like the economists, the behavioral researchers were also concerned with the rationality of consumers' decisions, but their concept of rational, purposive, and deliberate behavior was different than that of the economic theorists. To them, any behavior consistent with achieving goals is rational, not just optimizing behavior that is consistent with a set of utility goals.

One area of research focused on purchase decisions for the acquisition of large consumer durables, which were frequently obtained using credit. In this area, behavioral researchers examined consumers' purchase decisions in detail, collecting data on the circumstances giving rise to a decision, the amount of planning for a purchase, the extent of information seeking and shopping, and the evaluation of alternatives. One of the important contributions arising from this research was how characteristics of human thought processes influence economic decisions.

The decision process that emerges from this work differs from that suggested by traditional economic theory. One finding concerned how consumers often do not collect extensive information on alternatives or carefully weigh choices before making them. Instead, consumers typically take shortcuts and simplify decisions by focusing on one or a few aspects of the decision. They sometimes also engage in limited decision processes when faced by an urgent need or perception of a special opportunity. In these (and other) cases, past experience may allow consumers to make rational choices without an extended decision process. Consumers search for information and carefully consider alternatives most frequently in situations in which past experience does not offer clear and unambiguous guidelines. Although the situations in which consumers use an extended decision process were found to be not especially common, evidence indicated that, by far, most situations included at least some elements of deliberation, and nearly half contained several elements.

The early behavioral research included investigations of the role of credit in purchase decisions. Evidence indicated that few consumers were knowledgeable about the effective interest rate on installment credit before TIL and also that a considerable percentage of consumers using credit to purchase durable goods could have paid cash. These findings supported the view that many consumers were not well informed when they made credit decisions. Nevertheless, there appeared to be more at issue, because the same research suggested elements of purposive and deliberate behavior.

An important finding was that consumers tended to incur new debts if their expectations of future income and financial situations were favorable; they delayed purchases and repaid existing debts if their expectations were unfavorable. This meant that there was even more to the credit decision than costs, and cost disclosure might not always affect decisions. The research also suggested a rationale for the simultaneous holding of debt and low yielding liquid assets: Many consumers use credit as a budgeting tool; the discipline required to make the monthly payments on installment debt forces consumers to "save." Some consumers believed they would be less able to replenish liquid asset holdings if they paid cash for large purchases and had to rely on their own internal motivation to replenish cash balances.[24]

Buyer Behavior Theories

In the 1960s and 1970s, behavioral scientists began to assemble the breadth of motivational and environmental influences on consumers into comprehensive theories known today generically as *buyer behavior theories* (see Nicosia 1966; Engel, Kollat, and Blackwell 1968; Howard and Sheth 1969; and Bettman 1979). Redefined and altered by more than forty years of subsequent consumer research, the buyer behavior models and their associates, descendants, and derivatives remain an important underlying conceptual framework for posing and testing hypotheses about a range of cognitive, social, and motivational influences that potentially affect consumers' purchases of goods and services. Importantly, these influences include the usefulness of information, the willingness to search for information, information processing capability, and factors that influence the effectiveness of information disclosures.[25]

The buyer behavior and related theories and their descendants are conceptually interesting and useful in themselves for helping observers to understand, classify, and describe important aspects of human motivations, including use of required disclosures. Their original purpose, however, was much more practical, namely, to facilitate marketing of products. In the decades following World War II, marketers found that if they were to be successful, they needed to understand the successive stages in consumers' buying decision process and be aware of the determinants and differences in consumers' ability and capacity to process information. Consequently, developing and testing comprehensive theories and their components became important to the marketing profession over subsequent decades, featuring substantial empirical efforts on every aspect.

Essentially, the buyer behavior approach argues that consumers engage in problem-solving activities to bring about need satisfaction.[26] In providing an overlying structure, buyer behavior theories explicitly argue that many factors at each stage will shape the final outcome of the purchase process. These include personal differences among consumers, internal motivations, and external and environmental influences such as social pressures and marketing activities. Differences in psychological processes, including the individuals' ability to assimilate and process information, are also very important.

Blackwell, Miniard, and Engel provide a schematic diagram or flow chart of the updated Engel, Kollat, and Blackwell buyer behavior approach. Their flow chart diagram shows how the model suggests each of these variables enters the buying process (see Blackwell, Miniard, and Engel 2006, p. 82). The seven decision process stages occupy the central part of the flow chart and form the core of the model: (1) need recognition, (2) search, (3) prepurchase evaluation of alternatives, (4) purchase, (5) consumption, (6) post-purchase alternative evaluation, and (7) divestment. For evaluating the role of required disclosures the second step, search, is especially important, although the model is more properly considered an integrated whole. Their diagram also shows how each of these stages might be subject to outside influences. For example, the model hypothesizes that individual differences (consumer resources, motivation and involvement, knowledge, attitudes, personality, values, and lifestyle) can be significant at any of the stages. Likewise, environmental influences (culture, social class, personal influences, family, and situation) can also show their importance at any of these stages.

The comprehensive buyer behavior theories contend that each of the steps is present in some sense in every decision to purchase something, but some steps can become highly abbreviated under many common circumstances. Blackwell, Miniard, and Engel argue that consumer problem-solving behaviors exhibit a continuum from extended problem solving at one end through mid-range to limited problem-solving at the other end. The purchase of some products clearly is very complicated and requires more effort than the acquisition of routine household needs, such as bread or toothpaste. The purchases of the latter products can become so commonplace that they can be described as habitual problem-solving requiring almost no thought or effort at all. Under the circumstances, some of the stages in the buying process will become very abbreviated or even nonexistent. In contrast, some other purchases, such as cars or college educations, can be so complicated that significant effort becomes useful or even necessary. In these situations, it is reasonable to expect that all the stages in the decision process will explicitly come into play.

Obviously, the budgetary and other significant aspects of the purchase are important components of the distinction between the extended and limited problem-solving cases, but the buyer behavior approach suggests that much of the variability in effort between the different manifestations of the purchase process arises specifically from personalized needs for information. This view then quickly leads to the conclusion that the differentiating factor between extended and limited problem-solving and, therefore, in the amount of time and effort that goes into the decision process, as a whole, depends upon another list of outside factors such as: (1) whether the purchase is one time or repeated, (2) the extent of product differentiation, (3) the amount of time available for shopping and analysis, and (4) the degree of personal involvement with the product. Any of these factors can move a purchase decision into the extended problem-solving category recommending additional information acquisition.[27]

Information Search

Within this context, consumers can and do search for information. In studying consumers' search processes, many behavioral scientists have implicitly employed Stigler's (1961) cost-benefit framework as a working description of consumer search behavior, even though they have not always focused explicitly on *price* search, as Stigler did. Relatively few empirical studies in the marketing literature investigate Stigler's concern for price differences per se. Rather, they have applied Stigler's propositions concerning price variability to a more general concept of *offering variability* which applies broadly to product search and could even apply to brand-search situations (see, for example, Urbany 1986). It seems like a truism that consumers will evaluate, at least implicitly, whether the benefits of further search for information on products, brands, or prices are worth the costs before undertaking a purchase. A *no* answer leads to limited problem-solving approaches, sometimes referred to as repeated or habitual decision-making. An affirmative reply leads to more extended approaches. Consequently, the cost-benefit basis of search behavior has become a core analytical concept for marketing as well as economic analysis.

Internal and External Search

The buyer behavior approach shows that information search can be either low-cost internal search (through long-term memory and the individual's information processing system), or higher cost external information seeking (looking for new information not currently in memory). As suggested, internal memory scanning is frequently sufficient. It typically will be adequate for many habitual purchases like toothpaste and many others, for which recollections are strong and the product class in question has not changed appreciably since the last purchase or external information search. In many cases, internal search may be sufficient even for substantial purchases. The fourteenth business trip to the coast this year, for example, probably will not set off a new round of hotel evaluations. It should be clear, however, that the absence of an external search in a given instance does not mean no search has taken place. Rather, a lower cost internal search may be substituting for external forms.

In other instances, an internal search may be insufficient and a higher cost external search becomes necessary. Sometimes, for example, memory may fail or enough time has elapsed since a prior purchase that conditions or products have changed. Sometimes consumers' needs and resources may be different the second time around, or a consumer may contemplate purchasing an unfamiliar item.

External search covers a range of activities. It includes directly inspecting products at retail outlets and consulting experts including relatives and acquaintances. It also encompasses reviewing advertisements, published articles, studies, and product reports in print sources and on the Internet; and discussing products with salespersons (who, of course, are not disinterested parties). Clearly, it is more likely to be extensive for less common purchases, especially expensive ones. For many people, there is also the phenomenon of *ongoing search*, which refers to the acquisition of information about certain products on a fairly regular basis for recreational reasons or just to be informed (see Bloch, Sherrell, and Ridgway 1986). Many people regularly read automobile, music, garden, photography, computer, antiques, wine, travel, and other specialized publications to gather information on an ongoing basis and not just before they purchase something. Some people even subscribe to publications on personal financial matters, like *Money* and various Kiplinger reports. As individuals become knowledgeable, this may change their prepurchase search activity, even for substantial purchases such as cars, computers, cameras, or various financial services.

Like the purchase decision itself, the information search phase (along with the other initial stages in the buyer behavior process) is subject to environmental influences and individual differences. They include culture, social class, personal influences, family, and situational factors (*i.e.*, factors specific to a particular time and place). Each may be more or less important to a given search process concerning a particular good or service. Even though we know that search clearly is an important component of the theories of consumer decision-making, the research does not tell us a great deal about the relative contribution of each of these specific environmental factors to the differences in search among individuals for financial products.

In addition to environmental influences, individual differences among consumers themselves will certainly also be critical in determining the amount of external search. Individual differences include consumer resources, motivation and involvement, knowledge, attitudes, personality, values, and lifestyle. Search undoubtedly will vary with previous knowledge, for example. Those who are highly informed may rely on their memories for internal search and not engage in much formal external looking. Consumers who are moderately well informed may be the most likely to search because they may know what to look for and can best use the information that they find. Still, they may search because they are uncomfortable about relying solely on their memory. In contrast, the less well informed may search less and well rely more on the opinions of others. Thus, the best- and worst-informed may engage in the least external search, and the search function may take on an inverted U shape with respect to previous knowledge (see Punj and Staelin 1983 and Moorthy, Ratchford, and Talukdar 1997). Ratchford (2001) suggests the possibility that level of search can also depend upon expectations that the information gathered will be useful not only for purchasing now, but also for future purchases (e.g., human knowledge and skill capital). It might be that there will be more searching in situations in which the gathered information will also be useful in the future.

Other personal influences also affect the amount of external search. Some people, for example, are simply more interested in shopping than others; some consumers just are very interested (involved) in certain products—antiques, cameras, cars, computers, and travel are common examples). In the shopping lovers' case, the result may be more shopping or search on an ongoing basis, other things equal, but less shopping immediately before purchase, because the product is so well known already.

Certain demographic differences may also be important in explaining variations in amount of search. Older consumers often have more knowledge and experience and may shop less, for example. They also can have well-established shopping proficiencies and product preferences. Higher income consumers may value their time more, and, consequently, may shop less. Some studies of shopping behavior have used income as a proxy for the value of time in studying shopping behavior (see, for example, Board of Governors of the Federal Reserve System 1987). Also, more education should increase the effectiveness of shopping time. Other things equal, better educated consumers may search more, expecting a better payoff. Surely, product differences themselves should be important in explaining search. It stands to reason that the degree of differentiation among the choices of a product and its close substitutes is significant in determining the amount of effort necessary to make decisions. If products have a lot of differentiating features, such as cars or college educations, more search will normally be necessary. There simply is a larger payoff to the careful gathering of information. The level of price should also be important; higher priced products will typically receive greater attention, other things equal.

Murray (1991) argued that one particular product difference, the difference between goods and services, is an important distinction that contributes to variations in the search effort. He contended that consumers perceive that the purchase of services is inherently riskier than the purchase of goods, other things (like price) being equal. Therefore, the search will be more extensive for services. Services ranging from haircuts to surgical procedures are customized and nonstandard. They are intangible and often cannot easily be evaluated in advance by product inspection, the distinction noted by Nelson (1970) and discussed above among the economic theories. Services usually are consumed as they are produced, typically with no return policy. They may be experimental in nature, and they often are unpredictable in outcome. Consequently, direct product evaluation can come only after purchase, production, and consumption.

According to Murray, the differences between goods and services suggests greater perceived uncertainty and risk with services, including performance, financial, social, psychological, and even safety risks, in some cases. This should mean a greater search for information about services than goods, other things equal. Such considerations caused Murray to propose, and subsequently to find experimental evidence consistent with, a number of hypotheses about information search in the case of services. These hypotheses include the suggestion that consumers will use more personal sources for information about services, and that consumers who have had experience with a particular service will more often use internal sources of information for evaluating services than for evaluating goods.

Many financial services are more analogous to goods than they are to other services, however. Deposit services, for example, are much the same from one source to the next for many, maybe most consumers. The physical location of a bank or credit union and ATMs may be important to some consumers making initial purchase decisions, and the interest rate paid on deposits may have some continuing importance. Nevertheless, banks and deposits are merely commodities to many consumers; the institution and the specifics of the plan are otherwise of little concern to them on an ongoing basis. Such services are hardly customized and nonstandard, as contemplated by Murray. The same is largely true for many credit plans and insurance programs. Many consumers likely cannot even name their life insurance company if the policy is through their employer.

Some financial services, such as investment advice, tax preparation, and estate planning, are more customized and nonstandard. They may well be difficult to evaluate in advance and less predictable in outcome, and therefore, they may be riskier in the sense considered by Murray. These considerations predict more use of personal information sources and more extensive information search for these services. But the more ordinary financial services may well not attract any more significant attention or search than other goods not purchased every day.

Summary: Cost Benefit Basis of Search

Russo (1988) has argued that consumers' cost-benefit review of the need for information may be brief in a given situation, but it always takes place at some level. In this context, he also contended that, to be worthwhile, proposals for information disclosure policies should take consumers' cost-benefit framework into account. Thus, to have any impact, required disclosures either must enhance the usefulness of information for consumers or reduce the cost of using it.

In Russo's view, both benefits and costs of acquiring information can be either tangible or intangible. On the benefits side, tangible advantages involve economic considerations, such as maximizing the utility from the purchased product while minimizing the purchase and post-purchase out-of-pocket expenditures. Intangible benefits typically are more obscure, but they also are important in determining consumers' use of information. They include increased mental certainty that the purchase is the best choice, greater satisfaction with the information and decision process itself, the enhanced entertainment value of the purchase process (some people find shopping more enjoyable than others), and others considerations such as reduced risk and greater safety, and enjoyment in the ultimate use of the product.

On the cost side, consumers' search costs are again both tangible and intangible. Tangible costs are largely monetary, including the costs of publications and documents. Intangible costs essentially involve the physical and mental effort necessary to acquire and process product information. For many products and decisions, the potential effort and the intangible cost of the effort are not trivial. Acquiring information about many products with complex legal components, for example, can involve substantial work for many individuals. Finding the right car or college can also require diligence. Ultimately, the total information costs equal the sum of tangible and intangible components; they are more than merely the tangible costs, which often are relatively small by themselves.

Ratchford (1988) and others have noted that, despite the importance assigned to information by the economic search equilibrium models, explicit information search is relatively uncommon. It seems that some contentions of the buyer behavior theoretical structure described here can help explain this phenomenon. To try to shed some light, Moorthy, Ratchford, and Talukdar (1997) have proposed an economic model grounded in buyer behavior to explain the phenomenon of search variability and have tested it with data on car purchasing. From their theoretical work, they contend that search among brands depends not just upon uncertainty about features of the brands themselves but also upon the strength of prior overall convictions. There will be no search if either pre-existing convictions about a brand are strong, or there are neither convictions nor a current view that there is a lot to gain from searching (because brands are believed to be largely alike), or the costs of search are high.[28]

Like that of many of the other economic models, the discussion by Moorthy, Ratchford, and Talukdar is quite technical, but it offers some testable predictions. It is a bit gloomy in that it suggests there are many plausible circumstances in which consumers' search for information will be relatively uncommon, despite the potential for some (unknown) gain from the activity. Their empirical findings are consistent with their theory in that they find evidence that prior convictions can reduce search and that when it takes place, search can have an inverted U shape with respect to experience with given products. That is, experience increases search up to a point and then greater experience reduces search. Consumers with relatively high levels of experience apparently do not see a need for much search.

Disclosure Policies and Information Processing

More information, especially at a low cost, can lead to both better and more satisfactory decisions for consumers and the more efficient functioning of markets overall. But acquiring sufficient information sometimes carries a high cost. Therefore, it is hardly surprising that requiring disclosures would become an important element of government policy to protect consumers in the marketplace. If required disclosures lower the costs of acquiring useful information, then consumers can be better off if they receive disclosures.

Nonetheless, despite these advantages of disclosures, the work of the behavioral researchers suggests a further concern about requiring disclosures, particularly at the point of sale. Both the buyer behavior models and the information search component contemplate an important role for consumers' information-processing capacity. Required disclosure by itself is not enough; somehow, someone must do something with the disclosed information if it is to make any difference anywhere. This consideration highlights the significance of consumers' internal systems for processing and using information.

The concept of information processing arose from cognitive psychology and refers to the "process by which a stimulus (such as a piece of information) is received, interpreted, stored in memory, and later retrieved" (Engel, Blackwell, and Miniard 1995, p. 472). People are bombarded with thousands of stimuli daily, and their information-processing systems determine which stimuli receive attention and generate responses. Thus, consumers' information-processing ability will be important to anyone desiring to employ information disclosures, either for marketing products or for consumer protection.

The buyer behavior model argues that information processing also consists of a number of distinct stages: exposure, attention, comprehension, acceptance, and retention. A piece of information must go through all of them to reach memory.

The first of these stages, *exposure*, means the presence of information that stimulates one or more of the five senses. This is the arrival stage for incoming stimuli. A number of roadblocks can stand in the way even of exposure to a marketing or consumer protection disclosure stimulus, including wrong target market and ineffective timing (see Federal Trade Commission Staff 1979).

Attention refers to actual activation of the information processing capacity. At this stage, the limitations in individuals' cognitive capacities force a screening process to separate the stimuli that will receive further attention from those that will be ignored. The selection process depends on internal and external factors. Internally, a consumer is more likely to attend to a useful stimulus. An individual already mulling over the purchase of a car, for example, is much more likely to devote attention to stimuli in the form of car advertisements. Likewise, an individual contemplating the need for a loan is more likely than someone else to notice advertisements for annual percentage rates (APRs) or a brochure on the pitfalls of credit use. Obviously, as well as unfortunately, this fact complicates campaigns to enhance financial literacy if these campaigns are not directly connected with specific purchases.

External factors at the attention stage include the nature of the stimulus itself; some stimuli are simply more noticeable because they are more intense or more distinctive. Some advertisements, for example, are designed to be colorful, loud, attractive, funny, or even annoying for the purpose of gaining attention. Direct mail ads that mimic window envelopes from the Internal Revenue Service (IRS) may attract more attention than many other pieces of mail, given the nature of the agency being imitated. Likewise, TILA disclosures probably receive more attention than some other documents concerning credit because of their nature as legally required information.

Attention is (sometimes) followed in the processing hierarchy by comprehension, which involves the attachment of meaning to the information. *Comprehension* refers to classifying stimuli according to previous knowledge and experience. As with attention, comprehension will vary both among individuals and according to the nature of the stimulus. Interest in the subject, experience in the area, and general knowledge all can affect the comprehension of stimuli. The source, type, and features of the stimulus itself, including its complexity, also can be important.[29]

The next stage, *acceptance*, refers to the degree to which a stimulus influences knowledge and possibly attitudes. A message or stimulus may register and be comprehended perfectly but may have little or no impact. For example, information that is contrary to previous experience or belief may not be accepted as readily by these recipients as by others. Likewise, certain individuals may barely notice information that merely confirms their existing knowledge or beliefs.

Retention, as the word suggests, means the transfer of the information into long-term memory, the mind's storehouse of information. Actual processing, however, is through short-term memory where classification and categorization (*i.e.*, thinking) take place at the attention stage. Although there are limits to how much information the brain can process at one time through the short-term memory system, the storage possibility of long-term memory is virtually limitless.

For either advertising or for consumer policy-oriented disclosures, the excessive flooding of the sensory system with information can result in overload of the short-term memory, which is limited in the number of pieces or "chunks" of information it can process at one time. Limitations in the ability of the short-term system to process pieces of new information simultaneously does not mean that the long-term system cannot retain all of the information necessary for decisions, however. Individuals can maintain in long-term memory many more chunks of information obtained over time than they can process at any single time through the sensory and retention system.

Conclusions and Questions from Buyer Behavior

Contrary to the recognized limits of short-term retention, on occasion, advocates of disclosure proceed by assuming that the information processing capability is large and required disclosures should always be extensive. In contrast, opponents of additional disclosures contend that such capabilities are insufficient for handling vast quantities of newly disclosed information. To a large degree, such disputes fail to focus on the important issues; both are correct and not in conflict. Consumer capacity to respond to volumes of disclosures at one time through the short-term memory processing system is indeed limited, but the ability of the long-term memory to retain and retrieve processed information is much larger. The challenge for disclosures is to make use of the different capabilities of the short- and long-term memories without overloading the processing system at the decision point. It seems unlikely, for example, that any disclosure scheme at the point of sale can overcome the prior failures of education and experience to inform consumers about all the features of credit. Fortunately, providing information at the point of sale is not the only goal of TILA and other financial disclosures, as will be discussed further in Chapter 7. If it were, TILA probably would indeed be the failure its critics sometime allege it to be.

The positions of those favoring and those opposing additional disclosures beg the question of the underlying policy motivation for requiring disclosures. For economists, as discussed in the first portion of this chapter, the answer to this question is clear: to improve the competitiveness and efficiency of markets, which implies the importance of price and quality disclosures, while recognizing that not all market participants need be perfectly informed to foster this desirable outcome.

Behaviorally-oriented marketers tend less to think in terms of required disclosures. For them, disclosures are advertisements, and should be crafted in whatever way they believe will sell products the best. Advocates of requiring disclosures often go beyond the position of the economists and emphasize the shortcomings of individual knowledge and behavior. But they stop well short of the position of marketers (sell more products). For those advocating required disclosures, it often seems the underlying hope is to change the patterns of product usage to some policy-preferred alternative, not necessarily more use.

Public policies to increase the benefits of information for consumers, in some cases, might prove more difficult to implement than procedures to reduce the costs of information assimilation and use. Enhancing benefits might require wholesale changes in the consumers themselves, such as through raising education levels. Such changes might be a prerequisite to convincing the consumers that the benefits of knowledge are greater than previously realized. In contrast, reducing the cost of acquiring information might often prove to be a better public policy strategy because it would require fewer changes in consumers themselves. Thus, it seems that much of the advantage to be gained from disclosure policies is likely to come from reducing the intangible costs of information acquisition and processing.

Effective disclosure policies could reduce consumers' information costs in a number of ways, thereby increasing search and knowledge, other things equal. Providing price lists on the Internet or in newspapers, for example, could reduce information-collection costs. Using consistent summary measures (like unit prices) could reduce the effort needed for computation and comparison. In general, any disclosures that take advantage of consumers' existing knowledge could reduce comprehension efforts and costs, easing the transfer of information into long-term memory and making it useful at the point of consumer decisions.

In contrast, it will probably cost consumers more to assimilate and use new information that is disclosed to them, rather than to rely on familiar information. Even if the information disclosed is not essentially new, its use can still be aided by reducing the costs of information processing. If the proposals do not fit the search needs and information-processing capabilities of the consumers they are to protect, it seems they are not likely to be of much use to them.[30]

In sum, the issues raised by the traditional behavioral scientists are wide ranging, and they quickly suggest additional empirical questions about consumers and information use and search in the context of financial services. These questions on the behavior side expand upon the six suggested areas of research listed above at the conclusion of the economic theories:

1. How do consumers search for information about financial services? Since financial products, including both loans and some

asset services, are likely to be relatively complicated and legalistic for many consumers, will consumers more often use personal information sources, such as recommendations from friends and relatives, as important and lower cost sources of information for financial services than they do actual shopping among service providers? Does behavior vary across financial services or types of services?

2. How do consumers use the disclosures currently required for financial services? Are there current disclosures that are particularly useful and, if so, what are they and how are they used? Do the uses vary among consumers, and if so, on what basis?

3. Are there substantial demographic or other segment differences in propensities to search for information about financial services or in the types of information consulted and used? Will, for example, better educated consumers search more, since they can better use the information they glean? In contrast, will older consumers search less, other things equal, on account of more experience, since they can use prior experience as a way to reduce perceived risk? Will lower income consumers search less, either because they perceive they have fewer alternatives or for other reasons?

Recent Research on Cognitive Errors and Behavioral Biases

The behavioral research discussed above indicates that consumers do not always make the cognitive efforts required for an extensive decision process. Individuals often take shortcuts, simplify, and use heuristics (problem-solving strategies). Extended cognitive effort tends to be reserved for situations in which the commitments of money and duration are great, past experience and information are insufficient or obsolete, or outcomes of previous decisions are regarded as unsatisfactory. In situations in which consumers have previous experience and are satisfied with past decisions, they often make choices with little further deliberation. Nevertheless, none of these findings suggests that consumers behave irrationally when using credit or making financial decisions or that information policies are ineffective.

More recently, new lines of behavioral research have produced evidence that raises questions about consumers' ability to make rational financial choices. Evidence is primarily from two sources. The first is experimental studies of choice under uncertainty and risk that have found that individuals are prone to make choices in statistical or logical problems that violate normative rules for rational behavior. Influential articles in *Science* by Tversky and Kahneman (1974 and 1981) describe many of the cognitive biases in choices, examined in the following subsections.

Examined later in this chapter, the second source of questions from behavioral research about consumers' ability to make rational decisions involves mostly experimental studies of time preferences. These studies have found that individuals discount proximate prospects more than more distant prospects. This tendency leads individuals to make impatient choices when outcomes are close in time but more farsighted choices when outcomes are more distant. As a consequence, choices can be inconsistent over time, which violates the normative rules for rational behavior (see Frederick, Loewenstein, and O'Donoghue 2002).

The findings from these two sources have stimulated development of models of consumer behavior with various psychological assumptions that are asserted to be more realistic than those underlying standard economic theory. Behavioral models of this kind have been proposed to explain, for example, the observation that consumers fail to reallocate income or wealth to smooth monthly consumption (Thaler 1985), United States workers' low levels of saving for retirement (Thaler and Benartzi 2004), and Ausubel's (1991) conjecture that consumers systematically underestimate their future credit-card borrowing (Prelec and Loewenstein 1998). Cognitive errors and behavioral biases have been alleged to cause market failure (for example, Ausubel 1991 and Gabaix and Laibson 2006) and are cited as a possible justification for regulatory intervention (Lynch and Zauberman 2006; Barr, Mullainathan, and Shafir 2009). Exploring these issues requires further examination of the concept of heuristics.

Heuristics and Cognitive Errors

Heuristics are decision rules that individuals use to reduce complex tasks of assessing values to simpler judgmental operations. They allow individuals to make decisions quickly using limited information. Heuristics may be specific to certain tasks or more general. Heuristics are not optimizing techniques. They are methods that take account of the computational limitations to achieve satisfactory outcomes with moderate amount of computations (Simon 1990). In the economics lit-erature, the term *satisficing* has been coined to designate such behavior.

Common heuristics include *availability* (predicting the frequency of an outcome, good or bad, based on how easily an example can be brought to mind). Another is *representativeness* (judging outcome frequency by considering how much the hypothesis resembles available data), and a third is *recognition* (inferring that a recognized object has a higher value with respect to some criterion than an object that is not recognized). A heuristic for credit decisions is choosing the lowest monthly payment from among consumer credit contracts with the longest available term (see Juster and Shay 1964).

Research has shown that heuristics work well under many circum-stances. Limited theoretical analysis suggests that a satisficing heuristic (*i.e.*, choosing an action again if it previously satisfied aspirations; search-ing otherwise) produces optimal long-run outcomes in some circum-stances and changes the result to improved though not optimal outcomes in others (Bendor, Kumar, and Siegel 2009).[31] Several empirical studies have found that that simple heuristics often perform as well as extensive information and weighing of alternatives.[32] For consumer credit deci-sions, for example, Juster and Shay (1964) demonstrated that the lowest monthly payment heuristic is equivalent to optimizing behavior for credit-constrained borrowers.[33] But, if heuristics are used, certain cogni-tive processes or biases can produce outcomes that violate the normative rules for rational choice. For example, considerations that influence one's ability to imagine an event (such as recent coverage of an airline accident) or misperceptions about statistical influences (such as ignoring the effect of a small sample size in assessing observed sequences or frequen-cies) may bias estimates produced by availability or representativeness heuristics.

Researchers have identified and investigated numerous cognitive biases, but the nature of the problems and the research issues involved are similar in the many examples. The following pages and the next three subsections discuss some of the observed biases, psychological hypoth-eses, and the robustness of the evidence associated with them before returning to the buying decision.

Tversky and Kahneman's (1983) *Linda Problem* is one of the best-known experimental tests of a cognitive bias attributed to use of a heuris-tic. For the test, participants were presented with the following problem:

Linda is thirty-one years old, single, outspoken, and very bright. She majored in philosophy in college. As a student, she was deeply concerned with issues of discrimination and social justice, and also participated in anti nuclear demonstrations.

Which is more probable?

1. Linda is a bank teller.
2. Linda is a bank teller and is active in the feminist movement.

The correct answer to this statistical problem is (1) because the probability of any one of two events is always equal to or greater than the probability of the two events occurring together. That is, the probability that Linda is a bank teller has to be at least as great as the probability that she is a bank teller *and* a feminist.

Tversky and Kahneman presented this problem to three groups of students, whose experience with statistics ranged from casual to advanced. Eighty-nine percent of participants with no formal statistics training said that the correct answer was (2), that Linda was a bank teller and active in the feminist movement was more probable than that Linda was a bank teller. Surprisingly, about the same percentages of participants with introductory and advanced statistics coursework (90 and 85 percent, respectively) also said that the correct answer was (2). Apparently, the representativeness heuristic caused study participants to view Linda as more typical of someone who is active in the feminist movement rather than someone who is a bank teller. This view led participants to provide an incorrect response to the statistical problem, even though they should have known better.

Framing and Loss Aversion

Tversky and Kahneman proposed other cognitive biases that they attributed to framing and loss aversion. *Framing* is the manner in which an option is presented. *Loss aversion* is a tendency to prefer avoiding losses much more strongly than acquiring gains, which leads to risk aversion if individuals evaluate a possible gain, since they prefer avoiding losses to making gains. In other circumstances, if individuals are facing a loss, loss aversion may cause them to prefer a riskier prospect if the riskier prospect provides the possibility of mitigating a loss.[34] Because of these cognitive biases, the possibility of suboptimal or inconsistent decisions arises.

For example, Tversky and Kahneman (1981) presented experimental evidence that individuals' risky choices depend on whether an option is framed as a loss or a gain. In the experiment, participants were asked to choose from among hypothetical public health programs to prevent the death of 600 persons from a disease. One problem was presented in terms of saving lives or gains, the other in terms of deaths or losses. Otherwise, the problems are identical:

Public Health Programs:

Problem 1

Program A: 200 lives will be saved.

Program B: 1/3 probability of saving 600 lives, and a two-out-of-three probability of saving no lives.

Problem 2:

Program C: 400 people will die.

Program D: A one-in-three probability that no one will die; a two-in-three probability that 600 people will die.

Participants who were presented problem 1 were more likely to choose program A than program B: certain saving of 200 lives over a one-in-three chance that no one will die. In contrast, participants who were presented problem 2 were more likely to choose program D than program C: a one-in-three chance that no one would die over a certain loss of 400. In problem 1, in which outcomes were framed in terms of gains, participants' choices were risk averse, but in problem 2, in which outcomes were framed in terms of losses, participants' choices were risk seeking.

In another example, Tversky and Kahneman also pointed to inconsistencies in preferences for options due to framing and loss aversion if contingencies are involved, such as two-stage process in which an uncertain outcome in the first stage determines whether the individual proceeds to an uncertain second stage. In one experiment, a group of participants was presented a choice between (A) a certain win of $30 or (B) an 80 percent chance to win $45, contingent in both cases on being selected with a probability of 25 percent in a first stage. Participants in this experiment were asked to state their preferred option before the beginning of the first stage. Their choices were similar to choices of a second group that was presented with options (A) and (B) without any first stage contingency. Seventy-four percent of the first group and 78 percent of the second group chose option (A).[35]

A third group was offered a choice with the same expected values as the choice offered the first group: (C) a 25-percent chance to win $30 and (D) a 20-percent chance to win $45; but, in this case, no contingency was involved. Only 42 percent of this group chose option (C), which was equivalent to option (A) for the first group. Tversky and Kahneman concluded from the responses of these three groups that participants tended to overlook the 25-percent chance of moving to the second stage, focusing only on the outcomes of the second stage in making their choice. For participants in the first group, option (A) appeared more attractive because it had the appearance of being certain. Thus, whether or not prospects are framed as contingencies may affect individuals' choices.

Kahneman and Tversky (1979) developed prospect theory to address such deviations from expected utility theory as differentiated reactions to losses and gains.[36] *Prospect theory* argues that for making choices, expected outcomes are first edited and then evaluated. Editing organizes and reformulates options to simplify subsequent evaluation and choice. This feature of prospect theory is consistent with earlier behavioral research indicating that individuals tend to simplify decisions. Kahneman and Tversky identified several possibilities for simplification:

- Prospects can sometimes be simplified by combining probabilities of identical outcomes. For example, two $200 outcomes having probabilities of 0.25 and 0.33 can be combined into a single outcome having a probability of 0.58.
- Sometimes prospects can be segregated into risky and riskless prospects. A prospect paying $100 with probability of 0.67 and $300 with probability 0.33 could be segregated into certain receipt of $100 and a risky prospect paying $200 with probability of 0.33.
- For two prospects having a common component, the common component can be discarded. For example, in the two-stage process described above in which participants were presented a choice in the second stage between (A) a certain win of $30 or (B) an 80-percent chance to win $45, the first stage might be ignored because it was common to both choices.[37]
- Prospects can also be simplified by rounding outcomes or probabilities ($101 to $100 or 0.49 to 0.50) and discarding extremely unlikely outcomes. In addition, clearly inferior prospects can be rejected without further consideration.

Kahneman and Tversky suggested that many anomalies and inconsistencies in preferences result from the editing phase. The experiment involving the contingent two-stage prospect is an example in which ignoring information in editing (the 25-percent probability of being eligible to the second-stage lottery) may have changed preferences.

Edited prospects are then evaluated, and the highest valued prospect is chosen. The value of each prospect is a weighted sum of the utility of possible outcomes associated with the prospect. The utility of each outcome is an individual's personal evaluation of a monetary value of an edited expected gain or loss (that is, a *value function*). The weight employed for each outcome (*decision weight*) reflects the personal evaluation on the basis of the likelihood of the outcome and is not a true probability.[38]

Kahneman and Tversky argued that individuals overweight very small probabilities. Hence, individuals are willing to buy insurance (incur a certain small loss, the insurance premium) in order to avoid a smaller expected value of loss (a very small actual probability of incurring a large loss) but also to purchase lottery tickets for a higher price than the expected payout (a large payout received with a very small actual probability).[39] Over the entire range of probabilities, Kahneman and Tversky argued, individuals are not especially sensitive to variations in probabilities, and decision weights need not, and typically do not, sum to unity.

Mental Accounting

Thaler (1980, 1985) adapted elements of prospect theory to develop the concept of mental accounting, a set of cognitive operations for individuals to organize, evaluate, and manage their budgets. Thaler focused his attention on the value function $v(x_i)$. He maintained the assumption that individuals define utility derived from potential outcomes in terms of gains or losses relative to a reference point. Considering Kahneman and Tversky's evidence on loss aversion, he proposed additional rules for editing prospects:

- Evaluate gains separately (because utility increases less than proportionately with the amount of gain);
- Combine losses (because utility decreases less than proportionately with the amount of loss);
- Integrate smaller losses with larger gains (to offset disutility arising from loss aversion); and
- Segregate small gains from larger losses (because the utility of a small gain may be greater than the utility from a small reduction in the amount of a loss).

He cited evidence from a small experiment in which most participants judged events consistent with these rules more favorably than events not edited according to these rules. In a later experimental study, Thaler and Johnson (1990) found support for three of these four rules. The exception was that most study participants did not prefer to combine losses.

Individuals then evaluate edited prospects. Thaler posited that individuals consider two types of utility in evaluating prospects: (1) *acquisition utility,* which depends on the value of the prospect relative to the outlay required to obtain the prospect; and (2) *transaction utility,* which reflects the outlay relative to a reference price. The reference price Thaler defined as a "fair" price. This evaluation process, he suggested, might explain why an individual would pay a higher price for an item in one context but not in another. For example, an individual might be willing to pay a considerably higher price for a bottle of water at an expensive hotel than at a supermarket. Because the hotel price would be considered unreasonably expensive at a supermarket, an individual might refuse to pay the hotel price at the supermarket.

Thaler proposed that individuals group prospects in categories of expenditure. The purchase decision takes place within the context of a category and subject to a local temporal budget constraint. That budget constraint is more likely to be based on current income flows (perhaps augmented by access to credit that the income can service) than the more general concept of the present value of lifetime wealth, which is commonly assumed in neoclassical economic models.

Thus, the mental accounting system consists of a set of expenditure categories or mental accounts with a portion of monthly income allocated to each category. The individual would normally restrict monthly expenditures in each category to the income allocated to the category. This simple heuristic likely works well in most circumstances, but can be nonoptimal. For instance, it prevents an individual from shifting income from one category to another to equalize marginal consumption across categories.

Mental accounting, then, is a heuristic that simplifies decision-making and may facilitate self-control. For credit decisions, mental accounting may help explain the often-cited observation that many consumers focus on monthly payments in making credit decisions (because it simplifies decision-making). It also may help explain why many consumers simultaneously have substantial liquid assets and owe credit card debt (because it prevents the depletion of funds saved for emergencies). Researchers have also suggested that mental accounting may help explain consumers' unwillingness to use credit to smooth income over time, as opposed to smoothing expenditures on durable goods. The explanation is developed more fully in a mental accounting model proposed by Prelec and Loewenstein (1998).

Prelec and Loewenstein (1998) argued that if individuals make purchases, the pain of paying undermines the pleasure derived from

consumption. To evaluate the interactions between the pleasure of consumption and the pain of paying they proposed a double-entry mental
accounting model in which an individual evaluates both the utility from
consumption after subtracting the imputed cost (the net utility of consumption) and the disutility of payments after subtracting the imputed
benefit associated with payments (the net disutility of payment). If benefits or costs occur over time, they are discounted to the present but not
necessarily at a constant rate. Prelec and Loewenstein's net utility/dis-
utility concepts are analogous to Thaler's (1980, 1985) acquisition and
transaction utilities.

Three significant additional assumptions underlie Prelec and
Loewenstein's mental accounting model. First, they assume that past
events are largely written off (*prospective accounting*). This assumption
implies, for example, that if a vacation is paid in advance, the cost is
essentially zero, and the vacation feels as if it were free. In contrast, much
of the utility of a vacation financed by credit would be forgotten, and the
pain of future debt repayments would be paramount in the mind.[40]

The second assumption is that individuals allocate future payments
to consumption or allocate consumption over future payments (*prorating
over multiple events*). In other words, individuals try to match consumption to payments. The third assumption is that individuals do not always
fully link payments and consumption (*decoupling*). The extent to which
payments and income are coupled, they suggested, varies according to
the situation, payment method, and individual.

From these assumptions, Prelec and Loewenstein hypothesized that
prepayment enhances consumption. The prospect of future consumption diminishes the pain of prepayment, while the prospective accounting assumption implies that past payments are largely written off at the
point of consumption. In contrast, debt financing tends to diminish the
utility of consumption. Future payments are discounted for current consumption, but past consumption is written off when future payments are
made. Thus, consumers would tend to have an aversion to debt.

These considerations do not imply that prepayment would always
be preferred and credit purchases avoided. An individual may well
prefer prepaying a vacation because the payments would be a memory
when consuming the vacation (and no thought of future debt payments
would diminish the pleasure). However, an installment purchase of a
durable good may be attractive if the durable good provides a series of
surpluses of consumption over the periodic payment or the durable provides services after the loan is paid in full. Indeed, this is typically the

case with the installment purchases of durable goods. Consumers consume the items as payments are made, enjoying contemporary benefits that exceed the payments and may outlast the payments.

Prelec and Loewenstein suggested that debt aversion resulting from mental accounting may help explain why individuals with temporarily low incomes fail to borrow sufficiently against future income to maintain a constant consumption profile over their lifetime. They also suggested that mental accounting might prevent consumers from paying off credit card debts. The pain of repaying a credit card debt immediately would be relatively large and possibly greater than the discounted disutility of making relatively small minimum payments to repay the debt. And if expenditures financed by credit cards provide little or no stream of future consumption, any benefits experienced in the past would tend not to be recalled and are therefore unavailable to offset the pain of repayment. Prelec and Loewenstein speculated further that credit cards may actually enhance the consumption paid by credit card if the payment is associated with the monthly credit card payment rather than the event of signing the credit card slip. This possibility arises because mental accounting enables the consumer to decouple the consumption from thoughts about paying.

Prelic and Loewenstein's provided evidence from several small-scale experiments involving hypothetical choices to support the theoretical predictions of their mental accounting model. Experiments included the rankings of schedules for taking vacations and making payments, the preferences for fixed or variable fees for different services, the pleasure associated with a windfall used to pay various types of bills or purchases, and the preference for saving or borrowing to pay for a party or miscellaneous expenses. This approach brings up the question of the reasonableness of experimental approaches to studying these matters.

Robustness of Experimental Evidence of Cognitive Errors and Biases

The replication of the results of experimental studies strongly supports the existence of certain cognitive biases; the significance of observed biases is uncertain, however. It turns out that the experimental tests are sensitive to the format of the problem and the experimental procedures. Changing the format of the question or implementing different procedures can make cognitive biases disappear. There is no generally accepted theory to explain why cognitive biases occur or what causes them to disappear, although some hypotheses have been suggested. Further, the extent to which cognitive biases affect actual behavior, including purchasing behavior, remains unresolved.

Researchers in the field of evolutionary psychology have proposed hypotheses to explain why cognitive biases are observed in some situations and not in others. Evolutionary psychologists have approached the problem on the basis of a theory that humans have many specialized cognitive processes that underlie their reasoning and that these responses are adaptations to humans' evolutionary natural environment.[41]

Evolutionary psychologists argue that human cognition of statistical processes occurs naturally through the observation of a series of events. Thus, human cognitive processes have adapted to process frequency information rather than probabilities. Therefore, experimental studies that frame problems in terms of probabilities may not adequately replicate the situations in which individuals make decisions under uncertainty.

Based on their theory, researchers in evolutionary psychology have hypothesized that presenting statistical problems in terms of frequencies would produce fewer errors than problems presented in terms of probabilities. In one study, Fiedler (1988) replicated Tversky and Kahneman's experiment using the original formulation of the Linda problem. He found that 91 percent of participants responded that the feminist bank teller option was more probable than the bank teller option. He conducted a second experiment in which he asked which option is more frequent rather than which is more probable.[42] In this experiment, only 22 percent of participants responded that the feminist bank teller option was more probable than the bank teller option. Similarly, Hertwig, and Gigerenzer (1993), reported in Gigerenzer (1994), found that 88 percent of participants made cognitive errors for the probability format, but only 20 percent made errors for the frequency format.

The frequency format reduced cognitive errors in other experimental problems as well. Gigerenzer and Hoffrage (1995) and Cosmides and Tooby (1996) conducted experiments comparing responses to probability and frequency formats in medical diagnosis problems. In both studies, participants were considerably more likely to provide correct responses to frequency formats than probability formats. Such results support the hypothesis that frequency formats facilitate statistical inference under some circumstances. They do not indicate that cognitive biases do not exist, but they do refute the notion that all statistical reasoning is biased.

The context of the problem may also influence how individuals respond. Hertwig and Gigerenzer (1999) investigated this possibility, again using Tversky and Kahneman's Linda problem. Recall that participants were asked whether it was more probable that (1) Linda is a bank teller or that (2) Linda is a bank teller and active in the feminist movement. Hertwig and Gigerenzer pointed out that that the opening statements in the problem (that Linda is thirty-one years old, single, out-spoken, and very bright; that she majored in philosophy in college; and that as a student, she was deeply concerned with issues of discrimination and social justice, and also participated in antinuclear demonstrations) are not needed to answer the statistical problem. They hypothesized that these statements can be interpreted as asking for a typicality judgment. In that case, a representativeness heuristic might well be an efficient process for producing an appropriate judgment.

Hertwig and Gigerenzer's empirical analyses supported this hypothesis. In a small-scale experiment, they found that by far most participants chose (2) as the correct answer. When asked about their understanding of the word *probable*, most provided responses suggesting a non-statistical understanding. In a second experiment, Hertwig and Gigerenzer presented the problem in the original format to half of the participants and a modified format asking for both typical and statistical judgments. Participants responding to the modified, two-part, format provided correct answers to the statistical problem much more frequently than participants responding to the original format.

Hertwig and Gigerenzer conducted a similar analysis of participants' understanding of the question in a frequency format. When participants were asked about their understanding of *frequently*, only one of 55 responses was non-statistical. Thus, it seems that the findings of considerably lower cognitive error rates for the frequency format than the probability format are not surprising, regardless of the validity of evolutionary psychologists' theories about frequency data.

Krynski and Tennenbaum (2003) proposed another potential source for observed cognitive errors in experimental studies. They argued that human reasoning under uncertainty naturally operates over causal mental models, rather than purely statistical representations. Typically, individuals make correct statistical inferences only if the data can be incorporated into a causal model consistent with individuals' theories of the environment. The problem focused on predicting the incidence of cancer, given a false positive test result. The possible cognitive error for this problem arises from a failure to consider the overall base rate of cancer in the population. They hypothesized that lacking an explanation for a false positive test result, individuals will tend to believe the test and focus only on the information from the test.

Krynski and Tennenbaum conducted two experiments. In the first, they tested whether describing false positive test results as uncertain would lead participants to believe the false positive rate and incorporate that information in their estimates. In the second test, they compared responses to a statistical question with those to a question that attributed false positive results to benign cysts.

In both experiments, they found that providing a way for participants to make sense of false positive results improved estimates. The number of participants who failed to consider the low base rate was lower, and the number of correct or near-correct estimates was higher for the causal format. They interpreted these findings as evidence that human probabilistic reasoning operates over causal mental models. These findings suggest that failing to consider or misunderstanding causal structure may be an important source of error in experimental studies of problem-solving involving uncertainty. In order to construct such causal models, theories of cognitive processes for specific environments are needed.

Even without accepting the theories of evolutionary psychologists, the sensitivity of experimental results to the format, context, and content of the problem suggests that some skepticism about the extent and impact of cognitive biases is warranted. For instance, economists have questioned the significance of experimental evidence of alleged cognitive biases such as the so-called endowment effect.

Plott and Zeiler (2005) conducted a particularly thorough investigation of differences in preferences attributed to an endowment effect. The *endowment effect* is the contention that individuals value an item they own more than an identical item that they do not own. This effect is hypothesized to arise from loss aversion and causes individuals' willingness to pay for an item to differ from their willingness to accept payment to do without the item. As a result, they demand much more to do without the item than they would pay to obtain it, which is not consistent with normative concepts of economic rationality.[43]

Plott and Zeiler examined in detail previous experimental studies of the endowment effect. They noted that the different studies employed various procedures to avoid participant misunderstanding of the nature of the problem, but participants may well have misunderstood anyway. They contended that the previous studies did not agree on the nature of potential misunderstandings, and no study had included all possible procedures they identified to avoid participant misunderstandings.

They also noted that even without focusing on the misunderstanding difficulty, the experimental evidence is not robust, despite some claims to the contrary (see, for example, Kahneman, Knetsch, and Thaler 1991). Twelve of the thirty-nine experiments Plott and Zeiler examined reported no significant difference in willingness to pay and willingness to accept. For these reasons, they contended that evidence of an endowment effect is not conclusive.

In the absence of a theory of how perceptions might influence experimental results, Plott and Zeiler developed an experimental design to avoid all possible sources of misunderstanding identified in previous studies. They initially chose the experimental design reported in Kahneman, Knetsch, and Thaler (1990) and replicated the results: The median willingness to accept was significantly greater than willingness to pay.

Plott and Zeiler then modified the survey procedures to avoid possible participant misunderstandings previously identified in the literature. For example, to elicit valuations, they used a market mechanism that provides incentives for participants to provide true valuations. They explained to participants that providing true valuations maximizes earnings, and they provided practice rounds for both selling valuation (willingness to accept) and buying valuation (willingness to pay). Participants kept any earnings from the practice rounds, so they did not think they were wasting their time. Participants also were told that strategic behavior (gaming the system) was not optimal, and practice rounds allowed participants to learn that such behavior reduced earnings. Plott and Zeiler also ensured that decisions and payments were anonymous so that participants would not be tempted to consider how others (either experimenters or other participants) would view their valuations.

The results of the modified experiment indicated that participants' willingness to accept was not significantly different from their willingness to pay. Based on their findings, Plott and Zeiler concluded that the observed differences between the willingness to accept and the willingness to pay do not reflect a fundamental feature of preferences and do not support the endowment effect hypothesis:[44] (Plott and Zeiler 2005, p. 542)

> The fact that the gap [between willingness to pay and willingness to accept] can be turned on and off demonstrates that interpreting gaps as support for endowment effect theory is problematic.

The mere observation of the phenomenon does not support loss aversion, a very special form of preferences in which gains are valued less than losses. That the phenomenon can be turned on and off while holding the good constant supports a strong rejection of the claim that WTP–WTA [willingness to pay, willingness to accept] gaps support a particular theory of preferences posited by prospect theory.

In sum, the experimental evidence indicates that the results are sensitive to experimental procedures, and this must be taken into account before arriving at strong conclusions. Further, Plott and Zeiler's findings provide evidence that market environments may influence cognitive process and produce different results than controlled experiments.

Heuristics and Market Performance

Ultimately more important than the results of experimental studies alone is the relationship to market outcomes. As mentioned earlier in this chapter, limited theoretical evidence indicates that a satisficing heuristic produces long-run optimal outcomes, in some circumstances, and empirical evidence from experimental economics (the branch of economics that applies experimental methods to study how markets and exchange systems work), supports this theoretical conclusion. The studies consistently indicate that individual decisions based on limited information in experimental markets produce prices and allocations that converge quickly to the neighborhood of optimal equilibrium values, an important contention. (See Smith 1991 for references and a summary of the findings of various studies.) The results occur even though participants do not engage in extensive weighing of alternatives. Smith proposed that markets and institutions serve as social tools that reinforce or even induce individual rationality, even though how this happens is not well understood. The important point is that the behavior of participants using various heuristics with limited information produces efficient market outcomes.

Experimental studies have also found that market environments reduce the incidence of preference reversals for risky prospects and losses from failure to recognize sunk costs and opportunity costs.[45] Smith (1991) argued that the findings of these studies suggest that markets reinforce or even induce individual rationality, although, as indicated, the manner in which markets promote rationality is not yet well understood (see Smith 1991, p. 881).

In a later paper, Smith (2005) speculated further on how markets promote rationality: Market prices provide stimuli that cause individuals to take actions that better their situations. These actions move prices and allocations toward competitive equilibrium. According to Smith, focusing on whether or not individual decisions *always* are optimal misses the point (p. 146). Individuals can still benefit from market processes, even if their decisions are not optimal. From a behavioral standpoint, this ultimately is analogous to the economic point advanced by Schwartz and Wilde (1979) and Wilde and Schwartz (1979) and discussed above: Limitations in individuals' information do not necessarily preclude the achievement of competitive market outcomes. In such markets, individuals do not need complete information in order to make purposive decisions and receive the benefits of the market processes.

Time Discounting and Time Preference

Beyond cognitive biases, as indicated earlier, the second source of questions arising from relatively recent behavioral research on consumers' ability to make rational decisions concerns experimental studies of time preferences. This researched reawakened economists' interest in psychological assumptions underlying intertemporal choices, which had become dormant after Samuelson's (1937) paper, "A Note on Measurement of Utility." In this paper, Samuelson developed a discounted-utility model as a generalization over multiple time periods of the economic model of intertemporal choice formalized a few years earlier by Irving Fisher (1930). Before Samuelson's paper, psychology played a major role in economists' discussions of intertemporal choice. Fisher, for example, extensively discussed the personal characteristics that contribute to or lessen impatience. These characteristics include short-sightedness, a weak will, the habit of spending freely, an emphasis on the shortness and uncertainty of life, selfishness, and a slavish following of whims of fashion; and their opposites.[46]

Utility and Time Preference

Samuelson's (1937) discounted-utility model posits that an individual behaves so as to maximize the sum of all future utilities. Future utilities are reduced to comparable magnitudes by discounting. For simplicity, Samuelson assumed that individuals discount by a single, constant discount rate, which is the same for all types of consumption and across all time periods. Assuming the same discount rate across all types of consumption precludes different discount rates for different items, such as gains being discounted more heavily than losses (that is, the loss aversion discussed earlier in this chapter).

More recently, assuming the same discount rate across all time periods also precludes discounting items closer in time more than more distant items. (A declining rate of time preference is often termed *hyperbolic discounting* because a hyperbolic function provides a better fit to a model of this kind than a constant, exponential function.) Samuelson did not claim that individuals actually discounted using a single constant rate. Instead, he maintained that a single, constant rate was a hypothesis, subject to refutation by the observable facts.

Many researchers have observed behavior consistent with hyperbolic or other non-constant rate of time discounting. Thaler (1981) is one such study (see Frederick, Loewenstein, and O'Donoghue 2002 for a comprehensive list). In Thaler's study, participants were asked to imagine that they had won a lottery. They could receive an amount of money immediately or a larger amount if they wait. Participants were asked how much money they would need to receive to wait different periods of time. For one set of options involving receipt of $15, for example, the median amount participants required to wait three months was $30, which implied a discount rate of 277 percent; a one-year wait required $60 or 139 percent, and a three-year wait required $100 or 63 percent. For another set of options also involving receipt of $15, the median amount participants required to wait one month was $20 or 345 percent per annum. The median amount for three months was $30 or 277 percent, for one year $50 or 120 percent, and for ten years $100 or 19 percent. Other researchers, also using experimental data, have found similar patterns. Such findings suggest that individuals are more impatient about shorter than longer delays.

Available evidence from many different studies suggests that discount rates decline sharply during the short run and then level off and become practically constant. Frederick, Loewenstein, and O'Donoghue (2002) examined the relationship between estimated discount rates and the time horizon from different studies. They found that the discount rate was inversely related to the length of the time horizon. The highest discount rates were for time horizons of one year or less. Discount rates decreased with the length of the time horizon. After a year, the discount rate was nearly constant, on average about 25 percent. This relationship is quite imprecise, however. Estimates from the individual studies varied quite substantially.

Constant, exponential discounting ensures that decisions are time consistent (Strotz 1955–1956). Time consistency means that if receiving Y tomorrow is preferred to X today, then receiving Y in 101 days will be preferred to X in 100 days. With hyperbolic discounting, the discount rate for evaluating options received tomorrow instead of today is greater than the discount rate for evaluating options received between the 101st and 100th day. Consequently, an individual could well prefer receiving X today instead of Y tomorrow, while preferring to receive Y in 101 days to X in 100 days. In words, the individual's preference over options X and Y reverses as the decision gets closer. Such preferences are called time-inconsistent. Time-inconsistent behavior may lead individuals to deviate from prior optimal intertemporal allocations in future time periods.

Besides a constant discount rate, the discounted utility model involves several additional assumptions. (Empirical evidence indicates that individuals do not behave in accordance with these assumptions either; see Frederick, Loewenstein, and O'Donohue 2002.) They include:

- *The integration of new prospects with existing plans:* Individuals evaluate a new prospect by considering how accepting the prospect will affect consumption in all future periods. This assumption is a consequence of the effect that accepting the prospect alters the budget constraint. Such integration requires that individuals have well-formed plans for future consumption and reallocate future consumption every time a decision is made.
- *Utility independence:* Utility is the discounted sum of each period's utility. Aside from discounting, the distribution across time does not matter. This assumption rules out preferences for a flat or improving utility profile over a highly uneven utility profile.
- *Consumption independence:* The utility of consumption in any period is unaffected by consumption in any other period. Consumption independence rules out, for example, that an individual's preference between lobster and steak for dinner depends upon having steak last evening or expecting to have steak tomorrow evening.
- *Stationary instantaneous utility:* An individual's well-being from an outcome in any time period is constant regardless of the time at which utility is evaluated. This assumption precludes changes in preferences over time.

Departures from some of the assumptions of the expected utility model do not seem to be problematic. That individuals may prefer to

spread consumption over time or allow variety to influence their choices
for dinner today and in the future does not suggest irrational behavior.
The failure to integrate new prospects in existing plans and hyperbolic
discounting are more problematic.

New prospects alter the intertemporal budget constraint. To evaluate a new prospect, an individual must consider both the existing consumption plan and the optimal consumption plan if the prospect is
accepted. This decision is difficult, but the failure to integrate new prospects may preclude reallocations that equalize the marginal consumption over time, resulting in a suboptimal intertemporal allocation of
consumption. It seems more plausible that individuals consider many
new prospects independently of existing consumption plans. Mental
accounting may play a role in simplifying such evaluations.

Hyperbolic Discounting

Hyperbolic discounting has raised the most concern. As mentioned, the
higher valuation of present over future utilities may lead individuals to
deviate from prior optimal intertemporal allocations in future time periods. For example, individuals might postpone or abandon earlier plans
for setting aside money in savings. As a consequence, individuals might
not save enough for future expenses or retirement. Hyperbolic discounting has also been be linked to behavior that can be or is harmful, such as
procrastination (O'Donoghue and Rabin 1999) and addiction (O'Donoghue
and Rabin 2000), for instance.

Whether or not hyperbolic discounting is irrational is not clear.
Individuals make numerous intertemporal choices, in most cases, apparently, without suffering great harm. In some cases, choosing a smaller
proximate reward may be sensible, such as if future prospects, preferences,
and resources are risky and uncertain or the proximate reward ensures
survival (see Becker and Mulligan 2001, Smith 2005).[47] Further, individuals
may exercise self-control to prevent impatience from jeopardizing long-
term plans. Individuals may also enter into contractual arrangements that
obligate them to carry out long-term plans (pre-commit).

Individuals have cognitive self-control structures that provide
the ability to direct thought and action to achieve internal goals. The
activation of these cognitive control structures enables individuals to
inhibit automatic processes that are susceptible to impulses.[48] Benhabib
and Bisin (2005) model such a structure for a consumption–saving decision. The structure trades off impulsive immediate consumption with a
saving rule requiring self-control for its implementation. Self=control

requires actively maintaining attention to the saving rule. An individual facing temptations might yield to a temptation only if it does not perturb the saving plan too much and does not have large permanent effects on the prescribed pattern of wealth accumulation. To be effective, the saving rule requires that the internal inhibitions become stronger as the awareness of the cost of impulsive consumption increases.

To enforce previous decisions, individuals sometimes pre-commit to future actions, such as having automatic contributions from pay to tax-deferred savings accounts or using installment credit to purchase relatively expensive household durables (see Strotz 1955–1956 or Laibson 1997, for example). Casual observation and empirical evidence indicate that individuals frequently exercise self-control through pre-commitment.

Ariely and Wertenbach (2002) provide experimental evidence that in circumstances where time inconsistent behavior is costly, many individuals self-impose binding constraints to overcome perceived self-control problems. The evidence consists of two studies. One involved course requirements for students' class papers, with one class being allowed to choose deadlines for each of three papers and the other being assigned three evenly spaced deadlines. A grade penalty was imposed for missing a deadline. Given a choice, most students chose deadlines before the end of the course: Only 12 of 51 students chose to submit all three papers on the last day of class. Comparing the performance of students in the two groups, Ariely and Wertenbach found that overall students in the no-choice class performed better than students in the free-choice class.[49] However, the performance of students in the free-choice class who chose approximately evenly spaced deadlines was not statistically significantly different from the performance of students in the no-choice class. Together, these findings suggest that some individuals did not set self-imposed deadlines optimally. Ariely and Wertenbach did not report the number of free-choice students for this test, but the chart of the frequency distribution of declared deadlines by week shows that declared deadlines clustered around evenly spaced intervals.

The second study involved a paid proofreading task, in which participants were randomly assigned to three experimental groups: (1) self-imposed deadlines, (2) mandatory evenly spaced deadlines, and (3) an end-of-study-period deadline. Payments were $0.10 per correctly identified error, and a $1.00 penalty was imposed for missing a deadline. The results of the experiment indicated that the number of errors correctly detected, timely submissions, and payment amounts were highest for the mandatory evenly spaced group and lowest for the

end-of-study-period deadline. Again, Ariely, and Wertenbach found
that performance for self-imposed evenly spaced deadlines were not
statistically significantly different from mandatory evenly spaced deadlines. Thus, they concluded that individuals self-impose costly deadlines
to overcome procrastination, self-imposed deadlines improve performance, and self-imposed deadlines are not always optimal (if optimal is
defined as evenly spaced).

Significance of the New Behavioral Economics

That cognitive errors and time-inconsistent discounting exist is well
established in the behavioral literature. However, the significance of
these phenomena for purchasing behavior is less clear. The mostly experimental evidence of these behavioral biases is not robust; the evidence is
sensitive to the format, content, and context of the problems presented to
study participants.

Some of the problems presented to participants of experimental
studies likely do not reflect the problems actually experienced by most
individuals in making decisions under uncertainty. Moreover, participants in experimental studies may not use the same decision processes
that they use in making actual decisions. Experimental problems often
appear more similar to test questions than choices that consumers actually face in the marketplace. Hypothetical situations are likely perceived
as such by study participants. There is little cost to making an error and
not much reward for the efforts to provide a correct response. Therefore,
participants in experiments likely do not make great efforts to analyze
the problems.[50]

Individuals may be predisposed to impulsive behavior but they also
have the capacity to exert self-control to implement forward-looking
plans. Self-control requires actively maintaining attention to the plan.
An individual facing an impulse might yield to the impulse if it does not
perturb the plan too much. To be effective, self-control requires that the
internal inhibitions become stronger as awareness of the cost of impulsive behavior increases. It is not clear that participants exert the same
cognitive efforts in experimental situations as they do in actual situations
that involve big commitments in money and duration, past experience
and information are insufficient or obsolete, or the outcomes of previous
decisions are regarded as unsatisfactory.

Statistical, logical, or other rational models of decision-making may
not necessarily be the appropriate norm for evaluating decisions

(Samuels, Stich, and Faucher 2004). Another concept of rationality is behavior consistent with the achievement of one's goals or objectives.[51] Heuristics often perform as well but require less information to implement as these rules are based upon full information and the weighing of alternatives. Heuristics may efficiently facilitate the achievement of goals in an environment of limited and costly information.

It seems reasonable to conclude that individuals sometimes do make cognitive mistakes. We cannot conclude from this, however, that all, most, or even a large percentage of human decisions are influenced by cognitive biases. Assessing decisions requires understanding the cognitive process and the environment in which the decision is made. Research in evolutionary psychology has contributed to this understanding and deserves to be taken seriously. Precise and falsifiable models that predict specific circumstances that elicit various heuristics are needed. To date, theories have been applied only to relatively simple problems. Theories on the use of specific heuristics in consumer credit decisions or cognitive biases arising from such use have not been vigorously tested.

In the financial area, empirical evidence indicates that consumers generally use credit to finance the purchases of relatively expensive consumer durable goods, not to smooth consumption. In doing so, behavioral concepts such as pre-commitment and mental accounts may be used to manage behavior. Some research suggests that these psychological considerations influence consumers' credit behavior. The extent to which cognitive biases and time-inconsistent discounting affect actual credit decisions is not known at this time.

Evidence from analyses of actual credit card behavior indicates that consumers are sensitive to price, consistent with the predictions of economic theory. If a credit card company increases the interest rates on an account, consumers reduce new charges, reduce existing balances, and shift charges to other credit card accounts; and over the course of a year, they reduce total credit card balances from the level before the price increase (Gross and Souleles 2002). Based on subsequent account use, consumers generally make cost-minimizing choices, trading off interest rates and annual fees when choosing new credit card accounts. If they make mistakes, the mistakes are usually relatively small. If the mistakes are large, consumers generally correct the mistakes. Although some consumers do not correct large mistakes, persistent large mistakes are not the rule (Agarwal, Chomsisengphet, Liu, and Souleles 2005). Analyses of credit card behavior based on survey data also suggest that consumers are sensitive to cost and do not incur costly mistakes (Zinman 2007, 2009).

And, evidence suggests that, by far, most consumers believe that credit cards provide a useful service and are satisfied with their dealings with credit card companies (Durkin 2000).

New behavioral models provide useful hypotheses on consumers' credit behavior. However, the theories are incomplete and have not been thoroughly tested. Our understanding of the processes is insufficient to justify specific policy actions or even to judge whether or not a problem exists. At this time, neither behavioral nor conventional evidence supports a conclusion of pervasive failures of household credit markets due to behavioral biases. None of this, of course, argues against requiring disclosures, whose benefits are clear enough from traditional economics and behavioral science. If the new behavioral economics does not demonstrate that the existence of cognitive biases is sufficient to show that credit use is irrational, then it does not undermine the contention that well-designed disclosures are useful. This is especially true if the disclosures reduce such costs.[52]

Conclusion: What Theory Tells Us about Required Disclosures

Both economic and behavioral theories promise a net beneficial return from required disclosures. The economics of information argues for the importance of information for the functioning of markets and contends that imperfect information about prices can result in price dispersion and divergence from production costs, even with otherwise competitive market conditions and a homogeneous product. Economics further maintains that information conditions are rarely going to be perfect, ultimately because both disseminating and gathering information is costly; information providers and users will act only as long as their individual expected private benefits exceed their private expected costs. Fortunately, there are important incentives at work for both groups. On the buy side, consumers understand that fuller information can provide them with better prices and more satisfactory purchases, leading to information demand. On the sell side, there are incentives for those with low prices and high-quality products to supply that information to potential customers. Finally, theory suggests that it is not necessary for all consumers to be completely informed for markets to function reasonably efficiently and provide a beneficial outcome even to those who do not gather information themselves. Newer branches of behavioral research do not undermine this contention.

Required disclosures have the potential to make the information dissemination process simpler and less costly for both providers and users. TILA and other required disclosure programs can improve the usefulness of information by defining and standardizing important terms and procedures, thereby improving market conditions, as long as the requirements do not involve excessive production costs. Nonetheless, the chance for policymaking disputes and errors is obvious. Also, though less commonly noted or emphasized, the better availability of information *about* consumers helps the functioning of credit markets by reducing the likelihood of credit rationing.

Traditionally, behavioral scientists have focused more than economists on the impact of information on individuals. Like the economists, they conclude also that perfect information is more a theoretical concept than a reasonable goal, but they emphasize the process necessary for information cues to become stimulants of individual action. This is the province of the marketers, who have an obvious reason for wanting to translate cues into actions, but also to those who believe that consumers will be better off if they behave appropriately, as suggested by the information. Like the economists, the behavioral scientists and marketers cite the costs of disseminating and gathering information, but the important motivation of the behaviorists is to spur individual action.

Consequently, economists and behavioral scientists may largely focus on different aspects of information availability, but the fact of their dissimilarity in approach does not argue that they are in dispute. Economists emphasize the functioning of markets using theory and mathematical modeling as guides, and the behaviorists and marketers focus on the behavior of individuals using experiments and surveys as guides. Both groups of analysts emphasize the overall importance of information availability, examine the costs of improving information conditions, and realize the importance of required disclosure regimes.

The information-processing theories of the behavioral scientists also suggest the need to consider carefully how any proposed disclosure regime is going to reach its intended goals. The theory in this area argues that the greatest likelihood of success for required disclosures probably arises from the chance to lower consumers' costs of information acquisition rather than convince them of the benefits of obtaining information. Further, the difficulties of information processing argue that extensive point-of-sale disclosures are a different regime and do not necessarily even promote, better long-term understanding.

4

What is Truth in Lending?
Key Conceptual Problems Facing
the Truth in Lending Act

In many ways, the Truth in Lending Act (TILA), enacted by Congress as Title I of the Consumer Credit Protection Act of 1968 (Public Law 90-321, May 29, 1968), is the centerpiece of federal consumer protection efforts in the credit area: It was the first federal intervention into consumer credit markets to regulate the activities of creditors in peacetime, its disclosure scheme is the most extensive of any federal financial consumer protection, and it regulates disclosures in possibly the most controversial area of consumer financial services — price and terms in the market for credit.

More fundamentally, TILA answered the question, at least for the four decades after its implementation, whether federal consumer protection in the credit area would be approached primarily through the disclosure of information to the consumer or through the regulation of contracts and practices. As discussed in Appendix A, "Financial Disclosures in the Federal Consumer Protection Statutes," TILA contains some provisions regulating practices, mostly concerning the rescission rights on loans secured by homes; credit card solicitations; credit card billing; home equity lines of credit; and high cost mortgages. Nevertheless, the law remains first and primarily a disclosure statute. Of all the federal financial information-based protections, TILA is probably the one most dependent upon the usefulness of the information it mandates for a favorable consumer protection outcome.

This chapter looks at some conceptual difficulties with TILA's central disclosures — the finance charge and the annual percentage rate (APR) — that have contributed so greatly to TILA's checkered evolution.

To preview, the concepts of the finance charge and the associated APR illustrate how the law (1) mandates the disclosure of transaction components that often cannot be separated easily or neatly and (2) tries to provide for the disclosures about future outcomes of transactions that are contingent on unknowable future developments. Attempts to overcome these fundamental conceptual problems through the extensive disclosure of bits and pieces of other information is a good part of why the disclosure scheme has become so massive and unwieldy. In turn, the complexity generates calls for more disclosures, especially if there is any evidence or belief that some segment of the population does not fully understand some aspect of existing disclosures. The ensuing demand for summaries, explanations, and more details has produced a constantly expanding regulatory structure that is supposed to aid consumer understanding.

This progression of disclosures leading to more disclosures is visible throughout the history of TILA but probably no more obviously so than for the example of credit cards. Disclosures for revolving credit, including credit cards, were not part of the precursor to TILA, the 1960 draft of Senator Paul Douglas's Consumer Credit Labeling Bill, but they found their way into the 1968 law. Two decades later, apparently not satisfied with the outcome, Congress provided for summary disclosures of existing requirements in the Fair Credit and Charge Card Disclosure Act (Public Law 100-583, November 3, 1988). After almost another two decades of experience, the Federal Reserve Board (FRB) in 2007 proposed a further revamping and more summaries of the information previously provided, portions of which were already in summary form, and approved the proposed rules in December 2008. The changes emerged from a team of lawyers working on the recommendations for about a half decade and also involving three public comment periods and the work of a significant team of consultants from a consumer behavior research company. (The 2008 changes are discussed in more detail in Chapters 5, "The Outlay and Unknown Future Events Issues: Closed-End Credit," and 6, "The Outlay and Unknown Future Events Issues: Open-End Credit.") Apparently still not satisfied, Congress legislated new requirements for credit cards in early 2009. Then, in 2010, Congress established a Bureau of Financial Consumer Protection (BFCP) whose proponents have promised further revisions of credit card disclosures. And so the beat goes on for credit cards, now into their fifth decade of disclosure evolution.

After a review of some of fundamental conceptual difficulties with TILA in this chapter and some illustrative examples of how things can go wrong in Chapters 5 and 6, it will be time to take another look at the underlying goals of TILA and attempts to measure its success (Chapter 7, "The Rubber Meets the Road: Evaluating the Effectiveness of the Truth in Lending Act") and to discuss ways out of the dilemma (Chapter 8, "Suggestions for a Way Forward").

The Key Cost Disclosures: Finance Charge and the Annual Percentage Rate

There is general agreement that the primary disclosures required by TILA are, in the terms used in the law, the "finance charge" and the "Annual Percentage Rate" or "APR." The finance charge is the cost of credit (that is, the cost of the amount borrowed) in dollars and cents. The APR expresses the finance charge as the unit price per year.

The APR is the summary, standardized unit price measure intended to free disclosed costs from variations due to the credit amount, maturity, and the timing of advances and payments. The APR's role in the credit area is analogous to cents per pound for dry goods or dollars per gallon for milk or gasoline, but, importantly, it also encompasses time (that is, the unit price per dollar of credit per measure of time). It is the time dimension that constitutes the essence of a credit transaction and differentiates credit from other purchases. The idea of the APR was to provide a measure of credit cost that can summarize all the dimensions, including time, in a standardized way that is consistent for all transactions.

The importance attached to the finance charge and the APR in the act is easy enough to see: These terms must be disclosed more conspicuously than other terms; they are among the terms that trigger statutory damages, required re-disclosure, and administrative reimbursement for mis-disclosure; and they are among the terms that can trigger rescission if not disclosed properly in mortgage transactions.

Both the finance charge and APR are fundamentally simple concepts, despite their mythology and their noteworthy operational and legal complexities. For the closed-end credit plans that constituted the bulk of consumer and mortgage credit at the time of passage of TILA, the finance charge is the (undiscounted) sum of credit costs over the credit period, stated in dollars and cents. The APR, in turn, is the annualized nominal discount rate that equates the payment stream to its present value; the present value is referred to in TILA as the "amount financed." (More will be said later about finance charges and APRs on open-end credit.)

The APR is the TILA analogue of the interest rate, but it encompasses in its calculation *all credit costs included in the finance charge, not just interest*. For intricate closed-end credit transactions with multiple credit advances and/or variable time periods between payments, calculating the APR can become quite complex. But the basic mathematics for most transactions is not very complicated, although when expressed in words, as it is in the act, it might seem so. Section 107 of the act defines the annual percentage rate ("in the case of any extension of credit other than under an open end credit plan") as:

> (T)hat nominal Annual Percentage Rate which will yield a sum equal to the amount of the finance charge when it is applied to the unpaid balances of the amount financed, calculated according to the actuarial method of allocating payments made on a debt between the amount financed and the amount of the finance charge, pursuant to which a payment is applied first to the accumulated finance charge and the balance is applied to the amount financed; … .

Paragraph 226.22(a)(1) of Regulation Z says the same thing in somewhat less formidable terms before directing the reader to Appendix J of the regulation for formal mathematical statement:

> The Annual Percentage Rate is a measure of the cost of credit, expressed as a yearly rate, that relates the amount and timing of value received by the consumer to the amount and timing of payments made.

The general equation for calculating the APR is in section 8 of Appendix J to Regulation Z. The equation that annualizes the calculated periodic rate is in section 7 of Appendix J. Together, these two equations define the APR for closed-end credit. Thus, using the simplest example, a single credit advance and a stream of identical payments, the definition of the APR for closed-end credit in decimal form is the number of periods in a year, n (which equals 12 for monthly payments), times the rate, r/n, that provides the solution to the following discounting equation for the number of years, t.[1] Multiplying the decimal equivalent by 100 (equation 2) gives the rate as a percentage:[2]

$$\text{AmtFin} = \text{PV} = \sum_{i=0}^{nt} (\text{Pmts}_i)(1 + r/n)^{-i} \qquad (1)$$

$$APR = n(r/n) * 100 = r* 100 \qquad\qquad (2)$$

Importantly, these equations demonstrate how the APR on a typical closed-end transaction is the residual calculation in the process. The closed-end APR is calculated from the amount financed and the stream of payments that *includes* the finance charge; it is not calculated solely from the amount financed and the stream of payments consisting of the finance charge alone, as some observers sometimes seem to believe (including some TILA lawyers). For closed-end credit, the APR is dependent on the size and timing of the payments discounted to a present value (the amount financed). Equation 1 shows that the periodic discount rate r/n (and, therefore, by Equation 2, the APR) is the solution to a single equation (Equation 1) in which everything else is already known: the present value of the transaction along with the number, amount, and schedule of cash flows (payments). A single unknown is, of course, a requirement to make a single-equation system solvable.

The Conceptual Stumbling Block: What is a Credit Cost?

Since implementation of TILA in 1969, most of the disclosure questions and controversy surrounding the APR area have arisen not from the mathematical requirements for calculating the mandated APR disclosure (although there have been some difficulties there too), but rather from a central conceptual matter: what cost items constitute the cost of credit, called the *finance charge*, and what parts of the cash flows are something else? Since isolating the finance charge is necessary for disclosing it properly and calculating the APR correctly, this issue is a core concern for TILA. At first glance, the question might seem archaic now, more than four decades after the passage of the act, but as credit markets have evolved, it has remained remarkably unsettled.

Ultimately, the composition of the finance charge for required disclosures is the key operational question for truth in lending as a consumer protection, maybe the only really significant one. The resolution of the question cannot eliminate uncertainty and wrangling over legal details in other areas, including over mathematical methods, what else should be disclosed, and how and when. But with a clear answer to the question of what constitutes the finance charge, disclosure of the other required measures, including the APR, becomes much simpler.

This central conceptual uncertainty in TILA—the definition of the finance charge and, by implication, the APR—manifests itself in three sets of specific issues. The following names are our terms; they do not appear in TILA: the outlay issue, the unknown future events issue, and the compliance issue.

The outlay issue is the problem that arises because not all outlays in conjunction with a credit transaction are credit costs, and this frequently generates confusion over which outlays constitute such costs and which are something else. For example, outlays in a credit transaction also can include down payments, expenditures for other products, repayments of principal due on a prior transaction, and other outlays for a variety of ancillary services and taxes. Under full disclosure, everything must be accounted for correctly, however, added and subtracted correctly, and disclosed as necessary in the right boxes and formats "clearly and conspicuously" (Regulation Z 226.5(a)(1) and 226.17(1)).

The unknown future events issue arises because both the amount of credit costs and the cash flows arising from credit arrangements always depend on future actions and typically are not known with certainty before the transaction, which is when initial disclosures are due. Consequently, there must always be some assumptions in order to make initial disclosures. But assumptions necessarily introduce an element of arbitrariness into any proceeding, and there often are good arguments for employing some other reasonable assumptions. This means there is potential for ambiguity and mistakes in determining proper finance charges and APRs, sometimes leading to arguments over policy as well as legal disputes.

The compliance issue concerns the effects and implications of compromises, deviations from rules, and special rules generated to help creditors comply. Over the years, the operation and evolution of credit markets, products, and the uses of credit products, together with the range of size, sophistication, and technical skills of creditors, have produced a demand for simplifications, exceptions, shortcuts, and compliance aids. This demand has focused especially on the mathematical conception of the APR itself, and has produced a host of special provisions.

At the heart of the controversy over each of these three groupings of concerns about the finance charge is an inherent conflict of basic objectives. On one side is the laudable search for exactitude, completeness, consistency, and comparability in a complicated area despite complex and changing markets and an unknown future ("truth" in lending, after all). Against this is the difficulty for consumers to understand all the necessary concepts along with the equally praiseworthy goal, at least to those regulated and, importantly, to the political figures who constitute the Congress, of reasonable compliance ease for regulated institutions, especially smaller and less sophisticated ones and larger ones with a wide range of products. As so often is the case in legislative matters, a clear solution that is acceptable to everyone is not instantly obvious.

The ongoing search for resolution of the conflict among exactness, understanding, and reasonable compliance ease has produced decisions and compromises leading to multiple regulatory approaches in some areas, anomalies, various inconsistencies, and lots of disputes, along with mind numbing complexity in the law, the regulation, and the *Commentary*, which is itself the compilation of the set of annual official interpretations believed necessary. This complexity, in turn, has produced simultaneous criticism that the regulation is not exact enough to constitute *truth*, but also that the current regulatory structure is unworkable to the point that compliance is impossible.

Despite all the accrued complexity, the underlying fundamental approach of TILA has not changed much at all since its inception. With more than four decades of hindsight, it seems clear that any really substantive improvements to the current structure (further dramatic simplification, for example) will require a firmer decision on the fundamental question of exactitude, completeness, and consistency of understanding versus reasonable ease of compliance.

The Outlay Issue

The outlay issue poses the problem of including in the finance charge (and, consequently, in the APR) all expenses created by the extension of credit and excluding all others. If the separation of credit related charges from others that may arise around the credit transaction is successful, the finance charge will represent only a true credit cost and not a combination with something else. Section 106 of the Truth in Lending Act sensibly defines the finance charge as containing all credit costs but excluding other outlays:

> Except as otherwise provided in this section, the amount of the finance charge in connection with any consumer credit transaction shall be determined as the sum of all charges, payable directly or indirectly by the person to whom the credit is extended and imposed directly or indirectly by the creditor as an incident to the extension of credit. The finance charge does not include charges of a type payable in a comparable cash transaction.

The act gives a number of examples of finance charges, such as interest, time price differentials, points or discount amounts in discount systems of charges, and various fees. The corresponding part of Regulation Z (12 CFR 226.4(b)) elaborates on these examples and provides an additional listing of fees that are *not* finance charges, such as charges for late payments on accounts and overdraft fees. The relevant sections of the act and regulation are reproduced in the appendix to this chapter, where it is possible to see how complicated these requirements have become. Using the method of defining by providing examples means that any innovations or alterations in products or services are almost by definition going to be controversial.

The wording of the act and regulation show clearly that the definition of finance charge is intended to be highly inclusive of credit costs for federal disclosure purposes, regardless of how a credit contract characterizes a cost (for example, interest, fees, points, etc.) or what that cost is considered to be under the laws of the states. The comprehensiveness of the finance charge concept was intended to make it difficult for creditors to manipulate fees and other costs in ways that would exclude credit costs from the finance charge or the interacting calculation of the APR. At the same time, the act recognizes that some costs are logically not costs of credit, such as insurance or costs that would have been incurred for a purchase that did not involve a loan ("... not include charges... payable in a comparable cash transaction").

The Nature of the Outlay Issue

Over the years, the ingenuity of financial institutions in finding new ways to charge fees and that of attorneys in finding new issues to litigate have made the outlay issue an area of constant flux and uncertainty.[3] Congress itself complicated the matter by specifically excluding from the finance charge certain costs associated with residential mortgage financing that otherwise would seem to warrant inclusion.

A few examples can illustrate the complications of the outlay issue. Interest and discount points on a mortgage always seem to be finance charges, and voluntary insurance premiums to protect the debtor's life or collateral probably are not (they are the costs of additional, voluntarily purchased services, not the costs of credit). But what if the creditor requires the insurance as a condition of the credit—is the premium a finance charge? (Answer to quiz: TILA and its regulation currently say *no* for some kinds of insurance under some circumstances–homeowners' property insurance on a purchase-money mortgage, for example—and

yes for others or under other circumstances–credit insurance on installment credit, for instance.) Are fees to brokers in a mortgage transaction
finance charges or not? (For almost thirty years, the answer depended
upon whether the lender required the use of a certain broker or seller;
this changed in 1995, and now brokers' fees are always included.)

Further, how is a fee for a credit commitment handled? Need it be
disclosed as a finance charge? (*Yes.*) Suppose the fee varies according to
the use of the loan? (*Yes*, again.) If a credit arrangement is secured with a
deposit account, is interest paid on the deposit account a reduction in the
finance charge? (*No.*) Conversely, is interest foregone on an associated
deposit account an addition to the finance charge? (*Yes.*) Further still, is
the access fee for obtaining a cash advance on a credit card account at an
ATM a finance charge or not? (For years, *no*, if the charge is not greater
than the fee for accessing an asset account; otherwise, *yes*. The answer
changed to always *yes* by regulatory adjustments proposed in 2007 and
adopted with more clarifications in 2008.)

The questions are almost endless, deciding on answers is often difficult, and the results frequently lead to litigation. But TILA, Regulation
Z, and the Regulation Z *Commentary* must answer all the questions satisfactorily and consistently if creditors are to receive proper guidance and
consumers to receive useful shopping information.[4]

As noted, Congress itself added a few complications of its own in the
text of the act. For residential real estate transactions, TILA specifically
excludes certain costs from the finance charge that otherwise would
seem to be includable. Specifically, Section 106(e) states:

The following items, when charged in connection with any extension
of credit secured by an interest in real property shall not be included in
the computation of the finance charge with respect to that transaction:

1. Fees or premiums for title examination, title insurance, or other
   similar purpose;
2. Fees for preparation of a deed, settlement statement, or other documents;
3. Escrows for future payments of taxes and insurance;
4. Fees for notarizing deeds and other documents;
5. Appraisal fees;
6. Credit reports.

Normally, fees levied for the performance of at least some of these
tasks (appraisal fees, credit reports, and a few more excluded in the
regulation) would seem to be finance charges. Congress chose to make

exceptions for real-estate-related transactions, however, presumably for political reasons at the time of passage. The scope and specific nature of the exceptions have been the subject of review in the regulation, in the *Commentary*, and through four decades of court actions.[5] Congress held hearings in 1998 about possible changes in the real estate area, and more hearings plus legislative changes could be forthcoming at some point (see US House of Representatives 1998 and US Senate Committee on Banking, Housing, and Urban Affairs, Subcommittee on Financial Institutions and Regulatory Relief 1999). The Federal Reserve raised the same questions again as part of its updating exercise in 2009.

The Ultimate Source of the Outlay Issue: Joint Purchases

Each of these examples of the complexity in calculating and properly disclosing the finance charge arising from the outlay issue illustrates different aspects of the same general problem: the fundamental difficulty of dividing what are often inherently joint purchases (goods or services and payment over time, *i.e.*, credit) into components, allocating costs to discrete categories, and then disclosing information about costs of some components in a simple summary fashion so that no consumer ever needs further information about them. This is certainly a worthy intent of TILA for credit costs, but it turns out to be difficult in any ideal sense. To demonstrate, consider an unreasonably simple, but illustrative, hypothetical example.

Imagine two consumer lenders whose loans impose no charges on the borrower except interest — the lenders impose no other fees of any sort. Out of the interest charge, each lender pays all of its costs of doing business. Both companies are exactly the same and impose the same charges for loans of the same size and maturity to cover the costs of these services and the return on forbearance (cost of capital including risk). The companies are right next door to one another and customers always park at the municipal lot right across the street.

Now suppose company A provides "free" parking by stamping customers' parking passes and remitting $2.00 per customer to the municipal parking authority. Patrons of company B, in contrast, must pay $2.00 to the local parking authority for a visit to B's office. It stands to reason, everything else equal, that A's production costs are higher than B's because they include the use by A's customers of the municipal parking lot. Thus, other things equal, company A will charge a higher finance charge and higher a corresponding APR so that it can pay the parking authority.

The question is, which deal is better for the consumer, the one with the "free" parking and the higher APR or the one with the lower APR and the charge by the municipal authority? Ideally, customers should be economically indifferent between the transactions, if they fully understand them, but how can you guarantee that understanding through the required credit disclosures? Although (presumably) no one would suggest including parking authority fees in anyone's finance charge, the consumer cannot tell from the finance charge or APR alone which is the better credit deal, considering everything.

This example is simple and unrealistic, but the underlying necessity of understanding the nature of joint purchases is not. In some manner, the purchases of credit accompany purchases of some product or service: a family obtains a mortgage loan to purchase a house; a consumer buys a car on a five-year installment note; a student attends medical school by taking on large student loans; a homeowner obtains a second mortgage to remodel the basement and replace the heating system. The simultaneous purchase of insurance may accompany any or all of these transactions, and there may be other services involved. There may also be expenditures for related taxes, which raises the question of whether they are credit costs. A court decision in 1994 concerning the proper disclosure of outlays for a tax and a FedEx courier charge in connection with a mortgage transaction caused the Congress to decide on a major revision of the Truth in Lending Act itself.[6]

The underlying essence of the outlay issue is that in every credit-related transaction, there are really at least two purchases, namely, the product or service bought and the credit itself (the right to pay over time). In fact, it is correct to say that the demand for credit is a derived demand; there is never a purchase of credit without the purchase of something else or a refinancing of such a purchase. Credit use involves the intertemporal shifting of receipt and payment for goods, services, or assets. As a result, at best, it is often difficult to separate the numerous components associated with each purchase into discrete costs that can be allocated between the good or service purchased and the timing rearrangement.

It becomes especially difficult to differentiate transaction components if both the product and the credit are supplied by the same retail source and the prices can interact. Even in the simple example above, in which the reason for borrowing is completely separated from the credit source (and not even revealed in the example), there is still the cost issue associated with the parking lot. Most examples are much more complicated.

Automobile shopping, for example, is especially confusing because there are multiple components to the financial calculations: the vehicle price, the trade-in value of a different vehicle, the price of associated services and products, the down payment, the finance charge, and the number of payments, and they all can vary. It seems obvious that the finance charge and the derived APR as defined in TILA are only partly helpful in these cases because they do not by themselves provide all the information needed for effective shopping. (For most purchases, the credit package is actually the smaller component of the transaction anyway.) Consumers are not necessarily better off by choosing the arrangement with the lowest APR; the price of the automobile can vary in the opposite direction, confounding a credit decision based solely on the required credit disclosures. Consequently, to be fully informed, consumers are always going to have to exercise some thought and care, even with the mandatory disclosure of the finance charge and APR. Clearly, though unfortunately, the Truth in Lending Act is not a panacea.

The difficulty for automobiles is readily visible by simply considering the automobile advertisements in the daily newspaper. It has become standard practice in recent years to compete for automobile sales by quoting low APRs (3.9 percent, 1.9 percent, and even 0.0 percent financing according to the advertisements). Probably some consumers, possibly many, fully realize that there is a likelihood that low finance rates are associated with less flexibility in other areas of pricing or that these rates are somehow bound up with the disposition of factory rebates or the price of the vehicle, but it becomes very difficult to sort all the components of the joint purchase easily. Comparing becomes especially difficult if the maturities of the arrangements compared differ. What consumers really need is some sort of unit price of the *joint* purchase, but this is not readily available and is certainly not a disclosure required under TILA. Again, this means that if consumers want the best deal for themselves, they are not exempt from care and thinking, even if they have the disclosed finance charge and APR.[7]

Although retail purchases on credit are the clearest example of the difficulties that arise from joint pricing, even simple personal cash loans not associated with specific purchases can produce the same concerns if the loans are combined with ancillary services like credit insurance or product insurance. In the days before TILA, creditors often tried to divide the lending process itself into multiple components as a way of removing some costs from finance charges and interest rates that were subject to rate ceilings frequently set too low to make consumer lending feasible.[8]

To divide the lending process, creditors on occasion defined some aspects of loan processing as additional services outside of the lending process, necessitating separate prices, sometimes called *brokerage fees* or even *paperwork fees*.[9] As mentioned earlier, this proliferation of fees, rates, and the methods of calculating and disclosing them was the ultimate rationale for proposing TILA in the first place, even though Congress itself also specifically excluded certain of these paperwork fees from the finance charge on mortgage credit as it legislated TILA. It can hardly be surprising that such issues have continued to prove troublesome since then.

Rohner and Durkin (2005) proposed and discussed general guidelines for how to classify charges and fees as finance charges or not, focusing especially on credit card credit, in which some of the severest problems have arisen. Their proposal is so straightforward that the need for it seems surprising at the end of the fourth decade of the TILA era. The core of their proposal, which is not limited conceptually to credit cards, is to include within the required finance charge disclosure (and the accompanying APR) only those fees and charges that pay for the characteristics of credit (origination, servicing, forbearance, and risk) and to exclude those charges that pay for other things. Thus, their approach encompasses interest, points, and the other elements of finance charges characterized as such by TILA and Regulation Z, but it would also include some of the mortgage-related fees excluded by statute in 1968. It would also tend to exclude many of the specific fees associated with credit card plans that have caused controversies in recent years, including fees such as those levied for the expedited delivery of a credit card by FedEx or similar means, but which are not determining characteristics of a credit account relationship itself. Their suggestions have not explicitly been adopted as a component of the TILA regulatory structure, although they seem worth considering; they are discussed in a bit more detail in Chapters 5 and 6.

In any case, the "Is it in or is it out?" and often unclear nature of calculating and disclosing finance charges and the associated APRs has tended to increase uncertainty for creditors and consumers over the years and has spawned a substantial amount of controversy. It also has contributed significantly to the demand for the full disclosure of everything under the assumption that somehow highlighting everything will enable consumers to understand what is going on. Over time, the realization has grown that it is likely impossible to develop an internally consistent, unvarying, complete, and, therefore, theoretically satisfying solution that correctly covers all circumstances every time but is also operationally feasible, simple, easily understandable, and not controversial.

At a minimum, someone has to introduce some definitions and assumptions, and make some decisions. Congress made many of these decisions in the act in 1968, and from time to time has modified them as times and conditions have changed (for example, after litigation in 1995), but the basic conception of the finance charge and the APR, along with the basic approach of the law, has remained essentially unchanged over the decades. The regulation and the *Commentary* elaborate on the provisions of the act, but they do not fundamentally alter its underlying structure or approach. As a result, although various observers have, on occasion, proposed alternative schemes, the act largely retains the conceptions of the finance charge and APR adopted in 1968. In the 1980 simplification, Congress did decide that the disclosure of a detailed itemization of the components of the finance charge would no longer be required. This requirement had produced substantial amounts of litigation in the years before the reform. Many of the remaining difficulties caused by the outlay issue still arise because there are multiple components of charges associated with credit transactions, especially mortgage loans, even if all need not be disclosed separately for nonmortgage credit. These issues are discussed further later.

Unknown Future Events

Even if it were possible to solve the outlay problem satisfactorily and easily, the second basic issue for disclosing credit costs properly is equally (or more) vexing: How is it possible to calculate and disclose a prospective finance charge and the APR unit price based on it when these key terms depend fundamentally on future events that are unknown when disclosures are required to be made? The problem is obvious for revolving credit like credit card transactions in which the amount of the finance charge depends on the consumer's future usage of the credit line, but it exists as well for other types of credit. Home purchase mortgage contracts, for example, seldom run all the way to maturity (maybe thirty years into the future) and so consumers rarely pay the entire disclosed finance charge. Likewise, consumers agreeing to automobile finance contracts with a specific balance and projected finance charge often trade in their cars early and never pay the full contractual amount before entering into a new deal. Or, consumers sometimes pay slowly and then owe additional interest plus late or default charges for nonpayment. In this case, the total charges are higher than contemplated at the outset. On variable rate mortgage contracts, the finance charges, payment sizes and numbers, and, therefore, the resulting APR all can change depending on the future circumstances. In any of these cases, the amounts actually paid often differ substantially from the amounts contemplated in contracts. The question is how to make disclosures if the outcome of the events requiring disclosures is not known when the information must be given.

To answer, the Truth in Lending Act divides credit arrangements subject to the disclosure requirements into two segments, closed-end and open-end credit, and then makes assumptions about the cash flows for the former and defines a group of answers for the latter. *Closed-end credit* refers to credit generated for a single, specific transaction. It includes common kinds of credit such as familiar purchase-money mortgage loans, automobile credit, and personal loans with a specified maturity. Open-end credit refers to arrangements that typically contemplate multiple transactions, like credit cards or credit lines.[10]

Closed-End Credit

For closed-end credit, the full scope of the transaction can be anticipated on the basis of a transaction-related contract, even if that basis is not always achieved exactly as set out. The regulatory scheme for the disclosure of both the finance charge and the APR, in this case, adopts the convention that the contract proceeds exactly as initially envisioned until the payoff; legally correct disclosure assumes this outcome. There is no requirement to provide multiple or alternative disclosures for a typical transaction or some other example, even if the completion of the full contract exactly as outlined in the original document is not very likely (paying off a full thirty-year mortgage loan at completion under the original contract, for example). Even variable-rate closed-end loans make this basic assumption, although for them, there must also be a disclosure of the conditions and circumstances governing rate changes.[11]

Abstracting from the outlay issue and focusing only on timing, the decision to assume that a closed-end contract proceeds to maturity permits the use of the conceptually simple and straightforward mathematical principles associated with calculating the closed-end finance charges and APR, as noted above in Equations 1 and 2. Over the years, however, many observers have called attention to the potential inappropriateness of a single solution if the future is unknown. Among others, Guttentag and Hurst (1985) have pointed out that for both variable-rate and fixed-rate mortgages, the assumption of an invariable APR (or finance charge) is almost never correct. From their perspective, the problems of disclosing an APR on mortgage contracts are so severe that they recommend a wholesale change in the TILA scheme (Guttentag and Hurst 1985, p. 558):

> In our view, the APR as it is now disclosed for mortgages, whether ARMs (adjustable-rate mortgages) or FRMs (fixed-rate mortgages) is worse than useless because it biases the decisions of borrowers; they are better off without it!

Guttentag and Hurst suggest two sources of the problems they perceive: (1) the fundamental nature of variable-rate credit whereby the rate, by definition, can and does change; and (2) the typical structure of a mortgage loan that includes advance fees that are amortized over the life of the loan, a difficulty that exists even on fixed-rate mortgages. Because of the fee problem, the true post hoc APR on these loans never equals the disclosed APR (even for fixed-rate mortgages), unless the contract runs fully to maturity, which happens in only a minority of cases. They contend these problems may mislead many consumers into choosing the wrong mortgage based on differing patterns of cash flows among products. In this view, the single prospective APR required under TILA does not capture these differences, so the implications of the different cash flows are not obvious to consumers.

All of this leads Guttentag and Hurst to be critical of the whole scheme of TILA for mortgage credit (and, by implication, for all of closed-end credit), which they disparagingly call a "checklist approach." In their view, TILA merely requires listing all the variables that might affect the APR (such as the effect of advance fees, frequency of rate adjustments, rate caps, initial rates; see Table 1 in their paper, p. 554). Then, it somehow expects consumers to be able to understand the implications of all these variables on the APR, under reasonable assumptions concerning their own individual cases. They contend that even experts cannot do this—a point well taken.

To remedy the situation, they recommend replacing the essence of TILA with another method, which they dub the *performance approach*. Fundamentally, their recommendation consists of disclosing the results of computer simulations using multiple sets of assumptions, just the sort of outcome TILA has avoided. These results would be shown in tables of three columns for monthly payment, the year-end balance, and (post hoc) "APR when terminated." What the professors have done, of course, is demonstrate and highlight the unknown future events problem of

TILA for closed-end credit and propose a solution of exactly the opposite approach to existing TIL: multiple disclosures.

Clearly, Guttentag and Hurst have described a real problem (especially concerning the disclosures for closed-end mortgage credit, on which they concentrate their attention), and they propose a solution at least worth considering. Their proposal also is probably more plausible today than when they advanced it; in recent years, the increased availability of personal computers and ubiquitous spreadsheet software have made such calculations relatively easy and straightforward. The problem is that their approach does not solve the difficulties of an unknown future; it merely substitutes multiple groupings of assumptions about unknowable future prospects for the single assumption set now required.

One important unanswered question of their approach is how many sets of disclosures to make. There would have to be tables for multiple interest rate and repayment scenarios on variable-rate loans, and none would necessarily be better than any other. Moreover, even for fixed-rate loans with fees, tables for multiple repayment scenarios would be necessary, and consumers would have to project the likely pattern of their own future behavior concerning moves, housing upgrades, mortgage refinancing, etc.[12] In any case, even if better in some (a few? many?) instances, Congress has not made the decision that this is the proper approach for truth in lending. Furthermore, the cost of changing to a new program and the likely additional ongoing costs of more numerous disclosures would have to be considered versus the prospects of really improving consumers' information situation under a new scheme.[13]

Open-End Credit

Calculating finance charges and APRs for prospective disclosures on open-end credit is even less straightforward than for the closed-end variety as a result of unknown future events peculiar to open-end credit. Two additional major classes of difficulties arise uniquely with open-end credit: (1) the unknown pace concern (by far the more important issue) and (2) inconsistencies caused by so-called grace periods.

For open-end transactions like credit cards, future use and payment schedules are unknown, unknowable, and cannot even be assumed in advance. Because future account use is variable and unpredictable, TILA concludes for open-end credit that no prospective calculation of a finance charge is more sensible than any other, and so none is necessary. Only disclosure of the method of determining the finance charge is required prospectively: at the account opening, during any period in which a finance charge is imposed, and at any time the method changes. TILA also has long required retroactive or retrospective disclosure of the actual finance charge during any cycle following the one in which a charge is actually imposed. Rules changes in 2008 and 2009 also required, beginning in 2010, monthly summaries of amounts charged in the year to date and a break-down into "interest" and "fees," some of the latter not finance charges.

For the unit price, open-end requirements have entailed disclosure of *three* rates: (1) the periodic rate used in calculating periodic finance charges (usually daily); (2) a defined prospective APR that equals the periodic rate times the number of periods in a year; and, for many years until changed in 2008 by amendment to Regulation Z, (3) the retroactive, retrospective, or effective APR calculated after the fact from finance charges and balances during the previous single period, using the rules of Appendix F to Regulation Z. Changes to the regulation in 2008 repealed the latter requirement.

Until the 2008 revision to Regulation Z, the prospective and retro-spective open-end APRs were both defined as the APR and disclosed as such on periodic (usually monthly) statements. They were not calculated the same way and often differed in practice, however, sometimes sharply, which certainly could be confusing. Moreover, neither open-end APR was directly comparable to the closed-end APR calculated from pro-jected cash flows using a mathematical discounting expression and the contract parameters necessary for the calculation.

More specifically, differences between the prospective APR and the long required retrospective open-end APR could come about whenever there was some sort of finance charge assessed that did not arise from the application of the prospective periodic rate. The most common examples were transaction charges, cash advance charges, and fees for the use of convenience checks attached to a credit card account. Fees of this kind became more prevalent in recent years as open-end creditors (especially credit card issuers) have responded to marketplace pressures by unbun-dling their charges. As competition became intense, typical open-end creditors responded by lowering periodic rates on many accounts, but simultaneously instituting fees for specialized transactions and events affecting only some customers.[14] These charges arose from specific credit extensions and so there was little question that they were finance charges; the problem was how to allocate such fees and related repayments to time periods, so that APRs could be calculated and disclosed.

For prospective disclosures, the equations in sections 7 and 8 of Appendix J to Regulation Z (simplified above in this chapter as Equations

1 and 2) could easily take all such fees into account in closed-end credit arrangements in which their timing is contractual and the charges and the prospective balances can be calculated and related directly to one another mathematically (under the assumptions that the contract runs to stated maturity and the payments arrive on schedule). Fees like transactions fees and cash advance charges on open-end credit cannot be predicted, though, because they are up to the consumer after the time the disclosures must be given. Furthermore, such fees may initially be associated with a particular transaction and related balance, but they quickly become unattached from their originating transaction as new credits, and partial and variable payments become blended in monthly. Even for a given fee for a specific event, outstanding balances can vary substantially from account to account and month to month as a result of customers' individualized account use and payment behavior. Consequently, unlike closed-end credit, on open-end credit there are simply too many variables underlying consumers' behavior to reduce the relationship of fees and cash flows to a simple mathematical formula for prospective disclosures. Unfortunately, there also are no convenient, reasonable assumptions for open-end credit to lead the way out of this box.[15]

The solution adopted of requiring disclosure of *three* rates, including a retroactive or retrospective APR calculated after the fact for those periods during which a finance charge was imposed, had difficulties of its own. For one, by definition, this retrospective rate was backward-looking and provided the disclosure only well after the fact of the transaction. More significant, the impossibility of forecasting cash flows necessitated calculating the retroactive APR disclosure by amortizing the transaction fees over the single-month period following their imposition. This was usually a false condition, since most customers with cash advances and other transactions leading to a fee do not pay off the account in full the next month. This meant the calculating approach for the retroactive APR produced an erroneous disclosure, in most cases, though required by law.

There is no obvious solution to this difficulty for a retroactive APR, short of the multiple disclosure solution of Guttentag and Hurst. Changing the assumed time period for amortizing the fee does not eliminate the problem. The timing of amortizing the associated balance remains unknown, and any other assumption is also false in the majority of cases. Furthermore, any alternative that distributes fees over more time periods runs the risk that the retroactive APR, which includes such fees, may not make any sense at all, even if it is possible to calculate mathematically. For example, choosing to distribute occasional fees over a longer period such as six months or a year, rather than a single month, would lead to fluctuating impacts on monthly APRs as balances changed (unless fees and credit balances are amortized over the same number of months with consistent payment size and no additions to the balances from the subsequent use of the card). Worse still, any allocation of a finance charge to a month with no outstanding balance would produce the apparently nonsensical result that the disclosed APR increases without bound (approaches infinity as a limit) as the monthly associated credit balance approaches zero. Although in some sense this is a true result, disclosing an infinite rate to consumers is not especially helpful. All it really says is that there is a fee allocated to the time period, however small or large, and the outstanding balance in the period in question is zero.

A similar difficulty has been evident for years with annual or membership fees on credit cards, although, in this case, the regulatory structure has chosen a different outcome for these fees. In an attempt to increase revenues during a period of financial and regulatory stress, in 1980, many banks began to assess annual fees on all holders of open-end accounts, especially credit card accounts.[16] Competitive pressures dictated the removal of periodic fees from many accounts by the 1990s, but they still remain an important component of some programs, especially those featuring rewards like frequent flier miles. Such membership fees have always been important to the travel-and-entertainment card plans of American Express and Diners Club and remain so for some cards with these brands.

Certainly, these annual or membership fees would also appear conceptually to be finance charges, since they arise from the maintenance of a credit plan by a consumer. Because it is not possible to relate them to specific transactions or balances, however, the same difficulty arises in attempting to factor them into an APR for prospective (and retrospective) disclosure purposes. As a result, Regulation Z specifically excludes from the finance charge and the APR "fees charged for participation in a credit plan, whether assessed on an annual or other periodic basis" (Regulation Z 226.4c(4)). By regulation, the disclosure of such fees as "Other Charges" has been required. The argument, in this case, is that such fees are not "incident to" a specific credit advance and, therefore, are not finance charges under the reigning definition in section 106 of the Act ("... the sum of all charges, payable directly or indirectly by the person to whom the credit is extended and imposed directly or indirectly by the creditor as an incident to the extension of credit").[17]

Thus, excluding annual fees from the finance charge and APR on open-end credit is not an especially satisfying assumption, theoretically, because annual or membership fees would seem to be credit costs even though they do not become part of the disclosed finance charge or APR. Regulation Z solves the difficulty of factoring these fees into APR disclosures by defining away the problem. It is not clear that either the approach of the retroactive APR for fees like transaction charges or defining away the problem for fees like annual charges is better or worse; both are unsatisfying because they are conceptually wrong. One approach amortizes fees over a time period that is usually inappropriate, and the other makes the problem go away through tinkering with the definitions.

None of this means that a given open-end *prospective* APR is useless for consumers, even if it is not directly comparable to the closed-end rate. If a consumer assumes that his or her future spending pattern and behavior using credit card plan A will be exactly the same as prospective behavior if the choice is to use plan B, and if the fees charged are the same and the periodic rate is applied in the same way with the same balance-calculation approach, then the plan with the lowest disclosed prospective APR is the lowest cost plan for the consumer. The necessity of such assumptions on the consumer's part would seem to violate the original intent of TILA to make the APR a single summary measure (presumably without assumptions), alike in all transactions, but avoiding this outcome is impossible without substantive requirements that control how open-end credit plans operate. Simply put, it seems it will never be possible through disclosures to relieve consumers completely of all responsibility for thinking about their choices and understanding their implications.

As mentioned, a second unknown future events difficulty in disclosing finance charges and associated APRs on open-end credit arises not so much from the nature of the kind of credit as from vestiges of a cultural tradition of credit use in the United States known as the *grace period*. This addition to the litany of unknown events difficulties pokes up its head whenever there is any portion of a time period in which there is a credit balance outstanding on an open-end credit account but the periodic rate does not apply. If so, it means the periodic rate is not applied uniformly over time, and using it to calculate the prospective APR for disclosures will cause the disclosed rate to diverge from the actual rate of charge.

Credit plans vary, but many credit card programs involve a period with no finance charge, typically known as a grace period. This feature of many open-end programs arose in the days when thirty-day "same as cash" charge plans were common at retail stores. These plans contemplated that credit was a convenience for customers, who would resist being charged specifically for it. This grace period or free period lives on today in more modern revolving credit card programs, for those customers who still regard credit as a convenience and who pay their credit card bills in full upon receipt and might still object to an explicit credit cost.

A grace or free period might occur either at the beginning or ending of a period of actual indebtedness, or both. In a typical example, a finance charge does not accrue until the billing cycle following the period in which the credit balance begins, generating free credit during this period if the balance is paid in full on time. If not paid in full, finance charges would begin. In some programs in the past, the finance charge might then accrue from the earliest date with a balance (so-called two-cycle average daily balance billing programs, outlawed beginning in 2010 by regulatory and legislative changes in 2008 and 2009). For others, the finance charge might start at the date on which a periodic billing is not paid in full. In some programs, there might be another period at the end with no finance charge if the balance is paid in full at that time.[18]

The point is that as long as there is a grace or free period associated with a credit plan, multiplying the periodic rate times the number of periods in a year will never produce an APR that strictly reflects the actual rate that applies. In fact, if there is a grace period but no finance charges other than those arising from the application of the periodic rate, along with assumed end-of-period payments as with closed-end rate calculations, then the actual rate will always be less than the disclosed open-end prospective rate. It will approach the disclosed rate as the time the credit is outstanding increases and the free period becomes a proportionately smaller part of the whole. Some observers sometimes seem less disturbed by the grace period problem than other difficulties with disclosures. Nevertheless, since disclosed rates with grace periods exceed actual rates, it is not clear why this is not also an affront to the idea of truth in lending, even though a solution that would correct this difficulty without outlawing grace periods is not obvious.

Compliance Simplifications, Exceptions, and Shortcuts

The third grouping of fundamental difficulties with calculating and disclosing meaningful finance charges and APRs noted above is the compliance issue. It is not so much conceptual as practical. It concerns the implications of the requests made by regulated financial institutions at the outset of TILA (and sometimes over the years since) for a reasonable trade-off between mathematical perfection and ease of compliance, especially for smaller creditors and those with a wide range of products and product features. This desire has led to a host of simplifications, exceptions, and shortcuts from pristine APR mathematics, even on closed-end credit for which a reasonable hypothetical basis to forecast the payment stream exists. Most of the specifics in this area will only be mentioned in passing here.[19] Although always controversial, the violence to truth in lending from all these matters combined appears to be less than that potentially arising from the difficulties with either the outlay or unknown future events problems. In fact, for the most part, these issues seem to be of little interest to all but technically minded individuals, although it seems useful to introduce them at least briefly.

APR Formula

As noted earlier in this chapter, for closed-end credit, the APR is the mathematical analogue of an all-inclusive annualized interest rate that, for TILA purposes, discounts the stream of future payments (including the pattern of the payment of the finance charge) to its present value, the amount financed. It is more comprehensive than the concept of an interest rate, because it includes more than the return on forbearance; it also is intended to encompass, besides interest, any other fees that are really credit costs. For closed-end credit, the APR has a specific, strict mathematical definition found in Appendix J to Regulation Z.

But this is not the end of the story. As introduced earlier in footnote 2 in this chapter, even for closed-end credit in which (under the assumption that the contract runs unchanged to maturity) all the flows are predictable in advance, the proper choice of mathematical formula to relate the stream of future outlays to their present value (the amount financed) has generated some residual controversy over the years. In 1968, Congress decided what the mathematical representation of the closed-end APR would be, but this did not end the discussion (quoted in part earlier, from Truth in Lending Act Section 107):

> (A) That nominal Annual Percentage Rate which will yield a sum equal to the amount of the finance charge when it is applied to the unpaid balances of the amount financed, calculated according to the actuarial method of allocating payments made on a debt between the amount financed and the amount of the finance

charge, pursuant to which a payment is applied first to the accumulated finance charge and the balance is applied to the unpaid amount financed; or

(B) the rate determined by any method prescribed by the [Federal Reserve] Board as a method which materially simplifies computation while determining reasonable accuracy as compared with the rate determined under subparagraph A.

This passage from the act appears to make the APR the simple periodic discounting rate multiplied by the number of periods per year based on payment frequency. A *nominal rate of interest* was a common term of art in the days before TILA, referring to "the quoted *annual* rate which does not take into account that interest is compounded at intervals throughout the year" (Neifeld 1951, p. 59, emphasis in original). Today, the term is most often used to describe an interest rate that is also unadjusted for inflation; in other words, it is an unadjusted simple interest rate.[20]

From time to time, mathematical and financial experts have been critical of the specific mathematical derivation in Appendix J, recommending a true compound internal rate of return instead, but Congress apparently chose otherwise. Either the compound internal rate of return or the TILA approach of multiplying the simple discount rate times the number of unit periods per year qualify as actuarial approaches, as required by the law, because they fully amortize the total of payments. In most cases, the difference would be fairly small, and presumably a simple interest concept was chosen for easier calculation, in the years before inexpensive electronic calculators and computers were widely available.

Tolerances and Simplifications

Beyond this fundamental concern with the APR, there have also been other compromises, exceptions, and simplifications to the actuarial mathematics made to ease compliance. An important one concerns tolerances. To aid compliance and eliminate violations that might otherwise occur (for example, on account of the misclassification of minor fees), Congress, in 1980, as part of the simplification effort, permitted a range around the correct solution to the discounting equation to be considered correct for TILA purposes. The tolerances were fairly small at the outset (one-eighth of one percent on either side of the rate calculated under the rules of Appendix J, and one-quarter of one percent on irregular transactions). In effect, Congress increased them somewhat through amendments to TILA in 1995 that also permitted tolerances for finance charges.

These tolerances amount to the authorization of a general amount of inaccuracy in any APR disclosure, for any reason (even including careless error or incompetence), to ease compliance. On the positive side, they undoubtedly do aid some struggling creditors sometimes; on the negative side, they probably hide some error and shoddy practice. They still do not seem to complicate the concept of truth in lending as much as the difficulties associated with joint purchases and with unpredictable future events.

Another such simplification arises from a broad set of rules concerning minor irregularities. These rules permit the calculation of APRs based on a group of simplifying timing assumptions, such as permitting all months to be the same length. Using this example, the absence of such simplifications would produce slightly different daily actuarial rates for the same finance charge for the six months beginning in March versus the six months beginning in September. The minor irregularities rules also permit other relatively small timing divergences from the pure actuarial mathematics of Appendix J, such as slightly irregular first and/or last periods and/or payments, weekend payments, leap years, etc. In each case, it would be possible to calculate different rates that discount the same payment stream for the correct number of days (rather than months) and this would result in a more accurate rate. Such exceptions and simplifications do not dramatically alter the rate disclosed, however, and the policy has long permitted these differences to be ignored under specified circumstances. Although each of these factors (and some others in the regulation, such as the rules for fractional cents and a few other special cases) compromises the mathematical accuracy of the APR to a degree, none is really a major factor in the variability of the calculated and disclosed APR.[21]

The Extent Issue: How Much Disclosure is Enough?

Ultimately, the conceptual difficulties caused by the outlay and unknown future events problems have led to a good deal of the demand for extensive disclosures, summaries, and explanations of cost and cost-related information besides the basic finance charge and APR. But the approach of working around difficulties by disclosing extensive details and related information has produced problems of its own, complicating and checkering TILA's concept with the concept of full disclosure. As shown in Table A.1, "Required Financial Market Disclosures for Consumers in the United States," of Appendix A, "Financial Disclosures in Federal Consumer Protection Statutes," the finance charge and the

APR may be the key disclosures, but they are many others. The utility of these other disclosures has been a subject of debate all the way back to the hearings in the 1960s before initial passage of the law.

Focusing first on closed-end credit in Table A.1, section I, "Information-Based Protections," subsection A, "Closed-End Credit," it seems reasonable to require the disclosure of the payment schedule (line g), but the total of the payments is also required (line f). The total of the payments is merely the periodic payment from the payment schedule multiplied by the number of payments, also part of the payment schedule. Likewise, the total of the payments is also the sum of the amount financed and the finance charge. In effect, the disclosures include three ways of looking at the same information: once as components, once as the product of two components, and a third time as the sum of two others. Although no one disputes that all three disclosures potentially provide information that is useful at times to certain recipients, the mathematical redundancy also naturally raises the question what is gained and what is lost by requiring all the detail.

There also are other questions. For instance, although the amount financed is a required disclosure and is also necessary mathematically for solving the APR equation for closed-end credit, some observers have asked whether the concept is meaningful to consumers, especially if the credit finances certain prepaid finance charges or insurance premiums. A report by two federal agencies, in 1998, raised the question of whether this disclosure should be replaced with something new called the *loan amount* (see the Board of Governors of the Federal Reserve System and Department of Housing and Urban Development 1998). Then, should both the loan amount and the amount financed remain required disclosures? Would consumers understand the distinction?

Another ongoing question is, How much detail should be left in the contract and how much should become additional, separately required disclosures? What about name of the creditor, for example? Is this important to consumers, other than to show where and to whom the payments are due? Further, the provisions for late charges might be important if a consumer defaults, but how many consumers shop for this term? All such concerns cloud the answer to the extent question.

The extent of requirements on open-end credit is at least equally problematic. As discussed earlier, even the key disclosures can be lengthier for open-end credit: In addition to finance charges, there has long been a mandate to disclose "other charges," a requirement that changed substantially in 2008 and is examined further in Chapter 6. As indicated, there even has been required disclosure of more than one conception of the APR (prospective and retrospective), also reviewed further in Chapter 6.

Much of the debate over TILA disclosures has involved whether all the required disclosures are really needed as required disclosures in addition to being contract provisions; that is, what should be the proper extent of the disclosure requirements? Equally important but more forward-looking, are new disclosures sometimes needed and if so, what and when?

To a large degree, the answer, in both cases, depends on the underlying goals of the disclosure program in the first place. If, for example, the intent of the disclosures were to provide the information necessary for shopping, then maybe disclosure at the point of sale would be more valuable than the current formidable TILA forms. In contrast, if the goal is a full record of underlying transactions for record, tax, and dispute resolution purposes, maybe a fuller listing is appropriate. If, however, a program serves both goals, but at different times, maybe different disclosures would be useful at different times rather than the current compromise single-approach that is now mandatory.

The issue of goals is discussed further in Chapter 7; suffice it to say here that the goals of disclosure programs have not always been as well articulated as one might hope. The result has been that the extent of the disclosures required has remained controversial and probably will continue to remain so until a firmer conception of goals emerges.

In sum, despite the obvious advantages of the disclosure of credit costs in dollars and as a unit price, the implementation of TILA illustrates the difficulties of trying to compress all the information that a consumer might need into key summary disclosures. The extent question asks about what other disclosures might also useful enough to be required for everyone. Yet, it seems that consumers are going to have to be at least somewhat knowledgeable about what the numbers they receive stand for and mean, if they are to be adequately informed. Both the issue of joint purchases (the outlay issue) and the assumptions necessary to make TILA manageable (the unknown future events issue) are significant. They illustrate the fundamental complexities of disclosing costs in a meaningful way if they depend either on difficult distinctions among categories of outlays or upon unknown and unpredictable future behavior. Beyond this, the history of TILA involves a succession of compromises made for the sake of clarity, computational ease, and simplification, especially from the time when computer systems were much less common than today. All of these problems make the finance charge and the associated APR as the unit price a bit less uniform and accurate than might be hoped for in some imaginary world where there are no complexities.

All of the compromises and difficulties taken together have not returned credit cost disclosures to the inconsistent and sometimes chaotic condition that existed before TILA, however, or taken away its basic thrust or intent. For this reason, it seems probable that, despite residual ongoing difficulties that should have been expected and probably cannot be avoided completely, the Truth in Lending Act has had a favorable impact on consumer credit markets by improving information conditions overall. There are implementation difficulties to be sure and many aspects of the program over the years are likely unnecessarily costly, but it is still true that the act has developed for consumers a relatively consistent set of definitions for credit costs, albeit within the confines of assumptions necessary to make the disclosures workable and with the hope that consumers can understand the scheme. There certainly is improvement relative to the situation before mid 1969. Furthermore, disclosures must be made available upon account opening (and sometimes periodically, depending on account type), and it is difficult for creditors to hide anything significant.

There still are legitimate questions about consistency and the comparability of the methods of finance charge and rate calculation, but under reasonable assumptions about account features and consumers' behavior, the information disclosed about charges and rates likely is helpful, in many cases. Various consumers may well employ the information differently (or not at all), and the extent of other disclosures may or may not be useful to them, but the information is certainly available. Consumers undoubtedly know that low APRs are better for them than high, and both they and marketplace competitors can monitor market conditions if they desire. It seems likely all of these things have the potential for a favorable market impact, as discussed in Chapter 3, "Why Disclosures?" but this is ultimately an empirical question, as noted earlier.

All this notwithstanding, it is still difficult to say something favorable about the disclosure of the retrospective or retroactive APR in open-end credit if there is a fee that is a finance charge. The necessity of assuming a one-month period for amortizing the fee is certainly wrong in the majority of cases, making the resulting disclosure very frequently erroneous. The argument sometimes made by advocates favoring this usage is unfortunate. Sometimes referred to as the "shock theory," since it argues in favor of disclosing a high retrospective APR for one month to "shock" consumers, this disclosure is somehow supposed to discourage credit use. There is no available evidence that it does so, but the more important issue is philosophical. A requirement by the government for an often conceptually erroneous disclosure in order to "shock" citizens into adopting some behavior they would not otherwise prefer or exhibit (and which, in some cases, may not be in their best interest) raises an important question: Is this a proper role of government in a free society? One can and does find disagreement on the answer, but at least some large proportion of citizens likely would answer no. The Federal Reserve Board probably entertained at least some elements of this kind of thinking in 2008 when, on its own authority, it repealed the requirement for the disclosure of the historical APR on open-end credit.

Appendix to Chapter 4: Definition of Finance Charge in 2008

1. Truth in Lending Act §106: Determination of finance charge.
(a) Except as otherwise provided in this section, the amount of the finance charge in connection with any consumer credit transaction shall be determined as the sum of all charges, payable directly or indirectly by the person to whom the credit is extended, and imposed directly or indirectly by the creditor as an incident to the extension of credit. The finance charge does not include charges of a type payable in a comparable cash transaction. The finance charge shall not include fees and amounts imposed by third party closing agents (including settlement agents, attorneys, and escrow and title companies) if the creditor does not require the imposition of the charges or the services provided and does not retain the charges. Examples of charges which are included in the finance charge include any of the following types of charges which are applicable:
  (1) Interest, time price differential, and any amount payable under a point, discount, or other system of additional charges.
  (2) Service or carrying charge.
  (3) Loan fee, finder's fee, or similar charge.
  (4) Fee for an investigation or credit report.
  (5) Premium or other charge for any guarantee or insurance protecting the creditor against the obligor's default or other credit loss.
  (6) Borrower paid mortgage broker fees, including fees paid directly to the broker or the lender (for delivery to the broker) whether such fees are paid in cash or financed.

(b) Charges or premiums for credit life, accident, or health insurance written in connection with any consumer credit transaction shall be included in the finance charge unless

(1) the coverage of the debtor by the insurance is not a factor in the approval by the creditor of the extension of credit, and this fact is clearly disclosed in writing to the person applying for or obtaining the extension of credit; and

(2) in order to obtain the insurance in connection with the extension of credit, the person to whom the credit is extended must give specific affirmative written indication of his desire to do so after written disclosure to him of the cost thereof.

(c) Charges or premiums for insurance, written in connection with any consumer credit transaction, against loss of or damage to property or against liability arising out of the ownership or use of property, shall be included in the finance charge unless a clear and specific statement in writing is furnished by the creditor to the person to whom the credit is extended, setting forth the cost of the insurance if obtained from or through the creditor, and stating that the person to whom the credit is extended may choose the person through which the insurance is to be obtained.

(d) If any of the following items is itemized and disclosed in accordance with the regulations of the Board in connection with any transaction, then the creditor need not include that item in the computation of the finance charge with respect to that transaction:

(1) Fees and charges prescribed by law which actually are or will be paid to public officials for determining the existence of or for perfecting or releasing or satisfying any security related to the credit transaction.

(2) The premium payable for any insurance in lieu of perfecting any security interest otherwise required by the creditor in connection with the transaction, if the premium does not exceed the fees and charges described in paragraph (1) which would otherwise be payable.

(3) Any tax levied on security instruments or on documents evidencing indebtedness if the payment of such taxes is a precondition for recording the instrument securing the evidence of indebtedness.

(e) The following items, when charged in connection with any extension of credit secured by an interest in real property, shall not be included in the computation of the finance charge with respect to that transaction:

(1) Fees or premiums for title examination, title insurance, or similar purposes.

(2) Fees for preparation of loan-related documents.

(3) Escrows for future payments of taxes and insurance.

(4) Fees for notarizing deeds and other documents.

(5) Appraisal fees, including fees related to any pest infestation or flood hazard inspections conducted prior to closing.

(6) Credit reports.

(f) TOLERANCES FOR ACCURACY. — In connection with credit transactions not under an open end credit plan that are secured by real property or a dwelling, the disclosure of the finance charge and other disclosures affected by any finance charge —

(1) shall be treated as being accurate for purposes of this title if the amount disclosed as the finance charge —

(A) does not vary from the actual finance charge by more than $100; or

(B) is greater than the amount required to be disclosed under this title; and

(2) shall be treated as being accurate for purposes of section 125 if —

(A) except as provided in subparagraph (B), the amount disclosed as the finance charge does not vary from the actual finance charge by more than an amount equal to one-half of one percent of the total amount of credit extended; or

(B) in the case of a transaction, other than a mortgage referred to in section 103(aa), which —

(i) is a refinancing of the principal balance then due and any accrued and unpaid finance charges of a residential mortgage transaction as defined in section 103(w), or is any subsequent refinancing of such a transaction; and

(ii) does not provide any new consolidation or new advance;

if the amount disclosed as the finance charge does not vary from the actual finance charge by more than an amount equal to one percent of the total amount of credit extended.

2. Regulation Z §226.4: Finance charge (after revision of December 2008).

(a) <u>Definition</u>. The finance charge is the cost of consumer credit as a dollar amount. It includes any charge payable directly or indirectly by the consumer and imposed directly or indirectly by the creditor as an incident to or a condition of the extension of credit. It does not include any charge of a type payable in a comparable cash transaction.

(1) <u>Charges by third parties</u>. The finance charge includes fees and amounts charged by someone other than the creditor, unless otherwise excluded under this section, if the creditor:

> (i) Requires the use of a third party as a condition of or an incident to the extension of credit, even if the consumer can choose the third party; or
>
> (ii) Retains a portion of the third party charge, to the extent of the portion retained.

(2) <u>Special rule; closing agent charges</u>. Fees charged by a third party that conducts the loan closing (such as a settlement agent, attorney, or escrow or title company) are finance charges only if the creditor –

> (i) Requires the particular services for which the consumer is charged;
>
> (ii) Requires the imposition of the charge; or
>
> (iii) Retains a portion of the third party charge, to the extent of the portion retained.

(3) <u>Special rule; mortgage broker fees</u>. Fees charged by a mortgage broker (including fees paid by the consumer directly to the broker or to the creditor for delivery to the broker) are finance charges even if the creditor does not require the consumer to use a mortgage broker and even if the creditor does not retain any portion of the charge.

(b) <u>Examples of finance charges</u>. The finance charge includes the following types of charges, except for charges specifically excluded by paragraphs (c) through (e) of this section:

(1) Interest, time price differential, and any amount payable under an add on or discount system of additional charges.

(2) Service, transaction, activity, and carrying charges, including any charge imposed on a checking or other transaction account to the extent that the charge exceeds the charge for a similar account without a credit feature.

(3) Points, loan fees, assumption fees, finder's fees, and similar charges.

(4) Appraisal, investigation, and credit report fees.

(5) Premiums or other charges for any guarantee or insurance protecting the creditor against the consumer's default or other credit loss.

(6) Charges imposed on a creditor by another person for purchasing or accepting a consumer's obligation, if the consumer is required to pay the charges in cash, as an addition to the obligation, or as a deduction from the proceeds of the obligation.

(7) Premiums or other charges for credit life, accident, health, or loss-of-income insurance, written in connection with a credit transaction.

(8) Premiums or other charges for insurance against loss of or damage to property, or against liability arising out of the ownership or use of property, written in connection with a credit transaction.

(9) Discounts for the purpose of inducing payment by a means other than the use of credit.

(10) Charges or premiums paid for debt cancellation or debt suspension coverage written in connection with a credit transaction, whether or not the coverage is insurance under applicable law.

(c) Charges excluded from the finance charge. The following charges are not finance charges:

(1) Application fees charged to all applicants for credit, whether or not credit is actually extended.

(2) Charges for actual unanticipated late payment, for exceeding a credit limit, or for delinquency, default, or a similar occurrence.

(3) Charges imposed by a financial institution for paying items that overdraw an account, unless the payment of such items and the imposition of the charge were previously agreed upon in writing.

(4) Fees charged for participation in a credit plan, whether assessed on an annual or other periodic basis.

(5) Seller's points.

(6) Interest forfeited as a result of an interest reduction required by law on a time deposit used as security for an extension of credit.

(7) Real-estate related fees. The following fees in a transaction secured by real property or in a residential mortgage transaction, if the fees are bona fide and reasonable in amount:

> (i) Fees for title examination, abstract of title, title insurance, property survey, and similar purposes.

(ii) Fees for preparing loan-related documents, such as deeds, mortgages, and reconveyance or settlement documents.

(iii) Notary and credit-report fees.

(iv) Property appraisal fees or fees for inspections to assess the value or condition of the property if the service is performed prior to closing, including fees related to pest-infestation or flood-hazard determinations.

(v) Amounts required to be paid into escrow or trustee accounts if the amounts would not otherwise be included in the finance charge.

(8) Discounts offered to induce payment for a purchase by cash, check, or other means, as provided in section 167(b) of the act.

(d) Insurance and debt cancellation and debt suspension coverage.

(1) Voluntary credit insurance premiums. Premiums for credit life, accident, health, or loss-of-income insurance may be excluded from the finance charge if the following conditions are met:

(i) The insurance coverage is not required by the creditor, and this fact is disclosed in writing.

(ii) The premium for the initial term of insurance coverage is disclosed in writing. If the term of insurance is less than the term of the transaction, the term of insurance also shall be disclosed. The premium may be disclosed on a unit-cost basis only in open end credit transactions, closed end credit transactions by mail or telephone under § 226.17(g), and certain closed end credit transactions involving an insurance plan that limits the total amount of indebtedness subject to coverage.

(iii) The consumer signs or initials an affirmative written request for the insurance after receiving the disclosures specified in this paragraph, except as provided in paragraph (d)(4) of this section. Any consumer in the transaction may sign or initial the request.

(2) Property insurance premiums. Premiums for insurance against loss of or damage to property, or against liability arising out of the ownership or use of property, including single interest insurance if the insurer waives all right of

subrogation against the consumer,[22] may be excluded from the finance charge if the following conditions are met:

(i) The insurance coverage may be obtained from a person of the consumer's choice,[23] and this fact is disclosed. (A creditor may reserve the right to refuse to accept, for reasonable cause, an insurer offered by the consumer.)

(ii) If the coverage is obtained from or through the creditor, the premium for the initial term of insurance coverage shall be disclosed. If the term of insurance is less than the term of the transaction, the term of insurance shall also be disclosed. The premium may be disclosed on a unit-cost basis only in open end credit transactions, closed end credit transactions by mail or telephone under § 226.17(g), and certain closed end credit transactions involving an insurance plan that limits the total amount of indebtedness subject to coverage.

(3) Voluntary debt cancellation or debt suspension fees. Charges or premiums paid for debt cancellation coverage for amounts exceeding the value of the collateral securing the obligation or for debt cancellation or debt suspension coverage in the event of the loss of life, health, or income or in case of accident may be excluded from the finance charge, whether or not the coverage is insurance, if the following conditions are met:

(i) The debt cancellation or debt suspension agreement or coverage is not required by the creditor, and this fact is disclosed in writing;

(ii) The fee or premium for the initial term of coverage is disclosed in writing. If the term of coverage is less than the term of the credit transaction, the term of coverage also shall be disclosed. The fee or premium may be disclosed on a unit-cost basis only in open end credit transactions, closed end credit transactions by mail or telephone under § 226.17(g), and certain closed end credit transactions involving a debt cancellation agreement that limits the total amount of indebtedness subject to coverage;

(iii) The following are disclosed, as applicable, for debt suspension coverage: That the obligation to pay loan principal and interest is only suspended, and that interest will continue to accrue during the period of suspension.

(iv) The consumer signs or initials an affirmative written request for coverage after receiving the disclosures specified in this paragraph, except as provided in paragraph (d)(4) of this section. Any consumer in the transaction may sign or initial the request.

(4) Telephone purchases. If a consumer purchases credit insurance or debt cancellation or debt suspension coverage for an open end (not home-secured) plan by telephone, the creditor must make the disclosures under paragraphs (d)(1) (i) and (ii) or (d)(3)(i) through (iii) of this section, as applicable, orally. In such a case, the creditor shall:

(i) Maintain evidence that the consumer, after being provided the disclosures orally, affirmatively elected to purchase the insurance or coverage; and

(ii) Mail the disclosures under paragraphs (d)(1) (i) and (ii) or (d)(3)(i) through (iii) of this section, as applicable, within three business days after the telephone purchase.

(e) Certain security interest charges. If itemized and disclosed, the following charges may be excluded from the finance charge:

(1) Taxes and fees prescribed by law that actually are or will be paid to public officials for determining the existence of or for perfecting, releasing, or satisfying a security interest.

(2) The premium for insurance in lieu of perfecting a security interest to the extent that the premium does not exceed the fees described in paragraph (e)(1) of this section that otherwise would be payable.

(3) Taxes on security instruments. Any tax levied on security instruments or on documents evidencing indebtedness if the payment of such taxes is a requirement for recording the instrument securing the evidence of indebtedness.

(f) Prohibited offsets. Interest, dividends, or other income received or to be received by the consumer on deposits or investments shall not be deducted in computing the finance charge.

5

The Outlay and Unknown Future Events Issues: Closed-End Credit

Despite the fundamental usefulness of the Truth in Lending Act (TILA) and its likely favorable economic impact overall, the four concerns enumerated in the previous chapter—the issues of outlay, unknown future events, compliance, and extent—continue to generate problems. Each illustrates the ongoing complexity of characterizing a credit transaction correctly for TILA purposes. This chapter and the next focus on examples of litigation, legislation, and regulation surrounding two of those issues—the outlay and unknown future events problems. The examples chosen are by no means unique, but because they provide a look at fundamental concerns, and the flavor of the kinds of complexities involved in making the proper disclosures under the current regime, they are exactly the sorts of problems that keep coming back in new trappings. In each case, an appeal to economic concepts and legal definitions offers only a starting point to understanding and implementing the correct disclosure; the issues enumerated have made disclosure law much knottier than mere economic theory or legal principles. Each situation involves some sort of major concern and has resulted in significant revisions or expansion of the existing disclosure regime.

The first examples, covered in this chapter, involve closed-end credit arrangements, especially for mortgage credit, in which recent controversies in the closed-end area have been strongest. The next chapter turns to open-end credit in which, if anything, disclosure policy has in recent years been even more complicated and contentious.

A Mistake in Closed-End Mortgage Disclosing: The *Rodash* Case in Florida

Frequent changes in TILA by the Congress and, in the TILA regulations, by the Federal Reserve Board (FRB or the Board), have generated uncertainty over TILA's requirements, but the courts have also produced their share of alterations. This section looks at an important court decision that at first pointed to an upheaval in mortgage lending but instead led to a congressional revision of the Truth in Lending Act itself. Our discussion then turns to some proposed TILA reforms in the mortgage area.

The 1994 Florida court case known as *Rodash vs. AIB Mortgage Company* offers a good illustration of the potential for confusion that can arise from the outlay issue.[1] The decision created an uproar, and Congress, in 1995, took up the thorny process of settling the matter legislatively. Although the outcome of this congressional effort generally seems to have straightened out and answered the immediate legal questions, it also entailed just enough elements of political compromise to leave most close observers a tad dissatisfied on theoretical and policy grounds.

The *Rodash* case arose over accounting for two costs in a particular mortgage refinancing: the fee Florida charged the creditor for its state intangibles tax ($204) and the charge for FedEx® courier service ($22). The creditor included those costs in the loan amount and the amount financed rather than in the finance charge. This treatment meant the amounts were disclosed as fees for services purchased and received by the consumer, and then financed, rather than as loan costs. The court disagreed and made these two fees into finance charges. The decision was problematic because the rejected practice had been employed in good faith by knowledgeable market participants, and arguably the court could have gone the other way.[2] Consequently, the decision instantaneously left many lenders on the wrong side of the disclosure rules.

The lender's position was certainly reasonable as a matter of both economics and logic. The payment to the state for its intangibles taxation is not something like interest, points, or other compensating fees due to the lender for the specific characteristics of the loan. The courier fee incurred to deliver the payoff check to the former mortgage holder is likewise not something necessarily part of the new loan cost.

Also, as a legal matter, arguably neither payment appears necessarily to come under the TILA definition of a *finance charge*: an amount "payable directly or indirectly by the person to whom the credit is extended and imposed directly or indirectly by the creditor as an incident to the extension of credit" (section 106). For the courier fee, a consumer not otherwise required to purchase the courier service might well do so anyway, since payoff using the service probably saved the consumer money by stopping daily interest accruals on the old mortgage as soon as possible. This could well bring the payment under the cash exception in TILA: "The finance charge does not include charges of a type payable in a comparable cash transaction" (TILA, Section 106). That is, the costs that could be incurred if the consumer used cash instead of borrowing should not be counted as a finance charge in the case of a loan. Likewise, an intangibles tax goes to the state and not to the lender, and so it is easy enough to argue that it is not "imposed" by the lender.[3]

But it is also possible to argue these questions in the way decided by the court. In the court's reasoning, both fees are part of the cost of the credit transaction, "imposed directly or indirectly by the creditor as an incident to the extension of credit" — that is, finance charges.

The court acknowledged that this outcome might not always follow, depending on the structure of the transaction. According to the court, it makes a difference whether the tax is direct or indirect: "A tax imposed by a state... on the credit transaction that is directly *payable by the consumer* (even if the tax is collected by the creditor) when the charge is imposed on the consumer by someone *other than the creditor*" can be *excluded* from the definition of a finance charge [emphasis added]. But if the same tax is imposed on the *creditor* (which it was in this case), thereby becoming part of the creditor's costs and cash flows, even if the tax ultimately is paid by the consumer, then it *is* a finance charge, even if separately identified and billed by the creditor as a tax. With respect to the fundamentals of the transaction, these distinctions over form of billing of taxes begin to sound like musings about the dancing of angels on the head of a pin.

The problem is simply a classic example of the outlay issue: how to clarify when payments made in a credit transaction are the costs of credit (finance charges) and when they are something else. As a TILA *legal* matter, the court seems absolutely correct to point out that it makes a difference who pays these fees, even if the payment amount is the same and the consumer ultimately is responsible for them in either case. If the taxes and courier fee had been paid directly by the lender and covered out of its lending revenues arising from the transaction, then the amount from the consumer covering them would clearly be part of the finance charge, as would any component of expenditures covered by the lender out of its lending revenues, such as salaries of employees, for instance.

This situation is actually nothing more than the parking lot example of the previous chapter. If the lender pays the parking lot fee (or the FedEx charge, the intangibles tax, or whatever), then the customer's outlay to cover it is a finance charge legally. In contrast, if the third party bills the same fee directly to the consumer, then it is not a finance charge. As with the parking lot fee, however, neither disclosure is going to hand consumers a golden solution to the question: What is the best deal, with no need to consider any further implications?

As reviewed in the previous chapter, whenever expenditures that are parts of a whole must nonetheless be classified into subgroupings, the outlay issue raises its ugly head. In such situations, one must look for legal guidance on the proper disclosure to the wording of the law, regulation, *Commentary*, and court precedents for guidance, but it is always possible to make damaging mistakes, as transpired in *Rodash*. If the appellate court had decided against the creditor in *Rodash*, the possibility would have arisen that the borrower could not only seek damages but also rescind the transaction for wrongful disclosures. The upshot of *Rodash* was that everyone else who had received similar disclosures — potentially millions of consumers — also, consequently, held the right to rescind, even if the disclosures were otherwise correct and given in good faith with no intent to misinform.

The fear of a wave of rescissions along with massive class-action lawsuits over such a small matter apparently enabled creditors to convince Congress that some relief was reasonable. Congress responded first, in May 1995, with a moratorium on class-action suits in the area, pending substantive amendments to TILA and second, at the end of September, with the amendments. The changes included some additional Section 106(e) statutory exclusions from the finance charge on mortgage loans, changes in the rules concerning fees paid to mortgage brokers, and slightly eased accuracy rules for the finance charge. For the last of these, it provided explicitly for tolerances and permitted over-disclosure of the finance charge without potentiality for monetary penalties or enforcement actions.[4] Specifically solving the immediate *Rodash* issues, the Congress decided that:

> The finance charge shall not include fees and amounts imposed by third party closing agents (including settlement agents, attorneys, and escrow and title companies) if the creditor does not require the imposition of the charges or the services provided and does not retain the charges (Truth in Lending Act, Section 106(a)).

[Also not included in the finance charge:] Any tax levied on security instruments or on documents evidencing indebtedness if the payment of such taxes is a precondition for recording the instrument securing the evidence of indebtedness (Truth in Lending Act, Section 106(d)(3)).

In the revisions, Congress also expanded the liability for any residual situations in which violations might still occur and established somewhat different tolerances and rules for cases involving a foreclosure (details of the changes may be found in Cook and Wisner 1996). All of this settled the immediate legal questions raised in *Rodash*, but, of course, the outlay issue itself did not go away.

Some Proposed Changes for the Finance Charge

Courier fees and intangibles taxes have not been the only difficulties with determining and disclosing finance charges that have arisen from the outlay issue, and there have been many attempts to resolve them.

The original act attempted to obviate the outlay issue by carefully delineating the finance charge concept, and Congress looked at the matter once again at the time of the act's subsequent simplification, in 1980. Further, as part of the 1995 *Rodash*-inspired legislation, Congress requested, from the FRB, a new study on the concept of the finance charge for TILA purposes. The request specifically asked the Board to consider expanding the definition of the finance charge to include all costs associated with a mortgage transaction, an issue Congress had wrestled with the 1960–1968 period, in the run-up to passage of the original TILA.

As touched upon earlier, lenders have long had an incentive to exclude fees from the finance charge. Before 1980, mortgage lending, and indeed all of consumer lending, was subject to usury laws — interest-rate ceilings — established by the states. Most of the time and in most places, market interest rates on typical consumer mortgage loans were comfortably below these ceilings. But during inflationary times or in those periods of the business cycle when interest rates were high, usury ceilings significantly interfered with mortgage lending. The interaction of market cycles and usury laws accentuated the cyclicality of mortgage lending and helped perpetuate a certain element of boom and bust to the mortgage lending industry and its institutions, especially to savings banks and savings and loan associations.

Consequently, usury laws created an incentive for lenders to split the lending process into parts that could be excluded from the usury restrictions whenever possible. Charges such as *brokerage fees* and *paperwork fees* arose on both mortgage loans and on common, nonmortgage consumer lending. Lenders' success in convincing legislatures and courts to allow such pricing practices to continue outside the rate ceilings produced a lending culture in which prices, especially for originating mortgage loans, became fragmented into a variety of parts that could vary even by location of the lender.[5] Indeed, support for Senator Paul Douglas' truth in lending plan arose in large part as a reaction to the complications in loan pricing on consumer and mortgage loans that had grown up over the decades due to usury laws.

From its outset, TILA overlaid a legacy culture of fragmented pricing practices. For ordinary consumer lending, keeping fees out of the finance charge and annual percentage rate (APR) became mostly impossible following implementation of TILA, but mortgage lending was different for a number of reasons.

First, even though many separate fees became finance charges under TILA, regardless of their characterization under state laws, Congress retained some disclosure anomalies in the mortgage area after 1968, as mentioned in the previous chapter. This meant that even with the demise of usury laws on mortgage credit following passage of the Monetary Control Act in 1980, keeping fees separate when possible was still useful for mortgage creditors. Second, the fear of antitrust exposure that might arise from any joint discussions among lenders regarding improving mortgage pricing likely contributed to inertia in this area. Third, at least some lenders believed that a strict interpretation of the Real Estate Settlement Procedures Act (RESPA, discussed further in Appendix B, "Discussion of Disclosures in Selected Federal Consumer Financial Protection Statutes Other than the Truth in Lending Act") complicated their ability to offer packaged charges on mortgage loans if some of the fees were payable to third parties like brokers and appraisers. Finally, less scrupulous lenders and processors also believed that, with lots of fee categories, many consumers would pay a price higher than necessary out of confusion.

It seems that all of these factors have contributed to keeping both the mortgage lending industry fragmented and the disclosures required for mortgage loans complicated. Table 5.1 contains a list of fees that might be found on a typical mortgage settlement sheet. The table indicates which ones are included within the finance charge in the current TILA regime; the others, consequently, are (as of year-end 2009) outside the finance charge on mortgage loans. The sheer magnitude of the list in the table shows how extensive and convoluted these fees and associated disclosures can be.

The FRB responded in two stages to the 1995 congressional request for review of the finance charge on mortgage credit. First came a preliminary report in 1996 (Board of Governors of the Federal Reserve System 1996) followed by a lengthier discussion in 1998. The latter was part of the Board's joint report with the Department of Housing and Urban Development (HUD) on Truth in Lending and the Real Estate Settlement Procedures Act, often referred to as the Fed–HUD Report

Table 5.1 Fees That Might Be Found on a Typical Mortgage Lending Arrangement

	Part of finance charge in current TILA and Regulation Z
Loan origination fee	*
Loan discount	*
Per diem interest	*
Mortgage broker fee paid by borrower	*
Application fee	
Annual fee for open-end plan	
Credit report	
Appraisal and survey	
Lender's inspection fee	
Pest inspection	
Tax/flood certification	
Tax and flood service (life of loan)	*
Assumption fee (pre-consummation)	*
Document preparation (loan-related)	
Veterans' Administration application fee	*
Mortgage insurance premium	*
Credit life and disability insurance (optional)	
Settlement or closing fee	
Abstract or title search and title examination	
Title insurance and binder–lender's coverage	
Notary fee (for mortgage)	
Attorney's fee (lender)	
Recording fees: mortgage, release	
State/county/city tax/stamps–mortgage	
Lock in fee	*

Source: Board of Governors of the Federal Reserve System and Department of Housing and Urban Development (1998), Appendix C.

(Board of Governors of the Federal Reserve System and Department of Housing and Urban Development 1998).[6] A public comment period on the matter, the issuance of the two reports, and congressional hearings in 1998 and 1999 thoroughly aired the outlay issue for mortgages once again.

Both the FRB's 1996 report and the joint Fed–HUD Report in 1998 postulate the polar concepts of "what the consumer pays" and "what the creditor receives" as the primary possible alternatives to the reigning conception of the finance charge that Congress might consider. These alternatives are actually merely dusted-off and updated manifestations of the "consumer cost" and the "creditor yield" conceptions renamed from the truth in lending hearings of a generation earlier (and rejected then in favor of a cost of credit approach). Presumably, either of these alternative approaches could simplify compliance with disclosure requirements, by mandating that fees to third parties either be in the finance charge (what the consumer pays) or out of the finance charge (what the creditor receives). To prove that nothing ever goes away, the FRB asked for further comment in 2009.

The difficulty with these approaches is that they would move the definition of finance charge away from the cost of credit and toward becoming just a compliance convenience but one potentially misleading for consumers. As argued in the previous chapter, a fundamental reconsideration of the ultimate goals of TILA should be a necessary prerequisite for any meaningful wholesale conceptual realignment. Apparently, this has also been the view of the Congress, at least in effect, in that it did not take any action except to hold hearings and did not adopt any changes upon receipt of the reports responding to its request for review.

That said, there still seems to be room for improvement. If there is a desire to strike a reasonable balance between truth in lending and ease of compliance, without changing the overall approach of the TILA finance charge based on credit cost, then there is still merit to straightening out some long-standing anomalies in the definitions of the finance charge for mortgage credit.[7] The approach called the "Required Cost of Credit Test" in Chapter 2 of the 1998 Fed–HUD Report and in its Appendix C would remove some of the inconsistencies between the treatment of fees for mortgages and those for other consumer credit.

The changes recommended would include in the finance charge and APR certain fees currently excluded by statute or regulation for mortgage credit, some since 1968, that would otherwise appear to be finance charges. Fees for required appraisals or for obtaining credit reports would become part of the finance charge, as they are on non-mortgage credit, even if the fees are paid to third parties. A variety of other fees, generally only found on mortgage lending, would also become finance charges—lender-required title insurance, for example. As noted, Table 5.1 lists fees that frequently are features of mortgage loans, not necessarily each one on each loan. The devil of such recommendations is always in the details, but the prime candidates for revisions are fairly obvious in Table 5.1.

Though this approach of making the finance charge and the associated APR on mortgage credit more comprehensive contains the potential for answering questions, tightening up anomalies, and even simplifying compliance, it would come at the cost of altering the familiar disclosure regime for mortgage loans and introducing a variety of start-up costs for the mortgage lenders implementing the changes. Start up costs would arise from the need to evaluate and possibly change many lending systems and disclosures. The chance that old issues would need to be litigated again could further increase costs. Elliehausen and Lowrey (1997) and Elliehausen (1998) show that even limited change in disclosure regulations can be very costly, which argues that if proposed changes are pretty limited and not likely to alter consumers' conception very much, if at all, then the social benefit of frequently tinkering with disclosure rules may well be entirely lacking. (The next section of this chapter looks at the potential impact of proposed changes in mortgage disclosing on the comprehensive percentage discounting variable, the APR.)

Overall, a revision to the finance charge definition, along the lines recommended in the 1998 report, would not stray very far from the current conception and would amount essentially to housekeeping, but its adoption might still entail sizeable operational difficulties for creditors. Because of concerns over necessary changes, many lenders have been unwilling to sign on as supporters, even though, conceptually, the changes make sense. In effect, they have asked, "What's in this sort of proposal for me?" In their view, the changes often discussed simply seem too costly to be worth the trouble of undertaking the necessary alterations to their lending systems and required disclosures.

As of the end of 2010, Congress had not enacted the proposed reforms, and presumably it will not do so without extensive further study, although potential changes in this area again came under scrutiny by the FRB in 2009. For now, the current version of the cost of credit approach for mortgage credit, long enshrined in TILA, remains in effect. It continues to include anomalies and some inconsistencies between mortgage loans and other sorts of closed-end credit, but it soldiers on as the basic approach to truth in lending in this important area.

It appears that instead of constant upheaval over finance charges, over the years, Congress generally has tended to agree, at least in effect, that perpetual tinkering with the definition of the finance charge as credit markets change and new ideas arise produces its own sets of difficulties. Since change itself potentially involves substantial market disruptions, litigation, and adjustment costs, it seems proper to be cautious in amending TILA. As the lenders suggest, it is not always clear that new approaches are sufficiently better to warrant the costly disruptions that they often entail.[8] The next section of this chapter examines in more detail the effect on the APR for mortgages that arise from proposed changes to the definition of the finance charge.

Mortgage Reform and the Annual Percentage Rate

Whenever a proposal to redefine the finance charge arises, it immediately raises not only the outlay issue involving whether the proposed change is conceptually appropriate but also the mathematically interrelated operational question of the potential impact on other TILA measures, notably on the APR. Previous discussion argued that the mathematics of calculating APRs on closed-end credit are not conceptually complicated, although the more terms in the underlying equation, the more daunting the appearance.

To simplify the examination of impact, it is useful first to employ artificially simple examples that focus just on the basic interrelationships among the amount financed, finance charge, and the APR without all the equation detail arising from lengthy time periods and multiple other components. The examples that follow use a single-period loan to illustrate APR movement resulting from a variety of potential changes that might arise in the process of mortgage disclosure reform. After the preliminary examples with the single-payment loan, more realistic examples follow to illustrate the order of magnitudes of the potential impact on the APR that might come about from some of the finance charge changes actually discussed as part of possible mortgage disclosure reform.[9]

Consider a home purchase transaction and mortgage loan with the following characteristics:

Cost of house: $100,000
Down payment: $20,000

Contract amount of loan, therefore:	$80,000
Contract simple interest rate:	10%
Maturity of loan:	one year
Repayment:	Single payment at maturity
Interest on loan:	$8,000
Points:	None
Other closing costs:	$1,000

The way to determine the APR for this (or any) loan is to place all the things the consumer purchases or receives as part of the transaction on the left side of an equation and all the amounts the consumer pays on the right side. After this equation is set up properly (which involves satisfactorily answering the questions designated here as the outlay issue) it is easy to solve the example for the percentage rate, the remaining term that equates the two sides of the equation. The complicated part is to *set up* the equation correctly, accounting for all the terms properly. Correctly recording the terms clearly involves accurately specifying the timing of flows on both the left and right sides of the equation. Time differences of cash flows, after all, are the essence of a credit arrangement and the genesis of the APR concept.

In the example, we begin with the left side (what the consumer receives). For most loans, the timing of the left side flows is straightforward because the transaction and all loan advances are made at the present time. Multiple-payout construction loans with disbursements in the consumer's favor over some extended time period are the main, but uncommon, exception for typical consumer and mortgage credit. The example here does not contain a complexity of this sort.[10]

The timing of the flows that go on the right side of the equation is more complicated. Some of the payments the consumer makes might be current, but some are put off until later — notably, the payment of interest and principal (in this simple example, both are paid one year from now).

The amounts payable later are discounted to their present values by application of a periodic discount rate. In terms of TILA, the present value of the loan flows is called the amount financed. In the equation, it is the quantity that remains on the left side, after the algebraic cancellations. The APR for closed-end credit is then simply the annualized periodic discount factor that solves the equation by equating the left to the right side. In the simple examples outlined here, there is no need to annualize by multiplying the discount rate by the number of discounting periods per year, since there is only one period.[11]

Now we look at some examples to examine calculation of the APR and the impact of changes in finance charge components. The same examples are expanded upon in Appendix B to include the case of yield spread premiums (YSPs), which have been important for compliance with the RESPA.

Example 1: A Plain-Vanilla Mortgage Transaction. The above hypothetical mortgage transaction produces an APR equation for a very simplified mortgage transaction as follows. The consumer receives a house worth $100,000 plus a loan of $80,000 and $1,000 of loan closing services. Because the consumer receives the house, the loan of $80,000, and the closing services of $1,000, they go on the left side of the equation.[12] The consumer makes a down payment of $20,000 plus the closing costs of $1,000 immediately in cash, and the $80,000 loan principal is paid immediately to the seller along with the down payment amount. These amounts go on the right side of the equation and are not discounted since they are due immediately.

The buyer then repays the entire loan of $80,000 plus interest of $8,000 (that is, the $80,000 loan times the 10-percent contract interest rate) in one payment of $88,000 at the end of the year. These latter amounts go on the right side of the equation as well, but since they paid later, they are discounted to a present value by a periodic discount factor, r. Because the APR unit period, as defined in Appendix J to Regulation Z, is one year in this example, the APR equation is as follows:

$$\$100,000 + 80,000 + 1,000$$
$$= 20,000 + 80,000 + 1,000 + (80,000 + 8,000) * (1+r)^{-1} \quad (A1)$$

and cancelling and solving this equation for r:

$$\$80,000 = (88,000)*(1+r)^{-1} \quad (A2)$$

$$r = 8,000/80,000 = 10 \text{ percent} = APR \quad (A3)$$

Notes:
Finance charge: $8,000
Amount financed: $80,000

Consumer's cash out of pocket at closing: $21,000 (down payment and closing costs)

Not surprisingly, the APR on this transaction is the same as the contract rate; there are no complicating factors, such as fees, to make it otherwise.

In the example, the finance charge is $8,000 and the total of payments (due at the end of the year) is $88,000. The amount financed (left side of the equation) is $80,000, following algebraic cancellations, and the APR that solves the equation is 10 percent.

Example 2: A Mortgage Transaction with Financed Closing Costs. Next, suppose that the consumer does not want to pay the closing costs in cash because, from the consumer's standpoint, this expenditure amounts to an increase in the down payment requirement; instead, the consumer prefers to finance these settlement costs as part of the loan. Assuming this change in the loan-to-value ratio is acceptable to the lender so that the contract interest rate does not rise, this transaction produces a second equation. In this case, the consumer receives an additional loan advance of $1,000, which also must go on the left side of the equation along with the house value and the value of the closing services. This generates a corresponding additional repayment of the $1,000 after a year, plus the additional finance charge of $100 upon it at the contract interest rate of 10 percent. These amounts go on the right side:

$$\begin{aligned} &\$100{,}000 + 80{,}000 + 1{,}000 + 1{,}000 \\ &= 20{,}000 + 80{,}000 + 1000 + (80{,}000 + 8{,}000 + 1{,}000 + 100)*(1+r)^{-1} \end{aligned} \quad (B1)$$

and solving this equation for r:

$$\$81{,}000 = (89{,}100)*(1+r)^{-1} \quad (B2)$$

$$r = 8{,}100/81{,}000 = 10 \text{ percent} = \text{APR} \quad (B3)$$

Notes:
Finance charge: $8,100
Amount financed: $81,000
Consumer's cash out of pocket at closing: $20,000 (down payment)

Not surprisingly, the APR remains at 10 percent because Example 2 differs from Example 1 only through the loan of an additional amount at the same contract rate and repayable at the same time. The consumer is charged an additional $100 finance charge because of the addition of the $1,000 in closing costs to the loan balance. In TILA terms, the finance charge increases by $100 in this transaction and the amount financed (left side of the equation) increases by $1,000.

Example 3: A Mortgage Transaction Following a Regulatory Change that Makes Closing Costs a Finance Charge, Which Is Paid at the Closing in Cash.

Now suppose that, under some version of mortgage disclosure reform, the closing costs are declared to be a finance charge. This amounts to a redefinition, making closing costs not an additional service the consumer purchases and receives but rather an additional finance charge the consumer pays at the loan closing. In this case, the closing costs no longer go on the left side of the equation as something the consumer receives as part of the purchase, but they remain on the right side as a finance charge paid immediately. Because, in this example, the consumer pays the additional finance charge in cash immediately at the closing, this cash flow functions like an additional element of the down payment. The resulting equation looks almost like Equation *(A1)* above, although the APR is higher because of the additional finance charge paid at closing:

$$\$100{,}000 + 80{,}000$$
$$= 20{,}000 + 80{,}000 + 1{,}000 + (80{,}000 + 8{,}000)*(1+r)^{-1} \qquad (C1)$$

and solving this equation for r:

$$\$79{,}000 = (88{,}000)*(1+r)^{-1} \qquad (C2)$$

$$r = 9{,}000/79{,}000 = 11.392 \text{ percent} = \text{APR} \qquad (C3)$$

Notes:
Finance charge: $9,000
Amount financed: $79,000
Consumer's cash out of pocket at closing: $21,000 (the down payment and closing costs)

In this case, the finance charge is $9,000 and the amount financed is $79,000.

Example 4: A Mortgage Transaction Following a Regulatory Change that Makes Closing Costs a Finance Charge But with the Additional Closing Costs (Finance Charges) Financed by Increasing the Loan Balance. In this fourth example, suppose that the consumer does not pay the additional finance charge (the closing cost) in cash but rather prefers to finance it with another $1,000 of loan advance. In this case, the consumer receives additional funds of $1,000, which increases the left side of the equation. The closing costs and finance charge are paid at closing. The $1,000 of amount financed generated to make this initial payment is repaid together with the additional $100 of the finance charge it requires, along with the rest of the loan and the finance charge at the end of the one-year period. In this case, the equation looks more like Equation *(B1)* above:

$$\begin{aligned} &\$100{,}000 + 80{,}000 + 1{,}000 \\ &= 20{,}000 + 80{,}000 + 1{,}000 + (80{,}000 + 8{,}000 + 1{,}000 + 100)^*(1+r)^{-1} \end{aligned} \quad (D1)$$

and solving this equation for r:

$$\$80{,}000 = (89{,}100)^*(1+r)^{-1} \tag{D2}$$

$$r = 9100/80{,}000 = 11.375 \text{ percent} = APR \tag{D3}$$

Notes:
Finance charge: $9,100
Amount financed: $80,000
Consumer's cash out of pocket at closing: $20,000 (down payment)

In this example, the finance charge is $9,100 and the present value (amount financed) is again $80,000. The out-of-pocket cash again is $20,000, rather than $21,000, due to financing of the closing costs.

Significantly, these same simple equations may be employed to illustrate the direction of impact on APRs of other common aspects of lending, such as the financing of ancillary products like single premium credit insurance (a transaction like Example 1 or, more likely, Example 2 above), or the payment and/or financing of advance finance charges, such as the points on real estate loans (as in Example 3 or, more likely, 4). Table 5.2 contains some more common examples based on the same hypothetical mortgage loan. Taken together, all of these examples illustrate in a simplified way that it is not the mathematics of the APR calculation that is complicated; the daunting part of TILA is where to put the various quantities that go into the equation. Clearly, correctly managing this problem requires a full understanding of the outlay issue.

Now, moving away from these simplified examples, and with the benefit of spreadsheet software, it is easy enough to examine the impact of possible mortgage disclosure reforms in a more realistic manner, employing the more complicated form of the APR equations introduced as Equations 1 and 2 in Chapter 4. These equations are:

The discounting equation:

$$AmtFin = PV = \sum_{i=0}^{nt} (Pmts_i)(1+r/n)^{-i} \tag{1}$$

And the annualizing conversion:

$$APR = n(r/n)^*100 = r^*100 \tag{2}$$

Table 5.2 Some Additional Examples of APR Calculations[1]

Simplified, generic, transaction terms:	
Cost of house	$100,000
Down payment	$20,000
Contract amount of loan, therefore	$80,000
Contract simple interest rate	10%
Maturity of loan	1 year
Repayment	Single payment at maturity
Interest on loan, therefore	$8,000
Points	None (unless stated differently in example)
Other closing costs	$1,000

APR calculations:

1. With a financed credit insurance premium of $1,500:
100,000+80,000+1,000+1,500
$= 20,000+80,000+1,000+(80,000+8,000+1,500+150)*(1+r)^{-1}$
$81,500 = (89,650)*(1+r)^{-1}$
$r = (8,150/81,500) = 10$ percent = APR
Finance charge: $8,150   Amount financed: $81,500
Consumer's cash out of pocket at closing: $21,000 (down payment and closing costs)

2. With a point paid by consumer in cash at closing:
100,000+80,000+1,000
$= 20,000+80,000+1,000+800+(80,000+8,000)*(1+r)^{-1}$
$79,200 = (88,000)*(1+r)^{-1}$
$r = (8,800/79,200) = 11.11$ percent = APR
Finance charge: $8,800   Amount financed: $79,200
Consumer's cash out of pocket at closing: $21,800 (down payment, closing costs, and point)

3. With a financed point (equal to $800):
100,000+80,000+1,000+800
$= 20,000+80,000+1,000+800+(80,000+8,000+800+80)*(1+r)^{-1}$
$80,000 = (88,880)*(1+r)^{-1}$
$r = (8,880/80,000) = 11.10$ percent = APR
Finance charge: $8,880   Amount financed: $80,000
Consumer's cash out of pocket at closing: $21,000 (down payment and closing costs)

(continued)

Table 5.2   Some Additional Examples of APR Calculations *(cont'd)*

4. With a financed point and financed credit insurance premium of $1,500:
100,000+80,000+1,000+800+1,500
Simplified, generic, transaction terms:
= 20,000+80,000+1,000+800
+(80,000+8,000+800+80+1,500+150)*(1+r)^{-1}
81,500 = (90,530)*(1+r)^{-1}
r = (9,030/81,500) = 11.08 percent = APR
Finance charge: $9,030   Amount financed: $81,500
Consumer's cash out of pocket at closing: $21,000 (down payment and closing costs)

Employing these fuller equations, the question is, What is the impact on the APR of adding to the finance charge some specific fees that heretofore have not been finance charges? This is not the same question as that regarding the impact of fees on the APR, because many fees are already finance charges for purposes of calculating APRs; it is rather, What is the impact of a change in the classification of certain fees that are not previously finance charges? As indicated above by comparing Examples 1 and 3, the direction (not surprisingly) would be upward, but by how much in realistic examples?

One approach to answering this question is to designate some hypothetical examples and then estimate the impact on APRs of switching the designation of certain fees by newly counting them as finance charges. For example, on a $100,000 mortgage loan with a 6-percent APR and the fees of $1,000 due at settlement that would newly become finance charges under some reform approach, the APR increase can be calculated from Equations 1 and 2. The impact of any number of hypothetical examples can be calculated using this approach.

Table 5.3 offers a variety of such solutions for loans of different sizes with initial APRs at various levels and with 30- and 15-year maturities and two different increases in finance charge levels. For example, newly defining, as a finance charge, an additional $400 due as an initial fee plus $2 per $1,000 for title insurance would increase the APR for a 6-percent loan of $100,000 by 0.06 percentage points (to 6.06 percent) if the term to maturity is 30 years. The same increase in finance charges would increase the APR for a 6-percent loan of $100,000 by 0.09 percentage points if the term to maturity is 15 years. The impact is reduced as the loan size increases. It is easy to see from this sort of calculation that increases in

Table 5.3 Increases in APRs Disclosed Under the Truth in Lending Act, Due to Making Selected Not Finance Charge Initial Fees Into Finance Charges (in Percentage Points)

1. Initial fee increase of $400 for various purposes plus $2 per $1,000 of initial loan balance for title insurance

30-Year loans at initial APRs of:

Initial loan amount:	6 percent	8 percent	10 percent
$100,000	0.06	0.06	0.07
$200,000	0.04	0.04	0.05
$300,000	0.03	0.04	0.04

15-Year loans at initial APRs of:

Initial loan amount:	6 percent	8 percent	10 percent
$50,000	0.16	0.17	0.18
$100,000	0.09	0.10	0.11
$200,000	0.06	0.07	0.07

2. Initial fee increase of $800 for various purposes plus $2 per $1,000 of initial loan balance for title insurance

30-Year loans at initial APRs of:

Initial loan amount:	6 percent	8 percent	10 percent
$100,000	0.09	0.11	0.12
$200,000	0.06	0.06	0.07
$300,000	0.04	0.05	0.06

15-Year loans at initial APRs of:

Initial loan amount:	6 percent	8 percent	10 percent
$50,000	0.28	0.30	0.32
$100,000	0.16	0.17	0.18
$200,000	0.09	0.10	0.11

finance charges by these amounts do not change the disclosed APRs calculated according to the rules of Regulation Z by very much. This finding again raises the questions whether small changes of this kind influence consumer behavior very often and whether they are worth the costs disrupting long-standing practice for the sake of the small amounts of additional precision they bring.

6

The Outlay and Unknown Future Events Issues: Open-End Credit

It would be easy enough to extend Chapter 5, "The Outlay and Unknown Future Events Issues: Closed-End Credit," by providing more examples of disclosure difficulties for closed-end credit arising from the outlay issue. It would likewise be easy to supply illustrations of complications due to unknown future events, for example, by showing the impact of fees and points on yields to maturity, the effective annual percentage rates (APRs), in the case of early payoff or refinancing. It was the latter problem that produced a disparaging description of the Truth in Lending Act (TILA) by Guttentag and Hurst (1985). But some of the best illustrations of disclosure complications arising from the outlay and unknown future events issues have come from open-end credit, and this chapter addresses that beleaguered area.

Charges for Special Services: A Festering Issue in Credit Card Disclosures

In recent years, credit card accounts issued by financial institutions have proliferated. As transactions devices, these credit cards are used billions of times yearly for routine purchases. As generators of consumer credit, they have largely replaced the old style closed-end installment credit accounts at retail stores, the so-called "easy payment" plans prevalent in past decades for appliances, furniture, and medium-ticket home improvements. They also have largely replaced the charge and credit cards issued by retail stores. Most card credit today is provided by banking and other financial institutions (primarily in the United States with the American

Express, Discover, MasterCard, and Visa brands), and these institutions compete for customers in part by offering enhancements and special services, such as worldwide acceptability at automated teller machines (ATMs).

Not surprisingly, modern credit card issuers have demonstrated little interest in offering widely usable cards with enhanced services at a loss, and so they charge interest on the revolving credit employed, and typically tack on fees for special features and services when possible (for example, fees for access to non-owned ATMs, or cash advances on credit cards). They also try to sell additional products like insurance in conjunction with the accounts, through statement stuffers and other means. Then, there also are late payment fees and over-the-limit charges. As always, for truth in lending purposes, the question is how to characterize and disclose all fees and charges properly. Are the fees for specialized features or services finance charges as defined in Regulation Z or something else? What about penalty fees such as late payment charges? And, how do these fees impact the disclosed APR, if at all? Not surprisingly, the outlay and unknown future events issues have complicated the answers to these questions.

The Cost of Credit Approach

For many years, the starting point for the classification of fees for disclosure purposes on open-end credit was the same as for closed-end credit: the basic statutory definition of a finance charge as the cost of credit. It is found in section 106 of the Truth in Lending Act quoted above as:

> … the sum of all charges, payable directly or indirectly by the person to whom the credit is extended and imposed directly or indirectly by the creditor as an incident to the extension of credit. The finance charge does not include charges of a type payable in a comparable cash transaction.

As discussed earlier, this definition in the act is consistent with an economic conception of the finance charge as the cost of credit. As the reigning legislative definition of the finance charge, this formulation naturally also provides a lot of fundamental legal guidance, but differing interpretations of specific questions are still possible, even likely. Straightening out such situations is the responsibility of Regulation Z and its official staff *Commentary*, though it seems nothing with truth in lending is simple. For closed-end credit, a fee either is or is not a finance charge, but for open-end credit, there has been a third classification, other charges, that also is subject to disclosure rules. Other charges are not finance charges, but they are still within the TILA requirements for disclosures. There is no specific other charges concept for closed-end credit.

Examining sections 226.4(b), 226.6(b), and 226.14 of Regulation Z and their accompanying *Commentary* before the 2008 revisions produced a classification scheme reproduced in Table 6.1 for the various charges that might be features of modern credit card plans: finance charges, other charges (significant charges that were not finance charges), and some fees that were neither finance charges nor other charges and need not be disclosed in TILA documentation. The examples given in the regulation and *Commentary* were only illustrations and not meant to be comprehensive. They did not preclude the existence of other fees, including some maybe yet to come. The message from the table is daunting: Under the rules, it was not necessary to disclose all fees related to card accounts, or disclose all required ones in the same way, but they still had to be classified properly for disclosures (and woe be to those who made a mistake).

The reasoning behind some of the characterizations of the charges listed in the lower part of Table 6.1 seems obvious enough (interest is a finance charge, for example), but the classification of some other card-related fees seems more obscure. (For instance, fees paid periodically to

Table 6.1   The Classification of Charges on Open-End Credit

---

1) Finance charges:
   A) Finance charges that are included in the APR (for example, the interest based on a periodic rate, see 226.14(c)(1));
   B) Finance charges that are not included in the APR (for example "a loan fee, points, or similar charge that relates to the opening of the account...," see 226.14(c)(2), especially footnote 33).

2) Other Charges ("significant charges related to the plan (that are not finance charges)," see *Commentary* 226.6(b)-1):
   A) Other charges that require a change in terms notice (for example, membership or participation fees, see 226.9(c)(1));
   B) Other charges that do not require a change in terms notice (for example, late-payment charges, see 226.9(c)(2)).

3) Neither finance charges nor other charges (*i.e.*, insignificant charges or those not related to the open-end credit plan; for example, fees for making copies for tax purposes, see *Commentary* 226.6(b)-2).

(continued)

Table 6.1   The Classification of Charges on Open-End Credit *(cont'd)*

Taking these official sources together, the following indicates contemporary examples of guidance from the regulation and official staff *Commentary*:

Fee	Classification
1) Interest (arising from the application of a rate to a balance)	Finance charge
2) Minimum, fixed, transaction, or activity charge	Finance charge
3) Late payment or over-the-limit fee	Other charge
4) Fees paid periodically to participate in an open-end credit plan	Other charge
5) ATM fees for cash advances that do not exceed the fee for cash withdrawals from deposit accounts	Other charge
6) A fee to terminate an open-end credit plan (Note: similar in concept to an early payment penalty on a closed-end loan)	Other charge
7) Copy fees for records relating to a billing error	Other charge
8) A tax imposed by a state or other governmental body	Other charge
9) Other delinquency, default, or similar fee, such as fees for unpaid checks, attorney's fees	Neither
10) Copy fees for records for tax purposes	Neither
11) Payment with a check returned for NSF (not sufficient funds)	Neither
12) Premiums for optional credit-related insurance	Neither
13) Application fees paid by all applicants	Neither, whether or not credit is extended

participate in an open-end credit plan are not finance charges, but are *other charges*). Such classifications arose ultimately from attempts to manage the outlay and unknown future events issues: Some fees simply were defined into certain categories to answer TILA questions, as discussed in Chapter 4, "What is Truth in Lending? Key Conceptual Problems Facing the Truth in Lending Act." Including the periodic, usually annual, fee for participating in a card plan in other charges, rather than as a finance charge, for example, was not based in the economics of typical transactions, but was rather a compliance solution to a knotty unknown future events problem.

The fundamental, perplexing difficulty for this disclosure has always been how to calculate and disclose a meaningful and comparable APR if the finance charge includes a periodic fee but credit balances fluctuate, are not known or knowable in advance, and may equal zero in the relevant time period. To solve the disclosure problem, Regulation Z and its *Commentary* have just defined an answer. They simply have placed membership fees outside the finance charge by defining them as other charges. This means they were, by definition, included neither as finance charges nor in the APR, but they must be disclosed in appropriate manner regardless. The readily available rationale for excluding such fees from the finance charge was that they were not "incident to the extension of credit" since they were not directly related to some particular credit advance. But the outcome of excluding membership fees from the finance charge and APR is not very theoretically satisfying, since they clearly are charges for a credit plan and would otherwise appear to be finance charges. A better practical solution for factoring this charge into the APR disclosure is not obvious, however, since accompanying credit balances can fluctuate rapidly and unpredictably, and sometimes equals zero, making any associated APR highly volatile and sometimes even infinite.

Other questions about the classifications of fees on card accounts have also arisen, notably in 2002 with concern over the classification of some fees assessed on consumers for special or expedited services relative to normal operation of the card plan: (1) fees for the expedited delivery of a new or replacement access device (such as the charges for the FedEx® delivery of a new card to open an account or replace a lost or stolen credit card) and (2) charges for telephone-initiated request, or other special requests for a wire or other electronic funds transfer, in lieu of mail or other method of payment, to make a required payment by some specified time. In both instances, the credit card industry believed such charges were not finance charges within the scope, experience, examples, and traditions of Regulation Z, but their status was murky.

To clarify the situation, in late 2002 the FRB staff issued, for public comment, a draft interpretation for insertion in the Regulation Z *Commentary* that charges for the expedited delivery of access devices were neither finance charges nor other charges within the scope of the open-end credit rules of Regulation Z, and that the electronic funds transfer fees for occasional expedited payments were other charges.[1] Previously, many credit card issuers had not been disclosing these fees either as finance charges or other charges, even though the FRB staff had informally telegraphed its view, through discussions at industry meetings and the like, that both might be finance charges, at least under some unspecified circumstances.

Though informal, the staff view that charges for specialized services might be finance charges was unnerving to creditors fearful of violations. The informal staff view seemed to hinge somehow on how the charges were imposed by the creditor in a transaction related to a credit account, rather than whether, theoretically, they were costs of credit or not. For at least the delivery charge, this was reminiscent of the *Rodash* issue all over again, now applied to open-end credit: Does a FedEx courier charge for a special delivery service constitute a finance charge or not? For both expedited delivery and expedited payment services, the underlying issue ultimately was the same: What does a fee for a special service constitute for purposes of TILA disclosure?[2]

At the time, this issue surfaced openly in 2002 in the request for public comments on fees associated with open-end credit accounts, the question of the correct treatment of these fees was already important for banks, who potentially faced both regulatory agency enforcement actions and consumer class-action lawsuits in this area if they made disclosure mistakes. At the time, banks apparently were receiving different guidance about the correct disclosures from different regulators, and they became concerned about the possibility that some agencies might require restitution to consumers for improper disclosures. A letter by a banker in South Dakota to his attorney and shared by the attorney shows the frustration felt by the industry:

> … [W]e believe that the ad-hoc manner in which the bank regulatory agencies are handling this question inhibits the consumer's ability to comparison shop among credit card offers. Currently, the consumer is faced with the real possibility that like charges are disclosed differently in their credit card disclosures based on the issuer's supervisory agency. In South Dakota, for example, FRB banks (i.e. banks supervised by the Federal Reserve Board, which are state chartered banks that are members of the Federal Reserve System) are generally disclosing the fees as finance charges; FDIC banks (state chartered banks that are not members of the Federal Reserve System) are generally not; and OCC banks (national banks, supervised by the Office of the Comptroller of the Currency) are in limbo.

What is the answer? The long-standing approach to such questions has been to engineer a response through a three-step process: (1) examining the definition of a finance charge; (2) looking at the facts of the specific outlays in question to see whether they provide an answer in the context of this definition; and (3) specifying any necessary alterations of outcome that might be required because of ambiguities due to the outlay and unknown future events problems, such as done in the past for membership fees. To illustrate, let us undertake such an examination for these fees.[3]

First, looking at the finance charge definition, if a fee is to be a finance charge under the current legislative definition, then it must be "imposed... as an incident to the extension of credit," and it must "not include charges of a type payable in a comparable cash transaction." Appending the latter clause seems both sensible and important in that it eliminates from the finance charge amounts also required in cash arrangements. Fees also paid in cash transactions hardly seem to qualify as credit costs. But credit cards, by definition, involve credit accounts, necessitating a careful review of all associated fees. The exception for cash clearly establishes the principle that not all costs associated with all credit arrangements are necessarily finance charges, however. This makes sense on its face.

Stage two involves a review of the facts of the individual situation: Are these specific fees "imposed... as an incident to the extension of credit? As with any other goods or services, credit costs are the amounts paid for the characteristics of credit, in other words, for the characteristics of deferring payment.

To get at the essence of the cost of credit, it is worth recalling that, ultimately, there are four fundamental components or basic characteristics of the deferred payment (credit) services that creditors provide to consumers: credit origination, servicing, funding or forbearance, and risk bearing. Credit types can be quite different—closed-end or open-end, fixed- or variable-rate, secured or unsecured, large (home mortgage) or small (payday loans)—but these are differentiations among credit products that reflect mixes of product characteristics (and their resulting prices). At their base, all of these transactions share a core of common characteristics that distinguish extensions of credit from other products or financial services. Economically, the finance charge is the cost of providing these elements of deferred payment.[4]

Looking at the specific fee examples in question, suppose that a consumer has an existing credit card account but loses the plastic card. Suppose, then, that the card account holder calls the issuer on the telephone to report the lost card. If the account holder is in good standing with the card company, then the issuer likely would be willing to issue a new plastic card quickly. Although the account number might change for security reasons (to prevent the fraudulent use of a found card by someone else), there would be no need for a credit investigation or further underwriting (new or different origination). For all practical purposes, this is the same card account with the same history, credit limit, balance outstanding, and accrued finance charges payable, even if there is a new account number. There is no necessity for the outstanding balance to be repaid on different terms (new or different servicing), or for any other characteristics of the account to change (forbearance or risk bearing). All that takes place is the mailing of a new plastic access device.

Now, suppose that during the same telephone conversation, the customer service representative says that the new card will come in "about ten business days," but the customer decides this is not soon enough because of an upcoming trip. Suppose, then, that the customer service person says that FedEx delivery is available, but that it will cost an additional twenty-five dollars. The same situation might arise in the case of a new credit card account: A consumer newly approved for credit might want the card in an expedited manner. In either case, this part of the conversation might even be initiated by either the customer service representative selling an additional delivery service or the consumer. Likewise, for a consumer wanting to change the timing of a payment with an electronic funds transfer of some sort, an electronic payment might be first brought up by either the consumer or the customer service person. The question is whether the related fee outlay is a finance charge, not who brought it up.

In the example of expedited delivery, under these given circumstances, it does not appear that the fee, economically, is a finance charge (credit cost) because none of the characteristics of the credit account changes in any way. The card account exists before and after the delivery of the new card and would continue to exist without incurring any fee for card delivery. With these facts, the consumer's contract with the issuer does not impose a fee for the expedited delivery of the access device; the delivery and payment could take place in due course, typically by mail, without any special services or fees. Under the circumstances, the fee does not seem to qualify within an economic definition of a finance charge as a credit cost, and, therefore, the facts as described qualify the charges as uses of funds rather than costs. The outcome would be the same in the case of the consumer who calls and requests an expedited payment on the account by electronic transfer. The fee charged for the payment made would not change the characteristics of the credit account or the agreement between the cardholder and the issuer. If the fee payment is not for the characteristics of the credit (deferred-payment) arrangement, then it follows that it is not a finance charge.

This outcome next raises the question of whether the conclusion that these fees are not finance charges might change if they were among the contractual terms of the account. In this second instance, although there still would be no comparable cash transaction to permit exploration of whether the charges would be imposed in that situation, they become fees that are part of the price of the credit service itself. Under these circumstances, they might seem economically to be finance charges, since they could appear to be "imposed... by the creditor as an incident to the extension of credit." The issue here is where to draw the line in classifying these fees so that regulatory compliance is clear and simple.

Rohner and Durkin (2005) examine this line-drawing exercise at some length and discuss some general principles for classifying fees as finance charges or not. They state their general principles, intended specifically for situations like this one, quite succinctly, and so it is worth quoting them completely, as follows (Rohner and Durkin 2005, p. 202):

> Some charges that consumer borrowers pay for optional products or services are either not *imposed* by the creditor, or are not *incident to* an extension of credit. In general, a fee incurred by a consumer for an optional product or service offered by or through the creditor is not a finance charge if
> (a) The fee is designated for a product or service that is voluntarily purchased by the consumer pursuant to an agreement that is severable from or additional to an underlying credit transaction or plan;
> (b) The creditor discloses the fee for the product or service to the consumer in a reasonable manner before or at the time the consumer agrees to incur the charge; and
> (c) The consumer's purchase, or failure to purchase, the product or service does not alter the amount of the credit, the consumer's access to it, the timing or method of repayment, or the allocation of credit risk, as provided in the underlying transaction or plan.

They then offer some explanations of this formulation:

> The preamble is meant to confirm the general proposition that while some optional fees may be finance charges, some such fees are not. This is generally consistent with the current [Federal Reserve] Board view. It rejects the notion that merely because a product or service is optional, the charge for it cannot be a finance charge.
> To fit under this exclusionary principle, the product or service must satisfy all three of the criteria in subsections (a) through (c).

Subsection (a) emphasizes the voluntariness of the purchase, as a distinct option or add-on to what is otherwise a complete transaction or plan. Creditors will need to be prepared to demonstrate and defend the contractual independence of the optional product or service, but this language does not prescribe any particular method for doing so (one can imagine that creditors might devise an "agreement" mechanism similar to that used now for credit insurance and Debt Cancellation Agreements—a separately signed authorization). This criterion could include optional add-ons at the time the transaction is consummated or the open-end plan is established, as well as optional after-market add-ons.

Subsection (b) contemplates that the optional product or service, and the charge for it, must be disclosed before the consumer is committed. It does not specify the language or format of the disclosure, only that it be in a reasonable manner, which could be oral. Again, the creditor would have the burden of demonstrating that it made an appropriate disclosure. Nothing in this proposed principle limits the amount of the charge or the manner in which it may be shared by the creditor with third parties.

Subsection (c) zeroes in on the essential cost of credit aspect. Whatever the optional product or service is, the consumer's action or inaction with regard to it must leave the underlying credit relationship intact. If the optional product or service changes any of the original credit terms or adjusts the credit risk, the fee is not excluded under this principle. These essential credit terms include the amount of credit or credit line, the timing of the availability of funds or the consumer's means of accessing a credit line, the schedule of payments (including minimum payments in an open-end plan), and the medium through which payments are made.

Following their approach, it seems that the decision of the FRB staff, following the 2002 request for public comments, was correct: Neither the expedited delivery charge nor the expedited payment charge are finance charges if they are not part of the characteristics of the underlying credit agreement. In contrast, if the charges are part of the credit plan the customer chooses, then they are finance charges.

It should be evident from this discussion that although a consumer's choice of product features is an important indicator of whether a fee is a finance charge under this approach, it is not the essential criterion.

Rather, the pivotal element is whether or not the fee agreed to is a cost of credit. If, in the example, the consumer does not agree to expedited delivery or payment as part of the contractual characteristics of the credit relationship, then the associated fees are not finance charges since they do not meet the statutory definition of finance charges as credit costs. In contrast, if the consumer agrees to them as part of the contractual features of the credit account, then the fees may be finance charges, but they also may be other charges if there is no other way to address them under TILA.

Ultimately, it seems that the regulatory proceeding in March 2003 revising the Regulation Z *Commentary* came out correctly after a lot of angst: Neither fees for occasional expedited payment nor expedited card delivery were deemed finance charges nor other charges under normal circumstances. As always, the ongoing difficulty was that, in the absence of clear legal guidance concerning fees on credit card accounts, card issuers are going to remain concerned that some court decision or the action of a regulatory agency will put them on the wrong side of some then-unclear or changing compliance criterion or regulatory concern.[5] As it turned out, in 2008 precisely this happened for disclosures of finance charges on open-end credit.

The third stage for determining the disclosure status of a fee on open-end credit involves whether or not the regulators simply change the definitions to solve perceived compliance or other issues. The 2003 decision concerning fees for expedited card delivery or occasional payments did not, at that time, involve redefining the outcome for compliance convenience or other purposes. But, as part of broad revisions to the open-end credit disclosure regime made in 2008 (discussed at greater length later in this chapter), the FRB undertook a massive redefinition in the specific area of card fee disclosures. At that time, it solved the question of whether redefinition is ever needed between finance charges and other charges by eliminating the distinction for disclosure purposes! As a result, by regulatory fiat, the cost of credit concept for open-end credit disclosures disappeared with the stroke of a pen.

The No-Definition Approach

In late 2008, apparently impressed by reports from consumer focus groups indicating that distinctions between finance charges and other charges on open-end credit were not very interesting to consumers, the FRB concluded that all fees should be grouped together by source (interest, cash advance fees, late fees, etc.) but disclosure of whether or not they were finance charges would no longer be necessary. In outcome, this meant that none of the fees other than interest needed to be included in calculating the APR, thereby also eliminating, by defining away the problem, any pretense of a need to disclose a historical APR. Consequently, it was easily decided to drop the historical APR as well, although the reason given for this decision was also attributed to consumer confusion in focus groups. (The range of problems with the historical APR is discussed further later in this chapter.)

This new approach, merely grouping fees by source, was scheduled in 2008 and implemented in 2010, and it may well enable consumers to visualize the extent of fees on their credit card monthly statements at a single glance. It also changes the concept of the Truth in Lending Act in this area away from disclosure of the finance charge as the cost of credit, to make this easier single glance the norm. The conceptual change entailed in the new disclosure approach was made without any discussion (and apparently without any realization) of how it diverges from the historical TILA approach requiring disclosure specifically of credit costs as such. However, this new definitional bow to a desire for convenience is certainly well within the TILA open-end tradition, in which other definitions also reflect compliance or other convenience (for example, as discussed above, characterizing annual fees on credit cards as not being finance charges). In the new case, the change requires massive new compliance efforts by card issuers.

The Anomalous Historical APR Disclosure on Open-end Credit

As outlined in Chapter 4, there also has long been a requirement for disclosure of a retroactive, retrospective, historical, or effective APR, calculated *post hoc* on open-end credit for any period in which a finance charge actually accrues. This requirement was part of the approach adopted in 1968 to address the unknown future events problem for this kind of credit. But the historical APR ultimately has the same difficulty as the prospective rate: how to assign properly to any one period those finance charges that arise in one particular period but that conceptually are part of a multiperiod transaction with an unknown future course. Changing the time period for calculating an APR does not solve this underlying problem; the future is still unknown and all other compromise calculations continue to run the risk of making no economic sense for any period. The FRB's regulatory change in 2008 that went into effect in 2010 eliminated this requirement going forward — not for the conceptual shortcomings of the requirement, which are clear enough, but rather as a compliance convenience and because consumer focus groups indicated that the disclosure of multiple APRs that did not agree was not especially helpful.

Historically, the calculation method decided upon for the effective APR requirement mandated retroactively dividing the total finance charge accruing in the previous month by a measure of the balance outstanding that same single month and annualizing the result. Leaving aside whether any *post hoc* rate is useful for shopping, and the operational issue of whether the ratio denominator (discussed later) and the annualizing methods chosen for the calculation were appropriate, the basic approach may be reasonable if the finance charge in the period arises only from the application of the periodic rate to the credit balance outstanding. In that case, the historical APR disclosed will equal the annualization of the periodic rate. (For example: 1.5 percent per month times 12 months equals 18 percent without compounding.) But problems develop if there is a finance charge during some period of time that does *not* result from the application of a periodic rate to a credit balance outstanding and actually should apply economically to the whole period over which the associated credit extension is open; a transaction fee, for instance. It is not at all clear that the historical APR method produces an appropriate and useful APR disclosure in this circumstance.

The classic example of a transaction giving rise to a finance charge disclosed in one month but economically applying to a longer period is the common transaction of a cash advance on a credit card with a transaction charge for the advance. A finance charge of this kind does not arise from the application of any periodic rate; it simply is assessed once for each cash advance, even if calculated using a percentage; for instance, 3 percent of the cash advance with a $5 minimum and a $75 maximum. Economically, this finance charge is not due solely to the moment or month of the cash advance itself, but rather is part of the whole consumer cost of the credit extension over the whole period until it is repaid. It accrues at a single moment in a particular month to be sure, but it is part of the cost of a credit advance that may not fully repay for many months into the future. As always, the difficulty is how to assign this finance charge and any associated APR, across the multiple periods during which cash flows for repayments are variable, unpredictable, and confounded with new purchases, cash advances, and payments in those later periods. The proper time period is simply unknown and unknowable when the disclosures must be given.

As indicated, the outgrowth of this problem has been to assign any imposed transaction charge to the single month when it arises, even if this assignment is conceptually wrong in most cases, and then calculate the historical APR based on that single month. As a result, the required disclosure is almost always conceptually wrong, which calls into question its appropriateness as a consumer disclosure. Extending the time period to more months obviously would not solve the timing problem. Because of the unpredictability of future events, the adoption of a horizon of one month may not be reasonable, but neither is the assumption at the outset of any other particular amortization time period.

Beyond these conceptual and philosophical concerns about the usefulness and appropriateness of a one-month historical APR disclosure in the first place, there are additional practical difficulties with the specific calculation long required by Regulation Z for this disclosure. Importantly, the results of the mandated calculation have some unusual properties for a rate that is supposed somehow to be useful for consumers trying to direct and possibly redirect their financial behavior. In particular, the correlation between total finance charges and the historical APR for months in which there is a transaction charge typically is inverse, not direct. In other words, under most conditions, at a higher total finance charge, the effective APR usually is lower, and vice versa. This is probably counterintuitive to consumers who are at least somewhat familiar with the uses of APRs. They probably expect that a higher disclosed APR is associated with a higher total finance charge and vice versa, but the mathematical approach for the historical APR as formerly required usually produces the opposite outcome. This counterintuitive result further damages the purported usefulness of the historical APR as a required disclosure. Such an inverse relationship would probably appear anomalous to most consumers, if they knew enough about it to understand and care, even if it is mathematically correct as required by the regulation.

More carefully specified, whenever, in some period, there is a fee that is a finance charge under Regulation Z that does not arise from the application of a periodic rate to a balance (a transaction charge, for example), and this fee is added to a finance charge that arises from the application of a periodic rate to a balance, then the combination of the two finance charges has an inverse relationship with the APR over the period, unless the transaction amount, the associated charge, and finance charges arising from the application of the periodic rate to the balance constitute the only changes in credit outstanding during the period. (This last condition means there are no payments made during the period and no further use of the credit account in the period.) Since this scenario does not describe typical credit card accounts, and because most card users probably expect that finance charges and associated APRs move higher and lower together in typical transactions, this is a matter worth examining further. It is hard to imagine that there will not, sometime, be a serious discussion about reinstituting this disclosure, which was required for forty years.

Calculating the Historical APR

It is easy enough to see the difficulties with the properties of the required single-month historical APR from a few examples. First, imagine the existence of a consumer's credit card account with a $100 unpaid balance outstanding as of the end of last month. For this account, this means a finance charge will accrue daily this month on the outstanding daily balance. The periodic rate assessed on the account is 18 percent APR, or 0.0493151 percent daily (18 percent divided by 365 days). Assume also, at the outset, that no payment arrives during the month and the late charge is assessed immediately after the month ends. (The essence of the example does not in any way depend upon any consequences of a late charge; this is just a means of assuring, for the illustrative purposes of this first example, that there are no other balance changes, like a payment, during the course of the month.) This set of conditions gives rise to a hypothetical set of historical disclosures at the end of the month (day 30) designated here as Hypothetical Disclosure 1, Month 1:

Hypothetical Disclosure 1, Month 1:

APR	Finance charge for month	Balance, end of month	Average daily balance	Effective APR
18.00	$1.49	$101.49	$100.72	18.00

To complete the initial example, assume also that the consumer is assessed a late charge of $29 on day 31 (not a finance charge under Regulation Z) but makes a payment of $100 on day 30 of the second month. Then the second month's disclosures (day 60) would look like those designated below as Hypothetical Disclosure 1, Month 2. In each month, both the (prospective) APR and the historical or effective APR each month would be 18 percent:

Hypothetical Disclosure 1, Month 2:

APR	Finance charge for month	Balance, end of month	Average daily balance	Effective APR
18.00	$1.94	$32.43	$131.43	18.00

Now, assuming again the same initial conditions, suppose that this account holder instead uses a convenience check to obtain a cash advance of $1,000 on day 2 of the first month but everything else remains the same. The terms of the convenience check involve a transactions-charge finance charge of 3 percent of the cash advance and the new balance accrues new periodic finance charges at the same periodic rate as a previously existing balances. After the date of the transaction, this amount adds to the balance and accrues periodic charges like any other balance outstanding. The account holder still does not make a payment in the first month, which again produces a $29 late fee on day 31 (not a finance charge), but again pays $100 on day 60 and avoids a second late charge. This second set of conditions produces another set of disclosures for the two months:

Hypothetical Disclosure 2, Month 1:

APR	Finance charge for month	Balance, end of month	Average daily balance	Effective APR
18.00	$46.31	$1146.31	$1102.28	51.11

Hypothetical Disclosure 2, Month 2:

APR	Finance charge for month	Balance, end of month	Average daily balance	Effective APR
18.00	$17.51	$1092.82	$1183.75	18.00

This second set of hypothetical disclosures is different from the first in a number of important ways. Notably, in the first month, the finance charge has jumped to $46.31 for two reasons: There is a charge of $30 for using the $1,000 convenience check, and the periodic finance charge is higher in the first month (now $16.31), as a result of the higher average daily credit balance outstanding. The disclosures also reflect the higher month-ending balance and average balance outstanding. The prospective APR remains the same at 18 percent in the two months, but there is a sharp leap in the effective APR in the first month, to 51.11 percent.

The divergence of the historical APR from the prospective APR in the first month arises from the requirement that the transaction fee also be included that month in the calculation of the historical rate along with the finance charge from application of the periodic rate. Whenever there is a finance charge not arising from application of the periodic rate (a transaction charge, in this example), there is going to be a divergence of the effective APR from the prospective APR. The sharpness of the divergence, easily visible in this example, comes from the necessity of factoring the entire fee arising from the source outside the periodic rate into the APR in a single month, even though the related credit amount might be repaid over many months.

It seems likely that the sharp divergence of the two required APRs from one another in the first month of this example could give rise to many questions from consumers. Whether or not the level of the effective APR the first month shocks anyone into changing behavior as postulated by the shock theory described in Chapter 4, the reasons for the sharp divergence are probably not going to be immediately evident to many consumers. Even if they realize the jump is due to the fee, the magnitude of the APR jump still may be surprising, even shocking. The sharp drop in the effective APR from month 1 to month 2 in Hypothetical Disclosure 2 may be surprising as well.

Hypothetical Disclosure 2 also demonstrates that if the only change in the balance outstanding is the transaction that gives rise to the finance charge, together with its associated finance charge, then the total finance charge and the effective APR move upward together if there is a transaction charge. But the movement in the same direction is not going to follow if the balance outstanding changes for any other reason, say, from any further use of the card account or from making a payment. This fact casts some further doubt on the usefulness of the shock theory as a guide to proper consumer behavior (or to policy). A moment's reflection reveals why finance charge and effective APRs will move in opposite directions in these common situations.

Notably, if the APR is higher because there is a finance charge that arises from some source other than the application of a periodic rate to a balance, then the APR drops if there is a larger balance outstanding from other sources for the same time, or the balance from other sources is outstanding longer. (The opposite is true for a smaller balance or one outstanding for less time, in which case, the rate would be higher.)

The reduction of the APR occurs if there is a larger other balance or it is outstanding for a longer time because the portion of the finance charge due to the transaction charge component looms smaller within the total finance charge. This lowers the effective APR calculated under the rules, even as the total finance charge rises. Again, an example demonstrates this effect.

Suppose that in Hypothetical Disclosure 2 above, the account holder still uses the convenience check for $1,000 on day 2, causing a transaction fee of $30, but the consumer this time also makes a normal purchase on the credit card of $1,000 on day 5, not using a convenience check for the purchase. This produces a larger balance outstanding and a larger finance charge due to the larger balance. Other things remaining unchanged, this situation would give rise to the following disclosures at the end of months 1 and 2:

Hypothetical Disclosure 3, Month 1:

APR	Finance charge for month	Balance, end of month	Average daily balance	Effective APR
18.00	$59.21	$2159.21	$1974.31	36.49

Hypothetical Disclosure 3, Month 2:

APR	Finance charge for month	Balance, end of month	Average daily balance	Effective APR
18.00	$32.61	$2120.81	$2203.93	18.00

In this case, the effective APR in month 1 is 36.49 percent, lower than 51.11 percent from the previous example. It seems that since the APR is lower, the consumer should be better off, but being "better off" entails paying a finance charge higher by $12.90 in the first month (that is, $59.21 less $46.31). The finance charge in the second month is also higher, of course, due to the larger balance.

The inverse relationship between the finance charge and the APR might be counterintuitive to a consumer receiving the disclosure in question and expecting a direct relationship (higher APR means a larger finance charge and vice versa). The relationship would be direct except for the finance charge from the transactions charge. Without the transaction charge, a higher APR would be associated with a higher finance charge for a given balance, and a higher finance charge would be associated with the same APR at a higher balance. Both cases would probably make sense to typical consumers, in contrast to the inverse relationship between finance charge that occurs if there is a transaction charge and further account activity. The inverse relationship between the two disclosed quantities in the example is an artifact of the mathematical calculations required if there is a finance charge not from the application of a rate to a balance, and its changing relationship to the other components fluctuates with the balance. Assuming away for a moment the question of whether calculating the historical APR over a single month ever has any conceptual integrity at all, the inverse relationship revealed by the example is not likely going to be obvious to the consumer and may not be very helpful. It is still truth in lending in the sense that the mathematics is correct as required, but, at the same time, it probably will not be much of a practical aid to understanding.

Suppose this consumer experiences a disclosed APR of 36.49 percent due to a transaction charge and is "shocked." Nonetheless, this same consumer is faced by another short-term financial emergency a few months later and decides it is necessary to use another convenience check, despite knowing the finance charge is going to lead to a higher disclosed effective APR. Suppose also that this consumer's account now exhibits exactly the same condition as before using the previous convenience check: There is an outstanding balance of $100 at the beginning of the month in question and the consumer decides to use the convenience check to obtain $1,000 on day 2. Further, as in Hypothetical Disclosure 3, the consumer uses the credit card for a normal purchase transaction of $1,000 on day 5. So far, this case is exactly the same as Hypothetical Disclosure 3, except that this time the consumer remembers the shock of the higher APR and thinks (rationally, it would seem) that making a partial payment later this month should reduce the cost. Assume, then, that the consumer has received a paycheck bonus or a tax refund and is able to make a partial payment of $500 on day 10 of month 1 (this also eliminates the $29 late charge in month 2). This set of circumstances gives rise to the following set of hypothetical disclosures at the end of this and the following month:

This disclosure might really shock this consumer. By trying to reduce the shocking effective APR of 36.49 percent by making a payment of

Hypothetical Disclosure 4, Month 1:

APR	Finance charge for month	Balance, end of month	Average daily balance	Effective APR
18.00	$54.25	$1654.25	$1639.41	40.26

Hypothetical Disclosure 4, Month 2:

APR	Finance charge for month	Balance, end of month	Average daily balance	Effective APR
18.00	$24.60	$1578.60	$1662.55	18.00

$500, this consumer finds the effective APR has risen to 40.26 percent, although the finance charge is lower. This shocking revelation comes about mathematically because the portion of the finance charge due to the transaction charge looms larger in the total as the portion due to the periodic rate falls along with the smaller average daily balance caused by making a payment. There is nothing wrong with the mathematics. It just appears anomalous (and may be annoying to the consumer), but it still is truth in lending within the confines of the historical APR concept. The total finance charge has indeed fallen with the changes from Hypothetical Disclosure 3 to 4, but the transaction charge component looms larger in the total charge and the total and APR have moved inversely. This disclosure may not be very helpful to a typical consumer.

Under the long-standing disclosure regime, potential examples of anomalous outcomes abound. Suppose this now-disgusted but persevering consumer finds him- or herself faced by another financial need a few months further on. The account has again returned to the base conditions: There is there is an outstanding balance of $100 at the beginning of the month and the consumer decides to use a convenience check to obtain $1,000 on day 2. Further, again as in Hypothetical Disclosure 3, the consumer uses the credit card for a normal purchase transaction of $1,000 on day 5. So far, this example is again exactly the same as Hypothetical Disclosure 3. But this time, the consumer remembers the shock of the higher APR both times previously and thinks making an early partial payment to reduce the APR seems silly under the circumstances, since the APR rose more than with no payment. Nonetheless, this consumer wants to avoid the late charge that will accrue after the end of the month and so again makes a partial payment of $500, but this time on day 25 instead of on day 10. This new set of conditions gives rise to another set of hypothetical disclosures at the end of this and the following months:

Hypothetical Disclosure 5, Month 1:

APR	Finance charge for month	Balance, end of month	Average daily balance	Effective APR
18.00	$57.97	$1657.97	$1890.89	37.30

Hypothetical Disclosure 5, Month 2:

APR	Finance charge for month	Balance, end of month	Average daily balance	Effective APR
18.00	$24.71	$1582.68	$1669.89	18.00

This disclosure may again surprise the persevering consumer (to the extent the consumer pays attention at all to disclosed rates by this point). By making the payment later, the effective APR at 37.30 percent is lower this time than the effective rate disclosed following the early payment last time (40.26 percent, Hypothetical Disclosure 4), and it is still higher than the rate disclosed when making no payment at all (36.49 percent, Hypothetical Disclosure 3). The disclosed total monthly finance charge is higher in this case, reflecting the higher average daily balance, again moving inversely relative to the effective APR.

Apart from not using the convenience checks at all, which the consumer in these examples has decided to use because of an unavoidable financial emergency, the only way of reducing the effective APR if it combines the finance charges associated with balances and other finance charges not based on the periodic rate, is to increase the amount of credit outstanding. Expanding the amount of credit outstanding just to reduce the effective APR is probably not a behavior to be expected of consumers very often, and is unlikely the preferred option of any consumers anyway. By itself, this inverse relationship of total finance charges and effective APR calls into question the overall usefulness of the disclosure of the effective APR.

To see how effective APRs might be reduced, if this is the goal, imagine this same consumer has used the convenience check for $1,000 on day 2 and made a payment of $500 on day 25 as in Hypothetical Disclosure 5. If this consumer understood the mathematics and, for some reason, decided that he or she preferred an effective APR of 20 percent rather than some higher rate, then this consumer would have to use the card more. It would be possible to reduce the effective APR to 20 percent, in this example, by making a purchase of about $23,200 on day 10 and repaying it plus finance charge on day 31. If the consumer deferred the purchase to day 20 but again repaid it with finance charge on day 31, the necessary purchase would almost double to $44,500. In the former case, the total finance charge for the month would be $299.18 and in the latter it would be $299.72. It seems more likely the consumer would prefer the higher effective APR to the sharply higher finance charge.

In sum, to reduce the effective APR following the introduction of a finance charge not based on the periodic rate (a transaction charge, for example) one would increase the proportion of the finance charge arising only from sources subject to the periodic rate (that is, not subject to the transaction charge). It is possible to do this in either of two ways: (1) by using more credit and/or using it earlier; and (2) making payments smaller and/or making them later. Since either of these strategies raises the total finance charges, it is not at all certain that consumers are better off or would prefer these strategies. All of this draws into question the appropriateness of the effective APR anchored in a short period as a useful consumer disclosure. A better approach might well be to tell consumers simply and generically that transactions fees raise the total finance charges and the effective APR without attempting to relate the latter to some particular time period or other credit transactions.

The Appendix F Anomaly

But the inverse relationship of the total finance charge and the effective APR is not the only anomaly associated with the retroactive, historical, or effective open-end APR. Another arises from Appendix F to Regulation Z, the appendix that specifies part of the mathematical requirements, in particular, the denominator of the required ratio. Appendix F says, "In determining the denominator of the fraction…, no amount will be used more than once when adding the balances subject to periodic rates to the sum of the amounts subject to specific transactions charges [footnote omitted]." So far, so good, the denominator should hardly be more than the sum of its components. But the appendix continues: "In every case, the full amount of transactions subject to specific transaction charges shall be included in the denominator."

This second sentence, in effect, provides for a ceiling on the effective APR by mandating a floor on the denominator used in the calculation: The denominator cannot be less than the amount of the transaction subject to the transaction charge.

Finance theory would not suggest this outcome. Theory would require instead that the charges be related mathematically to the balances outstanding to which the charges apply, over the time in which the balances are outstanding. Violation of this standard gives rise, of course, to the primary objection to the historical APR already discussed: It relates a charge that typically actually applies to a longer period to an amount outstanding in a single period. But this provision of Appendix F monkeys even more with the calculation of the historical APR by specifying that the balance can never be smaller than the transaction amount, regardless of any repayment that might occur.

In most cases, this provision of Appendix F would not come into play and, therefore, would seem to have little practical effect. In most cases, the amount outstanding (average daily balance or some other measure) would exceed the amount of the transaction, due to prior balances outstanding, the amount of the transaction itself, and accrued finance charges this period. Unless payments made this period exceed the transaction amount sufficiently to make the average daily balance decline, then this floor on the denominator would not come into play.

However, there certainly are situations in which payments would reduce the balance below its Appendix F floor of the transaction amount. In fact, three of the specific numerical examples in Appendix F are directly dependent on this provision for the calculations given, and all three appear anomalous relative to financial theory for that reason (Appendix F, examples 3, 4, and 6). Extensive research into the FRB's historical records surrounding development of the original Regulation Z has not produced an indication of the reasoning behind this provision. It almost seems, in the absence of any other explanation for this provision, that someone believed that the historical APR was misleadingly high in typical cases, and that inflating the required denominator, in some cases, could reduce the overstatement. If this was the reasoning behind how the appendix was written, why it should be a guide to good public policy has also long remained a mystery. With good reasons, but relying again on its consumer focus group results rather than the other reasons, the FRB in late 2008 repealed, on its own authority, the TILA requirement for the disclosure of the historical APR, beginning in 2010.

The Disclosure of Time to Payoff on Open-end Plans

By now, it should be clear enough that the unknown future events problem makes it impossible to predict, and, therefore, disclose in advance to
consumers, many of the key variables for open-end credit accounts.
Among the key credit terms, only the method of determining the finance
charge need be disclosed in advance for open-end credit, along with the
periodic percentage rate applied and its annualization as the APR. The
disclosure of additional important variables like credit used, payments,
and periodic finance charges, can only be retroactive, but after-the-fact
availability of the information on periodic statements has not eliminated
suggestions for changing the rules.

Hypothetical Disclosures

From time to time, interested observers have argued that more information about open-end credit could help consumers. Since providing actual
information about the future is impossible, proposals often run to hypo-
theticals, which raise concerns over the reasonableness, and even the
truthfulness, of the proposed disclosures. They also raise the extent issue
of TILA: Even if another disclosure is reasonable in construction and
occasionally useful to someone, is it reasonable enough and useful enough
to justify one more TILA disclosure competing for consumers' attention?

Beginning in the late 1990s, various proposals to require the disclosure of the length of time it would take to repay an advance of open-end
credit under specified assumptions about the pace of repayment surfaced in legislative agendas at both the state and federal levels. The
length of the repayment period on open-end credit varies directly with
the amount of credit extended and the APR, and inversely with the payment size. Credit balance and the repayment rate are, of course, two of
the unknown variables that depend upon the unpredictable preferences
of the individuals making the decisions. Some credit users use a lot of
credit and others do not. Some make large and steady payments on their
monthly credit card bills, while others make small and/or variable ones,
or even large but variable payments; some credit users pay everything at
once, either occasionally or every month. This variability in behavior is
going to confound the accuracy of any hypothetical disclosure of time to
payoff based upon assumptions.

Those who have proposed disclosure requirements in this area implicitly have maintained at least one of two underlying arguments: Either that

consumers do not know that minimum payments will take a long time to pay off or that somehow they will benefit anyway from a specific, personalized calculation of a time period based upon a subjective set of assumptions. Under the proposals advanced, new requirements in this area would involve much more than a monthly generic notice that repayment will take a long time with minimum payments, however. Supporters, typically, have preferred an account-specific monthly calculation and statement of the number of months repayment of an outstanding balance would take, prepared under the assumption that only minimum payments are made consistently, possibly for decades, without any other changes to the balance of the credit account except finance charges and minimum payments. Because these assumptions will rarely be correct, the disclosures will almost certainly be incorrect as well.

Nonetheless, both Congress and some state legislatures looked at this matter and Congress passed a version of this proposal in 2005 as an amendment to the federal Truth in Lending Act.[6] The TILA amendment that finally emerged in 2005 from the legislative process was a somewhat restricted version of the plan preferred by supporters of this disclosure, in that it contemplated that the account holder must call by telephone for the estimate; the account issuer needed not automatically report the information on the normal monthly billing statement. Legislation in 2009 changed this to monthly disclosure. Much of the impetus behind both requirements arose from policy and political discussions surrounding reform of the federal bankruptcy law; the 2005 TILA revision was passed as Section 1301 of the Bankruptcy Abuse Prevention and Consumer Protection Act of 2005, Public Law 109-8. From the standpoint of observers favoring this disclosure, credit is simply too readily available. In this view, if consumers only knew how long it would take to repay open-end credit outstanding when making the minimum permitted payment, then maybe they would not use so much of it and not find themselves in bankruptcy court.[7]

Evidence on Consumers' Account Use Behavior

Beyond the myriad other difficulties with the assumptions necessary for making the calculations underlying this disclosure, there is also the question how often the statutory assumptions (*i.e.*, only required minimum payments constantly and no further use of the card while making minimum payments) reflect actual credit card account use behavior. Variable credit use and payment size constitute the essence of open-end credit and are unknown future events when disclosures are made at the beginning of the period. This raises the question how often the required disclosure will reflect an accurate representation of a consumer's circumstances, even if the other calculating assumptions and information on other original conditions are reasonable.[8]

Some information on the accuracy of the core statutory assumptions is available from consumer surveys. To learn more about minimum-payment behavior, questioning on these subjects, sponsored first by the FRB and later by the Credit Research Center, was included in the monthly *Surveys of Consumers* undertaken by the Survey Research Center of the University of Michigan. Interviewing on these issues took place in the summer of 1999 and the following January. In all, two thousand consumers were questioned.[9]

The surveys found that just over one-third (35 percent) of holders of bank-type credit cards with a revolving feature said they hardly ever pay their balance in full. When asked for more detail about the payment sizes they actually made, 7 percent said they hardly ever pay more than the minimum, and another 9 percent of cardholders reported that they only sometimes pay more than the minimum amount due, for a total of 16 percent reporting they pay the minimum amount at least more than infrequently. A cross-tabulation of the minimum payers against those who responded to another question by stating that they stop using the card when making minimum payments found only about 4 percent of bank-type cardholders fall jointly into both groups. Thus, based on the consumer survey evidence, it appears that the proposed new disclosure would be reasonably accurate for only a very small proportion of holders of bank-type credit cards, even if the other calculating assumptions and initial conditions were appropriate.

Beyond such consumer surveys, specific information about consumers' payment patterns has heretofore been available only to the creditors who issue the cards. Creditors are able to review their own credit files to ascertain the patterns of card use and repayment, but even they do not have access to the account information of their competitors, and such information has been mostly unavailable to outside analysts.

Fortunately for the illustrative purposes here, a number of large credit card banks made available a sample of account information to the Credit Research Center for studying just such questions. Overall, they provided twelve-month account histories for more than 300 thousand randomly selected credit card accounts during the year 2001. Originally, the data samples of individual credit card accounts were collected from three groups: college students, young adults who were not college students, and a third, larger group of more typical accounts, neither college students nor exclusively young adults (see Barron and Staten 2004). An appropriate weighting of the data according to frequency of each kind of account in the underlying population of accounts permits the construction and examination of a data set believed to be representative of the relatively new card accounts of five very large issuers of bank-type credit cards. All accounts in this large data set were held by the top fifteen card issuers, by volume, of managed credit card receivables at the time of the sample. There is every reason to believe that this is a representative sample of the account experience of card issuers generally. But even if it is not a perfect sample of the universe of card accounts, the data set is large enough and representative enough to provide interesting descriptions of the card-use behavior of millions of consumers at the micro-level. The appendix to this chapter, "Sample of Credit Card Accounts," contains some more details about the data set and the sample selection process.

To answer precisely questions about making contractually minimum payments, it would be necessary to know the identity of the card issuers and their policies for the specific accounts of individual cardholders, but neither is available. Nonetheless, it is possible to designate an approximate minimum allowable payment amount and examine the frequencies of behaviors under this definition. For example, if paying 5 percent or less of the balance is defined as making approximately the minimum monthly payment allowable, then about 37 percent of accounts made the minimum payment in the second month of the twelve-month data set (Table 6.2, line 4).

A finding that about two-fifths of account holders making the minimum payment in a particular month does not mean that they always make minimum payments, however. Using more months of data, it appears that most of the minimum payers in the initial month considered do not always make minimum payments going forward. Notably, a bit under one-third of the minimum payers in the initial month continue to make minimum payments for another six months after the initial month, while the others at least sometimes paid more than the minimum, although not necessarily paying in full (see the notes to line 4 in the table). This means then that only about 12 percent of the accounts paid only the minimum for each of the seven months investigated (line 4A of Table 6.2). This proportion is much like the findings from the consumer surveys in which 7 percent said they hardly ever pay more than the minimum and an additional 9 percent of cardholders reported that they pay more than the minimum amount due sometimes, for a total of 16 percent reporting they pay more than the minimum amount only sometimes or hardly ever.

The credit card database further shows the reasonableness of the findings from the consumer surveys that only very few account holders

Table 6.2 Payment of Account Balances on Credit Card Accounts
(Percent of Active Accounts)

Payment experience in one month	Percent
1) No balance	16.3
2) Paid approximately in full (90% or more)	20.3
3) Paid more than minimum, but less than in full (paid more than 5%, but less than 90%)	26.4
Notes for item 3:	
A) Paid more than 5% but less than 10%	8.8
B) Paid more than 10% but less than 50%	13.9
C) Paid more than 50% but less than 90%	3.6
4) Paid approximately the minimum amount (paid less than 5%)	37.0
Notes for item 4:	
A) Then paid approximately the minimum for the following six months	11.9
B) Then paid off account at least once during the following six months	10.1
C) Exhibited all other payoff behaviors during the following six months	15.0
Total	100.0

Notes:
Source: The Credit Research Center credit card database.

Components may not sum to totals because of rounding.

make the minimum payment consistently and also do not use their card further. If those who pay the minimum for seven straight months are defined as hardly ever paying more than the minimum and then their accounts are examined further to see whether they continue to use their cards, then only about 4 percent of card accounts fall into the joint category of making only minimum payments and not further using the card (data not in a table). This is precisely the same as the measurements from the consumer surveys, one from account holders and the other from account issuers. This degree of inaccuracy on the statutory assumptions necessary for calculating the payoff time on credit card accounts does not argue that the new required disclosure is going to be strictly accurate in very many cases, even apart from the issues surrounding the other assumptions required for the calculations.

The credit card database also permits an exploration of the frequency of accurate and inaccurate disclosures of time to pay off under other definitions of accuracy. Notably, using the credit card database, it is possible to construct a set of disclosures that would be required under some set of assumptions about rates and payments, and then to calculate how accurate the disclosures turned out to be based upon consumers' actual card use behavior during some time period. This approach can even employ a variety of different definitions of accuracy.

For example, suppose that the APR of the finance charges on revolved card accounts reflects the example in the 2005 legislation: an APR of 17 percent and a minimum payment requirement of 2 percent of the balance outstanding or $20, whichever is greater, or the full amount owed if less than $20. Under this (or some other) set of assumptions, it is possible to calculate account payment durations. Then, after a month or some other time period has elapsed, it is possible to calculate another duration based upon the account balance at that time and then compare the two sets of calculations. The percentage by which the second calculation differs from the initial one (the original required disclosure) could then be defined as the percentage of inaccuracy of the initial disclosure over the time period. In a similar manner, percentage errors of this sort could be constructed for a variety of time periods. Each could be compared to the initial required disclosures according to some standard of accuracy. This would then make each initial disclosure either *accurate* or *inaccurate* according to the chosen standard for the given time period.

Employing this procedure, the credit card database was used to prepare an initial estimate of the payoff time for each card account under the assumptions listed above: 17 percent APR and a minimum payment of 2 percent of the outstanding balance or $20, whichever is greater, or the full account balance if less than $20. Then, the same calculation was undertaken after one month and the two calculations compared under an accuracy standard of not differing by more than 10 percent in month two from the initial disclosure required at month one.

Undertaking such an exercise shows that consumers' intervening actual use of their credit card accounts frequently renders such a payoff disclosure inaccurate (often very inaccurate) under such a standard, even over an interval as one month. Using the 10-percent divergence criterion of accuracy, only about half of initial month disclosures remain accurate one month later, not an especially promising outcome, and the degree of accuracy continues to decline sharply thereafter (Table 6.3). After six months, only about a quarter of the initial disclosures remain accurate under this criterion. Furthermore, the magnitudes of the percentage errors increase as well. After six months, about half of the initial disclosures are off by more than 50 percent (that is, a new disclosure would be at least half or twice the original duration). With a finding of this sort, it seems difficult to argue strongly that the initial account specific disclosure would be more useful than a simple generic reminder that constantly paying the minimum could lead to a long repayment period.

Even this dismal accuracy finding may be more optimistic than the facts warrant. It is possible that some supposedly accurate disclosuresare deemed accurate by coincidence rather than by fact. For instance, an account whose initial disclosure is still deemed accurate at the six months' point may receive this designation because its balance outstanding is similar, at that time, to the initial balance, even though the balance could have varied dramatically (and, therefore, the accuracy of the initial disclosure varied widely as well) within the time interval. Thus, in such cases, it seems a final designation as *accurate* seems more coincidental that actual.

To explore this possibility, calculations were made based on another definition of accuracy that eliminated the chance of accuracy in a later month only by coincidence. This second standard of accuracy requires that the original disclosure be accurate within 10 percent throughout the whole time period. Thus, a disclosure on an account that is off by more than 10 percent one month later is counted as inaccurate, even if, by coincidence, it should again become counted as *accurate* in some later month.

By this definition of accuracy, the approach of an initial payment duration disclosure appears mostly unpromising. This second definition

Table 6.3   Potential Errors on the Payment Duration Disclosure Arising from Assuming that the Minimum Payment Is Always Made Instead of Using Actual Historical Account Behavior Experience

	Percent of active accounts		
	Passage of time		
Accuracy of the initial disclosure:	After one month	After three months	After six months
1. Accurate (within ± 10 percent)	51.0	36.1	27.9
2. Inaccurate (error > ± 10 percent)	49.0	63.9	72.1
Total	100.0	100.0	100.0
Note:			
A) Very inaccurate (error > ± 25 percent)	37.2	52.2	61.6
B) Highly inaccurate (error > ± 50 percent)	27.8	41.3	50.7

Notes:
Source: The Credit Research Center credit card database.

Components may not sum to 100 because of rounding.

of accuracy reveals that only about 18 percent of the initial disclosures are accurate after six months (Table 6.4). The proportion deemed accurate also varies sharply by account use behavior. Not surprisingly, almost no convenience users receive disclosures that are still accurate after the passage of six months. This comes about, of course, because the accounts are used largely for the purpose of making payments rather than as a credit source, and the account balances can fluctuate substantially by month. In contrast, about half of the minimum payers, about 6 percent of the card accounts, receive an initial disclosure that is still accurate after six months. This proportion also is very consistent with the 4 percent of cardholders identified in the consumer surveys as minimum payers who are not further using their cards when they pay the minimum amount.

The Extent Issue Again: 2008–2010 Revisions

As noted earlier, in 2004, the FRB began the difficult process of the revision and reform of Regulation Z. In 2008, this effort resulted in huge changes to the structure and requirements of the regulation for open-end credit, effective July 1, 2010. An impatient Congress then amended TILA again in the same area in 2009. This led to more rulemaking in the winter of 2009–2010 and another eleven hundred pages of regulatory materials on January 12, 2010, much of which reorganized the 2008 rules to be consistent with the largely duplicative congressional action. Effective date now became February 22, 2010, for most of the changes.

The 2008–2010 changes to Regulation Z tend to equate disclosures with consumer education and seem largely designed to educate those with little or no understanding of financial matters (see Durkin (2007, Table 5 for the present authors' list of many of the changes proposed in the first part of this episode). The revised rules likely will be an improvement, although whether they will ultimately be worth the extensive underlying costs is the subject of an empirical study that would ideally have begun before the new rules were adopted.

Overall, the 2008–2010 revisions do not implement any new basic regulatory scheme, just extensively rearrange the deck chairs. For those consumers who understand the former disclosures, finding information may be somewhat easier and more straightforward under the new approach. Those who do not understand disclosures under the old rules may also be helped a bit in finding the information they need, but they also may become more confused by additional details, despite some new

Table 6.4 The Accuracy of Initial Disclosures of Payment Duration Throughout a Six-Month Period Based Upon the Payment Behavior of Account Holders

	Percent of active accounts within account categories					
	Payment behaviors					
Accuracy of initial disclosure	Pure conve-nience users	Conve-nience users	Payers	Fluctu-ators	Minimum payers	All
1. Accurate (within ± 10 percent)	3.1	0.4	3.0	18.9	58.1	17.8
2. Inaccurate (error > ± 10 percent)	96.9	99.6	97.0	81.1	41.9	82.2
Total	100.0	100.0	100.0	100.0	100.0	100.0

Notes:
Source: The Credit Research Center credit card database.

Pure convenience users are those who pay accounts in full at least five times in seven months.
Convenience users are those who pay account in full three or four times in seven months.
Payers are those who pay account in full one or two times in seven months.
Fluctuators are those who at least sometimes pay more than 5 percent of their balance but do not pay the balance in full in seven months.
Minimum payers are those who pay 5 percent or less each month over seven months.

clarifications within the details. The rulemaking in late 2008 also involved outlawing a variety of credit card practices as "unfair" or "deceptive" under the FRB's Regulation AA. Reorganization of all these efforts following the 2009 congressional action moved all these changes into TILA and Regulation Z.

The new disclosure requirements are a clear indication of how suggestions for changes in the TILA regime typically evolve into a legal and regulatory process of expanding disclosures, widening the scope, making them more extensive or more frequent or otherwise adding to their prevalence, all in the hope of influencing consumers in some preferred way. It is not obvious that underlying goals of the regulation were considered more carefully this time than were proposed changes in the past. Nevertheless, this time the effort did involve review by consumer focus groups aimed at evaluating clarity and basic understanding. Whether the proposal will lead to the outcomes preferred by the proponents is a matter that only the future will reveal. Certainly an extensive before-and-after research program would have been a useful accompaniment to the implementation of the changes.

Appendix: Sample of Credit Card Accounts

To examine aspects of account use behavior, a large pooled random sample of card accounts was assembled in 2001 from the portfolios of five of the fifteen largest credit card issuers at the end of 2000, ranked by managed card receivables. The random selection was done in such a way as to be representative of the new card accounts of the issuer. Together, these accounts likely are quite representative of the universe of domestic new card accounts overall, largely because of the size of the issuers. Accounts selected were restricted to those less than three years old at the beginning of the observation period.

Data from each account are a record of twelve to fourteen months of account activity for each of the approximately 336,000 selected accounts for a total of close to 4.5 million monthly observations.[10] These monthly observations included accounts open from one to forty-one months. However, the different sampling frameworks adopted by the various companies resulted in some differences in the distribution of accounts by account age (months since initial opening), as well as the initial month and subsequent duration of the observation period. To obtain a more uniform data set for analysis, the observation period for each account was restricted to the first twelve months of monthly statement data provided by each issuer. The sample was further restricted to accounts that had been open for thirty-two or fewer months as of the end of the observation period for each account. Thus, the final data set contains accounts open from one to twenty-one months at the beginning of the observation period, and for most of which twelve months of subsequent account information is available. Some accounts in the restricted sample have fewer than twelve months in the observation period because they charge off or close.

Weights were constructed to reflect the relative size of each issuer's portfolio in the pooled group. Due to the varying intervals over which the accounts were sampled across the five companies and the ranging levels of specificity across companies in reporting the underlying population from the different categories of accounts, it was not possible to construct statistically ideal weights. Nonetheless, the weights used can be considered to provide a database of the twelve-month experience of over 300 thousand accounts that were opened at major credit card issuers during the period from mid 1998 through early 2000 and were active during 2000–2001. The restricted sample contains approximately 316,000 accounts with about 3.8 million monthly observations.

All analyses exclude inactive or *dormant* accounts, that is, accounts with no-charge activity, payment, positive balance, or any other posting of activity at some point during the observation period. Dormant or inactive accounts may reflect a credit card being held in reserve by the individual for an emergency or a credit card that has been discarded or destroyed by the holder without notifying the issuer.

For analysis the following variables were available:

- Current balance
- Credit line
- Payment made
- Monthly fees
- Finance charges
- Cash advances
- Delinquency status (30 days, 90 days)
- Holder's birth date
- Date opened
- FICO score

The availability of these variables permitted calculation of the following additional variables:

- Utilization rate
- Proportion with a positive balance
- Proportion with a cash advance
- Monthly charge activity
- Proportion paying in full each month
- Proportion of dollars delinquent 90 days
- Age of account (months)
- Age of holder

7

The Rubber Meets the Road:
Evaluating the Effectiveness of the
Truth in Lending Act

To evaluate any consumer protection, the first concern is to identify a useful yardstick. Chapter 3, "Why Disclosures?" briefly explains the theoretical economic conclusion that the appropriate standard for information-based protections like the Truth in Lending Act (TILA) is the impact on overall market efficiency: An efficient market means the lowest possible price for each product variation for all purchasers. As discussed, the simplest manifestation of the theory argues that in a competitive, perfect-information market for a homogenous product, all sellers will charge the same price, and it will be the lowest possible price consistent with average and marginal production cost. (Monopolistic and oligopolistic market structures also normally lead to single prices, but not the lowest possible price.) This is the ultimate consumer protection for the purchasers of any product or service, including credit.[1] Unfortunately, the single, lowest price outcome is also unrealistic because, even leaving intact the competition and information assumptions, individual goods and services typically are not homogeneous, exhibiting no varieties.

Instead, there are many varieties in demand for most consumer products, and the differences in their production costs mean that varieties will sell for different prices, even if the market for each variation is individually competitive and characterized by perfect information. In this case, an efficient market means that value and price will fully reflect one another, but the presence of multiple (even though related) varieties with different features and production costs promises that the price will not be the same for all.

Financial products readily illustrate why related varieties do not sell at the same price. The users of financial products often demand different features for their purchases, or different risk characteristics may be associated with different transactions. Either situation will produce a range of production costs and market prices, even without information differences across the markets for product varieties. For example, there can be different loan sizes or limits for credit products, more or less willingness by the credit grantor to accept risk, different insurance, varying amounts of bookkeeping services or financial advice, convenient or relatively inaccessible offices and ATMs (automated teller machines), extended office hours or not, and a wide variety of customized features for individuals and businesses. As a result, the characteristics of the product offerings can and do vary among outlets, between individual deals, and according to the risk profiles of users. The unit price, the annual percentage rate (APR) of subprime mortgage loans, for instance, typically is higher than for prime mortgages, but the difference does not necessarily arise solely from information insufficiency of a sort that could permit excess profit among subprime lenders.[2] Origination, collection, and default costs also are higher for the subprime credits, maybe much higher. This means subprime loans must command higher rates in the marketplace than prime loans, and, consequently, a single price for loans cannot alone serve as a criterion for the information conditions in loan markets. Moreover, product variations and information insufficiency are not mutually exclusive. It is, indeed, possible to have both different cost structures and information imperfections, which certainly complicates the evaluation of outcomes.

All this shows that determining whether markets for consumer financial services are efficient, together with the subsidiary concern about whether legislation had any impact on information conditions, prove to be difficult analytical issues. Not surprisingly, relatively few studies of specific information-based protections for consumer financial services even acknowledge the market efficiency goal explicitly; most existing studies have focused instead on the knowledge or behavior of individual consumers. For information-based protections in the financial area, even the latter studies are uncommon enough.

The Goals of the Truth in Lending Act

Nonetheless, ultimately, the difficulties of specifying the impact on financial services pricing of product differences versus information

imperfections only concern the deficiency of the existing research methods. It is still worthwhile to try to ensure both competition and good
information conditions overall, and this is precisely what Congress was
attempting to do when it passed the Truth in Lending Act in 1968 and
the other financial information-based protections soon afterward. This
central goal of TILA is stated clearly in the act's *Statement of Findings and
Purpose* (Section 102). The research question is whether the act had its
intended effect:

> The Congress finds that economic stabilization would be
> enhanced and the competition among the various financial insti-
> tutions and other firms engaged in the extension of consumer
> credit would be strengthened by the informed use of credit. The
> informed use of credit results from an awareness of the cost
> thereof by consumers. It is the purpose of this title to assure a
> meaningful disclosure of credit terms so that the consumer will
> be able to compare more readily the various credit terms avail-
> able to him and avoid the uninformed use of credit. ...

Thus, the congressional intent is plain enough. It is to promote the
"informed use of credit" based on cost awareness and leading to strength-
ened competition. But, though enhanced competition through avoiding
the "uninformed use of credit" is undoubtedly the act's central purpose
and is certainly a goal consistent with market efficiency, stating this view
in the act still does not offer a convenient evaluative criterion for the effects
of the law. Filling this gap in the years before and since passage, observers
of consumer-oriented financial markets have suggested many other, more
specific goals for TILA. Examining the economic, legal, and behavioral
science literature, as well as congressional hearings and statements, reveals
that observers have articulated a wide variety of objectives for truth in
lending. It seems worthwhile to look at these goals more closely.[3]

Some of the goals offered for TILA concern broad aspects of economic efficiency, but most involve the knowledge and behavior of individuals. Congress itself apparently believed that TILA would influence
competition and individual consumer behavior directly (see discussion
in Landers and Rohner 1979). Other TILA objectives include regulating
macroeconomic conditions and influencing general educational and
philosophical aims. Some even involve totally extraneous matters,
including controlling specific behaviors of financial institutions in the
marketplace; the latter objectives mostly do not concern the usefulness of
information per se.[4]

Table 7.1 lists thirty-eight objectives for TILA that various analysts and interested parties have advanced at one time or another in eight separate categories. There probably are additional goals that might add to the list. By itself, the length of the table shows the difficulties of fully evaluating TILA and other information based protections to the satisfaction of everyone. Nonetheless, with this lengthy list of possible goals for

Table 7.1   Goals of the Truth in Lending Act

I. Credit Market Goals
  1. Enhance competition in consumer credit markets.
  2. Improve understanding of differences among classes of institutions
  3. Drive out high-cost producers.
  4. Encourage the credit industry to reform.
  5. Improve credit market products.
  6. Discourage risk shifting by institutions.
  7. Discourage *in terrorem* boilerplate clauses in contracts.
  8. Provide a vehicle for legal reforms.
  9. Protect legitimate businesses from unethical competition
II. Cognitive Goals: Awareness and Understanding
  10. Improve consumers' awareness of credit costs.
  11. Improve consumers' understanding of the relationships among credit cost terms.
  12. Improve consumers' awareness of non-cost credit terms.
  13. Simplify information processing.
III. Attitudinal Goals
  14. Improve consumer satisfaction.
  15. Improve consumer confidence.
IV. Behavioral Goals
  16. Reduce credit search costs.
  17. Show consumers how search can be beneficial.
  18. Encourage credit shopping.
  19. Improve consumers' ability to make comparisons.
  20. Enable consumers to match products and needs.
  21. Enable consumers to decide between using credit and using liquid assets.
  22. Enable consumers to decide between using credit and delaying consumption.
V. General Philosophical and Educational Goals
  23. Satisfy consumers' right to know.
  24. Enhance consumer education.
  25. Enhance consumers' general understanding of the credit process.
  26. Promote long-term rise in consumer sophistication.
  27. Promote the informed used of credit.
  28. Promote wiser credit use.

(continued)

Table 7.1   Goals of the Truth in Lending Act *(cont'd)*

VI. Macroeconomic Goals
29. Enhance economic stabilization.
VII. Institutional Control Goals
30. Promote control of institutions through compliance requirements.
31. Improve consumers' bargaining position relative to institutions.
32. Provide defenses for consumers.
33. Provide leverage for hard-pressed debtors.
VIII. Behavioral or Market Protection Goals
34. Require procedures for credit card billing error resolution.
35. Provide end-of-lease liability limits for consumer leasing.
36. Provide a cooling-off period for credit secured by residence.
37. Provide for limited liability on lost or stolen credit cards.
38. Eliminate unsolicited credit cards.

the legislation in mind, it is possible to articulate a few general principles or guideposts for evaluating truth in lending.

The first has already been stated. Because there are many objectives of truth in lending, evaluating the law on the basis of a single objective is not going to be sufficient to satisfy everybody.[5] For example, improvement in the functioning or efficiency of credit markets (Category I in the table), which economic theory and the economics of consumer protection suggest should be the central objective of TILA and other information-based protections, directly involves only one of the eight general categories of goals. Clearly, some observers will focus on the other objectives.

Table 7.1 provides many candidates. Categories II to IV in the table involve buyer behavior goals, including consumer knowledge, attitudes, behavior, and decision-making. These goals are easier to understand than the overall condition of the marketplace, and they are important to many observers for that reason alone. Individual goals among them are very important to some observers. Much more about buyer behavior goals is addressed later in this chapter.

Following the buyer behavior goals is a list of general philosophical and education goals (category V). These objectives involve a long-term improvement in consumers' understanding and abilities, apart from and beyond any immediate impact on knowledge and behavior concerning a particular purchase. Following them is the goal of influencing the macroeconomy (Category VI). This was an important aspect of the 1960s congressional hearings on truth in lending, although not mentioned frequently in more recent years.

The remaining groups of objectives in the table are the ones that go beyond information-based protections. Group VII concerns the direct control of the institutions themselves, to gain leverage for consumers, such as by providing legal defenses to creditors' collection actions. To a large extent, these objectives were minimized in the debate over passing TILA in the 1960s, but they have become more important since then. The final group (Category VIII) memorializes some specific provisions of TILA that are not information-based protections. The goals in this grouping were fully intentional all along, but they do not involve information per se. These goals include delays or cooling-off periods to be built into the processing of certain kinds of credit and a variety of requirements concerning the issuance and billing of credit card credit.

With such a lengthy list of objectives, it becomes obvious that even if economic information theory provides the fundamental economic underpinning for information-based protections, a favorable outcome on any one objective will not necessarily satisfy all interested observers of TILA. Accordingly, TILA, as a consumer protection, must withstand examination from many viewpoints and, indeed, even evaluation according to a single perennially favorite goal, credit shopping (goal 18 in Table 7.1) is not going to satisfy everyone. Apart from the general issue whether specific behavioral goals such as credit shopping are important in themselves or whether they are simply a means to some other end (such as enhancing efficiency of markets), specific behavioral goals are only one of eight categories in Table 7.1, and encouraging shopping is only one among thirty-eight suggested objectives.

As a corollary to this first evaluation guidepost — that not everyone is going to be happy with someone else's single criterion — if it is not sufficient to evaluate TILA on only one criterion, then it also seems questionable to recommend wholesale changes in the protection based on a single criterion. At a minimum, any proposed changes to the law should be examined in terms of the likely effects on a variety of goals. Again, the shopping criterion provides a useful example: It simply may not be reasonable to make wholesale changes in the regulatory structure to encourage one goal, shopping, unless it is clear that the market is inefficient or the changes simultaneously encourage other goals as well, or the beneficial changes can be made at small cost. It is possible that achieving small or no gains in allocational efficiency arising from the additional shopping of a few individuals may be at the expense of large losses of operational efficiency. This outcome could result if the market is relatively efficient, so that most consumers are receiving a price commensurate with risk; or if the costs of changing the law are large relative to the benefit; or if the impacts of reforms on other goals are small. Thus, wholesale changes could produce a net loss for society as a whole, exemplifying a serious risk with every episode of TILA tinkering; the larger the proposal, the greater the risk. The 2008–2010 credit-card episode could become a classic example, even if TILA's format and usefulness improve somewhat.

As a second guidepost, some goals do not suggest any directly measurable evaluative criteria and must be evaluated indirectly. The general philosophical and educational goals in Category V of the table offer good examples. The six goals listed there (such as satisfying consumers' "right to know" and enhancing their general sophistication) are almost universally recognized as important aspects of truth in lending, but they largely appear too general for direct analysis and invite only indirect conclusions. In this context, it might be worth noting again that if two disclosure programs each appear designed to satisfy these general goals, but one also appears likely to satisfy other goals as well, or the general goals at lower cost, then this method is preferable, other things equal.

Third, although some goals do offer evaluative criteria, the measured effects may differ among individuals, making it difficult to draw general conclusions. Many of the goals associated directly with consumer decision-making at the individual level in Category IV illustrate this phenomenon. Goal 20, for example, improving the ability to match products and needs, might be examined by studying choices made in the marketplace. But consumers' needs differ and, consequently, so will the choices made even under conditions of perfect information. Likewise, consumers faced with deciding between using credit and paying cash (goal 21) will not all reach the same conclusion. In a world of perfect information, some people will choose cash and others credit, depending on their individual circumstances (that is, depending on their own preferences, constraints, and resulting demand functions).[6] Consequently, a simple criterion related solely to the likelihood of taking one behavioral path or another cannot be expected to produce useful analytical conclusions.

Fourth, some goals may be more costly to achieve than others, and may become especially problematic if special attempts are made to reach them without sufficient regard to costs. Encouragement of credit shopping (goal 18) has already been mentioned, but there are other examples as well. These include, for instance, goal 12, improving consumers' understanding of the relationships among credit cost terms. Much of the complexity, litigation, and costliness of the original Truth in Lending Act and Regulation Z arose, in a large sense, out of attempts to satisfy this goal with extensive, detailed TILA disclosure statements. Possibly, a better approach might have been to consider whether all the details were necessary to enhance market efficiency and the other 37 goals or whether a simpler, less costly approach might have been sufficient. This question is an ongoing concern.

Nevertheless, unfortunately, there is relatively little direct evidence available about the impact of TILA on most of the goals listed in Table 7.1. Furthermore, since evidence must typically be gathered by surveys at discrete points in time, the evidence is always subject to potential methodological problems, particularly that alternative explanations of the changes over time may well be available (such as changes in the effectiveness of consumer education).[7] Nonetheless, it is still possible to discuss general findings concerning some of the goals in the table.

The Credit Market Goals

The first group of goals, the credit market goals, involves the economics of information most directly. Taken together, these goals refer to the improvements in credit markets that would result from better information. They potentially include such things as lower market prices, reduced price dispersion, discouragement of unfavorable contract devices, and protection of legitimate businesses from unethical competitors that might employ deceptive pricing in the absence of information.

The set of goals characterized here as the credit market goals is, of course, closely associated with the underlying motivation of encouraging marketplace competitiveness generally. Consequently, they were an important part of the original intent of TILA and were extensively discussed in congressional hearings before passage of the original act. Although it is difficult or impossible to undertake a reasonable direct test today for impact of legislation that became effective decades ago (say, a before-after control group research design or event study), available evidence on the competitive conditions in mainstream consumer credit markets since the passage of TILA is generally consistent with a favorable impact from the disclosure law.

Market Competitiveness

First of all, even a quick glance at basic market structure suggests that, today, the market for mainstream consumer financial services such as typical consumer credit is probably at least reasonably competitive in most areas for a variety of reasons.[8] There are literally thousands of entities offering financial services to consumers, and none of these firms appears large enough to dominate the market. Furthermore, it seems probable that the trend has been toward greater competitiveness, even given consolidation in the industry, as a result of the communications advances, and price and product deregulation at the state level in recent years. Today, many financial services firms can enter new niches in geographic and product markets, thanks to advances in communications. TILA and the other information-based protections undoubtedly have encouraged these trends in consumer-oriented credit markets, at a minimum by standardizing much lending terminology and making it more familiar to diverse consumers.

This kind of favorable outcome, arising from standardized information, seems probable, even if the number and scope of the specific disclosures themselves are daunting, at times, to consumers and regulated firms alike. Enhanced information seems especially useful in an environment in which other important forces are also encouraging competition. The possibility exists that some financial services firms still operate in geographically limited markets in which information does not flow well, but this likelihood is becoming steadily more anachronistic and less important, especially as both information availability and communications have improved.[9]

Typically, there are dozens of banks, savings and loan associations, credit unions, finance companies, retail stores, and other financial outlets operating in most urban and suburban markets that serve the bulk of the population, quite readily providing extensive information on credit costs if asked (in person, by telephone, and electronically through the Internet), as well as through advertising and actual required disclosures. Furthermore, there is competition from outside sources. In recent years, companies that operate nationwide have developed and grown. They include banks, finance companies, and others with extensive branch networks as well as those that operate through the mail or electronically from distant locations, often almost solely on a price basis. There are even purely electronic companies that have no retail physical presence anywhere except as mail-drops and Internet servers. Automated clearinghouses, direct payroll deposit, electronic debits and credits, automated banking machines, and Internet-based financial services all permit consumers easy access to financial institutions far from their places of employment and residence, and even in other areas of the country and potentially other countries. Moreover, there has been an underlying trend toward deregulation of the product markets for financial services to eliminate some historical legal barriers to entry, such as the restrictions on pricing, branching, and affiliations for banking companies. Certainly, today, it is hard to argue that the markets for mainstream consumer financial products, such as credit, are not structurally competitive or that information is not easily available, even if it is not possible to attribute all of the information flows specifically, directly, and solely to TILA.

Empirical studies on the competitive conditions among institutions in consumer credit markets are limited and mostly dated, but they largely conclude that these markets were relatively competitive years ago, consistent with the widespread availability of information. It is difficult to believe that this would no longer be true, even with a movement toward tighter regulation in the 2008–2010 period.[10]

The Truth in Lending Act and the Credit Market Goals

Evaluating the specific impact of TILA on credit market goals is difficult because of the potential competing explanations for any market phenomena and the lack of specific data so long after the fact. The only study that has attempted to analyze this question directly found that disclosures appear to have had a favorable impact on market competition, although the evidence is not overwhelmingly strong and the study could not evaluate the change from the period before TILA (see Board of Governors of the Federal Reserve System, 1987). Beyond this one limited direct study, which explored the usefulness of shoppers' guides in newspapers, that is, the lists of the prices charged for specific products by designated lenders in a market, theory and hypothesis must suffice in this area. Other things equal, a requirement that businesses provide pricing information, calculated in a uniform manner and using uniform terminology, should lower information costs and make markets more competitive, as theory suggests. The likely magnitude of any effect depends on the answers to a number of questions and is probably not quantifiable.

Survey evidence on some of these questions is consistent with a favorable outcome from the disclosure law, however. One issue is the importance that consumers attach to the information disclosed. If required disclosures highlight or make more understandable the information most desired by consumers, then the regulations can lower information acquisition costs and encourage positive impacts on the marketplace. TILA mandates many disclosures, but foremost are cost disclosures.

Available evidence immediately suggests that consumers regard cost terms as the most important credit terms. This is clearly visible from the results of surveys that have explicitly asked consumers which credit terms they regard as most important. For example, when asked an open-ended question about which terms are most important in automobile credit, 62 percent of consumers in a national survey, in 1977, mentioned interest rates or annual rates first, and the monthly payment size and size of finance charges followed in importance (see Durkin and Elliehausen 1978, Table 4-3). The same three terms were the answer to a follow-up, closed-end question asking specifically for rankings of the importance of cost and other credit terms (Durkin and Elliehausen 1978, Table 4-5). A smaller national survey in 1984 produced similar results to both questions. Again, 62 percent of consumers mentioned interest rates first; and rates, payments, and finance charges again were most important in the ranking question (unpublished Federal Reserve Board survey results).

More recent survey results concerning important terms on credit card accounts are similar, in that consumers continue to report they focus on cost terms as most important. In 2001, those both with and without credit card accounts were asked about information they would like to have if they were shopping for a new general purpose, bank-type credit card account such as Visa or MasterCard. Although respondents offered a variety of answers concerning important credit terms, cost items again predominated—notably the percentage rates of interest and finance charges. About two-thirds of those both with and without bank-type credit cards indicated that interest rates or finance charges were the most important terms (see Durkin 2002, tables 2-3 and accompanying text).

A second issue about the impact of TILA involves the probable information conditions in consumer credit markets without the law. If information was already widely available, then the gains from implementing or changing TILA to improve information availability would likely be small. Obviously, the evidence from before the enactment of TILA is limited, and, of course, there is no empirical evidence concerning how consumer credit might have evolved in the past forty-plus years without truth in lending. Still, what evidence there is from the period before the law suggests that consumers were not particularly knowledgeable about consumer credit costs before TILA, and many believed that consumer credit cost a flat 6 percent (see Juster and Shay 1964, Mors 1965, Board of Governors of the Federal Reserve System 1970, Appendix B, and National Commission on Consumer Finance 1972). In contrast, the evidence from the period after TILA's passage and its implementation (discussed below) suggests that consumers appear much more knowl-edgeable about the actual rates after TILA. Significantly, survey results also indicate that most consumers do not believe that obtaining informa-tion on credit terms is very difficult since passage of the disclosure law, likely a sharp change from the conditions prior to passage (although, of course, impossible to prove today). By 1977, only about 8 percent of respondents to a nationwide survey indicated their belief that obtaining information on credit terms was "very difficult," less than half the propor-tion who thought obtaining the information was "very easy" (Table 7.2). Overall, more than half of the respondents at that time indicated that obtaining information on credit terms was either "very easy" or "some-what easy." The remainder said "somewhat difficult" (29 percent) or indicated they did not know (one percent). The survey results from later years, posing the same question to credit users, including holders of bank-type credit cards (in 2001), yielded largely similar results.[11] Although the precise impact of TILA by itself in promoting these out-comes cannot be determined, this evidence appears consistent with reasonably well functioning markets after TILA.[12]

In a related survey question, many respondents also appear to believe that creditors offer information sufficient to enable consumers to make adequate credit decisions. Asked directly about this perception, in recent years about two-thirds of the credit users expressed the view that creditors provide enough information for good decision-making (second panel of Table 7.2). Since it seems unlikely that all consumers must be well informed for markets to function reasonably well, these results also suggest that TILA probably has had a positive impact on market compe-tition and efficiency, even though the decisions of some consumers are not as good as they think they are.

Beyond expressing an attitude that obtaining information is not especially difficult and is generally adequate, most consumers also report that they frequently peruse the disclosures made, at least on credit card accounts that sometimes are controversial because they are so easy to use. A survey of cardholders in early 2005 found that more than three-fifths of holders of general purpose revolving cards like Discover, MasterCard, or Visa reported that they examined the APRs on their cards at least four to five times per year, which was defined in the study as "frequently" (see first panel of Table 7.3, from Durkin 2006a, Table 1). Not surprisingly, the frequency of examination of the APR on credit cards appears to vary directly with the use of cards as credit, rather than transaction, devices. The survey found that, as the outstanding balance

Table 7.2   Opinions of Consumer Credit Users Concerning Ease of Obtaining Information on Credit Terms and on Adequacy of Information Provided, Selected Years, 1977–2001

Opinion	1977	1981	1994	1997	2001	
					For self	For others
Ease of obtaining useful information on credit terms:						
Very easy	23	28	23	23	21	11
Somewhat easy	39	48	48	49	44	32
Somewhat difficult	29	21	23	25	26	36
Very difficult	8	4	5	3	6	11
Do not know	1	*	1	*	3	9
Total	100	100	100	100	100	100
Creditors provide enough information:						
Yes	44	65	62	61	65	49
Some do/Some do not	13	7	5	9	2	4
No	38	27	30	29	31	43
Do not know	4	1	2	1	1	4
Total	100	100	100	100	100	100

Notes:
Source: 1977 Consumer Credit Survey; Surveys of Consumers, various years
Components may not sum to 100 because of rounding.
[a] For 1977, the percentage of families with closed-end installment debt outstanding; for 1981, 1994, and 1997, the percentage of families that had incurred closed-end installment debt in the past year; for 2001, the percentage of holders of bank-type credit cards.
* Less than 0.5 percent.

on the card increased, so did the likelihood that the cardholder would report examining the rate. Only about two-fifths of cardholders with no balance outstanding reported that they examined their APR frequently. In contrast, about four-fifths of those with a balance outstanding of $4,500 or more reported they examined the APR frequently. Consumers reported examining the descriptive material on the bill somewhat less frequently but, again, the likelihood of doing so rose with the balance outstanding on the card (second panel of Table 7.3).

In its final report in 1972, the National Commission on Consumer Finance (NCCF) indicated its belief that beyond specific cost-related information, consumers would also rely on their understanding of the differences among institutional sources of credit and that this institutional knowledge would supplement TILA. The commission argued that this institutional awareness supports experience with actual transaction

Table 7.3 Consumers' Responses in 2005 About the Frequency of their Examination of TILA Disclosures According to Balances on their Revolving General Purpose Cards After Last Payment

	Percent of respondents within groups				
	All	Balance outstanding after last payment			
		None	Positive but less than $1,500	Greater than or equal to $1,500; Less than or equal to $4,500	More than $4,500
Consumers who examine APR:					
Frequently:					
Every month	44.6	29.4	48.6	47.1	63.3
Every other month	5.6	2.1	7.8	13.9	2.8
Four to five times per year	11.3	9.3	12.0	13.0	13.6
Subtotal	61.5	40.8	68.4	74.0	79.7
Infrequently:					
Less often	29.6	40.7	25.0	26.0	20.3
Never (volunteered)	8.9	18.6	6.7	*	*
Subtotal	38.5	59.3	31.7	26.0	20.3
Total	100.0	100.0	100.0	100.0	100.0
Consumers who examine descriptive material on bill:					
Frequently:					
Every month	12.1	9.2	10.6	13.5	13.8
Every other month	6.2	4.4	3.9	8.6	9.7
Four to five times per year	15.5	9.9	24.3	14.9	16.2
Subtotal	33.8	23.5	38.8	37.0	39.7
Infrequently:					
Less often	57.7	65.1	54.9	53.8	57.2
Never (volunteered)	8.6	11.4	6.3	9.1	3.1
Subtotal	66.3	76.5	61.2	62.9	60.3
Total	100.0	100.0	100.0	100.0	100.0

Notes:
Source: Surveys of Consumers, January 2005.
* Less than one half of one percent.
Components may not add exactly to totals because of rounding.

information, and that both kinds of awareness could enhance competitiveness. Presumably, TILA would also encourage this second kind of awareness (goal 2 in Table 7.1). According to the commission (National Commission on Consumer Finance 1972, p. 177):

> The additional shopping fostered by TILA is significantly supplemented by consumers' knowledge of the relative rates charged by credit grantors. This so called institutional knowledge predates TIL. Recurring exposure to the information provided under TILA must certainly strengthen and refine that knowledge.

Because of this possibility, consumers' institutional knowledge has also been the subject of nationwide surveys after TILA, notably in 1971, 1977, and in 1984. The surveys are not strictly comparable for a number of methodological reasons, but they lead to the same conclusion: Consumers generally believe that depository institutions are the least expensive sources of credit, and non-depository institutions (dealers and finance companies) are more costly.[13]

Market conditions have changed substantially since the 1970s and 1980s, and a newer observation on consumer understanding of institutional differences would be interesting. But it seems unlikely that institutional knowledge would be less many years after TILA, even though inter-institutional rate spreads have lessened over time, as theory suggests they would with increasing competition. The available survey results show that many consumers differentiated among institutions and seemed, even decades ago, to have had a reasonable understanding of cost differences. It seems probable that TILA has enhanced this understanding.

In sum, a variety of pieces of information suggest that the markets for mainstream consumer credit likely are reasonably competitive, that credit cost information is readily available to consumers, and that TILA has had a positive impact on this outcome. Statistical studies suggest that competition exists in consumer credit markets and has increased since TILA; and that consumers regard cost information as the most important information about credit terms, do not believe that credit information is difficult to obtain, do believe that creditors supply enough information for them to make good credit decisions, examine APRs on credit card monthly statements, and supplement cost information with knowledge of differences among classes of institutions. Each of these indications is consistent with, although, of course, does not prove the existence of both a competitive market for consumer credit and the positive impact of

TILA on market efficiency, at least in the market for mainstream credit products. But, as the list of goals in Table 7.1 suggests, there is also more to the story of TILA.

The Buyer Behavior Goals

There is no question that proponents of TILA believed that it would impact the transactional behavior of individuals (see a discussion of this view held by others in Landers and Rohner 1979). This meant that there was another important line of research on the effects of TILA immediately after its implementation, which focused on the goals in Table 7.1 associated with buyer behavior. Such research in the 1970s focused especially on Category II, "Cognitive Goals: Awareness and Understanding," primarily on awareness of credit costs (goal 10).

Researchers studied the cognitive goals initially for two reasons. First, these goals, especially awareness of credit costs, offered a convenient operational evaluative criterion for testing. Consumers were either aware or not aware, under some definition of *awareness*, and the proportion that was aware could be estimated and analyzed. Thus, it was possible to draw conclusions without some of the kinds of complications associated with evaluating other goals, such as evaluating the impact of the law on market competitiveness.

Second, an important conception of buyer behavior theory at the time known as the *hierarchy of effects model* advanced the reasonable contention that cognition or knowledge logically precedes the use of information for decision-making, and so evidence of awareness is an important preliminary evaluation. The argument is that, since cognition precedes use, there must be awareness before information can be used. Although the evidence of awareness does not, by itself, demonstrate that information is used, lack of awareness probably indicates that disclosed information is *not* used. Consequently, the evidence of the lack of impact of TILA on awareness could be taken as an indication the law had little impact in other areas.

A paper by George Day (1976) is the clearest representation of the buyer behavior approach applied to credit disclosures. He explicitly employed the hierarchy of effects model to compose a list of hypotheses about the likely impact of information requirements.[14] He then interpreted a variety of empirical studies on credit and other areas with required disclosures within this context.

The Cognitive Goals

Day's observation, that relatively few studies over the years have examined the impact of the required financial disclosures on consumers, is
still true today. Studies of consumer credit most explicitly based on the
buyer behavior approach arose from the work undertaken for the
National Commission on Consumer Finance in the early 1970s (see Shay
and Schober 1973, Day and Brandt 1973, and Deutscher 1973.[15] Focusing
first on the cognitive impact, analyses of consumer surveys showed an
apparent sharp initial impact of TILA, at least as measured by changes in
awareness of APRs.

Using an operational definition of awareness they developed specifically for their project, Shay and Schober (1973) showed more than a
doubling in percentage rate awareness on most kinds of consumer credit
in the first fifteen months of TILA. By 1977, levels of rate awareness
defined this way had reached 54 percent for closed-end credit, 65 percent
for retail revolving credit, and 71 percent for bank credit card credit, up
from 14 percent, 35 percent, and 27 percent, respectively, in 1969 (see
Durkin and Elliehausen 1978, Chapter 2). A survey in 2000 found that
consumer awareness of APRs on bank-type credit cards continued to
increase in the next decades. Using the NCCF's measurement approach
awareness was recorded at 85-91 percent in 2000 for the "narrow" and
"broad" definitions of awareness employed in that year (see Durkin
2000, p. 630–31 for discussion).[16] Although many factors undoubtedly
affect credit knowledge, including gradually increasing educational
levels over time, it appears reasonable to conclude that TILA focused
attention on percentage rates and contributed substantially to the sharp
initial increases in this measure of awareness after implementation of the
act in mid 1969.[17]

Some other survey results, over the years, have been a bit less encouraging. One survey approach has involved exploring the public's basic
understanding of relationships among consumer credit rates and charges
(goal 11). To do this researchers have repeated in surveys a line of questioning originally designed by Day and Brandt in their study of the
effects of TILA for the National Commission (see Day and Brandt 1973).
These Day–Brandt questions do not ask about the awareness of rates or
charges on a specific recent transaction; rather, they inquire about the
perceptions of rates and charges that a consumer would have to pay on
a hypothetical consumer credit transaction involving a purchase of furniture for $1,000.[18] The advantage of a hypothetical case is that the same

generalized question can be asked of everyone, and not just of current credit users concerning a specific recent transaction. Consequently, the results can reflect a general understanding of credit conditions throughout the public at large, not just credit users. The disadvantage is that it involves a hypothetical situation and so does not actually indicate understanding of any real event. Over time, this line of questioning has provided an interesting perspective on credit understanding over the four decades since TILA:

    A. If you were to buy a room of furniture for a list price of $1,000 and you were to repay the amount to the dealer in twelve monthly installments, how much do you think it would cost in *total* for the furniture after one year—including all finance and carrying charges? (Can you give me your best estimate?)

    B. What interest rate per year do you think this would be? (Can you give me your best estimate?)

    Rather than a pattern clearly indicating long-term increases in understanding, responses to the interest-rate component of the Day–Brandt questions are relatively consistent over time, although it appears that respondents have become more willing to state an opinion rather than assert that they do not know. In the first study using these questions, Day and Brandt (1973) found about half of their sample of California consumers quoted a rate of 12 percent or more in 1970, whom the researchers classified as *aware*. Almost two-thirds of the remaining half of their sample quoted a rate below 12 percent, which the researchers believed was too low (and likely to contain many pure guesses), and the others (about 18 percent of the whole group) did not know or did not respond.

    In later national samples using the same questions, the portion giving a response greater than 12 percent to the rate question (and, therefore, in the *aware* zone used by Day and Brandt) has slowly risen over time, largely at the expense of the *do not know* category (Table 7.4, the first line). The aware group reached 56 percent in 1977 and 65 percent in 1993–1994 by this criterion. The number quoting a rate below 12 percent has stayed approximately the same at just under one-third of the respondents.

    It is true, of course, that the dramatic changes in the credit markets during these years may make long-term comparisons difficult. Today, it may well be that many consumers take advantage of incentive programs and finance furniture at rates below 12 percent, enlarging the zone appropriate for a correct answer. As a result, the lack of a dramatic trend in the distribution of responses to the rate question may reflect, to an unknown degree, the framework of the question and the chosen awareness cutoff rather than the quality of the answers. Nonetheless, it appears reasonable to state that, as a whole, the public's perception of consumer credit rates has improved only moderately in the three decades plus since the Day–Brandt study in the early 1970s shortly after implementation of TILA.[19]

Possibly more disturbing (even if not necessarily more surprising) is what appears to be an *unfavorable* trend in the results to the part of the question about finance charges. Day and Brandt noted that, in 1970, consumers generally seemed unable to estimate the finance charges within a reasonable range. Rather, to the extent that anything other than guesswork was taking place in consumers' response to their question about charges on a hypothetical transaction, Day and Brandt contended that they believed that some consumers seemed to be taking their mental percentage rate estimate and multiplying it times the original balance of the

Table 7.4   Consumers' Estimates of Annual Percentage Rates and Finance Charges on a Hypothetical Purchase

Percentage distributions of respondents					
1) Estimated annual percentage rates	1970	1977	1983	1994	1997
A) Less than 12 percent	32	28	**	29	**
B) 12 to 17 percent	17	24	**	28	**
C) 18 to 20 percent	30	26	**	27	**
D) More than 20 percent	3	6	**	10	**
E) Do not know; not ascertained	18	16	**	7	**
Total	100	100		100	
2) Estimated finance charges (converted to equivalent annual percentage rates)[a]	1970	1977	1983	1994	1997
A) 0 to 12.5 percent	3	3	2	1	4
B) 12.6 to 22.2 percent	20	13	6	5	6
C) 22.3 to 29.8 percent	13	8	5	5	3
D) 29.9 to 37.0 percent	31	28	26	20	18
E) 37.1 to 51.8 percent	5	7	17	6	5
F) 51.9 or more percent	17	28	34	55	51
G) Do not know; not ascertained	11	14	11	7	13
Total	100	100	100	100	100

Notes:
Source: Surveys of Consumers, various years.
[a]Intervals chosen to permit comparability with 1970 (see Day and Brandt 1973, Table 4-10).
** Not comparable due to methodological differences in questioning.
Components may not add exactly to totals because of rounding.

purchase to arrive at an estimate of the finance charge. This, of course, would be the add-on rate procedure and would produce an estimate of charges approximately twice the actual charge, since the actual charge would depend on the declining balance of a principal amount collected in installments. In any case, estimates of the finance charges on a hypothetical purchase tended to be too high in 1970 (Table 7.4, lower panel second line, first column).

Day and Brandt found that 53 percent of their sample in 1970 gave a response calculating to a rate of 29.9 percent or higher, and another 11 percent said they did not know. In contrast, in the 1990s, a total of more than 60 percent of surveyed consumers responded to the finance charge question by saying that they did not know, or gave an amount that converts to an APR of more than 51.8 percent, which appears unreasonably high for most consumers. This proportion is up from 28 percent in the same categories in the Day–Brandt California sample in 1970. It appears from these later national surveys, using the same questions, that consumers' understanding of the relationship of rates and charges has deteriorated, despite three decades of presumably better disclosures under TILA.

Thus, it seems that disclosures probably contributed to giving consumers the impression that consumer credit is expensive, certainly more than the 6 percent per annum apparently widely believed before TIL. But when asked to, consumers are largely unable to translate this impression into an estimate of a charge that is directly related to a particular percentage rate. Instead, they cite a charge that, in many cases, is far too high for the corresponding percentage rate. Day and Brandt noted this particular phenomenon in 1970, and it seems even more prevalent recently. Rather than a failure of TILA, however, this finding likely indicates a more general failure in the public to understand simple relationships among mathematical and financial concepts. TILA seems to have demonstrated that credit is expensive, but now it seems many consumers believe it has a larger budgetary impact than it actually does.[20]

In any event, the lack of awareness of finance charges (as opposed to APRs) may not be especially worrisome, because the finance charge on a loan ignores the time value of money. The finance charge is only strictly accurate for comparing the cost of loans of the same size for the same maturity, although for very small loans with very short terms to maturity, for example, typical "payday loans," the effect of ignoring the time value of money is negligible. In contrast, consumers need not understand financial mathematics or the concept of the time value of money to use APRs. Consumers see APRs in disclosure statements, monthly credit card bills, and in advertising; that they are generally aware of APRs suggests, by itself, that they find them useful.[21]

The Attitudinal Goals

The third group of TILA goals in Table 7.1, the attitudinal goals, concerns improving consumers' confidence in and satisfaction with the credit process. It seems probable that knowing that creditors must disclose certain costs and terms accurately under the watchful eye of regulatory authorities increases consumers' confidence in the integrity of an otherwise complex transaction, even if they do not pay a lot of attention to the specifics of the transaction. Increased confidence could produce psychological benefits for consumers beyond any immediate specific uses they make of the disclosure forms. Consistent with buyer behavior theory, this could enhance the purchase process and experience, and make consumers more willing to buy.

Limited consumer survey evidence indicates that consumers' attitudes toward credit improved after passage of the original Truth in Lending Act. Over the years, the results of a question asked in surveys of consumer finances concerning the appropriate reasons to use debt appear to show, on balance, an increase after 1967 (Table 7.5). Clearly, however, changes in attitudes over time cannot be attributed solely to any piece of legislation. Over time, income growth and employment stability for many members of the public may be equally or more important in explaining improved attitudes toward credit use. Inflation, which tends to reward the early purchases of goods and penalize accumulations of savings in the form of liquid assets, may also affect attitudes toward credit during inflationary periods. Furthermore, the various activities asked about may evoke differing degrees of acceptability. Today, for example, student loans may be more favorably viewed than in earlier years not because of more favorable attitudes to student loans, but because of more favorable attitudes toward going to college. It is interesting to note, though, that approval of purchasing luxuries on credit, the last two lines of Table 7.5, have also increased over time.

Nonetheless, there remains the possibility that consumer protection regulations have contributed to overall increases in consumers' satisfaction with the credit process. As one kind of direct test, surveys have inquired of consumers over the years about their perceptions whether TILA has had a positive impact on attitudes toward creditors. In particular, as part of a larger line of questioning, consumers were asked whether they agreed with the statement, "Truth in Lending makes people more confident when dealing with creditors." Consistently, about seven respondents in ten have agreed with the statement, with about two or three agreeing strongly (Table 7.6, fourth line). Since any gains in this area might be achieved just as well by simple rules, though, this finding argues for regulatory simplicity. Because obtaining these benefits does not require any specific uses of the information disclosed, this group of goals argues for a simple disclosure scheme. Rather than a highly technical regulation with strict requirements, by themselves this group of goals could be addressed with simple methods.

The Behavioral Goals

Turning to behavior, surveys after implementation of TILA were not able to demonstrate an impact on many of the behavioral goals as clearly as for certain cognitive goals. This is attributable to some difficulties of research design and cost, but also for more substantive reasons.

Foremost is the difficulty of specifying useful evaluative criteria for some of the behavioral goals listed in Table 7.1. Credit shopping might be studied with survey designs, but profiling the impact on some other goals, like improving consumers' ability to make comparisons, is more difficult and requires indirect evaluations. In some cases, micro approaches like experiments and focus groups might be appropriate, but, by their nature, such research designs are not likely to produce findings that are representative of the population and may not indicate real world choices. Also, they generally do not easily permit comparisons over time, which are necessary to any long-term evaluation. Consequently, for some of the behavioral goals in Table 7.1, it may not be possible to do much more than infer or assert that disclosure requirements have probably had a favorable impact.

For example, it may be difficult to demonstrate conclusively that TILA has improved consumers' ability to match products and needs (goal 20 in Table 7.1), but it certainly seems reasonable that more readily available information should do this. In this context, it is worth recalling that TILA does more than just require disclosures of pricing. It also requires that similar procedures be followed in making calculations and that similar contract content use the same terminology (such as, *finance charge* and *APR*). Such requirements should be important to satisfying the goal of matching products and needs, but also generally improving the quality of cash- and credit-delayed consumption

Table 7.5 Consumers' Attitudes Toward Installment Credit: Appropriate Reasons for Borrowing

	Percent of respondents										
	1959	1967	1977	1983	1989	1992	1995	1998	2001	2004	2007
Reason given:											
1) Cover expenses due to illness	86	80	85	83	*	*	*	*	*	*	*
2) Finance educational expenses	70	77	80	80	82	82	82	81	79	83	83
3) Finance car purchase.	67	65	84	82	80	78	81	79	79	81	80
4) Consolidate bills	44	43	47	49	*	*	*	*	*	*	*
5) Cover living expenses when income is cut	26	40	49	47	44	42	46	43	48	47	52
6) Finance boats, snowmobiles, and other hobby items	*	*	23	19	*	*	*	*	*	*	*
7) Cover vacation expenses	5	9	17	13	12	13	16	14	15	14	14
8) Finance the purchase of a fur coat or jewelry	2	4	6	5	5	5	7	6	6	6	5

Note:
* Question not asked in this year.

Table 7.6 Consumers' Agreement with Observations about Truth in Lending Act Statements (Percentage Distributions of Respondents)

Statement	1977	1981	1994	1997	2001
1) The Truth in Lending Act Statements are complicated:					
A) Agree strongly	38	31	41	49	45
B) Agree somewhat	35	37	36	32	30
C) Disagree somewhat	11	18	13	11	9
D) Disagree strongly	5	8	5	5	8
E) Do not know	12	6	5	2	8
Total*	100	100	100	100	100
2) Some information on Truth in Lending Act statements is not very helpful:					
A) Agree strongly	20	16	21	23	28
B) Agree somewhat	39	41	43	42	38
C) Disagree somewhat	16	23	19	21	18
D) Disagree strongly	5	6	9	10	7
E) Do not know	20	14	8	3	9
Total*	100	100	100	100	100
3) Most people read their Truth in Lending Act statements carefully:					
A) Agree strongly	8	7	9	7	NA
B) Agree somewhat	19	24	26	22	NA
C) Disagree somewhat	33	38	34	35	NA
D) Disagree strongly	31	26	27	34	NA
E) Do not know	9	5	4	1	NA
Total*	100	100	100	100	
4) The Truth in Lending Act makes people more confident when dealing with creditors:					
A) Agree strongly	31	28	24	26	26
B) Agree somewhat	42	44	46	43	41
C) Disgree somewhat	12	14	17	19	15
D) Disagree strongly	5	6	8	10	11
E) Do not know	11	8	5	2	7
Total*	100	100	100	100	100

Notes:
*Parts may not add exactly to totals because of rounding. NA: Not available

decisions, even though it is difficult or impossible to demonstrate these effects empirically.

Day (1976) pointed out that the impact of disclosure requirements could be expected to be less for behavioral than cognitive goals for a variety of reasons. In particular, he discussed how the issues of accessibility, comprehensibility, and relevance each could stand between TILA (or any information-based protection) as a concept and any visible effect on any aspect of behavior.

Accessibility of Information and Behavior

First, accessibility asks whether the disclosures are available when they might be most useful. The question then is, At what point is TILA information useful? Over the years, many observers have noted that the formal TILA disclosure notices for closed-end credit typically are presented to the consumer after the credit arrangements are negotiated (but before the contract is signed). Critics say this is too late for shopping usefulness. Creditors counter that this is the only time disclosures could be available, since only then are the details of the transaction in place and the specifics of the transaction are needed to prepare the required disclosures.

As with many other disputes over public policy, it seems that both sides here are correct; they just emphasize different aspects of the issue. Presentation of the completed TILA document for closed-end credit does come after the typical shopping period, but for the full disclosure required by the statute, this also is the earliest it could be prepared. But, as already noted, TILA is also more than just a set of formal disclosures given, after the fact, on closed-end promissory notes.

Notably, the law and regulations also govern how rates and finance charges are calculated for disclosure purposes and the form in which rates must be given to those who inquire while shopping (specifically, as APRs as defined in the law and regulations). TILA requirements also mandate disclosures at account opening for open-end credit and on periodic statements (usually monthly). TILA also governs credit advertising. Even after-the-fact disclosures on closed-end arrangements are intended to be more than shopping devices. They also serve as a formal record of the details of the transaction, and may be consulted repeatedly as either the intellectual interest or need arises. They may also be important for longer term learning about the credit process. In sum, it is hard to say conclusively that TILA provides only inaccessible information, especially because the law and its disclosures have become part of the financial culture. Ultimately, accessibility is an empirical issue bound up with consumers' perceptions of information needs. It has already been reported that consumers typically believe that obtaining credit information is very or somewhat easy, and their belief is that creditors generally provide enough information to make good credit decisions (Table 7.2).

This is, of course, not to say that the availability of information for shopping should not be accessible at the actual shopping stage.

Comprehension of Information and Behavior

Comprehension is another matter. As Day (1976, p. 67) pointed out: "Information availability does not mean comprehension. The barriers to comprehension involve issues of communication and education, notably the potential for misinterpretation and the ability of the buyer to absorb information." He contended that misinterpretations could occur for a number of reasons, including variability in product features other than price, newness of the information, and prior expectations. He specifically mentioned his and Brandt's TILA findings (discussed above) that consumers do not seem to be able to calculate finance charges in dollars from estimates of TILA APRs. Although this and later survey evidence suggested that consumers do not seem to be very knowledgeable about mathematical or financial concepts, they do seem to consider APRs to be important, and they likely well understand, other things equal, that lower APRs, finance charges, and payments, are better for them than higher ones.

By itself, TILA is unable to make up for failures of consumers to understand, especially if the failures arise from deficiencies of background or prior education. Simply stated, it is not possible to legislate comprehension of anything. This seems obvious for credit costs, and it has been well articulated by Rohner (Rohner 1996, p. 114):

> Even acknowledging the broad and optimistic statements of Congressional purpose in TILA, and the rhetoric of commentators, the realistic objectives of the TILA are quite limited and, given the breadth of consumer protection concerns in the marketplace, quite modest. TILA is meant primarily to assure that accurate, comparable information about credit costs is available to consumers....
>
> Nothing in TILA compels consumers to read, understand and respond to its disclosures. There is no TILA elixir to cure consumer illiteracy, "innumeracy," or plain disinterest. TILA cannot force economic rationality into a consumer's consciousness. About all that can be expected is that adequate amounts of credit cost information are available, at appropriate times, in a more or less standardized vocabulary and understandable format, so that consumers wanting to use it can do so.

TILA and its insistence on full disclosure also create problems in this area. By requiring transaction-specific disclosures of all relevant information rather than some scheme of more generic shopping or advertising disclosures of the credit terms, TILA has become immensely complex. It suffers from the difficulties broadly outlined above as the outlay issue and the unknown future events problem that are manifested in a lot of regulatory detail. It seems that the disclosure statements on closed-end credit, and especially those on mortgage credit, are often almost incomprehensible except to finance specialists where they interact with the additional disclosures required under the Real Estate Settlement Procedures Act (RESPA). Calculations of APRs in many instances, while mathematically correct in some sense (at least according to and within the boundaries of the law and regulations), will vary according to the accounting for the purchases of related services in ways that are complicated for creditors who must prepare the statements, and for any consumers who genuinely want to understand them. The TILA statements also contain detail on credit terms, such as prepayment and default charges, that probably are not of much concern to shoppers (regardless of how important they might be later to prepayers and/or defaulters).[22]

Despite the problems arising from full disclosure, it is also hard to argue that generic disclosures would be better in all cases. Such disclosures would suffer from lack of specificity to individual transactions, and they might add little to the general awareness and institutional knowledge that many consumers apparently already have. On occasion, they may even be susceptible to manipulation by the unscrupulous. Unfortunately, there seems to be no way out of the quandary of specificity versus simplicity and compliance ease without a fundamental reconsideration of the role of TILA in society. The absence of any clear political desire for change is likely the primary reason why TILA has retained its basic structure since its origination, despite almost constant tinkering through amendments. There can be little doubt, however, that understanding credit disclosures is daunting for most recipients and beyond the capabilities of some to absorb the information.

The "ability to absorb information" mentioned by Day (1976) as a potential barrier to comprehension refers to individuals' information-processing capacity. This refers to the ability of an individual to accept and sort the flow of information cues into coherent patterns without overloading the brain's natural approach to classification and comprehension. *Overload* itself is a concept arising from experimental studies in cognitive psychology suggesting that too much information presented too quickly reduces the ability to absorb and process the cues.

Ultimately, the concept of information overload arises from the distinction between short- and long-term memory, which an example should help make clear. Most people know five telephone numbers (home, office, parents, children, neighbor, weather report, etc.) because they are well entrenched in long-term memory. But if the same people receive five new telephone numbers in rapid sequence, they would suffer from an information overload in short-term memory and they would not remember all (or maybe any) of them.

The idea of information overload has a long association with TILA, and it was used as an argument favoring the simplification of TILA simplification in the late 1970s.[23] But, the overload concern again raises the question, What is the purpose of the disclosures? Certainly, information overload would be a concern for transactional disclosures required on closed-end consumer credit if this were the only element of TILA and the closed-end disclosure form was the only source of information. Too much, too fast clearly would be problematic. It seems likely, however, that consumers adopt their own simplification strategies for using the disclosures they receive.[24] From the surveys reported above, it becomes clear that consumers are interested primarily in rates, finance charges, and payment amounts. If the disclosures on TILA statements are consistent with their expectations on these aspects of the transaction, then the consumers receiving them may not often actually try to process all of the rest of the information on the form. In these cases, the form's primary usefulness may very well be its role as an official record of the transaction for future reference and use in the case of any difficulties.

To find out about consumers' views of the complexity of TILA statements, a line of questioning focusing on this issue has been included in national surveys over the years (Table 7.6). The basic question has three parts, asking how strongly respondents agree with three observations about TILA statements: people read them carefully; they are complicated; and some information on them is not very useful. (The exact wording of each part of the question is in Table 7.6. A fourth part of this question, asking for views on whether TILA makes people more confident in dealing with creditors, was discussed above).

The results of this line of questioning have been largely consistent over the years, if not especially encouraging: Consumers tend to agree with the negative statements that TILA statements are complicated and that some information is not very useful. Also, they generally disagree with the positive statement that most people read their TILA statements carefully. Offsetting this, to some degree, is agreement with the statement that TILA makes people more confident when dealing with creditors, noted earlier. None of these findings argues that the TILA statement is highly regarded for its specifics.

That consumers consider truth in lending statements complicated certainly raises questions about the effectiveness of the details in current disclosures. Recently, two economists at the Federal Trade Commission (FTC) studied the effectiveness of truth in lending disclosures for mortgages (Lacko and Papalardo 2007). The objective of the study was to investigate how well consumers understand current disclosures and whether better disclosures could improve consumers' understanding of mortgage terms.

They conducted tests with 819 recent mortgage borrowers in twelve different locations. Half of the participants received current disclosures, and the other half received prototype disclosures designed by the researchers. The tests included both prime and subprime borrowers. Lacko and Pappalardo tested disclosures for both simple fixed-rate purchase loans and more complex fixed-rate refinance loans with terms such as interest-only payments, balloon payments, prepayment penalties, optional mortgage insurance, no escrow, and zero cash due at closing.

The results of the tests indicated that current TILA mortgage disclosures fail to convey key loan terms to many borrowers. Eighty-seven percent of participants could not correctly identify total up-front charges; 74 percent could not identify the charges for optional credit insurance; and 68 percent could not identify the presence of a prepayment penalty. Participants had problems not just with terms of complex mortgages. Fifty-one percent of participants could not correctly identify the loan amount; 32 percent could not identify the interest rate; and 23 percent could not identify closing settlement charges. The responses of subprime borrowers were similar to those of prime borrowers for both the simple and complex loans, suggesting that the difficulty lies with the disclosure, not the type of borrower.[25]

The prototype disclosures were based on prior in-depth interviews with thirty-six consumers who recently obtained mortgages, agency experience in designing consumer disclosures, and problems encountered in deceptive lending cases investigated by the FTC. The principles for designing the form were that the form needed to contain information on key terms, the format and language should be easily understood, and less important information should be excluded.

Participants comprehended the prototype disclosures much better than the current disclosures. Increases in correct responses were 66 percentage points for up-front charges, 43 percentage points for optional credit insurance, 24 percentage points for the presence of a prepayment penalty, 37 percentage points for loan amount, 12 percentage points for the interest rate, and 15 percentage points for settlement charges.

Lacko and Pappalardo provide convincing evidence that current disclosures of some loan terms are not effective for many consumers. These findings do not necessarily suggest that consumers are uninformed about actual mortgage transactions; they may obtain information from a variety of other sources than merely the TILA forms. Lacko and Pappalardo's findings demonstrate, however, that credit disclosures can be improved. Consumer protection benefits from improving the disclosures have not been exhausted.

Relevance of Information and Behavior

Relevance, the third factor (after accessibility and comprehensibility) suggested by Day to explain why the behavioral impact likely is less than the cognitive impact, is potentially the most important aspect of the limitations of financial disclosures on any aspect of behavior. As already noted, TILA seems to require the disclosure on the TILA forms of any information that potentially might be useful to someone, sometime. This approach has produced a lengthy list of required disclosures, especially historically for closed-end credit but open-end credit has rapidly caught up.

The full disclosure approach has contributed to the frequent amending of the act. As new possibilities for disclosures arise or new problems surface in credit markets, new disclosures are almost certain to be among the recommended solutions. This was again demonstrated in 2001–2005. During those years, proposed TILA amendments specifically concerning disclosures for credit cards were advanced in the bankruptcy reform legislation that worked its way through Congress as a potential antidote to the increasing incidence of consumer bankruptcies. It also has been apparent in the Federal Reserve Board's rule-writing exercise in the open-end credit area 2004–2008 and further legislative revisions in 2009.

Day (1976) pointed out a number of reasons why disclosed credit information might not be relevant to some particular behavioral goals. First, the buyer may not have any choices. There are, of course, many options for a credit source (banks, credit unions, finance companies, etc.), but in a particular transaction, the consumer may not have any choice whether or not to use credit. Thus, under the likely circumstances that the consumer already knows that credit is expensive and the purchase will be more costly on credit than by paying cash, the specifics of the disclosures will have no impact on the cash versus credit decision, even if it profoundly influences the choice of credit source. The specifics of the credit cost are simply irrelevant for the cash-or-credit decision for most consumers contemplating a home purchase, for example. For them, the price of homes is prohibitively high for a cash transaction, and a loan is necessary to finance the purchase.

In their extensive study of credit decision making for the NCCF, Day and Brandt (1973) found that 72 percent of the credit buyers of durable goods in their study did not have sufficient cash on hand to make the purchase without credit. Even if some of these consumers were very sensitive to rates and would have postponed their purchase if rates had been higher, it is hard to argue that they would have used cash, even if TILA were able to produce cost disclosures that are perfectly understandable to all consumers.

Further, according to Day (1976), new disclosures might not be relevant to some TILA behavioral goals listed in Table 7.1 because existing choices may have been correct. This is obvious in the previous example of the purchase of a home with a mortgage loan. Before receiving the disclosures, the consumer may have been going to use credit, and still plans to use credit after receiving them. Consequently, any expectation of a behavioral change on account of the required disclosures is unreasonable.

Required disclosures still may not be relevant for affecting decisions even in cases in which the consumer has a choice. Imagine a relatively well-informed consumer who plans to use credit for a purchase but has not yet received the required closed-end credit disclosures. Because this consumer is relatively well informed, he or she has an accurate idea of the range of available APRs in the marketplace and the exact rate offered by this lender. There even may have been negotiations over the credit terms. Upon receiving the disclosures, this consumer determines that the disclosed APR is within the expected and acceptable range, and so goes ahead with the transaction. The previous decision to use credit at this credit source turns out to be correct, and so disclosures do not produce any change in behavior. For many informed consumers, this may well be the most common scenario; thus, disclosures will have no visible impact on behavior.

Third, according to Day, the disclosure may focus on an attribute the recipient believes is not important. This does not seem to be a significant problem with TILA. Its disclosures focus primarily on cost disclosures, and consumers seem to believe these are the most important. Nevertheless, much of the detail may seem much less relevant to consumers for decision-making purposes than the basic cost information, regardless of how important it might become after the fact if something goes wrong with the transaction.

In sum, each of these issues of accessibility, comprehensibility, and relevance suggests that visible behavioral impacts of TILA will be less than the cognitive. This seems to be the case. Although, in the 1960s, it seemed to some proponents of the law that the passage of TILA would finally cause consumers to realize that credit is expensive and should be avoided, experience has not produced this outcome.[26]

Information and Shopping Behavior

Available consumer surveys indicate that credit shopping by consumers was not universal either in the years immediately following the implementation of TILA or more recently, but this behavior does occur. For example, the 1977 nationwide survey found that about one-quarter of those with outstanding closed-end credit accounts had tried to obtain information about other creditors or credit terms before obtaining the credit, the same proportion found in 1981 (Table 7.7, line 1). The proportion who tried to obtain information about this sort of credit arrangement was a bit higher in later surveys, reaching about one-third of closed-end installment credit users in the 1990s.[27]

In each of the surveys, respondents were also asked open-end follow-up questions about what they had done to obtain information about creditors or credit terms and the kind of information they wanted. A difficulty of this approach is that open-end questions repeated over time always raise concern about the consistency of the coding of the responses, especially, as in this case, for the work done over many years by many different coders. This means that not much attention should be given to small differences or small changes over time, although the broad, overall pattern of responses should be indicative.

The notable thing about the pattern of responses to the questions about credit shopping is their general consistency over time. In all survey years, the most common action taken has been to shop institutions, including calling them (Table 7.7, line 2).[28] It is possible that the frequency of shopping or contacting individual institutions may have fallen off a bit in the more recent years in favor of other actions (indicated by vaguer responses like "calling around" or "checking around," Table 7.7, line 6), but this may be more an artifact of the coding than a real trend. There also

Table 7.7 Consumers Who Engaged in a Search for Credit Information on Closed-End Consumer Credit

	1977	1981	1994	1997
1) Tried to obtain information (percent of respondents):	26	26	37	33
What they did (percent of those who did something):				
2) Shopped other institutions	80	63	52	54
3) Shopped (not clear where)	13	*	19	10
4) Contacted people	4	*	2	3
5) Examined media and printed sources	1	4	4	7
6) Called or checked (not clear where)	7	*	31	34
Kind of information (percent of those who did something):				
7) Interest rates	73	83	81	88
8) Fees and charges	12	30	16	14
9) Payments and maturities	27	20	36	40
10) Amounts, limits, and collateral	21	9	3	4
11) Other	16	20	17	14
What they did (percent of those with closed-end credit):				
12) Shopped other institutions	20	17	19	17
13) Shopped (not clear where)	3	*	7	3
14) Contacted people	1	*	1	1
15) Examined media and printed sources	—	1	2	2
16) Called or checked (not clear where)	2	*	11	11
Kinds of information (percent of those with closed-end credit):				
17) Interest rates	18	28	30	28
18) Fees and charges	3	10	6	4
19) Payments and maturities	7	7	14	12
20) Amounts, limits, and collateral	5	3	1	1
21) Other	4	7	6	4
22) Able to obtain information sought (percent of those who searched):	91	96	95	88

Note:
* Not available in year indicated.

are more sources of information about credit today, including better-informed friends and advisers, and, of course, the Internet. In any case, shopping for credit information seems reasonably common and shopping individual institutions seems, by whatever means, to be the most frequent approach.

The finding of less-than-universal credit shopping is not especially surprising. Day and Brandt (1973) discussed how, for consumers in the process of purchasing durable goods such as automobiles and appliances, the details of the credit contract involve only one component of the purchase, and not necessarily the one most important to the consumer. There are decisions to make concerning the amount to spend, the features or model of the purchase, brand or make, store or dealer, cash or credit, and credit source. They found that most consumers ranked the product decisions in this list as more difficult than the credit decisions (see Day and Brandt 1973, Table 3-12). This was especially true among consumers who lack sufficient cash to make the purchase without using credit. It does not seem surprising that the product decisions loom large, since the amount of expenditure on the product dominates the amount for credit in the typical purchase of durable goods. According to these authors (Day and Brandt, 1973, p. 42):

> If the last three decisions in Table 3-12 [listed in the paragraph above] are defined as part of the overall credit decisions, for in many cases the store choice obviated the need to choose a credit source, we discover that even in this broad context the credit decision was considered as one of the *two* most difficult decisions by less than 25 percent of credit users in the study [emphasis in original]. The other three decisions, which might be labeled as product decisions, were considered far more difficult to make by more than three fourths of the respondents.

One significant market change in the years since the Day–Brandt study is the widespread use today of general purpose or bank-type credit cards, but it is not clear this change would alter their conclusions if the study were redone. It seems unlikely that today's consumer, armed with a bank card (or a pocket full of them), would spend more effort analyzing the credit decision at a retail store. Instead, knowing that credit is already available, consumers might well spend relatively even more time today analyzing the product decision. For the purchase of durable goods, such as automobiles and boats, for which credit cards are less useful, it is still not clear that product decisions have become easier relative to the credit decision.

If consumers do seek information about credit terms, percentage rates of interest are the most commonly sought information (Table 7.7, line 7).[29] About three-quarters to four-fifths of those who indicated they sought some information said they wanted *interest rates, best rates,* or something similar that showed they were looking for percentage rates. Respondents also gave a variety of other answers, including fees and charges (line 8), payment sizes and maturities (line 9), and other credit information (lines 10 and 11). There may be some indication from these responses that the availability of credit is of less concern among respondents in recent years than it was in the past (line 10), at least for closed-end financing.

More important than information sought is whether those who try to obtain information are generally able to obtain the information they seek. Consequently, respondents also were asked whether they were able to obtain the information they sought. In each year, approximately nine-tenths of those who inquired about creditors or credit terms were able to find the information (Table 7.7, line 22). Although this outcome cannot be attributed solely to TILA, it is not clear that passage of the law has led to a groundswell of opinion asking for disclosure of more information.

In 1993–1994 and 1997, interviewers asked the same questions of users of home equity credit, either in the form of home equity lines of credit or traditional second-mortgage loans. (For a discussion of these surveys, see Canner, Durkin, and Luckett 1994, 1998). The findings of the home equity surveys are generally similar to those of the other surveys (Table 7.8). Notably, about two-fifths of home equity credit users indicated they had searched for information about these credit products; shopping other institutions was the most common action and interest rates were the typical piece of information sought. A couple of differences are also worth noting. It appears that searching for information about fees (probably closing costs) is more common for home equity credit (Table 7.8, line 8) and there is relatively more use of media and printed sources (line 5). The latter may be true because home equity credit plans were aggressively advertised in print in the years during which these surveys were undertaken. Importantly, again more than 90 percent of those with either home equity loans or traditional second mortgages who sought additional information indicated that they were able to obtain the information they looked for (line 22).

Although certainly not conclusive, this finding of a measurable proportion of consumers shopping for credit cost information and a large
portion of those individuals able to obtain the information sought recalls
the views of the NCCF that a portion of consumers shopping for credit
would likely make the marketplace competitive (National Commission
on Consumer Finance 1972, p. 176):

> An individual creditor cannot know whether a consumer is
> "aware" or "unaware." If, as in the general market somewhere
> between one third and one half of the prospects are aware,[30] and
> if some portion shop for credit, a credit grantor is likely to offer
> each prospect a given package of credit terms for the same price.
> Most important, if the price is not competitive with similar pack-
> ages offered by other creditors, the credit grantor faces the ever
> present risk of losing the customer to a competitor. Indeed con-
> sumers' shopping is supplemented by comparison shopping of
> creditors. Credit grantors in the general market must compari-
> son shop if they are to maintain competitive rates because of the
> threat that many potential customers aware of APRs and differ-
> ences in rates may shop around for the best rate.

Not all consumers shop extensively for credit, of course, and the
NCCF was careful to point out (twice) in the paragraph quoted above
that its contentions applied only to the general market in which consumers have shopping skills, and not to the low-income market it discussed
elsewhere. Lack of shopping skills certainly is one reason why credit
shopping is not universal, but there is more: The general reason is that
shopping is costly, and, as both the economists and the other behavioral
scientists have pointed out, the costs of shopping can easily outweigh the
benefits. This is especially true for those who are generally aware of
credit costs and for whom much additional credit shopping can be
largely redundant. Regardless, it seems that those with higher education
and income are the ones most likely to shop for credit. Credit grantors
will be most interested in these customers and will compete fiercely for
them. More generally, the empirical evidence has been mixed from
survey studies looking for a measurable relationship between proxies for
either benefits or costs of search, and the amount of search. Urbany (1986)
reviewed a group of experimental and survey studies and offered possible explanations, although he did not focus specifically on financial services: Benefits or costs may not be well measured in customer surveys or
the circumstances of the purchase may be forgotten before the customer

Table 7.8 Consumers Who Engaged in Search for Credit Information on Home Equity Credit

	Home equity credit lines		Second mortgages	
	1993 to 1994	1997	1993 to 1994	1997
1) Tried to obtain information (percent of respondents):	40	45	44	54
What they did (percent of those who did something, by credit type):				
2) Shopped other institutions	53	40	50	53
3) Shopped (not clear where)	16	2	18	12
4) Contacted other people	8	12	10	4
5) Examined media and printed sources	14	32	13	8
6) Called or checked (not clear where)	31	33	32	35
Kinds of information (percent of those who did something by credit type):				
7) Interest rates	65	78	61	80
8) Fees and charges	29	26	20	13
9) Payments and maturities	37	26	21	44
10) Amounts, limits, and collateral	16	10	26	7
11) Other	23	15	33	20
What they did (percent of all thosewith credit type):				
12) Shopped other institutions	21	14	22	27
13) Shopped (not clear where)	6	1	8	6
14) Contacted people	3	5	4	2
15) Examined media and printed sources	6	13	6	4
16) Called or checked (not clear where)	12	14	14	18
Kinds of information (percent of all those with credit type):				
17) Interest rates	26	34	26	42
18) Fees and charges	12	11	8	7
19) Payments and maturities	15	11	9	24

(*continued*)

Table 7.8 Consumers Who Engaged in Search for Credit Information on Home Equity Credit *(cont'd)*

	Home equity credit lines		Second mortgages	
	1993 to 1994	1997	1993 to 1994	1997
20) Amounts, limits, and collateral	6	4	11	4
21) Other	9	7	14	10
22) Able to obtain information sought (percent of those who searched by credit type):	93	96	97	96

interview is conducted. Alternatively, Urbany's preferred hypothesis may be accurate: previous purchase experience creates strong customer opinions that may offset the impact of current price dispersion on the usefulness of the current search. In such situations, the benefits of a search are perceived as so low relative to its costs that additional search still seems unfruitful, even if benefits increase or costs diminish.[31]

Importantly, lack of shopping does not necessarily indicate unreasonable or irrational behavior. On the contrary, a failure to shop could indicate an awareness of credit costs on the part of the consumer and may reflect the view that further shopping is unwarranted. Consumers may sometimes be wrong in their judgments. Nevertheless, by itself, a failure to shop for credit terms does not indicate a failure of TILA. Probably more important for the evaluation of TILA are the questions about whether the regulatory structure increases cost awareness and permits effective shopping, if desired. The first of these questions has already been answered affirmatively, and the second answer seems positive as well. By establishing a consistent unit price and standards of terminology, TILA permits consumers to shop for credit to whatever extent they feel is appropriate.

Although the survey evidence indicates that disclosures influence relatively few credit users in their decision-making to take on debt, some unanswered questions may be as important. These include the extent to which cash buyers are dissuaded from using debt by its cost, and the extent to which consumers' attention and sensitivity to finance rates have changed over time. Regardless of answers to these questions, it seems that TILA has provided consumers with the necessary tools, for whatever purpose they want to use them.

One additional line of questioning employed in surveys a number of times, in the past decades, stated that the "federal Truth in Lending Law requires that credit card companies provide consumers with written statements of credit costs when a new account is opened and as part of the monthly bill." Then the interviewer asks, "Is the Truth in Lending statement helpful in any way?"

Three-fifths of consumers with bank-type credit cards indicated, in 2001, that the TILA statement was helpful and almost three-tenths responded it was not (Table 7.9). Most of those who said it was helpful gave a generic reason, namely, that it provided information on interest rates or finance charges, and about 10 percent said that it provided a good reference document if problems arose. These results are similar to past findings about closed-end credit, although the favorable proportion is a bit higher and the unfavorable somewhat lower than the earlier responses about TILA statements on various forms of closed-end credit. When asked in a follow-up question for their views about whether the TILA statement had affected their decision to use credit cards in any way, about 18 percent of card-holding respondents indicated the statement had affected their decisions, and 77 percent said it had not, results that are not shown herein in Table 7.9. About 5 percent said they did not know. Among the minority of consumers who reported that the TILA statement had affected their credit decision, about half said it helped in

Table 7.9 Opinions of Credit Users Concerning the Helpfulness of Truth in Lending Act Statements, Selected Years, 1981–2001 (Percent[a])

	1981		1994		1997	2001
Opinion	Installment	HELC	Installment	HELC	Installment	Bank-type credit card
Helpful	53	60	46	58	58	60
Not helpful[b]	45	32	49	39	39	29
Do not know	2	8	5	3	3	11
Total	100	100	100	100	100	100

Notes:
Source: Surveys of Consumers. The table is from Durkin (2002, Table 8, p. 207).
[a]For 1981, 1994, and 1997, the percentage of families that had incurred closed-end installment debt in the past year; in 1994 and 1997, the percentage of families with open home equity lines of credit (HELC), with or without an outstanding balance; in 2001, the percentage of holders of bank-type credit cards.
[b]Includes respondents who did not recall receiving statement.
Components may not sum to 100 because of rounding.

deciding whether to use a card and, if so, which card. A bit over one-quarter of this group said it made them more cautious in using credit. The proportion of users of home equity credit who reported being specifically influenced by their TILA statement was even smaller (see Canner, Durkin, and Luckett 1998, p. 245).

Other Goals

As with the credit market goals, little can be said definitely about the impact of TILA on the general philosophical and educational goals listed in Group V, "General Philosophical and Educational Goals," of Table 7.1. As a concept, it seems hard to argue that TILA disclosures have not fostered the general goals of satisfying the consumer's right to know and enhancing general educational aims. Similarly, it seems that consumers' general understanding of the credit process has probably been enhanced by TILA, and the law has probably contributed to increasing consumers' general sophistication over the long term. It seems unlikely, though, that the understanding and satisfaction of general education goals is ever going to be as complete as contemplated by the concept of full disclosure for this purpose.

TILA has probably also supplied the tools for the informed use of credit and the wiser use of credit by consumers (goals 27 and 28, Table 7.1). Although these two goals might seem quite similar at first glance, they are actually quite different, since the latter involves a value judgment concerning what is wise. To use an analogy from public health, it seems likely that the required disclosures of warnings by the surgeon general about smoking have contributed to a more informed use of tobacco, although possibly not to wiser use among those still smoking. In the case of tobacco, the value judgment is fairly obvious, but less obvious in the case of credit. Nevertheless, it seems likely that TILA has contributed to both more informed and wiser credit use, if only because it has provided necessary tools in the form of standardized disclosures and terminology.

Group VI, "Macroeconomic Goals," which were discussed extensively in congressional hearings before passage of the original act, but have received little attention since that time. The argument made in the congressional hearings was that the disclosure of the finance charges and APRs would discourage the use of credit during an economic boom if interest rates are high or rising and, conversely, encourage use in a recession or depression if rates were low or falling, other things equal.

Taken together, these effects would encourage economic stabilization by helping dampen business cycles.

The argument that the availability of credit cost information over the course of the business cycle might improve economic stabilization is consistent with economic theory. The question is the magnitude of the effect, which depends on the degree of fluctuation in consumer credit charges; consumers' knowledge of and sensitivity to credit cost fluctuations; and the importance of other factors that influence credit use, such as income changes or changes in expectations. The maturity of the credit will also be important because the finance charge will tend to be only a small portion of the total transaction cost for short-term credits. In such situations, the cost of the purchased item will tend to dominate the transaction price, and the price of the item may not fluctuate at all as interest rates change. Clearly, fluctuations in rates may be relatively much more important for the purchase of a home with 30-year mortgage credit than for a refrigerator using a one-year installment note or a credit card. Thus, if fluctuations in rates are small, if sensitivity to costs is low, if maturities are short, or if the impact of other factors is quantitatively larger, then disclosure of rates would not have much impact on stabilization. The answers to these difficult questions are not essential for reviewing TILA because the law has many goals, of which macroeconomic stabilization is only one and likely not the most important. Nevertheless, it is possible that regulatory rigidity in the past has limited creditors' willingness to change credit terms along with economic conditions.

Group VII, "Institutional Control Goals," in Table 7.1, is probably the group most directly affected by the new regulatory structure after the law was revised in 1980. As outlined previously, the Senate Banking Committee's stated purposes in drafting the Truth in Lending Simplification and Reform Act included making compliance easier for creditors and strengthening administrative authority over restitution enforcement. The latter enhances the regulatory control over lending institutions, while making compliance easier reduces leverage for pressed consumers.

It appears that the goals of providing defenses for consumers and leverage for hard-pressed debtors were not part of the original plans of Congress in 1969, although they may have been present in the minds of some observers. Instead, they arose quickly after implementation of the law from the complexity of the regulatory structure that made it difficult for creditors always to be in complete technical compliance. Collection actions initiated by creditors against delinquent consumers were sometimes resisted by debtors alleging TILA violations. Such actions frequently resulted in settlements or judgments for the debtor that reduced or eliminated the debt. Under the revised regulatory structure following the 1980 simplification revision, such situations have developed less often, although they still exist. Apparently believing that the private enforcement of TILA through consumer lawsuits had contributed to its growing complexity, Congress deemphasized private enforcement in the simplification act and increased the importance of administrative enforcement actions by the enforcement agencies relatively. This change reduced the importance of TILA as a defense or a device to obtain leverage over creditors and reemphasized the original goals of TILA as an information-based protection.[32]

Group VIII,"Behavioral or Market Protection Goals," do not generally concern TILA as an information-based protection; consequently, little will be said about them here. Rather, they involve the direct regulation of the credit-granting institutions, such as mandatory error resolution procedures, cooling-off periods for refinanced or junior-lien mortgages, and others that go beyond requiring information disclosures. Consequently, by their nature, they are not information-based protections, although they have proven to be important components of truth in lending.

Conclusion

Overall, despite a regrettable paucity of evidence in some areas, it seems clear that required disclosures likely have had a favorable impact on consumers' perceptions of availability of information on credit transactions. There are no corresponding measurements for the years before TILA, but it is difficult to imagine that two-thirds or more of credit users would have reported in those years that obtaining credit information was "easy" or "very easy" in those days. Although it seems unlikely that consumers spend a great deal of time thinking about information conditions, they do not appear to have widespread complaints either. The relatively consistent favorable responses to various lines of consumer questioning over many years also is heartening in that, during this period, consumer credit use has become more widespread while individual credit products have become both more numerous and more complicated.

8

Suggestions for a Way Forward

Required disclosure has become so widespread in federal consumer protection policy in the financial area that it is difficult to imagine it ever diminishing or becoming of secondary importance. This seems especially true for the federal centerpiece, the Truth in Lending Act (TILA) of 1968, regardless of the complaints about its costs or effectiveness. A careful observer of the whole history of TILA has reached a similar conclusion in a way that expresses both the hope and the frustration with this important law. The relevant paper is so succinct and wise that one is tempted simply to quote it in its entirety to serve as words of conclusion, but a brief excerpt will have to suffice (Rohner 1996, p. 114):

> It is most improbable, however, that TILA (Truth in Lending Act) will go away. It is also unlikely that its basic scope and methodology will be substantially reconstructed. ... This is not to suggest that TILA is perfect in its present form, nor that its future is controlled by some immutable inertia. Rather, I believe, TILA does its job tolerably well, enjoys widespread political and community support, and frankly serves an indispensable function in our complex and expanding consumer credit markets. Even if theoretically desirable, radical changes in an established regime like TILA have off putting costs in the short and long term: transitioning, reprogramming, retraining, and reimplementation.

Nonetheless, improvement should be possible, although perhaps that is the overarching source of frustration with disclosures in general and TILA in particular. Indeed, the secular trend since the law's inception has constantly been toward more disclosures. No major set of requirements has ever been fully repealed or substantially cut back as new ones have been added, even with the legislative simplification of

Truth in Lending in 1980, the Truth in Lending Simplification and Reform Act, enacted as part of the Depository Institutions Deregulation and Monetary Control Act of 1980 (Public Law 96–221).

When suggestions for changes to existing efforts surface, they typically involve proposals for enhancing disclosures, widening their scope, making them more extensive or more frequent or otherwise adding to their prevalence, all with the hope of finally influencing consumers in some preferred way.[1]

This is by no means to suggest that the disclosure approach to consumer protection is fundamentally flawed or misguided; in fact, there are many good theoretical arguments in support of the disclosure method. But after all the years of experience with the elaboration of disclosures, it is still startling to realize how much of the trend is based upon proponents' theory, faith, and hope about the effectiveness of disclosures as consumer protections rather than substantial evidence of the law's measured effects.

It is useful to recall that TILA is essentially an economic regulation, that is, a law concerned with the efficiency of the marketplace. It is easy enough, so many years later, to overlook the fact that Senator Paul Douglas, the original sponsor of federal truth in lending legislation, was elected to the Senate in 1948, the year after he was president of the American Economic Association. Although the economic theory of information was only in its infancy at the time he was in the Senate, it is difficult to imagine that Douglas did not have this view in mind in advancing consumer disclosure. The basic economic theory was that it would have a significant impact on the market, whatever it might do for consumers individually.

Congress then and now, however, approaches consumer disclosures in the credit area, and to a lesser degree in the other areas of federal information-based protections, more with the view of the behavioral or marketing specialist: Require disclosure of anything that might conceivably be useful to someone, sometime, for some purpose so that something appeals to everyone. For this reason, TILA and the other protections take a *full disclosure approach* that seeks to achieve a lengthy list of goals that in principle could well be endless. Unsurprisingly, the legislation has become enormously complex and is only getting more so.

The animating vision for this law seems to be that tinkering with it will eventually produce evidence of a clear impact on some specific, presumably key, aspect of consumer behavior (such as enhanced credit shopping or less credit use). Though cloudy, this vision, the holy grail of disclosures, continues to beckon to reformers and researchers. Arising far less often is a discussion of whether a targeted behavioral impact is a reasonable expectation or even an important one. This lack of specificity concerning goals (and, therefore, of the associated evaluation criteria for the program) seems destined to frustrate the process of fashioning effective consumer protection, not to mention the process of evaluation. In either establishing a program or evaluating its outcome, the first issue should always be whether the right question is under scrutiny.

Even the most knowledgeable observers sometimes forget to outline goals clearly. If, in an otherwise useful and illuminating article three of the most astute observers of the disclosure question do not focus on the goals of disclosure, then it is not surprising that others often do not do so either (Garwood, Hobbs, and Miller 1993, p. 790):

> More disclosure may be inevitable and necessary in the 1990s; we have already seen one major addition in the Truth in Savings Act. But as previously discussed, merely adding more disclosure can amount to less effective disclosure. Adding more detail or volume of information with no change in approach is probably not the answer. What are possible answers? Sometimes imprecise information may serve better than detailed information that is ignored or is not understood because of length or complexity. An illustration may be the limited information now required by TIL about charges for late payments, which is likely to be useful even though a contractual or statutory grace period is not required to be disclosed. Similarly, the required security interest information also is probably useful even if details about after-acquired property and other incidental interests are not permitted to be disclosed. There is evidence, however, that the need to keep things simple is a lesson that needs to be constantly relearned. [Footnote references to sections of Regulation Z omitted.]

"What are possible answers?" Indeed. First, what are the possible questions? Useful disclosures? Useful for what? The reader has no clue from the context. The goals and uses of information simply are not stated in the paper. To be fair, throughout the article the authors appear, not surprisingly for experts in the field, to realize that there are multiple goals to disclosure regulation; they just do not articulate this fact clearly or discuss its implications. This leads to statements such as (p. 783), "Thus, sometimes summary disclosure rather than detailed descriptions are best." Why? When?

Specific disclosures have been expected to satisfy multiple objectives. Even if such diffuse aims were possible, they should have been well articulated before the disclosure program was instituted. The resulting ambiguity about goals complicates any evaluation process and tends to generate unfortunate cynicism about government in the process.

Consumer protection laws may be economic or behavioral in content, but they are political in passage. The political compromises made upon the passage of TILA and the other information protections were made years ago, and they reflected the issues of the time, especially those concerning usury laws. Many of those issues are now settled. Hence, the efforts to improve the regime of information-based disclosures have a new opportunity to establish clear goals and devise optimal, rather than maximal, means of achieving them. In short, we may be at the point that the ever-present aim of TILA—to improve the consumer finance marketplace by making consumers' decision making easier and more productive—can be decisively advanced.

Some Specific Proposals for Resolving the Principal Difficulties

Chapter 4, "What is Truth in Lending? Key Conceptual Problems Facing the Truth in Lending Act," contends that there are three overarching conceptual difficulties with the full disclosure approach to truth in lending: the outlay issue, the unknown future events issue, and the compliance issue. Difficulties arising from the multiple components of outlays and unknown future events argue that there is no simple approach to solving these intractable issues. But this does not mean that no improvements are possible. In fact, if the difficulties with TILA stem from those three issues, then addressing them can give focus to reform, with the above-mentioned need for goal clarification firmly in mind.

Addressing the Outlay Issue

Because the greatest complexities appear to arise in deciding which fees to designate as finance charges (the outlay issue), the first attack should be here. If, in some situations, there is no clear way to differentiate outlays, or it is fundamentally difficult to do so, then it is reasonable to try to specify a simple rule.

In arriving at such a rule, it is helpful to recall that Congress specifically intended truth in lending to involve the disclosure of the cost of credit and not some other quantity. Retaining that overall intent, which seems both reasonable and appropriate, would tend to rule out such alternative proposals as disclosing cost conceptions like "what the consumer pays" (consumer cost) or "what the creditor receives" (creditor yield). These formulations simply do not appear to be consistent with the intent of disclosing credit costs, even if less difficult to manage. The reason the Congress excluded outlays in alternative cash transactions from credit costs is to make the finance charge disclosure refer to the cost of credit and not to something else, such as total outlays for credit and other purposes.

To establish this intent anew, Congress could state in some sort of resolution that cost of credit *is* the intent of TILA disclosure, and not some alternative. This, at least, would offer a starting point for finding a clear rule and would relegate to back benches any proposals to disclose something else.

Next, the clear rule should include some sort of criterion for credit cost dependent on the characteristics of the credit contract itself and not just whether a cost is imposed on consumers. In some sense, prices are always imposed if a product choice is made, even if there is negotiation over the size of the price. It is the seller's price, after all, that is imposed in order for the transaction to go to finality. Consequently, price imposition or finality cannot very well serve as the only element of distinction between the price of credit and other outlays. Rather, the issue is, how did ancillary features and products, for each of which the marketplace imposed a price, come to be purchased? If they are essential aspects of the credit contract, then their price would seem to be a finance charge. In contrast, if product features are not essential to the contract, then their cost would seem to be something else. Other costs can be disclosed as other costs as needed, whether for closed-end or open-end credit.

Congress offered such an example in the original Truth in Lending Act in 1968. The premiums for credit insurance on loan products were to be finance charges, unless the insurance was voluntary. If so, the premiums were to be a use of funds and not a cost. This founding example offers a normative model: If the product is a separate, subsequent, or otherwise differentiable purchase that is not an inherent aspect of the credit contract itself, then its price is not a finance charge. This formulation would go a long way toward clarifying the outlay issue. Rohner and Durkin (2005) offer a plausible approach to how this might be done in practice (discussed in detail in Chapter 5, "The Outlay and Unknown Future Events Issues: Closed-End Credit"). Their approach seems worthy of further consideration.

Addressing the Unknown Future Events Issue

Future behavior is always a determinant of future finance charges and other credit terms, and future behavior is typically unknown and often unknowable. Thus, relevant amounts cannot accurately be disclosed in advance, a problem called here the unknown future events issue. TILA handles such matters by making assumptions, some for closed-end credit and others for open-end credit. That approach has been criticized since the earliest days of TILA because actual outcomes often, perhaps usually, stray from those disclosed. However, the alternative, offering many assumptions simultaneously to produce multiple disclosures at the point of sale, has always seemed unworkable, if only because of the overwhelming amount of information that would be presented to consumers.

The advance of information technology since passage of the original Truth in Lending Act more than four decades ago presents the opportunity to consider an improved disclosure scheme for credit costs based upon interactive disclosures, at least under some specified circumstances. In effect, consumers could be guided in modeling their own assumptions about future events and see the results in a manageable way. Designing an interactive disclosure system would be aided by legislation that clearly sets out the goals of the approach. The promise is that consumers could control and potentially increase the amount of information they receive on the matter of the unknowable future while getting a range of answers that offer more realism than the current system. As with any proposal to resolve the three main issues regarding TILA, whether the promise offers enough incentive for creditors and consumer advocates to sign on to a disruption of the status quo is the key problem of political strategy.

Addressing the Compliance Issue

The third and probably least important cause of concern over TILA arises from matters designated here as the compliance issue—the sum total of the deviations from the basic provisions of TILA to ease compliance burdens. The deviations encompass special decisions to accommodate problems ranging, for example, from leap years, fractional cents, and months of unequal length all the way to the form of the annual percentage rate (APR) equations themselves. Here, technology might also be employed to reduce the need for exceptions and special rules, but as mentioned earlier, all the distortions of truth in lending from these sources are probably less than those due to the simplest assumptions necessary to address the outlay and unknown future events issues. Again, the specifics of reforms will depend on the goals of the legislation itself, especially on what it declares to be the wants and needs of consumers.

Broader Principles for Reform

The above discussion of specific possibilities suggests some closely related general principles for improving disclosure programs as consumer protections:

1. *Articulate the goals.* The design of an effective disclosure system requires a clear motivation. Some of the goals outlined in the past for TILA (see Table 7.1, "Goals of the Truth in Lending Act," in the preceding chapter) may no longer be relevant or may better be addressed today by other means. If encouraging credit shopping is a key goal, one approach may be best, but if a record of the transaction is most important, then some other approach might be better. If yet another goal is the key objective, then yet another approach may be appropriate or it may be useful to rethink entirely.

2. *Include all the important goals explicitly.* Do not permit unstated objectives to dominate. Unstated objectives promote costs, delays, legislative dilemmas, political opposition, and even cynicism.

3. *Keep the attainment of the goals foremost.* If the initial choice of approach is not likely to be successful, it is better to go in some other direction than to hope and pretend the initial approach is going to work.

4. *Recognize the limitations of the consumer's decision-making process.* Consumers generally do not make the effort to become fully informed and compare all alternatives; they simplify and take shortcuts, and their decision process may not be optimal in terms of economic theory. Often, their decision process is deliberative and purposive but not extended. Thus, disclosures will tend to be ignored if they seem complicated, require careful

consideration, or do not appear to be directly relevant to their present circumstances.

5. *Minimize costs whenever possible.* Consumers receive the benefits of disclosure regulation, but they also pay all the costs. There is no good reason for them to pay more than necessary.

6. *Take into account the difficulties facing practitioners.* Practitioners can make important contributions to the attainment of the two preceding goals. They know the markets and their customers and can often provide useful suggestions. This does not mean that they should always get their way, but ignoring their concerns is foolish. In the workings of the competitive marketplace, which disclosures are meant to facilitate, consumers are going to pay for whatever costs the regulatory structure imposes on service providers.

Strategies for Reform

These principles point to the following strategies in designing a revitalized disclosure regime:

1. *Keep a sharp focus on the disclosure of costs.* Advocates of disclosure sometimes become so enamored of full disclosure that the core of the program becomes lost in the details. Consumers indicate they want and shop for cost information. In this area, it seems that Congress took the right approach at the outset by focusing, especially, on cost terms.

2. *Take diverse approaches to diverse goals.* It is easy enough to see that encouraging competition and overall marketplace efficiency is an important goal of TILA, but so is producing a record of the cost aspects of the transaction. These diverse goals might well suffer from a single-disclosure approach. More consumer shopping might enhance overall market competitiveness and efficiency, but consumers are not going to be able to use required disclosures for shopping if they are available only at the closing of the transaction. On the other hand, requiring full disclosures early is likely counterproductive as a result of information overload. Full disclosure is probably impossible anyway since, when shopping, the consumer may not yet have decided on the other main parameters of the deal (make and model of the car, for example, or location

and cost of the house). It seems that hybrid approaches like the long-standing, lengthy, but inexact early good-faith estimate (GFE) required under the Real Estate Settlement Procedures Act (RESPA) have not been a great success. Dissatisfaction with the GFE has been at the heart of Department of Housing and Urban Development's useful dialogue over recommendations for reform of this regulatory area. The presence of many goals argues for a diverse approach to disclosures, namely, greatly simplified shopping disclosures if they are needed, and a fuller record of the transaction details at the closure of the deal.

3. *Pay attention to the requirements of competing interests.* A proposal for a new disclosure regime will be politically dead on arrival without careful management of the economic incentives. There is great inertia in the status quo: changes in disclosures impose costs by requiring the retooling of documentation by creditors and posing the threat and reality of litigation. Likewise, any shift in the strategy of disclosures also threatens the advocates for the current strategy. So, no matter how virtuous a proposal may be, its advocates will have to anticipate and be prepared to address opposition from various parties. All parties will have to see something in it for themselves.

4. *Take advantage of technological change; above all do not stifle it.* Encourage the use of modern means of communication, like the Internet—and even of low-tech means of providing information, such as printers on ATMs—to broaden and deepen the availability of information and lower costs. Shopping disclosures—even multiple disclosure approaches, such as those recommended by Guttentag and Hurst (1985)—could be made available early by the Internet, for example. Disclosures for the record can still be made later by some other means. Above all, do not stifle new technologies; the failure to update regulations as needed does just that by smothering innovation under obsolete regulatory structures.

5. *Remember that disclosure is no panacea.* In fact, there are some problems it cannot solve. Making shopping easier, for example, is a worthy goal for required disclosures and is consistent with market efficiency, but it does not mean that everyone will understand and use the disclosures or that everyone will shop. As Rohner (1996, p. 114)) noted in a more extensive quote in Chapter 7:

Nothing in TILA compels consumers to read, understand and respond to its disclosures.... . About all that can be expected is that adequate amounts of credit cost information are available, at appropriate times, in a more or less standardized vocabulary and understandable format, so that consumers wanting to use it can do so.

None of this means that the Truth in Lending Act and other information-based protections do not work. It is just a further indication, like so many others in so many other areas, that solving all of life's problems is and will remain a never-ending goal. This is one of the tragedies of human existence, but it also provides its most exciting challenges.

Appendix A

List of Financial Disclosures in Federal Consumer Protection Statutes

More than forty years of congressional legislation in the area of financial disclosures for consumers has created a massive body of law. By the early 1990s, most aspects of consumer financial services had come under one or more federal disclosure statutes (the main exception being insurance, which has always been largely state regulated). To illustrate the extent, Table A.1, "Required Financial Market Disclosures for Consumers in the United States," at the end of this appendix, divided into two major sections and fourteen subdivisions, outlines in summary form the length and breadth of these federal financial disclosure requirements. Subsections 1, "The Truth in Lending Act," and 9, "The Fair Credit Reporting Act," each has multiple further significant subcategories. Even the summary of federal disclosure requirements in this area is quite impressive.

Over the years, many observers have mused about the question why are the disclosures so complicated and extensive? The underlying advantages of disclosures as consumer protections, a subject of Chapter 2, "Disclosures in the Regulatory Scheme," are certainly suggestive of disclosure usefulness in complicated situations, but are financial transactions really *this* complicated? To achieve the benefits, are all these disclosures *really needed*? Ultimately, that question was raised by Acting Comptroller of the Currency Julie L. Williams in her speech quoted in the preface to this book: Is the volume of information consumers receive actually informing them?

Even the short answer to this question is long. First, parts of the answer certainly arise from the complicated nature of some modern financial transactions, especially consumer mortgage loans. Providing all the details means lengthy, complicated disclosures.

Second, because complete information on the outcome of any given transaction is likely unknowable at the outset when disclosures must be forthcoming, it has led to a demand for extensive disclosures as a replacement for what is unavailable. If everything is disclosed, the implicit argument goes, then maybe important things that cannot be known can somehow be inferred as needed. This issue is the subject of Chapter 4, "What is Truth in Lending? Key Conceptual Problems Facing the Truth in Lending Act."

Third, technological change has dramatically increased the range of available financial transactions in recent years, and the pace of change as well. In this fluid environment, a competitive marketplace has led to many financial services that are tailored almost to the individual level. This leads to a demand for extensive disclosures to enhance individual understanding, certainly a concern of the Congress over the years. Over this time, it seems that financial transactional disclosures have morphed into a substitute for financial education, lengthening their extent.

And fourth, of course, decisions for consumer protection mandates are made through a political process, which itself produces demand for disclosures. Representative government responds to needs as it sees them. New financial services, along with the unacceptable results of the occasional sharp practices of unscrupulous vendors, constantly reinforce the belief that consumers would be better off if only they understood the marketplace better. It is easy to see how more disclosures may serve as a potential "quick fix" to some perceived consumer need under these conditions.

This appendix examines the length and breadth of federal financial disclosure requirements commonly considered consumer protections and suggests how they might be classified.

The Hierarchy of Disclosure Importance

Table A.1 summarizes federal financial disclosures for consumer protection, beginning with the Truth in Lending Act (TILA) and extending to the other federal disclosure rules for consumers. It omits corporate financial reporting required by the Securities and Exchange Commission (SEC), including such periodic statements as 10K and 10Q Reports. These documents are also widely referred to as required disclosures, but they are mostly employed by professional investment analysts and researchers and are not what typically is meant by consumer protections. Even leaving out these SEC disclosure mandates, the remaining consumer protection requirements are quite lengthy.

Table A.1 demonstrates in some detail that disclosure is the common requirement of federal financial consumer protections. Each of the individual federal protection laws mandates disclosures of some kind, but each law also contains a variety of other provisions, and this suggests the beginnings of a classification scheme. Information-based protections like TILA and the Consumer Leasing Act (CLA) are fundamentally different in regulatory approach than market protections like the Equal Credit Opportunity Act (ECOA) and the Fair Credit Reporting Act (FCRA), even though all these laws mandate disclosures. The former laws employ disclosures as the main element of their area of protection, while disclosure is secondary in importance in the latter, even though extensive, as in the case of the FCRA.

Organizing these statutes this way also shows that, within both groupings, disclosures are more important to the totality of some laws than others. For example, within information-based protections, TILA is closer to pure information-based protection than some of the other laws such as the Electronic Fund Transfer Act. Likewise, within market protections, disclosures are relatively more important to the totality of the Equal Credit Opportunity Act and the Fair Credit Reporting Act than they are to the Expedited Funds Availability Act.

All this, taken together, reveals a natural hierarchy of federal financial consumer protection statutes by disclosure importance, presented as Part I, "Information-Based Protections," and Part II, "Market Protections" in Table A.1. Each of these broad subdivisions contains a continuous ranking according to the importance of information disclosure to the regulatory scheme. The order is, of course, according to the authors' subjective rankings.

Next, it is also true that, within individual rules, certain specific disclosures are more important than others. Most observers consider the finance charge and the annual percentage rate (APR) the most important disclosures under TILA, for example, although they are only two of the many disclosures mandated by the act and its implementing regulation. Other statutes also have key disclosures like the annual percentage yield (APY) of Truth in Savings, but Table A.1 does not reflect this third level of differentiation. The disclosures listed in the table are arranged according to their underlying order of appearance within each implementing rule, rather than by importance. Incidentally, this facilitates further review of the body of each regulation, by providing an outline of the order of the disclosure requirements of the regulation.

By the authors' subjective ranking, the borderline area between information-based protections and market protections lies with three laws: the Electronic Fund Transfer Act (EFTA), the Home Mortgage Disclosure Act (HMDA), and the consumer financial privacy provisions of the Gramm-Leach-Bliley Act (GLBA). The EFTA and the GLBA privacy provisions could probably have gone into either grouping. The EFTA is included with the information-based protections because when Congress passed the law it probably seemed more like an information-based protection than it actually turned out to be; the nondisclosure portions have gained in relative importance over the years since passage. In contrast, the GLBA privacy provisions end up in the market protection category because the Congress likely did not believe the disclosure provisions of this law were as important as the market protection provisions. The Home Mortgage Disclosure Act is largely a disclosure statute, but is also a special case in that its disclosures are aimed less at consumers than at organized community groups and regulators. Because it is less focused on consumers directly, it is placed in the middle of the rankings.

Information-Based Protections and Market Protections

TILA and the Consumer Leasing Act have always been primarily disclosure laws; therefore, they receive the top spots in the first part of Table A.1. The Real Estate Settlement Procedures Act (RESPA), listed next, is also an important disclosure statute, but other aspects of this law have been more important to its totality than nondisclosure parts of TILA or the Consumer Leasing Act, and so it follows them in the listing.

The Truth in Savings Act (TISA), as passed by Congress is primarily a disclosure statute, but its information components have proven to be generally less important than were initially envisioned; consequently, it ranks here subjectively only fourth among the information-based protections. It seems that as interest rates have generally fallen since passage of the act in 1991, the discussion and controversy over the disclosure of these rates on deposit accounts has become less pronounced. Further, much of the law simply made mandatory many disclosures that were largely normal business practices for deposit accounts. An important feature of the law was to mandate the disclosure of a key term, the effective yield or APY. Competition in the market had already led most financial institutions to disclose this yield anyway, although sometimes with different definitions and nuances, and so the role of TISA was to mandate standardized calculation and disclosure. Since most institutions already provided written disclosure documents before the law required them, overall the disclosure sections of this law have not brought about changes of major importance and they now seem less important than when the law was new.

Next in order comes the Electronic Fund Transfer Act.[1] As mentioned, this law began life and still remains subjectively (but barely) within the information-based protection category. Over time, its disclosure aspects seem to have become less important relatively as its nondisclosure protections, like maximum time limits for institutions to investigate alleged errors and correct them, have tended to loom larger within the regulatory framework than the required disclosures. After more than thirty years, it appears that few consumers even notice the disclosures required by the EFTA, although there also seem to be few complaints that the act is "not working." Because the disclosures are still required and are fairly lengthy, the act remains in the information-based protection section of the table, but not near the top of the list.

Last in the information-based protection division of the table is the Home Mortgage Disclosure Act. Although its primary regulatory requirement is disclosure, its information component is not aimed primarily at consumers, and typical consumers likely are largely oblivious to its provisions. Rather, its disclosures have become a tool primarily for regulators and pressure groups. Because of this difference from the other information statutes, it will not receive further attention in this review of disclosures as consumer protections.[2]

Even in outline form, the listing of disclosure requirements among the information-based protections clearly is imposing. In fact, financial disclosure requirements under federal law are so broad that relatively few people, maybe almost no one, might be considered knowledgeable about the full range, and especially not about the details. In order for even this summary to be manageable, for the most part Table A.1 does not attempt to enumerate the requirements concerning the scheduling, timing, frequency, or format of required disclosures, although the statutes and their implementing rules regulate in all of these areas.

Scheduling of mandatory disclosures varies widely within and among the acts. Some disclosures are required upon or shortly after a consumer applies for the financial service in question, while others are required at account opening. Some are required both times and others upon "adverse action" (for credit applications and credit account changes). Some disclosures are made once, while others are necessary periodically as long as an account is open. Still others apply to advertising and solicitation, which may not even result in a particular consumer's purchasing or using the service in question. Some of the periodic disclosures are required annually, while others must be semiannual or monthly. Others surface upon any change in terms. Many rules have requirements for formatting matters such as type size and placement. Fully understanding and complying with all the disclosure requirements has proven to be so complicated that it has generated an industry of lawyers, consultants, compliance specialists, publishers, and trade associations to assist the regulated institutions.

Required Disclosures Among Information-Based Protections

Disclosures in the lending and credit area have received the greatest congressional attention. This is the province of TILA (1968), the first enacted and probably the centerpiece of federal information-based protections in the financial services area. Requirements arising specifically from TILA are found in six subgroups of Table A.1, one each for closed-end credit, closed-end credit secured by a residence, open-end credit, open-end credit secured by dwellings, certain mortgages that qualify as high-cost mortgage transactions, and finally for so-called reverse mortgages.

TILA covers all consumer credit (not commercial or agricultural credit) in amounts of $50,000 or less plus other credit transactions of any size involving consumers if secured by real property (mortgage credit). Besides mandating specific disclosures, the act and its implementing regulation, Federal Reserve Board (FRB) Regulation Z, 12 CFR Part 226, specify precise definitions and calculation methods to assure uniformity. The act also contains some nondisclosure regulations of creditor behavior, often referred to as *behavioral* or *substantive regulations*, but disclosures have always been its main purpose. The key substantive provision in the original act involved the right of rescission on non purchase-money credit to consumers secured by the consumers' principal dwelling. This provision allows borrowers on a second lien and all who refinance a mortgage loan to rescind or cancel the loan within a three-day period after receiving all the disclosures. Since 1968, amendments to TILA have added additional substantive requirements, particularly in the areas of credit card solicitations, credit card billing, credit card repricing, and credit secured by dwellings.[3]

Subgroup 1A, "Closed-End Credit," in Table A.1 lists the main required TILA disclosures on closed-end consumer credit, that is, on credit typically involving one extension of credit and a fixed schedule of payments (common automobile loans, for example). The requirements for closed-end mortgage credit are in subsection 1B, "Closed-End Consumer Credit: Certain Residential Home Mortgage Transactions." Both closed-end lists are quite comprehensive, including written notification of amounts of credit extended, finance charges, and APRs, plus information on the payment schedule, security interests, default events, and rescission rights, if they exist (certain mortgage credit). TILA has also always contained provisions governing advertising, but these mandates are not included in Table A.1 because advertising is not required.

Open-end credit, such as typical credit card credit and check overdraft credit that permits multiple credit advances and variable payments, has its own set of disclosure requirements, found in subgroup 1C, "Open-End Consumer Credit, Including Credit Card Accounts." Section 1D, "Open-End Consumer Credit Secured by Consumer's Dwelling," in turn, contains the requirements for open-end mortgage credit. The open-end credit lists are also lengthy, requiring disclosures of individual transactions under the open-end plan, outstanding balances, finance charges, fees, APRs, and error-resolution policies.

An amendment in 1988 substantially expanded disclosure requirements for credit card applications and solicitations, extending requirements to solicitations as well as at account opening and with periodic billing statements. Any changes in terms generate further special disclosure requirements. Newly enacted Amendments to Regulation AA ("Unfair or Deceptive Acts or Practices") and Regulation Z in December 2008 cover many practices in the credit card area and substantially rearrange many of the required disclosures.

Another important TILA amendment in 1988 greatly expanded the number of required disclosures on open-end credit secured by a consumer's residence, producing the requirements in subgroup 1D of the table. The revision required disclosures if (or shortly after) a consumer receives an application, as well as additional disclosures at account opening. After November 7, 1989, when the revisions took effect, those who obligate themselves on an open-end credit account secured by a dwelling receive, in effect, two sets of required TILA disclosures. The newer requirements (subgroup 1D) include extensive details about the account, as well as examples and historical experience with interest rates.

Subsection 1E, "Home Ownership and Equity Protection Act of 1994 (HOEPA) Requirements," contains the disclosure requirements that arose from HOEPA, an amendment to TILA in 1994. These provisions resulted from the view in Congress, at that time, that consumers who enter into high-cost mortgages need additional protections beyond the normal TILA mortgage disclosure requirements. Beside additional disclosures, the HOEPA mandated different timing rules and more precision for disclosures on mortgages judged to be high-cost mortgages, and a variety of other substantive provisions.[4]

The HOEPA also contained new provisions for reverse mortgages, a product normally intended for older, retired consumers who prefer to stay in their home after retirement. This product, typically packaged with an annuity, permits consumers to receive payments from a financial institution, usually monthly, with the payments added to a mortgage balance until the property is sold (or, in some cases, the consumer passes away). Because of the complexity of this product, Congress believed that additional disclosures were appropriate; they are found in subsection 1F, "Reverse Mortgages," of the table.

Subgroup 2, "The Consumer Leasing Act," initiates the outline of disclosures required under other statutes, beginning with disclosures required under the Consumer Leasing Act for consumer leases of personal property. Congress extended TILA-type disclosures to consumer leases in 1976 as long-term consumer leasing began to become more prevalent as an alternative to credit purchases, especially for automobiles. As with credit disclosures, consumer leasing disclosures are quite extensive; the requirements include details on the type, amount, and timing of charges, fees, and payments. There are also mandatory disclosures of property maintenance provisions and terms, and the conditions surrounding the termination of the lease. Although credit and leasing differ in a number of ways, including tax- and ownership-obligation differences, Congress inserted the Consumer Leasing Act as Chapter 5 of TILA. Unlike the rest of TILA, however, the implementing regulation is Federal Reserve Regulation M (12 CFR Part 213), rather than Regulation Z.

TILA is not the only source of required disclosures on credit transactions. Subsection 3 of the table lists the requirements of the Real Estate Settlement Procedures Act. The RESPA disclosures arise from Congressional concern that consumers did not well understand the process and fees associated with real estate transfers and refinancings. Requirements specify the use of required disclosure Form HUD-1, which calls for well over one-hundred lines of information (some of which are blank for supplementary items), and a mandatory explanatory booklet.

Congress passed TISA in 1991 because of the view that additional disclosures would enable consumers to make better decisions in this area and improve the competitiveness of deposit markets; Federal Reserve Regulation DD (12 CFR Part 230) implements the law. This rule applies to all financial institutions except credit unions, which have their own rule, that is required to be substantially similar but under the jurisdiction of the National Credit Union Administration (NCUA). TIS also contains advertising rules that apply to deposit brokers as well as financial institutions.

The truth in savings regulation also specifies methods of calculation of the APY to guarantee consistency, a requirement that is of potentially greater importance than the details of the disclosures. As discussed more fully in Appendix B, "Discussion of Disclosures in Selected Federal Consumer Financial Statutes Other than the Truth in Lending Act," the disclosure provisions of this law have proven to be relatively less important than the other disclosure laws because this mandatory disclosure scheme largely appears to follow existing industry practices found in the marketplace at the time of implementation. As a result, the impact on consumers' financial knowledge or behavior does not seem to have been especially substantial. Declining interest rates over the decade following implementation of Regulation DD requirements have tended to make them less important.

The EFTA requires disclosures on any consumer deposit accounts with an electronic transfer feature. This law resulted from congressional concern in the late 1970s, when electronic transfers were relatively new, that consumers might not be fully informed about how such accounts work. As financial services and the institutions that provide them have evolved over the years and electronic banking has become much more common, it seems that the disclosure requirements under EFTA and its implementing regulation (Federal Reserve Board Regulation E, 12 CFR Part 205) have not turned out to be as important as likely envisioned at the outset. Besides disclosures, the act and regulation also mandate specific procedures and timing for resolving any account errors that involve electronic funds transfers. Over time, it appears that these substantive protections have tended to become more important and the disclosures less important than probably foreseen.

The last subgroup of disclosures in the information-based protection section of Table A.1 concerns geographic lending patterns of depository institutions. As mentioned earlier, the requirements of the Home Mortgage Disclosure Act and its implementing regulation (Federal Reserve Regulation C, 12 CFR Part 203) differ from those of the other subgroups in the first part of the table. Rather than focusing on individual account information for consumers' purposes, this law and its regulation require cumulative disclosures of institutions' behavior across all accounts. These disclosures involve revealing geographic patterns of institutions' mortgage-lending behavior within their communities and elsewhere. These requirements resulted from congressional concerns over possible *redlining*, the contention that some lending institutions draw a "red line" around certain neighborhoods and refused to lend there.

Although the disclosures required under the HMDA are available to any individual in the community, it appears that Congress did not pass this legislation with the primary intent of influencing the behavior of individual consumers. Rather, it apparently believed that community organizations, pressure groups, and regulatory agencies would be the most likely users of these disclosures, and this has proven true.

Required Disclosures Among Market Protections

As indicated, the second major grouping of Table A.1 denotes the disclosure provisions in the federal financial regulatory statutes that are not primarily information-based protections. The consumer privacy provisions of the Gramm-Leach-Bliley Act require disclosures of the institution's privacy policy and the right to opt out of the institution's ability to share non-public information with its affiliates and others. The law provides for the disclosure of substantial detail on privacy policies, including information on the categories of non-public sorts of information covered by the policies. The extent of the details involved has led to the dense little brochures of disclosures that all consumers receive from time to time on all their accounts with financial institutions.

The Gramm-Leach-Bliley Act consumer privacy provisions require a list of disclosures, but also that covered institutions establish administrative, technical, and physical safeguards concerning the security, confidentiality, and protection of customer records. There also are substantive requirements concerning the release of non-public information by institutions to non-affiliated entities. A group of federal agencies received the responsibility to flesh out and specify in detail how institutions falling within their jurisdictions should carry out the mandatory responsibilities, for both disclosures and the substantive requirements.[5]

Another market protection with important disclosures is the Equal Credit Opportunity Act. This act and its implementing regulation (Federal Reserve Board Regulation B, 12 CFR Part 202) mostly involve controlling the credit-granting practices and the procedures of the regulated entities, but there are required disclosures upon the occurrence of a credit denial or other adverse action. The disclosure provisions reflect congressional belief that consumers would benefit from greater knowledge of the credit process, particularly the specific reasons for any adverse actions.

Subgroup 9, "The Fair Credit Reporting Act," in Table A.1 arises from the 1971 passage of this act, which governs the activities of credit reporting agencies and the use of information files about consumers. Most of the act involves the permissible reporting and activities of consumer reporting firms (credit bureaus), but it always has also contained disclosure provisions. In late 2003, Congress substantially lengthened the disclosure list, but many of the additional requirements apply only to special cases and are not general requirements for all credit transactions. The range of possibilities produces multiple subsections in Table A.1.

A long-standing requirement of the act mandates that if consumers are denied credit on the basis of information from a third party, such as a consumer reporting agency, then they must receive notice of the name and address of the third party and their right to receive additional information from the third party about the file. Consumers can then request a reinvestigation of the disputed information and place their own statements in the file. The act also contains provisions concerning the deletion of old or obsolete information and, after 2003, permits consumers to access their credit files even if there is no adverse action associated with the request.

Subgroup 10, "The Expedited Funds Availability Act," in Table A.1, concerns the timely crediting of deposit accounts and the availability of deposited funds for withdrawal. These provisions arise from concerns in Congress that at least some depository institutions were not crediting consumer deposits rapidly enough or making them available for withdrawal in a timely manner. The result was the Expedited Funds Availability Act of 1987 and Federal Reserve Board Regulation CC (12 CFR Part 229) to implement the law. Most of the law and regulation involves regulating the behavior of depository institutions concerning funds transfer and availability schedules. They also include significant disclosure provisions, however, reflecting the congressional view that consumers will be better off with fuller information in this area. The main element of the disclosures is descriptive material on funds availability policies.

The following two subgroups concern more limited or special lending situations. Subgroup 11, "The National Flood Insurance Act," involves additional disclosures for real estate credit secured by property in a recognized flood hazard area. It arises from the congressional concern that both financial institutions and consumers could benefit from greater attention to the possibility of damaging floods. The National Flood Insurance Protection Act of 1973 mostly concerns procedures for lending in the flood-prone areas, but also necessitates consumer disclosures.

Subgroup 12, "The Federal Trade Commission Improvements Act," involves disclosures of responsibilities and obligations of consumer credit co-signers. Its basis is in a trade regulation rule of the Federal Trade Commission (FTC), which extends to banks and credit unions, under provisions of the act. It responds to FTC concerns that co-signers did not always fully understand their obligations.

Subgroup 13, "The Community Reinvestment Act," or CRA, contains some disclosure provisions in addition to its requirements that a depository institution meet the "credit needs of its community, including low and moderate income neighborhoods... ." Like the Home Mortgage Disclosure Act, this statute does not concern itself with disclosures involving individual account relationships; rather, its disclosures focus on the lending pattern of the institution as a whole. Although the required disclosure of an institution's policy and its institutional rating from the regulatory agencies may, on occasion, become newsworthy and be widely reported, it does not seem that Congress envisioned that the disclosures would likely be of much interest to individual consumers very often. Instead, the disclosures are of great interest to pressure groups and to the agencies that enforce the act as a way of influencing favorable behavior from the institutions. A new disclosure mandated in the Gramm-Leach-Bliley Act, passed in November 1999 and dubbed the CRA "Sunshine Provision," requires the disclosure of the nature of agreements between regulated institutions and certain other parties like community groups. Again, this provision is intended to influence the behavior of the signatories of such agreements and not individual consumers.

Finally, SEC rules that govern disclosures that must be available to purchasers of mutual fund shares are in Subgroup 14, "Mutual Fund

Investments," of Table A.1. They have long been requirements for direct distributors of funds and for broker–dealers, but their reach has recently expanded as distribution of mutual funds through banking affiliates has become more common. As depository institutions have moved more aggressively into this field, the banking regulatory agencies have supplemented the SEC rules with their own additional guidelines, also indicated in the table.

As lengthy as Table A.1 may seem and be, it is only a summary. As indicated earlier, it omits timing requirements, advertising rules, formatting matters, and other highly significant details. Fully understanding the full range of the disclosure requirements is an ongoing work not only to understand the laws and regulations but also thousands of judicial precedents, which involves immersion into hundreds of legal thickets.

Table A.1   Required Financial Market Disclosures for Consumers in the United States

I. Information-Based Protections

1. The Truth in Lending Act (See Title I of the Consumer Credit Protection Act, 15 USC 1601 *et seq.*, and Federal Reserve Regulation Z, 12 CFR Part 226.)
    A) Closed-End Consumer Credit
        a) Identity of the creditor
        b) Amount financed
        c) Itemization of amount financed
        d) Finance charge
        e) Finance charge expressed as an annual percentage rate (APR)
        f) Total of payments
        g) Payment schedule
        h) Demand feature
        i) Total sales price (if applicable)
        j) Prepayment rebate or penalty (if applicable)
        k) Late payment fees (if applicable)
        l) Security interest charges (if applicable)
        m) Insurance and debt cancellation features
        n) Separately priced insurance charges
        o) Certain security interest charges

(continued)

p) Statement referring customer to the contract clauses concerning defaults, nonpayment, right of acceleration, and prepayment rebates and penalties

q) Assumption policy (for purchase-money mortgages)

r) Required deposit (if applicable)

s) Statements about the right of rescission if there is a security interest in debtor's residence and the credit is not for purchase of the property (if applicable)

t) Variable-rate features (if applicable)

B) Closed-End Consumer Credit: Certain Residential Home Mortgage Transactions

a) The redisclosure required if the APR at the time of consummation varies from the APR disclosed earlier by more than one-eighth of 1 percent in a regular transaction or more than one-quarter of one percent in an irregular transaction

b) Variable-rate transactions (if the APR may increase after consummation in a transaction secured by the consumer's principal dwelling with a term longer than one year):

1) Booklet entitled *Consumer Handbook on Adjustable Rate Mortgages* or a suitable substitute

2) The following loan program disclosures for each variable-rate program in which consumer expresses interest:

i. Whether the interest rate, payment, or term of loan may change

ii. Index used in making judgment and source of information about item i

iii. Explanation of interest-rate and payment determination and how the index is adjusted

iv. Statement that consumer should ask about current margin value and interest rate

v. Interest rate will be discounted and consumer should ask about amount of discount

vi. Frequency of interest rate and payment changes

vii. Rules relating to changed in index, interest rate, payment amount, and outstanding loan balance

viii. An example of a $10,000 loan illustrating the effect of interest-rate changes

ix. Explanation of how consumer may calculate payments for the loan amount to be borrowed

x. Whether the loan contains a demand feature

xi. Type of information that will be provided in notices of adjustments and timing of such notices

xii. Statement that disclosure forms are available for creditor's other variable-rate loan programs

c) In an assumption, new disclosures must be made to consumer, based on the remaining obligation

(continued)

Table A.1   Required Financial Market Disclosures for Consumers in the United States *(cont'd)*

---

    d) Variable-rate adjustments subject to item b above:
        1) Current and prior interest rates and the index on which
        these are based
        2) Extent to which the creditor has forgone any increase
        in the interest rate
        3) Contractual effects of the adjustment
        4) Payment required to fully amortize the loan at the new interest rate
        over the remainder of the term
C) Open-End Consumer Credit, Including Credit Card Accounts
    a) Finance charges
    b) Other charges
    c) Security interest (if applicable)
    d) Statement of billing rights and error resolution policy
    e) Home equity plan information, if applicable
    f) Previous balance
    g) Transaction summary
    h) Credits to account
    i) Periodic rates
    j) Balance on which finance charge is computed
    k) Amount of finance charge
    l) APR
    m) Other charges to account
    n) Closing date of billing cycle and new balance
    o) Free-ride periods without finance charge
    p) Address for notice of billing errors
    q) Supplemental credit devices and additional features
    with a different finance charge
    r) Change in terms
    s) Notice of fee to renew credit or charge card
    t) Change in credit card account insurance provider
    u) Fees for issuance or availability
    v) Minimum- or fixed-finance charge
    w) Transaction fees
    x) Name of balance computation method
    y) Statement that charges incurred by use of charge card
    are due when periodic statement is received
    z) Cash advance fees
    aa) Late-payment fees
    bb) Over-the-limit fees
    cc) Balance-transfer fees
    dd) Statements about the right of rescission if there is a security interest
    in debtor's residence and the credit is not for purchase of the property
    (if applicable)
    ee) Grace period

(continued)

Table A.1 Required Financial Market Disclosures for Consumers in the United States *(cont'd)*

D) Open-End Consumer Credit Secured by Consumer's Dwelling
(in addition to the open-end credit requirements in Section 1C)

    a) The length of the draw and repayment periods

    b) Explanation of determination of minimum payment

    c) Information about balloon payments (if applicable)

    d) Fees imposed by the creditor and by third parties

    e) Statement concerning negative amortization (if applicable)

    f) Limitations on number of extensions or amount of credit

    g) Any minimum-balance and minimum-draw requirements

    h) An example, based on a $10,000 outstanding balance, and a recent APR, showing the minimum periodic payment, any balloon payment, and the time it would take to repay the $10,000 outstanding balance if the consumer made only those payments and obtained no additional extensions of credit

    i) Advice to consult a tax advisor regarding deductibility of interest

    j) Statement that the consumer should retain a copy of the disclosures

    k) Statement of the time by which the consumer must submit an application to obtain specific terms disclosed

    l) Statement that, if a disclosed term changes prior to opening the account and therefore the consumer decides not to open the account, then the consumer may receive a refund of all fees paid in advance

    m) Statement that the security interest may result in loss of dwelling if default occurs

    n) Statement that the creditor may terminate the plan under certain circumstances and require payment of the outstanding balance in a full single payment and impose fees, prohibit additional credit extensions or reduce the credit limit, or implement certain other changes and that the consumer may receive information about the conditions under which such actions can occur

    o) Home equity brochure explaining the nature of home equity lines of credit including benefits and disadvantages

    p) Statement that the APR does not include costs other than interest and the recent APR imposed under plan

    q) For variable-rate plans:

        1) APR, payment, or term subject to change

        2) APR includes only interest costs

        3) Index used in making rate adjustments and the source of information for the index

        4) Information about how the APR will be determined and how the index is adjusted

        5) Statement that consumer should ask about current index value, margin, discount or premium, and APR

        6) Statement that the initial APR is not based on the same information as later rate adjustments and the period of time such initial rate will be in effect

---

(continued)

Table A.1 Required Financial Market Disclosures for Consumers in the United States *(cont'd)*

7) Frequency of changes in APR

8) Rules regarding changes in the index value and APR

9) Statement of limitations on changes in the APR

10) Statement of the maximum APR

11) Statement of minimum payment required and maximum APR for a $10,000 outstanding balance

12) Statement of the earliest date or time the maximum rate may be imposed

13) Historical example based on a $10,000 extension of credit and past APRs

14) Statement that periodic statements will include rate information

E) Home Ownership and Equity Protection Act of 1994 (HOEPA) Requirements (in addition to other TILA requirements, for non purchase-money, closed-end loans secured by residential real estate with rates or fees above specified amounts)

a) Statement that the consumer need not complete the transaction even though the disclosures have been received and that consumer must meet loan obligations to avoid losing home

b) APR

c) Regular payment and balloon payment

d) For variable-rate plans, the interest rate and monthly payment may increase

e) For a mortgage refinancing, a disclosure of the amount borrowed, which consists of the amount financed plus prepaid finance charges (if any), in early disclosures

F) Reverse Mortgages (in addition to other required disclosures on mortgages)

a) Statement that the consumer need not complete the transaction even though the disclosures have been received.

b) Good-faith projection of the total cost, expressed as a table of total-annual-loan-cost rates

c) Explanation of the total-annual-loan-cost rates table

d) Itemization of loan terms, charges, age of the youngest borrower, and appraised property value

2. The Consumer Leasing Act (See consumer leasing provisions of the Truth in Lending Act, which is Title I of the Consumer Credit Protection Act, 15 USC 1601, and Federal Reserve Regulation M, 12 CFR Part 213.)

Consumer Leases of Personal Property

a) Description of leased property

b) Total amount of any initial payments

c) Payment schedule and total amount of periodic payments

d) Itemized amounts of any other charges

e) Total amount to be paid

f) Payment calculation

(continued)

Table A.1 Required Financial Market Disclosures for Consumers in the United States *(cont'd)*

---

g) Early termination conditions, charges, and notice

h) Identification and details of maintenance responsibilities

i) Statement concerning option to purchase property

j) Statement that lessee should consult lease for additional information

k) Statement of and information concerning lessee's liability, if any, at the end or termination of the lease

l) Statement concerning independent appraisal of value at the end or termination of the lease

m) Description of liability at the end of the lease term, based on residual value, if necessary

n) Total fees and taxes

o) Identification of any insurance

p) Identification of any warranties

q) Amount or method of determining any default or delinquency charges

r) Description of security interest

s) Rate information disclaimer

3. The Real Estate Settlement Procedures Act (See 12 USC 2601, and Department of Housing and Urban Development Regulation X, 24 CFR Part 3500.) Residential Mortgage Credit, in addition to the TILA requirements in Section 1A-1F.

a) Special information booklet concerning real estate settlement procedures

b) Loan origination fees

c) Loan discounts (if applicable)

d) Appraisal fees

e) Credit report fees

f) Lender's inspection fee

g) Mortgage insurance application fee

h) Mortgage broker fee

i) Assumption fee (if applicable)

j) Interest accrued or accruing

k) Mortgage insurance premium

l) Hazard insurance premium

m) Mortgage insurance deposit

n) Hazard insurance deposit

o) City property tax deposit

p) County property tax deposit

q) Annual assessment deposit

r) Settlement or closing fee

s) Abstract or title search fee

t) Title examination fee

u) Title insurance binder fee

v) Document preparation fee

w) Notary fees

x) Statement concerning possible transfers of mortgage servicing rights

---

(continued)

Table A.1 Required Financial Market Disclosures for Consumers in the United States *(cont'd)*

y) Attorney's fees
z) Title insurance fee
aa) Lender's coverage
bb) Owner's coverage
cc) Deed recording fee
dd) Tax stamp fees
ee) Survey fees
ff) Pest inspection fees

4. The Truth in Savings Act (See Federal Deposit Insurance Corporation Improvement Act of 1991, 12 USC 4301 *et seq.*, and Federal Reserve Board Regulation DD, 12 CFR Part 230.)
Consumer Deposits.
  a) APY
  b) Interest rate
  c) Variable-rate feature, if applicable
  d) Frequency of compounding
  e) Effect of closing an account
  f) Minimum balance requirements
  g) Explanation of balance computation method
  h) Statement of interest accrual
  i) Fees
  j) Transaction limitations
  k) Maturity date, for time accounts
  l) Early withdrawal penalties, for time accounts
  m) Withdrawal of interest before maturity, for time accounts
  n) Renewal policies, for time accounts
  o) Bonuses
  p) Provisions for changes in terms
  q) Notice before maturity
  r) APY on periodic statement
  s) Amount of interest on periodic statement
  t) Fee summary on periodic statement
  u) Coverage length of periodic statement

5. The Electronic Fund Transfer Act (See 15 USC 1693 *et seq.*, and Federal Reserve Regulation E, 12 CFR Part 205.)
Accounts with an Electronic Transfer Feature
  a) Details of consumer liability on any unauthorized transfers
  b) Telephone number and address for unauthorized transfer notice
  c) Business days of institution
  d) Type of transfers the consumer may make and limitations on their frequency or amount
  e) Fees
  f) Documentation of consumer's right to transaction information and regarding preauthorized transfers

(continued)

Table A.1 Required Financial Market Disclosures for Consumers in the United States *(cont'd)*

g) Information concerning the stoppage of transfers

h) Liability of institution

i) Circumstances under which consumer's account information may be provided to third parties

j) Information on error resolution

k) Notice of ATM (automated teller machine) fees

l) Change in terms notice

m) Error resolution notice

n) Receipts at electronic terminals must include the following transfer information: amount, date, type, identification of account, terminal location, and third-party name

o) In addition to the immediate above, periodic statements must include the following transaction information: account number, fees, account balances, address and telephone number for inquiries, and telephone number for preauthorized transfers

6. The Home Mortgage Disclosure Act (See 12 USC 2801 *et seq.*, and Federal Reserve Regulation C, 12 CFR Part 203.)
Residential Lending and Home Improvement Lending.

a) Notice of availability

b) Type and purpose of loan and application

c) Type of property

d) Owner occupancy status of property

e) Amount of loan and application

f) Request for preapproval

g) Type of action taken

h) Location of property

i) Ethnicity, race, sex, and income of the borrower

j) Type of entity purchasing loan if sold within the calendar year

k) Rate spread between APR and applicable Treasury yield for home purchase, refinance, or home improvement loan subject to HOEPA

l) Date interest rate was set

m) HOEPA status

n) Lien status

II. Market Protections

7. The Gramm-Leach-Bliley Act Provisions Concerning Disclosure of Non-Public Personal Information (See Gramm-Leach-Bliley Act, Title V, Subtitle A, 15 USC 6801 *et seq.*, and Federal Reserve Regulation P, 12 CFR Part 216.)
Protection of Non-Public Personal Information

a) Notice of the financial institution's privacy policy at account opening or revision of policy, not less than annually

  1) Categories of non-public personal information collected

  2) Categories of non-public personal information disclosed

(continued)

3) Categories of affiliates and non-affiliated third parties to whom non-public personal information disclosed

4) Categories of non-public personal information about former customers disclosed and the categories of affiliates and non-affiliated third parties to whom non-public personal information can be disclosed about former customers

5) Separate statement of the categories of information disclosed and the categories of third parties with whom financial institution has contracted, if non-public personal information disclosed to non-affiliated third party

6) Notices regarding ability to opt out of disclosures of information among affiliates

7) Explanation of polices protecting confidentiality and security of non-public personal information

b) To the consumer who is not customer, at the same time of opt-out notice, a statement that privacy notice is available upon request and the methods by which it may be obtained

c) Notice stating that the financial institution reserves right to disclose non-public personal information to a non-affiliated third party; consumer's right to opt out of disclosure and the methods by which this right may be exercised

8. The Equal Credit Opportunity Act (See title VII of the Consumer Credit Protection Act, 15 USC 1601 *et seq.*, and Federal Reserve Regulation B, 12 CFR Part 202.) Consumer Credit and Commercial Credit.

a) Notice within 30 days of actions taken on applications

b) Statement in writing of reasons for adverse actions on applications (or written statement of the right to receive such reasons)

c) Name and address of the creditor (in cases of adverse action)

d) Statement of prohibition of discrimination (in cases of adverse action)

e) Name and address of enforcement agency (in cases of adverse action)

f) Statement that the information collected on race, sex, marital status, and age on residential real estate credit is for government-monitoring purposes

9. The Fair Credit Reporting Act (See 15 USC 1681.)

A) Using consumer reports for employment purposes

a) Notice to consumer that report may be used for employment purposes

b) Statement that adverse action has been taken based on consumer report, if applicable

c) Name, address, telephone number of consumer-reporting agency that furnished report (in cases of adverse action)

d) Statement that the consumer-reporting agency did not make the decision to take adverse action and cannot provide reasons for such (in cases of adverse action)

e) Statement that consumer may obtain a free copy of the report and may dispute its accuracy with consumer reporting agency (in cases of adverse action)

(continued)

Table A.1 Required Financial Market Disclosures for Consumers in the United States *(cont'd)*

B) Election of Consumer to be Excluded from Marketing Lists Furnished by Consumer-Reporting Agency
- a) Notice that information in consumer files may be used for marketing
- b) Address and toll-free telephone number to use to notify agency of the consumer's election to be excluded from such lists

C) Fraud Alerts
- a) Statement that consumer may request a free copy of report in any case in which fraud alert is placed on file

D) Block of the Reporting of Information in Consumer File Resulting from Identity Theft
- a) Notice that consumer's request for block of information has been declined or rescinded by consumer reporting agency, if applicable
- b) Notice of the decision to block the file, including the name, address, and telephone number of each consumer reporting agency from which the consumer's information was obtained for resale (resellers only)

E) Disclosure of Investigative Consumer Reports
- a) Statement that investigative report may be made
- b) Statement that consumer has right to request a complete disclosure of the nature and scope of the investigation

F) Disclosure of File to Consumers, Upon Request
- a) All information in the consumer file, with some specific exceptions
- b) Sources of consumer file information
- c) Identification of each user of consumer report in preceding year (or two years for employers)
- d) Dates, original payees, and amounts of any checks upon which is based any adverse characterization of the consumer
- e) Record of all inquiries during previous year that identified consumer in connection with credit or insurance transaction not initiated by consumer
- f) Statement that consumer may also request credit score

G) Summary of Rights to Obtain and Dispute Information in Consumer Reports and to Obtain Credit Scores
- a) Statement of the consumer's right to obtain copy of report upon request
- b) Statement of the frequency and circumstances under which consumer is entitled to receive free report
- c) Statement of the consumer's right to dispute information in file
- d) Statement of the consumer's right to obtain credit score and description of how to obtain it
- e) Description of the method by which consumer can contact and obtain free report, if eligible
- f) Toll-free telephone number of consumer reporting agency
- g) List of all federal agencies and their addresses and telephone numbers responsible for enforcement of this statute

---

(continued)

h) Statement that the consumer may have additional rights under state law

i) Statement that the consumer-reporting agency is not required to remove accurate derogatory information from the file unless it is outdated or cannot be verified

H) Information Available to Victims of Identity Theft from Business Entity that Has Made Commercial Transaction With Person Who Has Stolen Consumer's Identity.

a) Copy of application and business transaction records that are evidence of identity theft

I) Disclosure of Credit Scores by Consumer Reporting Agency, Upon Request of Consumer

a) Statement that information and model used by consumer reporting agency to calculate credit score may be different than that used by lender

b) Current or most recent credit score calculated by consumer reporting agency for use related to extension of credit

c) Range of possible credit scores under the model used

d) Date on which credit score was created

e) Four or fewer key factors that adversely affected credit score

f) Name of the person or entity that provided score or file on which score was created

g) Standard copy of Notice to the Home Loan Applicant, as written in statute (required of certain mortgage lenders only)

J) Procedure in Case of Disputed Accuracy of Information in Credit File (See Fair Credit Reporting Act, 15 USC 1681.)

a) Information about the outcome and nature of disputed information reinvestigation

b) Notice of the consumer's right to add own statement to file regarding the accuracy of disputed information

K) Disclosures Involving Public Record Information Likely to Have an Adverse Effect Upon Consumer's Ability to Obtain Employment (National security investigations are exempt.)

a) Statement that public record information is being reported, together with name and address of the person to whom such information is being reported

L) Written Credit or Insurance Solicitations Made on the Basis of Information Contained in Consumer Files

a) Solicitations not initiated by consumer

1) Statement that the information in consumer's credit report was used in connection with solicitation

2) Statement that the consumer received offer of credit or insurance because of satisfying certain criteria of creditworthiness

3) Statement that the credit or insurance may not be extended if consumer fails to meet other criteria for creditworthiness

(continued)

4) Statement that the consumer has right to prohibit credit file information from being used for credit or insurance solicitations

5) Address and toll-free telephone number of appropriate notification system to opt out of such solicitations

b) Red flag guidelines

1) If the card issuer received a notice of change of address for an existing account and subsequently receives a request for additional or replacement card for account, before issuing card, the issuer must notify the consumer of the request at the former address of cardholder and provide means by which cardholder can promptly correct address.

c) Debt collector communications in situations in which the debt may be the result of identity theft

1) All information to which consumer would be entitled if the debt were to be disputed under provisions of law applicable to that collector, upon request

d) Credit extension based on consumer report, on terms that are less favorable than the most favorable terms available to a substantial portion of consumers

1) Statement informing consumer that terms offered are based on information in report

2) Identification of consumer reporting agency furnishing the report

3) Statement that consumer may obtain free copy of report and the contact information for that consumer reporting agency

e) Consumer credit denials (adverse action), based on information from a consumer reporting agency

1) Name, address, and telephone number of reporting agency

2) Statement that reporting agency did not make the decision to take adverse action and cannot offer specific reasons for such

3) Statement that consumer has right to obtain a free copy of consumer report within a 60-day period

4) Notice of consumer's right to dispute the accuracy or completeness or any information in the report

M) Duty of Furnishers to Provide Accurate Information

a) Written notice of financial institution's furnishing of negative information to consumer reporting agency, if applicable

b) Notice of results of disputed information investigation

c) Notice of the reasons for determining that dispute is frivolous or irrelevant and identification of information required for investigating the dispute

N) Solicitation by Affiliates

a) Statement that consumer's information may be used for making a marketing solicitation

(continued)

Table A.1 Required Financial Market Disclosures for Consumers in the United States *(cont'd)*

10. The Expedited Funds Availability Act (See 12 USC 4001-4010 and Check Clearing for the 21st Century Act, 12 USC 5001-5018, and Federal Reserve Regulation CC, 12 CFR Part 229.)
All Consumer Deposits
   a) Summary of the institution's funds availability schedule (The schedules themselves are controlled by the same law and regulation.)
   b) Description of possible exception to funds availability policies
   c) Description of delayed-availability situations, such as those pertaining to different categories of checks and any case-by-case policies
   d) Notices on all preprinted deposit slips that funds may not be available for immediate withdrawal
   e) Description of how to differentiate between proprietary and nonproprietary ATMs if availability is later at nonproprietary ATMs
   f) Notice of changes of policies
   g) Notice of funds availability policy posted in any location where employees receive deposits and at ATMs
   h) For credit unions that start the accrual of interest on deposits at a date later than when the bank receives credit for the funds deposited, an explanation of when interest begins to accrue
   i) Notice to the customer of a depositary bank that the depositary bank received a returned check or notice of nonpayment from paying bank
   j) Notice that the consumer's claim for recredit is or is not valid; if valid, notice that account has been recredited
   k) Notice that amount previously recredited has been reversed, if such action occurs
   l) Description that substitute check is the legal equivalent of an original check and that consumer has right of recredit if substitute check is not properly charged to account

11. The National Flood Insurance Act (See National Flood Insurance Act of 1968 and the Flood Disaster Protection Act of 1973, 42 USC 4001-4129, and Federal Reserve Regulation H, 12 CFR Part 208.)
Residential Real Estate Credit in a Flood Hazard Area
   a) Statement that property is in a flood hazard area
   b) Statement about federal disaster relief
   c) Description of flood insurance purchase requirements
   d) Statement that flood insurance coverage may be available under National Flood Insurance Program or private insurers

12. The Federal Trade Commission Improvements Act (See 15 USC 57a(f), and Federal Reserve Regulation AA, 12 CFR Part 227.)
Consumer Credit Involving a Co-Signer
   a) Statement of obligations

13. The Community Reinvestment Act (See 12 USC 2901 *et seq.*, and Federal Reserve Regulation BB, 12 CFR Part 228.)

(continued)

Table A.1 Required Financial Market Disclosures for Consumers in the United States *(cont'd)*

Lending

    a) Written comments received from the public

    b) Copy of the public section of the bank's most recent CRA performance evaluation

    c) List of bank branches and addresses

    d) List of branches opened or closed by bank in previous years

    e) List of services offered at branches

    f) Map showing assessment area

14. Mutual Fund Investments (See Securities Act of 1933, 15 USC 78a *et seq.*, and Securities and Exchange Commission Regulation, 17 CFR Part 274.)
Prospectus Requirements for Mutual Fund Purchases

    a) Fund name

    b) Date of prospectus

    c) Statement that SEC has neither approved nor disapproved of these securities or judged the adequacy of prospectus

    d) Investment objective or goals

    e) Principal investment strategies

    f) Principal risks of investing in the fund

    g) Statement that the fund is not guaranteed by the Federal Deposit Insurance Corporation (FDIC) or any other government agency (for money market mutual funds)

    h) Statement that the investment in the fund is not a deposit and is not insured (if the fund is advised by or sold through an insured depository institution)

    i) Statement that the fund is not diversified and the effects of non-diversification (if applicable)

    j) Risk–return bar chart and table

    k) Shareholder fees

    l) Annual fund operating expenses

    m) Investment objectives

    n) Principal investment strategies

    o) Risks of investing in fund

    p) Location of information about portfolio holdings

    q) Discussion of fund performance (if not a new fund)

    r) Investment adviser and services

    s) Portfolio manager

    t) Legal proceedings

    u) Capital stock restrictions or non investment risks

    v) Explanation of the pricing of fund shares

    w) Procedures for purchase and redemption of fund shares

    x) Policy concerning dividends and distributions

    y) Tax consequences of buying, holding, exchanging, and selling fund shares

    z) Sales loads

(continued)

Table A.1   Required Financial Market Disclosures for Consumers in the
United States *(cont'd)*

aa) Financial highlights

bb) How and where to obtain additional information

cc) Banking agency (such as, the Office of the Comptroller of the Currency,
FRB, FDIC, and the Office of Thrift Supervision) Guidelines for Brokers Who
Sell Mutual Funds Through Banks (See the Federal Reserve Board's Version
of Interagency Statement on Retail Sales of Nondeposit Investment Products,
SR 94-11.)

    a) Product is not insured by FDIC.

    b) Product is not a deposit or an obligation of or guaranteed by a
depository institution.

    c) The fund is subject to investment risk, including possible loss
of principal.

Appendix B

Discussion of Disclosures in Selected Federal Consumer Financial Protection Statutes Other than the Truth in Lending Act

The Truth in Lending Act (TILA) is the first and undoubtedly the preeminent set of federal financial disclosure requirements for consumers, but certainly not the only one; others have developed over the last four decades. As discussed in Appendix A, "Financial Disclosures in Federal Consumer Protection Statutes," disclosure is required by all federal financial consumer protection laws enacted by Congress, but is central to five of them that have been designated here as *information-based protections*. After TILA, and listed in an order that roughly (but subjectively) ranks them according to the centrality of disclosure to their intended purposes, the others are the Consumer Leasing Act (1976), the Real Estate Settlement Procedures Act (RESPA, 1974), the Truth in Savings Act (TISA, 1991), and the Electronic Fund Transfer Act (EFTA, 1979). This appendix reviews each of these laws as information-based consumer protections.

For the most part, these laws are not as well known to the public at large as TILA, and their disclosure components generally have not posed TILA's compliance and litigation difficulties for regulated institutions. Among them, the Consumer Leasing Act, TISA, and EFTA have been relatively quiet areas of disclosure law and practice in recent years, while RESPA has been a somewhat more active area. In 2002, the Department of Housing and Urban Development (HUD) began a lengthy rulemaking to revise the disclosures required under RESPA, but the effort became highly controversial and was bogged down for some years before resurfacing in 2009.

The Consumer Leasing Act

The original Truth in Lending Act did not cover consumer leases. Granted that a strict interpretation of the wording of the act might suggest that it did cover leases, the legislative history convincingly demonstrates otherwise.[1] Noting the increasing prevalence of consumer leasing of automobiles, Congress amended TILA in 1976 by passing the Consumer Leasing Act (Public Law 94-240, March 23, 1976).[2] Since 1976, the Consumer Leasing Act has remained basically unchanged, although its implementing regulation, Federal Reserve Board (FRB or the Board) Regulation M (12 CFR Part 213), received a complete overhaul in 1996.

Leasing an automobile is an inherently intricate transaction, but this area of disclosure law has been quite calm since the revision of the disclosure rules in 1996, which is an intriguing combination of circumstances. For consumer leasing, the outlay and unknown future events problems are even more severe than for consumer credit, but it is the one area of federal financial consumer disclosure law in which there was a conscious decision not to try to solve all problems by merely extending the range of required disclosures. In fact, the leasing area is as interesting for what disclosures are *not* required as for the range of its mandates. Consequently, it receives the lengthiest and most detailed attention of the statutes covered in this appendix.

The following discussion of consumer automobile leasing and required disclosures reviews the basics of the leasing arrangement and compares leasing with purchase financing. That establishes the groundwork for a look at the disclosures required and rejected for the lease transaction.

Kinds of Leases

Acquiring and financing a substantial asset through purchase credit ranks among the most complicated financial transactions a typical consumer undertakes; in some ways, a lease is even more complicated. Since leases can provide convenient substitutes for credit purchases and frequently offer lower monthly payments, many vehicle acquisitions, in recent years, have involved a lease. In fundamental economic terms, a consumer's decision to lease rather than use more traditional forms of credit is relatively straightforward to a financial analyst, but it often is much less obvious to consumers. Stating the problem in its simplest form, a consumer should lease an asset rather than purchase it on credit if the risk-adjusted discounted present cost of all the lease payments and outflows (including down payments and any deferred payment for a residual value if relevant) is less than the comparable present cost of all outflows for the credit purchase over a comparable period of time.[3]

Clearly, there are difficulties that make this criterion less than straightforward for most consumers. Like closed- and open-end consumer credit, consumer leasing manifests the sorts of outlay and unknown future events problems discussed for credit in Chapter 4, "What is Truth in Lending? Key Conceptual Problems Facing the Truth in Lending Act," but they are even more severe for leasing. At the basic level, are the usual problems: Leases may exhibit a variety of outlay features and unknown future outcomes that can affect the results of transactions but must be disclosed properly in advance, and the consumer must understand these issues to make the proper choice. At a second level, leasing and credit are not economically identical, and consumers must also be able to understand and compare and contrast the differences if they are to make completely informed decisions. This means properly understanding the implications of streams of outflows – including acquisition charges, down payments, financing charges, periodic payments, disposal charges, taxes, insurance premiums, and other outflows – that can differ in both amounts and timing under the two alternatives.

As the leasing market has evolved over the years, the closed-end operating lease has become typical in consumer transactions, at least in the big market for automobiles and light trucks. An *operating lease* covers a period of time shorter than the whole economic life of an asset. There is an expectation that an asset will still have an economic value (usually called its *residual value*) at the end of an operating lease. With an operating lease, an asset user (lessee) agrees to pay for the expected depreciation of an asset during the lease period, plus a financing or lease charge to compensate the owner (lessor) for the use of the lessor's capital, including a profit. Common car rentals or apartment leases are examples of short-term operating leases.

Also very familiar today are longer term operating leases (possibly up to four to five years or even longer) that auto dealers offer consumers through leasing companies and banks. These are the operating leases that have become important substitutes for purchase financing for many consumers, and they are widely advertised by both automobile manufacturers and dealers. Like a car renter or apartment lessee, a vehicle lessee, under these plans, uses the asset for a term but must return it to the lessor at the end of the lease period, unless the parties make some other arrangement for disposition. An operating lease always assumes the asset will have some remaining economic life and value at lease-end. Consequently, the transfer of ownership at lease-end (to the lessee or another party) requires additional payment for the residual value.[4]

Among operating leases for consumers, the *closed-end operating lease*, sometimes referred to as a *walk-away lease*, has become the most common form of automobile lease agreement. On a closed-end operating lease, the lessee has no obligation concerning the market value of the lessor's asset at lease-end. The agreement merely requires the consumer to return the asset at lease-end and to pay, then, for any excess damage above normal expected wear and tear.[5] Common, long-term, closed-end lease agreements for automobiles and trucks typically contain an option for consumers to purchase their vehicles at lease-end at a price agreed upon at the outset, but there is no obligation to purchase.

The closed-end operating lease contrasts with the less common *open-end operating lease*, in which the lessee still does not have a requirement to purchase but there is an obligation at lease-end to make up to the lessor any shortfall from expectations in the actual market value of the asset. In effect, the open-end lessee guarantees the residual value of the lessor's asset. Under typical open-end automobile lease contracts, lessees also may purchase their vehicles at lease-end for a purchase price guaranteed at the outset, but open-end lessees cannot walk away. Rather, if they return their vehicles, they are liable for any differences between assumed residual values and actual, realized market values at lease-end. The Consumer Leasing Act limits a consumer's liability for the difference between expected and actual market value on an open-end vehicle lease to no more than three times the amount of the monthly payment. This provision likely has encouraged the use of closed-end leases by making open-end leases less useful to lessors as a way of shifting risks to their customers.

From this brief description of the basic characteristics of leases, it is easy to see that closed-end operating leases offer consumers a different set of risks than open-end leases or credit purchases of assets: notably, closed-end lessees do not bear any risk of decline in the residual value of used assets below expectations over the lease period, but open-end lessees and purchasers do.[6] If, at lease-end, the value of the asset is below the deferred purchase price established at the outset, the closed-end lessee may return the asset and walk away (except from excessive wear and tear). If, in contrast, the market value at lease-end is *greater* than expected, the lessee may keep the asset (and can retain it or sell it) by paying the deferred purchase price agreed upon at the signing of the lease. For the closed-end lessee, this amounts to a heads-I-win, tails-you-lose proposition, at least with respect to the residual value of the asset. It seems reasonable to suppose that, as part of the lease cost, lessors will charge closed-end lessees for the purchase option feature that transfers the residual value risk to the lessor. Purchasers and open-end lessees bear this risk themselves. Ultimately, it is this difference in risk bearing, together with differences in the size and timing of cash flows (discussed in the next section, "Cash Flows and Decisions"), that characterizes the distinction for consumers between closed-end leasing and purchase financing.[7]

Cash Flows and Decisions

Beyond risk differences, closed-end leases also present consumers with a pattern of cash flows different than that of purchase financing. Ultimately, it is the comparison of the present values of the outflows that arise under the different financing schemes, together with the distinction in risks, that resolves the question of best choice for consumers. A comparison of the cash flows of a lease is complicated because of the many components. Because a fully informed consumer must satisfactorily solve the outlay and unknown future events problems for both the lease and the credit alternative in order to make an accurate comparison, it is worthwhile to outline the issues in some detail in this subsection of the chapter, though they are a bit complicated and tedious. Then, the following subsection, "Required Disclosures," can examine the required and omitted potential disclosures.

Decision Parameters

In the long run, in a competitive, perfect capital market with full information and without transaction costs or taxes, the financing arrangement for retail purchase of automobiles by consumers would be a matter of indifference to both consumers and creditors–lessors: Both costs to consumers and yields to creditors and lessors would be the same under the two financing alternatives. Clearly, capital markets are not perfect, however. First of all, there are transaction costs, including paperwork and legal costs, that may differ between leasing and debt financing. Also, taxes may differ between consumers and lessors, as well as between financing schemes, and, as noted, there may be risk differences among consumers and among types of transactions. On occasion, there also may be marketing promotions that encourage one transaction form over the other. Consequently, at different times, leasing may be more or less advantageous than purchase financing to either consumers or creditors–lessors, and both consumers and creditors–lessors have an interest in evaluating the alternatives.

Full statement of the parameters of either the purchase or lease decision is complicated. Fundamentally, consumers should choose a closed-end operating lease instead of debt financing only if the risk-adjusted present value of all the costs (outflows) arising from the lease (including any down payment) is less than the present value of outflows resulting from the credit purchase over a comparable period of leasing or ownership.[8] The present value of the purchase option embedded in a closed-end operating lease, which the consumer also pays for as part of the lease payments, must be subtracted from the present value of the lease payments in order to maintain comparability between the packages of transportation-related services purchased. (In a sophisticated analysis using the Black-Scholes option pricing methodology, Giacotto, Goldberg, and Hegde 2007 show that the value of this option can be substantial for consumers.) This presents the following decision criterion:

If Sum PV (LP) - PV (Option) < Sum PV (FP), then lease,
where PV ( ) = Present Value (of quantity in brackets),
LP = all payments on a lease,
FP = all payments on a financed purchase, and
Option = Value to lessee of purchase option.
That is,
If Sum PV (FP) + PV (Option) - Sum PV (LP) > 0,
then lease.   (1)

To analyze the decision, a consumer should discount the leasing flows at the APR available on the credit purchase or loan. If the discounted present value of the credit flows (which equals the purchase price) plus the present value of the option is greater than the discounted present value of the leasing flows, then leasing is the better choice and vice versa.[9]

Leaving aside the question of whether consumers understand present values and the discounting process, the difficult matter in analyzing the decision is to specify the flows properly for the two kinds of arrangements—in other words, satisfactorily solve the outlay and unknown future events problems—for both the purchase and the lease. Typically, the flows will differ in form, timing, and amount. Also, valuing the purchase option available on a closed-end lease might become an important aspect of the decision.[10]

Table B.1, "Cash Outflows Associated With Obtaining the Use of Assets Through Closed-End Operating Leases and Credit Purchases," provides a list of the four possible patterns of cash outflows arising from (1) a closed-end lease and (2) a purchase agreement for an automobile. For the lessee, there are two possibilities at lease-end: The lessee may return the vehicle to the dealer or may exercise the purchase option and buy it. For the credit purchaser, there are also two possibilities at the end of the payment period: The owner can keep the vehicle or sell it.

Table B.1 Cash Outflows Associated With Obtaining the Use of Assets Through Closed-End Operating Leases and Credit Purchases

	(Read Down Columns)			
	Lease		Credit Purchase	
	Retain Auto at Lease-End	Turn in Auto at Lease-End	Retain Auto when Paid	Sell Auto when Paid
1)	- Trans Serv	= - Trans Serv	= - Trans Serv	= - Trans Serv
2)	+ Trade in	= + Trade in	= + Trade in	= + Trade in
3)	+ CCR	+ CCR	+ Down Pay	+ Down Pay
4)	+ Secur Dep	+ Secur Dep		
5)	- PV (Dep Ref)	- PV (Dep Ref)		
6)	+ Sum PV (LP)	+ Sum PV (LP)	+ Sum PV (FP)	+ Sum PV(FP)
7)		+ Sum PV (PPT)	+ SumPV(PPT)	
8)	+ PV (Pur Price)			
9)		+ PV (Disp Chrge)		
10)			- PV (Sale)	
11)			+ PV (EL/S)	
12)	+ PV (EL/ET)	= + PV (EL/ET)	+ PV (EL/ET)	= + PV (EL/ET)

Abbreviations Used:

PV ( )	Present Value (of Quantity in Brackets)
Trans Serv	Transportation Services Provided
CCR	(Cash) Capitalized Cost Reduction
Down Pay	(Cash) Down Payment
Secur Dep	Security Deposit
Dep Ref	Security Deposit Refund
LP	Lease Payments
FP	Finance Payments
PPT	Personal Property Taxes
Pur Price	Purchase Price
Disp Chrge	Disposition or Drop-Off Charge
Sale	Sale Price
EL/S	Expected Loss on Sale of the Vehicle
EL/ET	Expected Loss Upon Early Termination of Lease or Credit Arrangement

The table adopts the convention that outflows are positive and inflows negative; thus, the table expresses the net costs of the transactions.

Under this convention, the consumer receives from a lease or a financed purchase an inflow (negative cost) of transportation and other services from the vehicle during the period covered by the agreement.[11] Over comparable time periods, the transportation services are assumed to be independent of the financing method (Table B.1, line 1). This is denoted in the table by equal signs between columns.[12]

For both types of financing, the consumer agrees to a series of outflows to satisfy the payment obligation; some of the outflows arising from the two alternative financing methods will be the same, but some will differ. Frequently, the first of these outflows is a trade in of a vehicle already owned by the consumer (Table B.1, line 2). With the assumption that the consumer trades in the same vehicle under both financing schemes, the trade in is the same under the two alternatives.

Often, the trade in is accompanied by a cash down payment (Table B.1, line 3). (On a lease, the down payment and the trade in are often called the *capitalized cost reduction*. In Table B.1, this term applies to the cash component.) A lessee typically must also provide a security deposit, which often approximates one monthly payment on the lease obligation (Table B.1, line 4). Upon satisfaction of the lease agreement, this security deposit is refunded at lease end (Table B.1, line 5).

In addition to these initial outflows, the consumer is also obligated for a series of further cash payments over the agreement period, usually monthly (Table B.1, line 6). On a lease, the first payment typically is due at signing, while a credit purchase agreement normally defers the first payment for a month.

In many jurisdictions, vehicle owners are also subject to personal property taxes on their vehicles owned or garaged within tax districts such as counties or states (Table B.1, line 7). On a lease in some jurisdictions, the lessor may be responsible for these taxes, which it recoups by upping the necessary periodic payments. Consequently, for lessees, the flows for personal property taxes may not appear as a separate, explicit outflow on a lease in many tax jurisdictions, even if personal property taxes are explicit for financed purchases. For comparability with a credit purchase, therefore, either the taxes in these jurisdictions must be subtracted from the lease payments or added to the finance payments.[13]

End-of-term outflows also differ between purchasing and leasing. In the credit purchase, the consumer owns the vehicle at the end of the financing period and holds the right to continued transportation services over the additional expected life of the vehicle; with a lease, the consumer does not have this right. To compare a lease with purchase financing, it is necessary to account for the remaining transportation services at lease-end.

One possibility, of course, is that the consumer purchases the leased vehicle at the end of the lease period, thereby obtaining the remaining transportation services. On a typical closed-end lease, the consumer obtains the vehicle and its remaining services by purchasing it at the optional purchase price disclosed in the original lease agreement, or at some other price negotiated between the parties. This price becomes another outflow (Table B.1, line 8), this one deferred until the end of the lease period.[14]

Because the lessee does not have to make the decision whether or not to retain the vehicle until the end of the lease period, at the outset the deferred decision amounts to a call option for the lessee, and, as noted previously, this option has value because it transfers risks of residual price fluctuations to the lessor. In effect, when lessees contract for the services of vehicles, they obtain options to call the residual values of their vehicles at the end of the leases by paying at lease-end a deferred optional purchase price agreed at the outset. This differentiates the lessee from the credit purchaser, who owns the vehicle and bears all of the residual price risk. To maintain comparability with a purchase, the present value of this option must be subtracted from the present value of the lease costs or added to the present value of the purchase finance costs (see Equation 1, above).

The other possibility is that the consumer returns the vehicle to the lessor at lease-end, thereby giving up any claim to transportation services remaining in the vehicle. In this case, the lessee returns the vehicle and pays any drop-off or disposition charge in the contract (Table B.1, line 9), but not any optional purchase price (Table B.1, line 8 is zero in this case).[15]

Purchasers who sell their vehicles receive a wholesale selling price upon sale (Table B.1, line 10). Those who sell them privately and not to a dealer may receive an amount closer to the retail price (if the cars are in good condition), less, of course, the costs of selling, including advertising expenses and the costs of personal time spent on the sale process (and the subjective personal costs of any accompanying aggravation).

Two contingencies might lead to additional outflows at the end of the relevant time period. First, there is a chance that a vehicle may be worth more or less at the time of eventual disposition than the consumer expects at the outset, which may be important to the consumer, in some cases. If the consumer expects to purchase the vehicle at lease-end or plans to retain the vehicle at the end of the purchase finance period, however, the planned disposition likely will take place far enough into the future that the consumer may well not have, at the outset, any expectation about the value many years hence. If so, this contingency probably need not enter into the present value calculations at the outset of the transaction (or into columns 1 or 3 of Table B.1).[16]

In the other situation, that is, if the consumer does *not* intend to retain the vehicle at lease-end or does plan to sell the purchased auto, the time before expected disposition is shorter and unexpected loss may become a factor in decision-making. For the closed-end lessee, the lessor bears this risk; the value to the consumer of avoiding the loss is subsumed into the value of the call option on the vehicle's residual value. Thus, of the four cases, only the purchaser who plans to sell the vehicle upon completion of the payments is subject to this potential risk (Table B.1, line 11, column 4).[17]

The second contingency is the chance of a loss upon an early termination of the lease or upon a sale of the vehicle before the end of the credit purchase agreement period. A loss on early termination might occur following theft or an accident not fully covered by insurance, or because the consumer desires to change vehicles before the end of the lease or purchase financing agreement. For both lessees and purchasers, this risk is independent of plans to retain the vehicle or not at the end of the payment period and can be assumed equal for all lessors or all purchasers (indicated by equal signs on Table B.1, line 12). Since a loss (outflow) is more likely than an unexpected gain under these circumstances, however, the expected value is probably positive. To minimize the size of such losses for lessees in the cases of accident or theft (and the financial and legal difficulties that might arise) gap insurance often is available from lessors, and typically included as part of the leasing transaction and charge. For most consumers, though, either the prior probability of unexpected early termination (and, consequently, the expected value of any associated loss) is probably small enough in the consumer's mind at the outset of the transaction, or the expectation of a difference in loss size in this area between leasing and purchase financing is probably small enough, that the expectation of a loss on early termination is probably not much of a factor in the choice between leasing and financing.[18]

The Lease Versus Purchase Decision

Now, the quantities in Table B.1 can be substituted into Equation 1 to derive the net advantage of leasing: In the first instance, the consumer keeps the vehicle at the end of the payment period (Equation 2, below); and in the second, the consumer does not retain the vehicle (equation 3).

To ease solution, a few simplifications of the equations are possible. First, because transportation services (Table B.1, line 1) are assumed to be the same for comparable periods of ownership and lease holding, they may be ignored and omitted from the equations. Likewise, since the trade in is the same (line 2), it may also be dismissed. Third, if the expected value of the loss from an early termination (line 12) either is not very large or does not differ much between a financed purchase and a lease, it also can drop from the equation, since it is the difference between these quantities for a financed purchase and a lease that would enter the equation anyway. Thus, with these assumptions and recalling that leases, but not purchases, commonly require one monthly payment in advance, this leaves the following specifications for Equations 2 and 3 for finance and lease periods of N months:

Equation 2: When the vehicle is retained, if

$$Down\ Pay_0 \qquad \text{(Initial)}$$

$$+ \sum_{t=1}^{N} (FP_t + PPT_t)(1+\frac{i}{12})^{-t} \qquad \text{(Periodic)}$$

$$- [(CCR_0 + Secur\ Dep_0 + LP_0) \qquad \text{(Initial)}$$

$$+ \sum_{t=1}^{N-1} (LP_t)\left(1+\frac{i}{12}\right)^{-t} \qquad \text{(Periodic)}$$

$$+ \left(Pur\ Price - Dep\ Ref\right)(1+i)^{-N} \qquad \text{(End of Term)}$$

$$- \left(Pur\ Opt\right)(1+i)^{-N}] > 0,\ Then\ Lease.$$

Equation 3: When the vehicle is not retained, if

$$Down\ Pay_0 \qquad \text{(Initial)}$$

$$+ \sum_{t=1}^{N} (FP_t + PPT_t)(1+\frac{i}{12})^{-t} \qquad \text{(Periodic)}$$

$$-\left(Sale-\frac{EL}{S}\right)(1-i)^{-N} \qquad \text{(End of Term)}$$

$$-[(CCR_0 + Secur\ Dep_0 + LP_0) \qquad \text{(Initial)}$$

$$+\sum_{t=1}^{N-1}(LP_t)\left(1+\frac{i}{12}\right)^{-t} \qquad \text{(Periodic)}$$

$$+(Disp\ Charge\text{-}Dep\ Ref)(1+i)^{-N} \qquad \text{(End of Term)}$$

$$-(Pur\ Opt)(1+i)^{-N}] > 0,\ Then\ Lease.$$

These equations exhibit some features that should receive special mention. First, as discount rates move higher, but other things are equal, leasing becomes relatively more attractive. Specifically, in the case in which the vehicle is retained (Equation 2), higher discount rates make leasing more attractive because such rates reduce the discounted future purchase price of the leased vehicle relative to purchasing. This decreases the second (subtracted) term in Equation 2 (the term in square brackets), tending the equation toward a positive value favoring leasing. In contrast, if the vehicle is not retained at contract-end (Equation 3), higher discount rates favor leasing for a different reason. In this case, as the discount rate rises, it relatively decreases the present value of the sale price of the vehicle in the future. Since this is a subtracted item in the first part of the equation, higher discount rates again increase the likelihood that the equation will be positive, again tending to favor leasing relatively.

Second, the non-retention case (Equation 3) requires a term, the future sale price of the vehicle, that is not known at the outset of the transaction. Even if an expected used car price some time in the future is available from some guidebook, there is no certainty concerning this price, and there is no certainty about advertising, sales and aggravation costs that properly should reduce the final sales price. Consequently, Equation 3 requires some estimating and cannot serve as a definitive guide.

Third, both Equations 2 and 3 contain a term for the discounted value of the purchase option available on a closed-end operating lease. Estimating the value of this option is not a simple matter, even if experienced automobile dealers are reasonably proficient at estimating the values of used vehicles some time into the future.[19] As already discussed, its value to many consumers may be enhanced by the absence of necessary haggling over used car values at time of trade-in.

In sum, a consumer's informed choice whether to lease or purchase an asset such as a vehicle depends on the amount and pattern of the stream of outflows and the discount rate that converts the stream of outflows to present values. Unfortunately, the presence in a closed-end lease of a purchase option with unknown value and consumer uncertainty about future used car prices mean that the single-equation optimal decision criterion will always contain multiple unknowns and be insoluble mathematically, even if the discount rate is known. Whether this is a major concern depends on the value of the option to consumers and how it is priced by producers. If the option has no value because residual values are easy to predict, presumably its value can be ignored. Because this seems unlikely, however, the equation cannot easily be solved by consumers, even if they understand the concepts and can outline all the cash flows. Thus, the search is not for the perfect set of disclosures, but rather for the set that enables most consumers to make good decisions most of the time.

Required Disclosures

As with the main body of TILA, it seems that the Consumer Leasing Act requires the disclosure of virtually anything that might be useful to some degree to someone, sometime, for some purpose. (The broad outline of the required disclosures is in Appendix A, Table A.1, "Required Financial Market Disclosures for Consumers in the United States"). Arising from a scheduled periodic review of Regulation M, which implements the act, the FRB promulgated a new disclosure regime in 1996 (effective in early 1998) that mandated a mathematical progression of the components of the disclosures in a manner designed to aid understanding. The redrafted regulation required that lessors make substantial changes in the format and content of required disclosures, but it seems that the new approach improved the quality and accessibility of useful information to consumers.

Not surprisingly, though, it does not provide all the information necessary to solve Equations 2 or 3 above. For a variety of reasons it does not even seem possible that any leasing disclosure scheme could provide all of the information required for consumers to solve Equations 2 or 3 for the theoretically correct choice between a lease and a financed purchase. Some of the difficulty arises, first, from the outlay problem, but in the lease–purchase decision case, it arises for both a purchase and a lease simultaneously. Leasing disclosures cannot reasonably be expected to provide information about the purchase financing alternative to a lease, which is necessary to solve either equation. Consumers would have to obtain this information themselves by shopping, even if this merely means obtaining the necessary information from the same dealer.

Second, some information such as personal property taxes and an individual's personal tax situation are idiosyncratic to each shopper and must be factored into the purchase or lease decision by that person.

Then, as already mentioned, there is the unknown future events problem. Both Equations 2 and 3 require some information, such as the future prices of used vehicles and the present value of the purchase option, that is not readily available to either party to the transaction except by crude estimation.

Nonetheless, much of the information that consumers might need to characterize the lease component is available from the required disclosures. Moreover, the 1996 disclosure scheme (effective 1998) seems to make this information easier for consumers to comprehend and use. This is visible more clearly from a rapid tour of the revised disclosure regime.

Regulation M

Revised Regulation M requires segregation of a group of key disclosures in a highlighted "federal box," and, as mentioned, the disclosure of the elements that go into the monthly payment in a mathematical progression that is intended to be intuitive and easy to understand. Although a segregated "federal box" of disclosures and a mathematical progression are not strictly required by the statute, they follow the general approach for credit disclosures that became part of Regulation Z under the Truth in Lending Act amendments of 1980. They include, for leases, disclosure of gross capitalized cost, adjusted capitalized cost, residual value, rent charge, and total of payments. These new disclosures arise as components of a mathematical progression leading to the monthly payment.

Gross capitalized cost is analogous to gross purchase price including lease acquisition charges, carried over balances on any previous transactions, initial taxes owed, registration fees, delivery charges, and any after-market products, such as extended warranties. Adjusted capitalized cost is gross capitalized cost less capitalized cost reductions, including trade-in allowances, cash-down payments, rebates, and any other reductions. The residual value of the lease is the estimated value of the asset at lease-end. The rent charge is the lessor's designated added-on charge to cover transaction costs and the charge for capital use, including any profit from financing.

There are also requirements for calculating and disclosing certain subtotals. Lessors determine periodic payments by subtracting the capitalized cost reductions and lease residual from the gross capitalized cost and adding the rent charge. They then divide the resulting quantity by the number of periods to determine the size of the base periodic payments, excluding any added amounts for taxes and insurance. Thus, each of these new disclosure requirements after 1998 (gross capitalized cost, adjusted capitalized cost, rent charge, and lease residual) are amounts that lessors had readily available to make their calculations, although there previously was no requirement for their disclosure. Likewise, newly required subtotals such as total capitalized cost reduction (including cash component, trade in, and rebate or other noncash component) and amount to be depreciated and amortized (adjusted capitalized cost less lease residual) are directly derived from amounts already calculated and did not represent dramatic departures into a new disclosure scheme.

The revised regulation also requires the itemization of the amounts due from the consumer at the inception of the lease in two columns, one listing amounts due at signing and the other designating the means of paying the itemized costs. Taken together with the mathematical progression leading to the monthly payment, these requirements include all of the cash flows for a lease that would be necessary to solve Equation 2 or 3 (except present value of the option), even if the corresponding figures for a purchase (also necessary to solve the equations) would have to be supplied independently by the consumer.

It seems that Regulation M, as revised and effective in 1998, is a reasonable basis to make consumers aware of important terms without searching through the contract. Before revision, Regulation M contained no placement requirement for the key disclosures except that they be clear, conspicuous, in meaningful sequence, and that they be on the same page and above the lessee's signature. Otherwise, lessors could spread the disclosures through the contract document. For disclosing monthly payments, the previous requirement had been the disclosure of the total amount required plus identification of the components. The regulation did not require disclosure of the amounts of the individual components, although some lessors had disclosed amounts of components and there had been some confusion concerning exactly what was required. The presentation of a mathematical progression for calculating both the amounts of monthly payments and amounts due at lease signing likely helps interested consumers understand the intricacies of their transactions.[20]

The Lease Charge and Rate

One disclosure that is almost conspicuous in its absence, when comparing required leasing disclosures under Regulation M to required credit
disclosures under Regulation Z, is any transaction-specific analogue to
the comprehensive TILA finance charge, call it the *lease charge*. Such a
requirement was considered and actually published for public comment
in 1995. In addition, the National Conference of Commissioners on
Uniform State Laws (NCCUSL) considered such a disclosure in earlier
drafts of the Uniform Consumer Leases Act it promulgated in 2001 for
consideration by state legislatures but without this provision (see
National Conference of Commissioners on Uniform State Laws 1999).
The state of Connecticut passed such a provision, originally effective
July 1, 2000, before postponing the effective date until 2002 and then
repealing the requirement before it went into effect.[21]

The Regulation M proposal, NCCUSL early draft, and the Connecticut action in 2000 requiring disclosure of a lease charge were essentially
the same: Attempts to calculate and supply consumers with a measure of
the cost of lease financing analogous to the finance charge on a credit
purchase. Each would have derived this measure essentially by adding
to the amount of the lease rental charge (1) amounts like administrative
fees that would qualify as prepaid finance charges, (2) any fees specifically associated either with including a purchase option in the contract
or with disposition expenses at lease end, and (3) the amount by which
any optional purchase price exceeds the lease residual used in making
the calculations. The assumption behind this last addition is that if the
offered optional purchase price exceeded the lease residual, then the difference must be a cost of financing that can be disclosed to consumers
both as part of a lease charge and in calculation of an annual percentage
lease rate (ALR) analogous to an annual percentage rate (APR). The reasonableness of this assumption is examined further below.

If disclosure of a lease charge had been required as part of the revised
Regulation M, it likely would have caused more administrative difficulties and regulatory burden than the other newly required transaction-
specific disclosures. Experience with Regulation Z has shown that the
issue of proper inclusions and exclusions from the finance charge (and
the amount financed) on credit transactions (that is, experience with the
outlay issue) has been subject to extensive litigation in the past. Apart
from the likely burden of this disclosure and the potential for litigation,
disclosing a lease charge in dollars would appear to have only limited
utility as a shopping tool for consumers anyway, like the finance charge

in TILA. It would not be useful for most comparisons because the amount of a lease charge would be directly dependent on the size and maturity of the transaction. Furthermore, a lease charge (as well as a finance charge) is merely a totaling of charges paid and payable regardless of timing; it is not a present value of these amounts that are due over time. For leases, as noted, the disclosure of the method of calculating monthly payment through a mathematical progression likely will be more useful in educating consumers about the intricacies of the leasing transaction.

But another leasing disclosure may be even more conspicuous by its absence: the analogue of the TILA APR, call it an ALR. This is not because the matter has not been considered. Ultimately, the difficulties with calculating and disclosing an ALR arise from the necessity of assuming for a lease the value of one or more unknowns to permit solution of the discounting equation. In effect, the ALR would be subject to all of the difficulties of the APR discussed earlier (the outlay, unknown future events, compliance, and extent issues) plus some special problems of its own.

The mathematical formula for calculating a percentage rate from a series of cash flows is well known and straightforward: The internal rate of return formula commonly used to discount cash flows (see, for example, Brealey and Myers 1991, Chapters 3-5; see also Appendix J of Regulation Z). For consumer credit, Appendix J to Regulation Z extensively describes the internal rate of return formula for unit period lengths of time, with many examples. But even an area as long established as calculating APRs on closed-end credit under Regulation Z can be subject to controversy and litigation. As noted earlier, it seems that turmoil rarely, if ever, arises from the mathematical formulas themselves, however. Instead, litigation comes from questions about the items included or not in the formulas, in other words, the outlay and unknown future events concerns arise.[22]

If anything, leasing is more complicated on this basis than closed-end installment credit. The additional difficulties associated with leasing disclosures come about because on a lease, as discussed above, a consumer does not contract, at the outset, for the ownership of the whole economic life of the asset, but rather for only a portion of it. This fact raises questions about how to account properly for economic depreciation in the various parts of the asset's life, offers more opportunities for differing good-faith interpretations and conclusions, and presents more potential opportunities for manipulation.

More specifically, mathematically calculating an internal rate of return from a series of cash flows requires knowing the amount of the credit and the pattern of the cash flows. For installment credit such as automobile financing, if assumptions are made that the contract runs to maturity and all payments arrive as scheduled, then all of these figures are known or readily assumable at the outset of the transaction. On a lease, they are not.

On a lease, the lessee contracts only to purchase a portion of the economic usefulness (depreciation) of the asset and merely holds an option on the rest. For this reason, it is not possible at the outset to know the complete pattern of the flows, even if the lease runs to maturity. Some automobile lessees will either pay or finance a balloon payment at the end of the lease term, as they acquire the vehicle by exercising their purchase option and paying the agreed-upon amount or refinancing it. Others will not purchase the vehicle and may have no intention at any time of exercising this option, and so the size of the balloon payment is irrelevant to them. Still other consumers will negotiate a continuation of the lease. To calculate a percentage rate at the outset of the lease, some assumption about the events at lease-end is necessary: a plain example of the outlay and unknown future events problems.

Although no assumption properly describes the lease-end event for all cases, one possibility might be to assume that the percentage rate calculation for a lease depends only on events of the lease term. This means that the calculation would not consider the purchase of the vehicle or negotiated continuation of the lease. In this case, the assumption is that the consumer returns the vehicle to the dealer at lease-end under the terms of the lease contract. Consequently, the cash flows used in the calculation would include only those for which the consumer is contractually liable. Other, hypothetical, possibilities would not have to become part of the calculation.

Under this assumption, specifying the stream of outflows during the period of the lease is relatively simple, except for the issue of valuing the purchase option. As is the case of calculating the net advantage of leasing over purchase financing (Equations 1–3, above), the present value of the purchase option embedded in a typical closed-end operating lease that permits a lessee to call the residual value of the asset at a prearranged strike price must be subtracted from the present value of the rest of the cash flows to compare the internal rate of return on a lease with purchase financing. The rest of the cash flows are reasonably straightforward. They are described in column 2 of Table B.1 and reviewed above.

Equation 4 employs these flows and using the methodology of Appendix J to Regulation Z calculates an annualized internal rate of return for a lease with these cash flows by solving for i.[23]

Equation 4:

$$\text{Lease Amount} =$$

$$Secur\ Dep_0 + LP_0$$

$$+ \sum_{t=1}^{N-1} (LP_t)\left(1+\frac{i}{12}\right)^{-t}$$

$$- (Pur\ Opt)(1+i)^{-N}$$

Importantly for a lease, however, this is not the end of the story. There is still the question of lease amount, the top line of Equation 4, which is necessary to solve for the ALR. On a credit transaction, the amount financed is known at the outset. What is the corresponding amount of the lease?

As indicated, a lease finances the economic use (depreciation) of the asset during the lease period. In present value terms, this is the difference between the asset price after all initial payments (called in Regulation M, the adjusted capitalized cost) and the present value of the residual value. Thus, using economic depreciation as the lease amount in Equation 4 and adding the present value of the residual value to both sides of the equation produces Equation 5. Solving Equation 5 for i calculates the ALR. This is the calculation contemplated in the drafting process before promulgation of the proposed Uniform Consumer Leases Act discussions and by the state of Connecticut:

Equation 5:

$$\text{Net Capitalized Cost} =$$

$$Secur\ Dep_0 + LP_0$$

$$+ \sum_{t=1}^{N-1} (LP_t)\left(1+\frac{i}{12}\right)^{-t}$$

$$+ (Disp\ Charge\text{-}Dep\ Ref)(1+i)^{-N}$$

$$+ (Residual\ Value_N)(1+i)^{-N}$$

$$- (Pur\ Opt)(1+i)^{-N}$$

Conceptually, other than the rate i, a lessor knows all of the variables in Equation 5 at the outset of the transaction, except the value of the purchase option. Consequently, some commentators have argued, in effect, that the option be valued at zero, which is not a correct assumption, and that lessors solve equation 5 for i and disclose the result, calling it an ALR.

But Equation 5 has a difficulty of its own, even disregarding the inappropriateness of valuing the purchase option at zero: The residual value used by the lessor for the purposes of making the calculations can never be better than an estimate. No one really knows what the value of the asset will be at the end of the lease, and different lessors may, in good faith, estimate depreciation over the lease period (and corresponding lease residual) differently. This means that, even in good faith, they can estimate different ALRs for otherwise identical transactions. Beyond good-faith differences, there is also the possibility that some market participants may want to manipulate the lease residual to alter a disclosed lease percentage rate.

These difficulties surrounding disclosure of an ALR may be illustrated by some examples. Table B.2, "Patterns of Disclosures, Hypothetical Financing and Leasing Transactions," provides simplified examples of ordinary automobile acquisition transactions using a disclosure format that, like Regulation M, follows a mathematical progression illustrating the components of the calculations. The first example is a base case of an automobile financing arrangement, included to illustrate the differences between credit flows and leases.

Assume a consumer and an auto dealer agree on purchase of a particular automobile for $20,000 (Table B.2, column 1, line 1). The consumer's trade in allowance is $1,000 and the cash-down payment is $1000 for total deductions of $2,000 (line 2), leaving an unpaid balance (amount financed in TILA terms) of $18,000 (line 3). For computational simplicity and ease of illustration, the finance charge is calculated at a rate of $5 per $100 of original balance per year (not an uncommon way of calculating finance charges, especially historically). This works through to a finance charge of $4,500 (line 6) and a total amount of further payments to be made of $22,500 (Table B.2, column 1, line 7). If payments are to be made over five years, this amounts to 60 payments of $375. The APR calculated from these flows under TILA rules is 9.15 (line 10).

Now, suppose that in the backroom of the auto dealership, where, it has been said, a good "F&I guy" (finance and insurance person) "can make anything happen with numbers," the dealer's employee asks,

Table B.2   Patterns of Disclosures, Hypothetical Financing and
Leasing Transactions

	1	2	3
	Base case financing	Base case lease	Lower residual lease
1) Purchase (gross cap. cost)	20,000	20,000	20,000
2) Trade+Down (cap. cost reduc.)	-2,000	-2,000	-2,000
3) Amount Fin. (adj. cap. cost)	=18,000	=18,000	=18,000
4) Residual value	-0	-12,000	-11,000
5) Depreciation	=18,000	=6,000	=7,000
6) Finance charge (rent charge)	+4,500	+1,800	+800
7) Total amount of periodic payments	=22,500	=7,800	=7,800
8) Maturity (lease term)	60	24	24
9) Base monthly payment	375.00	325.00	325.00
10) Annual rate (APR or ALR)	9.15	6.06	2.88

"How long do you plan to keep that car?" And, suppose the consumer's
response is "Oh, about two years, I guess." At this point, the F&I guy
might say, "Well, in that case, we have a plan that can save you some
money. We call it a SuperLease, but it is just as good as owning and costs
less." At the same rate of calculation of finance charge ($5 per hundred
per year), the hypothetical lease forthcoming is illustrated in Table B.2,
column 2.

The basic transaction remains the same in the leasing example: The
car is the same, the trade-in allowance is again $1,000 and the cash down
payment $1,000 (together, these amounts are now called the *capitalized
cost reduction*), which totals $2,000 (Table B.2, column 2, line 2). Subtracting
produces an *adjusted capitalized cost* of $18,000 (line 3). Next, the dealer
assumes a 60 percent residual value $12,000 (line 4) and, subtracting
again, calculates a depreciation component to be paid for of $6000 (line 5).
The next step is to add the rent charge, in this example, calculated at the
same rate as the finance charge on the loan ($5 per hundred dollars per
year). For two years, this rent charge is $1,800 (line 6). Added to the depre-
ciation, this produces a total of future payments of $7,800 (line 7), or, for
a lease period of twenty-four months, monthly payments of $325 (line 9).
There is no requirement at present to calculate an analogue percentage
rate on a lease, but an ALR is calculated here for illustrative purposes,
again using the TILA rules.[24] In this case, it is 6.06 percent (line 10).

Which deal is better for the consumer, an auto loan or a lease? Much
has been written on that question, but the best answer is, "It depends."

As set up in this example, clearly, the lease is better for the consumer: If the consumer sticks to the plan of two years usage of the car, the flows include, in both cases, an inflow of transportation services for two years (assumed to be the same for the two deals) and an initial outflow of $2,000 (trade-in and cash). But, the purchase case involves twenty-four payments of $375 (and a haggle and hassle at the end over the disposition of the vehicle and the unpaid note balance of $13,500), while the lease involves twenty-four payments of $325 (and no haggle at the finish, assuming no abnormal wear and tear). Not surprisingly, the calculated ALR for the lease is lower than the APR on the loan, given that the stream of payments is smaller over the two years.

It is obvious these days from a glance at the newspaper that auto dealers and manufacturers have turned to leases as an additional weapon in their arsenals to "move the metal." Column 2 of Table B.2 illustrates how, using reasonable, albeit hypothetical, assumptions about residual values and finance and rent charges. Basically, the financing plan produces larger payments than the lease because the former amortizes the purchase cost to zero over five years. The leasing plan amortizes the original amount to some other number presumed to represent the value of the vehicle after the passage of a shorter period of time (called the *residual value*). Because the lease does not contemplate payment for the whole value of the item, the payment size can be smaller, as Table B.2 illustrates. Thus, for a consumer with a specific time horizon, the leasing arrangement can be advantageous because the payments can be smaller. The arrangements also can be attractive to sellers if they can move more metal with smaller payments (there may also be certain tax advantages for the lessors). The downside for the dealers-lessors is that there may be more risk associated with the implicit forecasts of used car values necessary in assuming the residual values (and pricing to them).

It is worth noting again that, in this example, the hypothetical ALR, using TILA rules, would calculate to 6.06 percent, as shown. As also pointed out, a rate that is lower than the financing APR is not especially surprising, given that the payments are smaller than on the financing arrangement. But, unlike financing, this rate is not fixed for a given amount of finance (rent) charge. The reason is that the amount of the financing itself is not fixed because the amount of the residual value is not fixed. As illustrated by Equation 5 above, there is more than one unknown. Thus, the equation has no unique solution for the ALR; the solution simply must depend on the assumption made concerning the other unknown (and must ignore the value of the purchase option, as discussed above). And, since different people may arrive at different outcomes for the same estimation of a residual value (or they can use different guidebooks), they also can arrive in good faith at different implicit ALRs for the same transaction. Unfortunately, this also offers potential opportunities for sharp practices in that backroom, where anything can happen with numbers.

Imagine another example: A consumer leases a vehicle with many of the same financial aspects as in the first leasing example (Table B.2, column 3): gross capitalized cost after all negotiations and extras of $20,000, a trade-in allowance of $1,000 and $1,000 down payment in cash for a total capitalized cost reduction of $2,000, and adjusted capitalized cost of $18,000. Now, column 3 of Table B.2 illustrates the problem of different estimates of depreciation (and corresponding lease residuals). Suppose that another dealer–lessor uses a different guidebook (or guess) and estimates a higher rate of depreciation and, therefore, a lower residual value for the same vehicle. But, also suppose this dealer offers the same monthly payment by charging a lower rental fee. From a consumer's standpoint, the transaction illustrated in column 3 is exactly the same as the one in column 2: The vehicle leased in the column 3 transaction is the same, the trade-in allowance and cash-down payment are the same (each $1,000), and the pattern and total of the payments are exactly the same (twenty-four monthly payments of $325 for a total of $7,800). The calculated percentage rates are different, however, with column 3 leading to a lower ALR of 2.88 simply because the estimate of depreciation is larger for the same payment size. It would be misleading to assert that column 3 represents a better deal for the consumer, although the calculated ALR percentage certainly suggests that it is.

A comparison of the lease examples in Table B.2 easily illustrates how different good-faith assumptions about depreciation and residuals could change a calculated ALR for the same payment stream, apart from any issue of manipulation by dealer–lessors. If, in contrast, a dealer–lessor subject to a disclosure regime decides there is some usefulness in minimizing the disclosed percentage rate merely for the sake of enhancing appearances, lowering the expected residual would permit this outcome.

Common marketing practices could also lead to variations in calculated ALRs, even if, again, the transaction is otherwise exactly the same from the consumer's viewpoint. Table B.3 demonstrates this possibility. The three columns illustrate common marketing strategies that dealer–lessors often employ, each leading to price reductions for the consumer.

The examples are constructed so that, in the absence of a requirement for an ALR disclosure, the dealer–lessor and the consumer are financially indifferent among the strategies (there may be some accounting or tax differences for lessors that are ignored here) in that the timing and amount of outlays are the same. In the absence of a requirement for disclosing an ALR, which strategy lessors choose would seem to depend on their perceptions of the strategies consumers are most likely to notice and respond to. This may vary among dealer clienteles and for any given dealer over time.

Column 1 of Table B.3 illustrates the common marketing strategy of raising the anticipated residual on the vehicle, thereby lowering depreciation and the size of the monthly payments, a common marketing strategy known as subventing the residual. Column 2 shows the impact of offering a subvented rebate on the lease. This has the effect of lowering the adjusted capitalized cost and the recaptured depreciation. The third choice, column 3, contains the example of a subvented rental charge. In the example, this lowers the monthly payments by the same amount as the other strategies, although this time not by lowering the accounted for depreciation but instead by lowering the rental charge component of the monthly payment. The consumer pays the same amount at the same pace in each case. Thus, from the consumer's standpoint, apart from the ALR disclosure, these transactions are exactly the same (as long as the vehicle is returned at the end of the lease), but their ALRs are much

Table B.3 Patterns of Disclosures 2, Hypothetical Leasing Transactions

	1	2	3
	Subvent residual	Subvent rebate	Subvent lease charge
1) Gross Cap. Cost	20,000	20,000	20,000
2) Cap. Cost Reduction	-2,000	-3,500	-2,000
3) Adjusted Cap. Cost	=18,000	=16,500	=18,000
4) Residual Value	-13,500	-12,000	-12,000
5) Depreciation	=4,500	=4,500	=6,000
6) Rent Charge	+1,800	+1,800	+300
7) Amount of Periodic Payments	=6,300	=6,300	=6,300
8) Lease Term	24	24	24
9) Base Monthly Payment	262.50	262.50	262.50
10) Annual Lease Rate	5.76	6.37	1.01

different, 5.76 percent, 6.37 percent, and 1.01 percent, respectively. If disclosure of an ALR were required, it is not hard to predict which direction marketing would go. One approach clearly would be preferred, even though the two other methods would, other than the disclosed rate, produce exactly the same outcome for consumers because the cash flows would be the same.

Unfortunately, the opportunity for manipulation brought about ultimately by the existence of a single equation with multiple unknowns for calculating the ALR permits even more wonders in that backroom, where anything can happen with numbers. Suppose that a dealer believes that the possibility of lower payments from leasing also allows some margin for higher pricing. Suppose that this dealer adds another $700 to the rent charge of the base case lease in column 2 of Table B.2 and builds the higher rent charge into the monthly payments. Solving the equation for the ALR in this case produces a rate of 8.42 percent, illustrated in column 1 of Table B.4. This lease still looks more attractive than the purchase case (column 1 of Table B.2): both the payments and the disclosed percentage rate are lower than the purchase case, even if they are higher than on the base case lease (column 2 of Table B.2). This new example clearly is better for the seller and worse for the consumer than the base case lease example.

Now, suppose that competition over disclosed ALRs picks up and the dealer worries about losing customers to someone else but does not want to lower prices. One easy option is to make prices *look* lower by manipulating the percentage rate. This can be done by one method

Table B.4 Patterns of Disclosures 3, Hypothetical Leasing Transactions

	1	2	3
	Raise rent	Raise cap cost	Raise cap cost again
1) Gross capital cost	20,000	21,000	22,500
2) Capitalized cost reduction	-2,000	-2,000	-2,000
3) Adjusted capital cost	=18,000	=19,000	=20,500
4) Residual value	-12,000	-12,000	-12,000
5) Depreciation	=6,000	=7,000	=8,500
6) Rent charge	+2,500	+1,500	+0
7) Amount of periodic payments	=8,500	=8,500	=8,500
8) Lease term	24	24	24
9) Base monthly payment	354.17	354.17	354.17
10) Annual lease rate	8.42	4.89	0.0

already examined in the last column of Table B.2: lowering the residual value and keeping the payments the same. Lowering the residual by $1,000 while keeping the payments the same would reduce the disclosed lease rate to 5.23 percent (not shown in the table). Bumping this approach another notch could lower the rate further. Reducing the residual another $1,500, for example, could reduce the Annual Lease Rate to 0.0 percent (also not shown).

Another method would be to raise the gross capitalized cost, permitting higher depreciation for the same residual value. This again would permit lower percentage rates for the same payment size. Table B.4 contains two examples of this approach in columns 2 and 3. The argument might be advanced that the higher capitalized cost (a disclosure item under Regulation M) should be a tip-off to the consumer; nevertheless, it is hard to argue this strongly about consumers who have been bombarded, their whole lives, with the message that it is the percentage rates that are important. Column 3 of Table B.4 at 0.0 percent is the lowest percentage rate in any of the examples illustrated, but the arrangement it highlights is no better for the consumer than any of the others in that table (since the cash flows are the same), and it is worse than the two lease examples in Table B.2 that disclose higher percentage rates but require smaller real outflows.[25]

To try to minimize the possibility of the manipulation of residuals by lessors as a way of lowering ALRs, one alternative considered by Federal Reserve Board staff during the revision of Regulation M would have required that lessors not use the lease residual in their calculation of the lease charge or the ALR if the residual diverges from the optional purchase price. This is also the approach embodied in the discussion draft of the Uniform Consumer Leases Act and the legislation in Connecticut. If there is a divergence between the residual used for calculation purposes and the optional purchase price offered to consumers, then the lessor would have to use the optional purchase price in the calculation. The justification for requiring use of the optional purchase price is that it represents a better estimate of the true residual value of the asset, since it is the price at which the lessor really would be willing to sell the asset. Although this approach might appear to help to minimize absolute manipulations of the residual value by lessees, it has a number of problems of its own.

One difficulty is that many lease contracts do not state an optional purchase price for the asset. It is possible, of course, that the proportion of leases without an optional purchase price could rise as a result of the new disclosure regulation. Regardless of the frequency, because such leases do not contain an optional purchase price, only the residual could be used for calculations and disclosures on these leases. This would negate any purported advantage of requiring that the optional purchase price be used in place of the residual value, at least for these leases. More importantly, it would introduce a source of inconsistency into the methodology of calculations and disclosures: Some disclosures would be based on lease residuals, while the disclosures on other leases would be dependent on optional purchase prices. It is certainly not at all clear that the introduction of a methodological inconsistency of this sort would improve the quality of information for consumers or solve the problem of the potential for manipulation.

A second problem is that the use of the optional purchase price in place of the lease residual introduces into the calculations and disclosures a quantity for which the consumer is not contractually liable. Many consumers do not purchase their leased car at lease-end. Substituting the optional purchase price for the lease residual, for purposes of calculating the ALR while retaining the residual for calculating the monthly payment, in effect, adds the algebraic difference between the optional purchase price and the residual to the lease charge. But, the closed-end lessee is never contractually liable for this difference, at the time the dealer makes the disclosures. At the outset of the lease, consumers do not agree to the subsequent purchase of the vehicle or, consequently, for paying the optional purchase price or the difference between it and the lease residual. In many cases, lessees do not purchase their vehicles or ever pay these amounts. Thus, disclosures of a lease charge or an ALR based on an optional purchase price are never right for these consumers. Even for consumers who purchase their vehicles at lease-end, the price may be negotiated at that time anyway, and may well diverge from the optional purchase price originally disclosed.

A third difficulty is that the exercise price of a purchase option is not simply another estimate of the residual value of an asset. The exercise price of the purchase option may depend on the lessor's business strategy. Even if lessors have the same expectations about depreciation, they may quote different exercise prices because one may want to keep the asset, and the other may prefer that the lessee buy the asset at lease-end. Lessors may hedge against the possibility that certain high demand assets may not actually depreciate very much in value over time by quoting a high, but negotiable optional price. As a result, a lease charge or lease rate calculation that requires the use of this optional purchase price may not even approximate the lease charge or lease rate that a consumer actually pays, especially if the lessee declines to purchase the asset.

Fourth, it is not clear that optional purchase prices are free from manipulation any more than residual values, since future car prices are always matters of speculation at the time the original lease is negotiated. Dealers and lessors can also raise and lower them for purposes of making the transaction appear more attractive. It might be argued that lowering the optional purchase price to lower the ALR is a self-defeating business strategy, since then more people will buy the cars at the low prices and the dealers then cannot count on income from resale volume. This likely is true to a degree, but it must also be recalled that leases often are most attractive to those who specifically do not want to buy the cars at lease-end, and the disclosure of a reduced optional purchase price might not change behavior at all. Consequently, what might happen if the disclosure of an ALR is required remains speculative at best.

On another front, even if it were possible to solve all of the practical difficulties concerning the concept of a lease charge and rate, there still would remain the definitional and operational issues that, so often, have provoked uncertainty and litigation over aspects of disclosure requirements in the past. Many of these issues arise from differences in the operating practices, concepts, and definitions of terms that creditors and lessors use in their day-to-day operations. Frequently, these vary from company to company and, importantly, they do not necessarily correspond exactly to the terminology used in regulations as implemented.

The depth of the concern in this area among regulated institutions often can be gleaned from the public comments of firms and industry associations participating in the regulatory processes required for rule-making under of the Administrative Procedures Act that governs the development of federal regulations. Naturally, industry comments are self-serving, but this does not mean that they are essentially incorrect; in fact, no one else is in better position to comment on operating difficulties.

A portion of the joint public comment dated August 7, 1996 of the Association of International Automobile Manufacturers, the American Automobile Manufacturers Association, and the American Financial Services Association on revision of Regulation M (Federal Reserve Docket Number R-0892) provides such an illustrative list of difficulties. The letter is interesting both because of the size and economic importance of the members of these associations, and because the issues they cite have raised so many analogous difficulties with TILA in the past (potential for *deja vu* all over again, it seems):[26]

To achieve the goals of providing consumers with an understandable and meaningful ALR disclosure and lessors with workable rules to follow, we believe that the Regulation must both provide general guidance and address many specific situations. For example, the Regulation must contain a clear general rule that lessors can follow to determine whether or not an amount should be included in the Lease Charge for the purpose of calculating the ALR. There are also technical issues for which there may be a need for detailed rules. With this in mind, a process should be pursued to allow input to consider and to resolve at least the following questions:

1) Will there be direction about the classification of the different types of charges found in leases regardless of what the lessor labels the charges? Some of the possible charges are:

A) acquisition/administration fee

B) monthly or other periodic service charge

C) taxes (whether paid by or payable by the lessor or the lessee)

D) license, title and registration fees

E) credit insurance premiums/physical damage and liability insurance premiums

F) charges for gap waiver, gap protection, or gap insurance

G) service, extended warranty and mechanical breakdown protection contracts

H) default charges

I) documentation, dealer preparation or vehicle preparation fees?

While we believe that one option would be a listing or set of examples classifying each of these amounts, we suggest a general rule would be more desirable. Any list would likely be incomplete and not address charges developed by lessors for future services or products in connection with leases.

2) Will there be direction for handling charges if they are optional with the lessee rather than mandatory? What would be required to show that a charge was optional rather than mandatory?

3) Will there be direction for handling charges paid in cash at lease inception? Will the ALR be adjusted for prepaid amounts that would have been part of the Lease Charge had they been included as part of the monthly or other periodic payments?

4) Will there be direction for calculation of the ALR for a lease renewal? For example, will the Lease Charge include any renewal

charge, documentation charges and unpaid charges due under the original lease (such as unpaid parking tickets, unpaid late charges, or unpaid personal property taxes)?

5) Will there be a selection of accounting methods by which the Lease Charge is earned, for example actuarial method or US rule?

6) Will there be a tolerance for the accuracy of the ALR?

7) Will the method of calculating the ALR provide for the following: a regular or irregular schedule; where the due date is not a business day; where months have different numbers of days; leap year; odd first payment period; payment of Lease Charges in advance or arrears; single payment leases; etc.

8) Will the ALR be adjusted to take into account different methods of calculation for leases which disclose a purchase option price and leases which do not disclose a purchase option price, and, if not, how will disclosure of an ALR be made useful for comparison shopping purposes?

Because the rule adopted for disclosure of an ALR will be important to both lessors and lessees for years to come, we believe that it is essential that the rules governing such a disclosure be uniform. In the absence of comprehensive treatment at the federal level, state legislatures may adopt varying approaches to resolving these issues. Accordingly, the Board should preempt, to the fullest extent of its authority, state legislative mandates governing lease rate disclosure.

After reviewing this lengthy list of conceptual and practical concerns over the concepts of a lease charge and rate, the only thing that seems certain is that required disclosures of a lease charge or a lease percentage rate would provide enhanced prospects for litigators. Advantages for consumers is another matter entirely.

Research on Consumer Leasing

Despite continuing interest in consumer leasing in the press and in the regulatory arena, there has been relatively little empirical research either on consumers' response to the economics of leasing or the impact of required disclosures. Most of the published studies of leasing arise from the substantial body of theoretical and empirical work on the economics of leasing in the business context (see Schallheim 1994 for a discussion of the issues and many older studies). In particular, there are few published academic reports of experimental or survey studies of consumers' responses to leasing disclosures.[27] In fact, at a more fundamental level, there are not even any studies of the features and costs of consumer leases beyond anecdotal reports of the sort found in newspapers. Implementation of the revised Regulation M at the beginning of 1998, without any systematic information on the features and costs of leases, let alone on consumers' reactions to disclosures, unfortunately precludes any before–after studies of the impact of leasing disclosures. This paucity of information brings a list of interesting research questions to mind:

1. From a purchase financing transaction, we can derive the lease that would be equivalent for the consumer? Are actual leases less (or more) expensive for consumers (*i.e.*, do consumers share in the savings from lessors' interest and depreciation tax shields)?
2. Does leasing vary in attractiveness to consumers over the business cycle, for example, as interest rates change?
3. In deciding whether to lease or purchase, what is the consumer's sensitivity to changes in internal discount rates, payment amounts, residual values, operating costs, taxes, business cycles?
4. How do the yields to lessors of typical automobile leases compare to credit contracts? How sensitive are the yields to market interest rates, payment amounts, residual values, operating costs, and taxes? Do yields vary over the business cycle? If so, what factors are important in the variations?
5. What has been the trend in residual values compared to estimated residuals? What impact has this trend had on yields and the costs of leases? What has been the impact on willingness of consumers to purchase the cars at lease-end?
6. What is the value of the call option associated with a closed-end lease? Has it varied over time? Is it sensitive to the business cycle?
7. What disclosures do consumers need to make good leasing decisions? Good credit decisions? How do these compare to required disclosures under TILA and the Consumer Leasing Act? How do the new Regulation M disclosures improve consumers' ability to make decisions, if at all?
8. Is the value of the call option on a closed-end automobile lease a positive function of assumed residual values? (Presumably, it should be because the risk to the lessor is greater.)

Real Estate Settlement Procedures Act (RESPA)

Beyond TILA and its corollary Consumer Leasing Act, the Real Estate Settlement Procedures Act is another important federal financial disclosure law that addresses availability of information about credit matters. This statute focuses on the costs and procedures surrounding the process of generating consumer mortgage loans. Of all the various kinds of credit for consumers, those associated with residential real estate are the most significant for many reasons; for the same reasons, they also carry the most extensive disclosure requirements.

First, real estate credit for consumers (generally known as mortgage credit because of the security interest or mortgage held on the property) has long been the largest portion of consumer-related credit in volume. It includes credit for residential purchases as well as loans that use properties already owned as loan collateral, the latter typically known as home equity credit. Total real estate credit to consumers amounted to more than $10 trillion at the end of 200-98.

Second, for most consumers, purchasing a residence and financing it with a mortgage loan is the largest financial transactions they will undertake in their lifetimes. Furthermore, defaults on mortgage loans can mean loss of the property. Both of these facts make mortgage-related credit an important area for consumer protection.

Third, real estate credit has important interactions with the tax codes of the United States and its individual states and municipalities. Many aspects of real estate purchase, financing, and taxes directly and indirectly affect other tax liabilities and tax payments. This suggests that consumers will need a full record of all aspects of real estate purchases and financing.

And fourth, because of the inherently complex nature of the underlying transaction (involving, as it does, not only appraisals and titles to property but also complicated underwriting procedures for large loans), mortgage lending also is the most technical and legalistic form of consumer-related credit. This promises that many consumers will want to assure themselves of adequate information about the specifics of the arrangements, if only for their long-term record keeping. As a result of all these issues, mortgage credit has become the branch of credit for consumers with the most extensive and detailed disclosure requirements.

Background of RESPA

The main components of the disclosure requirements for mortgage credit are in Appendix A, Table A.1. In addition to the standard TILA disclosures necessary for all forms of consumer-related credit, TILA contains special provisions for mortgage credit. They include special sections for variable-rate loans secured by real estate, home equity lines of credit, and reverse mortgages. In addition, the Home Owners Equity Protection Act (HOEPA) added amendments to TILA in 1994, to mandate more disclosures as well as some product restrictions for certain high-cost mortgages that do not involve a purchase (specifically, for refinanced loans and second liens, but excluding open-end credit). One consequence of all the revisions is that they have left TILA quite complicated in the mortgage area.[28]

Beyond the full menu of the Truth in Lending Act, Congress in 1974 mandated another special set of disclosure requirements for real estate loans with passage of the Real Estate Settlement Procedures Act. This act came about specifically because Congress did not believe that consumers received enough information about the costs of closing and settling the loan transaction or about the escrow accounts that lenders sometimes require for payment of taxes and hazard insurance. These financial issues are apart from the costs of the credit itself, which is covered by TILA disclosures. Congress could have integrated these disclosures into TILA but for its own reasons chose not to do so at that time, preferring a separate law. The overall purposes are in Section 2(a) of RESPA:

> The Congress finds that significant reforms in the real estate set-tlement process are needed to insure that consumers throughout the Nation are provided with greater and more timely informa-tion on the nature and costs of the settlement process....

RESPA arises in real estate purchase transactions but also in refi-nancing of existing mortgage loans, even if no new money is advanced, because there is another loan closing (another settlement). An amend-ment in 1992 (effective August 9, 1994) extended RESPA to home equity loans, except home equity lines of credit covered by Regulation Z.[29] The Truth in Lending Act, of course, also covers purchase loans, refinanc-ings, and home equity loans, because in each case (including refinanc-ings) there legally is a new loan. Consequently, in most consumer real estate transactions (namely, on purchases with a mortgage, mortgage refinancing, and closed-end home equity loans) both TILA and RESPA disclosures apply. If both laws apply, there is necessary interaction among the disclosures, and it appears that the presentation of two sets of disclosures to consumers is behind many of the complaints by both industry and consumers of information overload associated with required disclosures on real estate purchase and related lending. This is apart from myriad complicating details that arise in the regulatory structures. Coverage rules, exceptions, exclusions, and the timing for TILA and RESPA disclosures actually are considerably more complicated than the fundamentals of the laws generically outlined here.[30]

Since Congress passed both laws, it is not surprising that it also has always recognized the interrelationship of the TILA and RESPA disclosures. In fact, under the provisions of TILA and Regulation Z, the laws now permit the RESPA settlement disclosure statement to substitute for the TILA disclosure of itemization of the amount financed. In Section 2101 of the Economic Growth and Regulatory Paperwork Reduction Act of 1996 (Public Law 104-208), Congress further acknowledged the closeness of purpose of the two Acts. It directed the FRB and HUD, the agencies responsible for implementing the regulations under TILA and RESPA, respectively, to work on combining, simplifying, and improving the required disclosures. The agencies were to produce a single, combined-disclosure statement for closed-end mortgage transactions if feasible through regulatory changes under existing law; if not feasible by regulation, the agencies were to make legislative recommendations.[31]

In 1997, the agencies reported their views that legislation would be needed to combine the disclosures. The following year, the agencies forwarded their more detailed recommendations for legislative changes for both TILA and RESPA covering closed-end mortgage transactions (see Board of Governors of the Federal Reserve System and Department of Housing and Urban Development 1998). Congress had held hearings on possible reform of the disclosure requirements for the real estate purchase and lending process, but did not take any action until 2010 when it mandated an integration of the two sets of disclosures (for Congressional discussion of the issues see United States House of Representatives 1998; and United States Senate Committee on Banking, Housing, and Urban Affairs, Subcommittee on Financial Institutions and Regulatory Relief 1999). Beyond the many questions that surfaced in the hearings about the basic usefulness of instituting major changes to well-known disclosure regimes and the form any alterations should take, there are some substantive provisions in Section 8 of RESPA involving allocations of fees that have been especially serious complicating factors for reform efforts.

Clearly understanding the political difficulties surrounding RESPA reform, and after much thought and preparation, HUD nonetheless began its own official process of rulemaking on an extensive reform proposal in the summer of 2002.[32] The proposal did not focus directly on combining TILA and RESPA. Rather, the HUD rulemaking was aimed at reforming its implementing rule, Regulation X (24 CFR Part 3500).

In effect, the agency, in 2002, proposed to implement by regulation many of the substantive reforms to the heart of RESPA disclosures that HUD had discussed in its section of the 1998 joint agency report to the Congress. Apparently, HUD believed, in 2002, it had the necessary legal authority to make the changes, and proposed a major reform without specific new authorizing legislation. In early 2003, however, it announced that a final rule would be delayed beyond its internal deadline of Spring 2003. Then, in March 2004, it withdrew the proposal altogether. Political opposition from a variety of factions had become intense and, apparently, HUD decided, at least temporarily, that the time was not right. Finally, HUD implemented part of the proposal in late 2008 with an effective date of January 1, 2010.

But the 2002 proposal was in many ways a remarkable document. It is not often that an agency proposes a change of such magnitude to the substance of a key federal financial consumer protection regulation without specific legislative direction. The only comparably sweeping instances that come to mind are the FRB's 1977 proposal for TILA simplification, which was a Congressional idea in the first place and required legislation before implementation (although the agency engineered many of the details); and the FTC's 1977 proposed Credit Practices Rule.[33] More will be said later about the HUD proposal and its outcome, following some discussion of RESPA's basic disclosure requirements.

The RESPA Disclosure Requirements

Current RESPA disclosure requirements are very lengthy and detailed, but they generally are not as conceptually complicated as the key provisions in TILA; there are no new concepts in RESPA similar to TILA's finance charge and amount financed, or the mathematical formulas necessary for an APR, for example. Essentially, required RESPA disclosures are of four main types, plus a generic consumer information booklet and a few other minor components.

First, lenders or brokers must provide early estimates of amounts due later at settlement, including property-related costs, financing figures, other costs, and the costs of settlement-related services, within three days after a consumer applies for mortgage credit. Together, these disclosures make up the so called good-faith estimate or GFE. Among the financing costs are mortgage origination fees, points, and odd-days interest. Other required disclosures include taxes and hazard insurance fees or escrows due. The disclosure of costs of specific settlement-related services, such as the amounts for title searches, title insurance fees, surveys, attorneys' fees, document registration, pest inspection fees, courier fees, are also required. The GFE must contain estimates of the fees due the creditor as well as the estimates of fees or escrows required by third parties, including government agencies. The HUD action in late 2008 was an attempt to improve clarity and usefulness of the GFE.

Second, RESPA requires that, at closing, there must be a final accounting for all the costs and amounts for settlement.[34] There must also be disclosures about whether the loan may be sold or transferred to another party, and later disclosures about the new creditor if a sale actually takes place. The regulations provide model forms and suggested formats for use in all of these disclosures. All of this has produced the well-known lengthy form HUD-1, which serves as the basis for closing cost disclosures (Table B.5). There is also a shorter form HUD-1A for loans covered by RESPA but for which there is no seller; for example, closed-end home equity loans. There also is a short version of the GFE for home equity loans.

Third, RESPA mandates an early revelation of any business relationships (defined in the act, as amended in 1983) between a creditor or settlement service provider and any (other) provider of settlement services required by the creditor, if the creditor (or service provider) has any ability to influence the selection of the service provider. The disclosure must be made at or before the time of the referral, must indicate the nature of the affiliation or relationship, set forth the charges, and provide notice that acceptance of that provider is not a condition of the property sale or loan and that use of the provider is not required.

Fourth, RESPA requires annual summary of the status of any escrow account for payment of real estate taxes and hazard insurance. It must reconcile payments into and out of the account and notify the borrower of any shortfalls or surpluses. If there is an excess or expected deficiency,

Table B.5 RESPA Disclosure Form

 A. **Settlement Statement (HUD-1)**

B. Type of Loan				
1. ☐ FHA 2. ☐ RHS 3. ☐ Conv. Unins. 4. ☐ VA 5. ☐ Conv. Ins.	6. File Number:	7. Loan Number:	8. Mortgage Insurance Case Number:

C. Note: This form is furnished to give you a statement of actual settlement costs. Amounts paid to and by the settlement agent are shown. Items marked "(p.o.c.)" were paid outside the closing; they are shown here for informational purposes and are not included in the totals.

D. Name & Address of Borrower:	E. Name & Address of Seller:	F. Name & Address of Lender:
G. Property Location:	H. Settlement Agent: Place of Settlement:	I. Settlement Date:

J. Summary of Borrower's Transaction		K. Summary of Seller's Transaction	
100. Gross Amount Due from Borrower		**400. Gross Amount Due to Seller**	
101. Contract sales price		401. Contract sales price	
102. Personal property		402. Personal property	
103. Settlement charges to borrower (line 1400)		403.	
104.		404.	
105.		405.	
Adjustment for items paid by seller in advance		**Adjustment for items paid by seller in advance**	
106. City/town taxes to		406. City/town taxes to	
107. County taxes to		407. County taxes to	
108. Assessments to		408. Assessments to	
109.		409.	
110.		410.	
111.		411.	
112.		412.	
120. Gross Amount Due from Borrower		**420. Gross Amount Due to Seller**	
200. Amount Paid by or in Behalf of Borrower		**500. Reductions In Amount Due to seller**	
201. Deposit or earnest money		501. Excess deposit (see instructions)	
202. Principal amount of new loan(s)		502. Settlement charges to seller (line 1400)	
203. Existing loan(s) taken subject to		503. Existing loan(s) taken subject to	
204.		504. Payoff of first mortgage loan	
205.		505. Payoff of second mortgage loan	
206.		506.	
207.		507.	
208.		508.	
209.		509.	
Adjustments for items unpaid by seller		**Adjustments for items unpaid by seller**	
210. City/town taxes to		510. City/town taxes to	
211. County taxes to		511. County taxes to	
212. Assessments to		512. Assessments to	
213.		513.	
214.		514.	
215.		515.	
216.		516.	
217.		517.	
218.		518.	
219.		519.	
220. Total Paid by/for Borrower		**520. Total Reduction Amount Due Seller**	
300. Cash at Settlement from/to Borrower		**600. Cash at Settlement to/from Seller**	
301. Gross amount due from borrower (line 120)		601. Gross amount due to seller (line 420)	
302. Less amounts paid by/for borrower (line 220)	( )	602. Less reductions in amounts due seller (line 520)	( )
303. Cash ☐ From ☐ To Borrower		**603. Cash** ☐ To ☐ From Seller	

The Public Reporting Burden for this collection of information is estimated at 35 minutes per response for collecting, reviewing, and reporting the data. This agency may not collect this information, and you are not required to complete this form, unless it displays a currently valid OMB control number. No confidentiality is assured; this disclosure is mandatory. This is designed to provide the parties to a RESPA covered transaction with information during the settlement process.

L. Settlement Charges

700. Total Real Estate Broker Fees		Paid From Borrower's Funds at Settlement	Paid From Seller's Funds at Settlement
Division of commission (line 700) as follows :			
701. $ to			
702. $ to			
703. Commission paid at settlement			
704.			

800. Items Payable in Connection with Loan				
801. Our origination charge	$	(from GFE #1)		
802. Your credit or charge (points) for the specific interest rate chosen	$	(from GFE #2)		
803. Your adjusted origination charges		(from GFE #A)		
804. Appraisal fee to		(from GFE #3)		
805. Credit report to		(from GFE #3)		
806. Tax service to		(from GFE #3)		
807. Flood certification to		(from GFE #3)		
808.				
809.				
810.				
811.				

900. Items Required by Lender to be Paid in Advance				
901. Daily interest charges from to @ $ /day		(from GFE #10)		
902. Mortgage insurance premium for months to		(from GFE #3)		
903. Homeowner's insurance for years to		(from GFE #11)		
904.				

1000. Reserves Deposited with Lender				
1001. Initial deposit for your escrow account		(from GFE #9)		
1002. Homeowner's insurance	months @ $	per month $		
1003. Mortgage insurance	months @ $	per month $		
1004. Property Taxes	months @ $	per month $		
1005.	months @ $	per month $		
1006.	months @ $	per month $		
1007. Aggregate Adjustment		-$		

1100. Title Charges				
1101. Title services and lender's title insurance		(from GFE #4)		
1102. Settlement or closing fee	$			
1103. Owner's title insurance		(from GFE #5)		
1104. Lender's title insurance	$			
1105. Lender's title policy limit $				
1106. Owner's title policy limit $				
1107. Agent's portion of the total title insurance premium to	$			
1108. Underwriter's portion of the total title insurance premium to	$			
1109.				
1110.				
1111.				

1200. Government Recording and Transfer Charges				
1201. Government recording charges		(from GFE #7)		
1202. Deed $ Mortgage $ Release $				
1203. Transfer taxes		(from GFE #8)		
1204. City/County tax/stamps Deed $ Mortgage $				
1205. State tax/stamps Deed $ Mortgage $				
1206.				

1300. Additional Settlement Charges				
1301. Required services that you can shop for		(from GFE #6)		
1302.	$			
1303.	$			
1304.				
1305.				

1400. Total Settlement Charges (enter on lines 103, Section J and 502, Section K)	

Comparison of Good Faith Estimate (GFE) and HUD-1 Charges		Good Faith Estimate	HUD-1
Charges That Cannot Increase	**HUD-1 Line Number**		
Our origination charge	# 801		
Your credit or charge (points) for the specific interest rate chosen	# 802		
Your adjusted origination charges	# 803		
Transfer taxes	# 1203		

Charges That In Total Cannot Increase More Than 10%		Good Faith Estimate	HUD-1
Government recording charges	# 1201		
	#		
	#		
	#		
	#		
	#		
	#		
Total			
Increase between GFE and HUD-1 Charges		$ or	%

Charges That Can Change		Good Faith Estimate	HUD-1
Initial deposit for your escrow account	# 1001		
Daily interest charges $ /day	# 901		
Homeowner's insurance	# 903		
	#		
	#		
	#		

Loan Terms

Your initial loan amount is	$
Your loan term is	years
Your initial interest rate is	%
Your initial monthly amount owed for principal, interest, and any mortgage insurance is	$ includes ☐ Principal ☐ Interest ☐ Mortgage Insurance
Can your interest rate rise?	☐ No ☐ Yes, it can rise to a maximum of %. The first change will be on and can change again every after . Every change date, your interest rate can increase or decrease by %. Over the life of the loan, your interest rate is guaranteed to never be **lower** than % or **higher** than %.
Even if you make payments on time, can your loan balance rise?	☐ No ☐ Yes, it can rise to a maximum of $
Even if you make payments on time, can your monthly amount owed for principal, interest, and mortgage insurance rise?	☐ No ☐ Yes, the first increase can be on and the monthly amount owed can rise to $. The maximum it can ever rise to is $
Does your loan have a prepayment penalty?	☐ No ☐ Yes, your maximum prepayment penalty is $
Does your loan have a balloon payment?	☐ No ☐ Yes, you have a balloon payment of $ due in years on
Total monthly amount owed including escrow account payments	☐ You do not have a monthly escrow payment for items, such as property taxes and homeowner's insurance. You must pay these items directly yourself. ☐ You have an additional monthly escrow payment of $ that results in a total initial monthly amount owed of $. This includes principal, interest, any mortgage insurance and any items checked below: ☐ Property taxes ☐ Homeowner's insurance ☐ Flood insurance ☐ ☐ ☐

Note: If you have any questions about the Settlement Charges and Loan Terms listed on this form, please contact your lender.

then there must be disclosure of the necessary action to be taken (additional escrow payment or refund).

Problems and Issues With Proposals for Revisions of the RESPA Disclosures

As indicated, a large part of the legislative difficulty with taking action to change RESPA disclosures, which, though lengthy, are not especially complicated conceptually, or to combine RESPA and TILA, arises primarily from the nondisclosure components of RESPA. Although RESPA is a significant disclosure statute, it contains a variety of other provisions that are not information-based protections by their nature. These nondisclosure provisions long have complicated reform suggestions because any discussion of possible changes always raises competitive fears among various current participants in the mortgage-lending process. Smaller companies, for example, sometimes fear that the lobbying efforts of larger companies will overshadow their own work toward any reforms, and that any resulting, significant changes in the marketplace will also be at the expense of their interests. In the past, such concerns have tended to limit political support for any particular reform proposal.

The most controversial nondisclosure aspect of RESPA is Section 8, which prohibits paying any unearned fees to participants in the lending and settlement process, so-called *kickbacks,* in the wording of the act. (RESPA also contains other important nondisclosure provisions governing the management of escrow accounts, one of the original motivations for the act, in Section 10.) Section 8 reads, in part:

> (a) No person shall give and no person shall accept any fee, kickback, or thing of value pursuant to any agreement or understanding, oral or otherwise, that business incident to or a part of a real estate settlement service involving a federally related mortgage shall be referred to any person.

> (b) No person shall give and no person shall accept any portion, split, or percentage of any charge made or received for the rendering of a real estate settlement service in connection with a transaction involving a federally related mortgage loan other than for services actually performed.

This wording immediately raises all sorts of questions about normal business practices. For example, what simple payments for services rendered are right, and what about true volume discounts? Do higher fees paid by lenders to high-volume mortgage producers (brokers), or volume-based discounts from funds providers on wholesale interest rates or settlement services, amount to kickbacks? The attempt by the act and HUD to make, in effect, this part of RESPA self-enforcing, by requiring the disclosure of business arrangements, affiliations, and fee paying among parties, has been highly controversial, to say the least—enough to produce both lengthy, complicated rulemaking, and large amounts of expensive litigation and enforcement efforts. Rulemaking has involved even issues such as whether mortgage lenders may compensate their employees based on origination (referral) volume involving affiliates, and whether there may be fees paid by borrowers to providers of computerized loan origination services (CLOs).[35]

As noted, the interaction of these issues means that revising the act has proven difficult politically. Without issuing an actual broadside to this effect, Congress nonetheless indicated, through statements of members and staff, that real reform would only follow the emergence of a general consensus among industry, consumerists, and government agencies. Extended discussions over longer than a decade failed to produce consensus legislative parameters. The HUD revision proposal of July 2002 would have undertaken significant steps toward reform without legislation, but it was also highly controversial politically. This is the reason why the department withdrew the proposal in 2004 and implemented only a part of it in 2008. Following congressional direction in 2010, the new Bureau of Financial Consumer Protection (BFCP) will pursue the matter again in 2011.

It is easy enough to see how much of the discussion of changes or reforms to RESPA, including the obvious suggestion of combining it with TILA, involves two interconnected questions, only the first of which directly concerns the disclosures themselves: (1) How can a simpler, better, and more useful set of disclosures of credit costs and closing costs be required earlier? 2) How can RESPA accommodate the changing mortgage market, where, over time, the lending and settlement process has tended to become more and more decentralized, but the law potentially questions or prohibits many forms of fee-sharing as possibly illegal "kickbacks."

On the disclosure question (better disclosures earlier), critics of the GFE have maintained, in effect, that there is not enough incentive for providers to be accurate in their GFE. In this view, expecting good faith is not enough; penalties are needed to combat low-ball estimates. To critics, the long-followed approach has, too often, led to significant underestimates of the amounts due and, therefore, to unpleasant surprises at closings. This contention, in turn, has produced discussion about two alternative proposals for change: (1) an approach that would guarantee settlement costs once stated, and (2) continuation of the good-faith approach but only within a specified tolerance to avoid some penalty.[36]

The 2008 revision focused on improving the GFE. It required a much longer disclosure form but also required specific tolerances beyond which the prices of individual settlement services could not rise between the GFE and the final statement of charges. For some, charges the tolerance (in the absence of the "unforeseen circumstances" discussed in the rule) became 10 percent; for others, including significant charges such as lender and broker origination fees, the tolerance for differences became zero (see *Federal Register*, March 14, 2008 and November 17, 2008).

Historically, the chief support for the guarantee approach came from a group of large lending institutions. They maintained that the frequent or bulk purchases of settlement services (such as surveys, title insurance, property inspection) from affiliated service providers or third parties would enable them to provide volume-based low costs for these services, plus guarantees of settlement costs. In their view, consumers typically are only interested in the total and not the components of settlement costs anyway, and the resulting lower costs with a package arrangement produce substantial consumer benefits.[37] They have contended that the bulk purchase of various settlement services enable them to provide lower overall prices and guaranteed costs to all customers, even though they know that they will lose money on some difficult cases, which have led to the surprises of the GFE approach.

Smaller lending institutions and some independent providers of settlement services were less enthusiastic about the guarantee approach because they feared loss of business to larger institutions able to advertise and promote their packages of services and guarantees of price. Consumerists have tended to like the concept of a price guarantee, but they have been skeptical of the claims of the large institutions that any cost savings would be passed on to consumers. Consumerists generally have supported the guarantee concept only if it is combined with a guarantee of interest rates and points. In their view, it is necessary to guarantee prices on the loans, too, to prevent substituting an increase in one area to offset guaranteed prices in the other. For them, the guarantees of rates and points seem to have become more important than improvements in the details or timing aspects of the disclosures.

In any case, many supporters of the guaranteed price concept have argued that this approach is fully feasible only with simultaneous reform of Section 8 of RESPA. They have maintained that changes are necessary to clarify, finally and definitively, what payments are "kickbacks, and what are not. In the view of those favoring changes to RESPA, it would be virtually impossible to package services and guarantee a price without being able to collect that price centrally and distribute parts of it to affiliated and unaffiliated producers of lending and settlement services. Their concern is that distributing revenues in this way could easily be characterized by litigious individuals or groups as illegal kickbacks. Furthermore, *requiring* the use of affiliated service providers, which those favoring changes say might often be necessary to produce the volume to acquire the discounts, has been illegal per se under Section 8 anyway. Class-action suits and criminal penalties for violations, including large fines and possible prison terms, make the question one of more than passing concern to lenders and providers of settlement services. All of this certainly further complicates the packaging of settlement service–guaranteed price approach, although many lenders have nibbled around the edges of the issue of providing some centralized settlement services, to the extent they believe they are able to do so legally.

Nonetheless, in the view of many supporters of change to RESPA, a large part of the difficulty with packaging lending- and settlement-related services, and guaranteeing prices arises simply from uncertainty over the applicability of Section 8. They have contended that Section 8 is based upon an outdated view of the mortgage-lending process. As discussed further below, they believe that mortgage borrowing no longer exemplifies the mechanics of the lending process prevalent when RESPA became law: Then, it was a process involving a consumer and a single institution (like a savings and loan association) that originates, funds, and services all its loans and generally does not have to pay fees to other parties for parts of the process, for example, for loan origination.[38]

Those favoring Section 8 revision argue that, in modern mortgage markets, much of the mortgage-generating process now is unbundled into its components of originating, risk bearing, funding, and servicing. Frequently, each of the components is parceled to specialists in that aspect of the transaction, and each of them requires compensation. With this view in mind, HUD issued a policy statement in March 1999 that such payments were not per se violations of RESPA. Nevertheless, it has been unclear whether and how, in the event of a lawsuit, such payments might be considered kickbacks.

Critics of the status quo maintain that Section 8 simply has not provided sufficiently clear guidance to those who might package settlement services to determine, in advance, whether payments are legal as reimbursement for services actually performed. The fear among lenders has been that if every payment can be characterized by someone as potentially illegal as a kickback, they will likely have to litigate every aspect of the packaging of settlement cost guarantees if the services themselves are provided by shifting groupings of different entities. Consequently, they argue that the consumer benefit of reduced settlement costs, along with improvements in disclosures that might result from reform, depends significantly on clarifications to the rest of RESPA, notably to Section 8.

Historically, in contrast to the guarantee approach, there has been little enthusiasm in any industry segment for the GFE with tolerances approach, with a bit more approval from consumerist observers and the rulewriting agencies. Larger institutions appeared to prefer the guarantee approach (with relief from Section 8) to the tightened GFE with limited tolerances, and the smaller mortgage providers have preferred no change to the GFE that has long been familiar to them.

Required to report legislative recommendations to Congress anyway, the Federal Reserve Board and the Department of Housing and Urban Development recommended in their joint report in 1998 that RESPA be tightened in the area of early disclosures of closing costs. Proposals for changes to the actual substance of the disclosures themselves were limited and largely cosmetic in effect, but the agencies made significant suggestions for the reform of other aspects of RESPA, which were generally not popular. Specifically, under the agencies' recommendations, each lender would have had a choice whether to guarantee closing costs (with Section 8 relief, if they also guaranteed interest rates and points) or a tightened GFE requirement with penalties for substantial underestimates. Industry support for the agencies' recommendations was limited, except among the relatively few large lenders who favored the guarantee approach. In 2008 the multi-year effort finally resulted in a version of the GFE with tolerances approach, with an effective date of New Years Day, 2010.

The Changing Marketplace

From this discussion of the past gridlock over RESPA disclosure reform, it seems clear that any improvement in this area has been closely bound up with the second RESPA issue: How can the old law accommodate changing industry conditions and practices? It appears essentially correct that RESPA is based upon an older model of mortgage lending in which the originating, funding, and servicing of mortgage loans typically took place within a single institution. In that environment, the payments required of consumers and paid to outsiders might be more readily identifiable as questionable practices. Today, however, mortgage lending is much more decentralized and often involves the payment of substantial fees to other, outside parties who are integral parts of the process. In some cases, they may be affiliated with the lender under some definition of affiliation, and in other cases not. All of this in turn raises and highlights the long-standing RESPA bugaboo of how to categorize and disclose affiliations. RESPA already mandates revealing affiliations properly and notifying consumers that purchasing services from affiliates is not required. Such disclosures are increasingly complicated in a modern high-tech world in which many competing firms nonetheless share systems, software, databases, and service providers. Identifying whether a service provider is a vendor and or an affiliate is a process that quickly becomes complex.

Financial institutions, of course, bring the ultimate providers of financial capital together with end users (in the final analysis, both are consumers, but with different financial needs), reducing the transaction costs of the transfer process and making the allocation of resources more efficient.[39] In providing mortgage credit transfers from savers to final users (borrowers), financial institutions supply four important services: origination, risk bearing, funding, and servicing. In 1974, when Congress passed the Real Estate Settlement Procedures Act, the typical mortgage loan was made by a depository institution, which held the loan in its own portfolio. In that case, there usually was no need to pay an originator (except the firm's own employees). Payments to settlement service providers (attorneys, title insurance companies, etc.) were also reasonably straightforward. After the loan was made, it became an asset of the originator who also funded it, bore the risk, and serviced it (*i.e.,* collected payments and the like).

In contrast, today the typical mortgage is originated by one institution (which may or may not service the mortgage), but the asset is held in the portfolio of a different institution, which may or may not bear the risk itself. Ultimately, the structure of a transaction and its cash flows depends (in the past or now) upon its costs. If there is a cost saving to be had from separating the components of a transaction, then there is a market incentive to separate them. That appears to be what has happened (see, for example, Jacobides 2001).

Today, many loans are originated by brokers or employees of mortgage bankers who specialize in this aspect of the process. Initial funding, often, is by a mortgage bank that may service the loan after closing, but typically sells the loan to investors. Much of the funding role, but not servicing, has passed to the large government sponsored enterprises (GSEs), notably Fannie Mae, formerly the Federal National Mortgage Association or FNMA; and Freddie Mac, formerly the Federal Home Loan Mortgage Corporation or FHLMC. Funding of the GSEs has been through the capital markets and includes investors worldwide, which was made abundantly clear in the financial crisis of 2008–2009. Risk bearing depends on the circumstances, but there has been an active market in risk trading, through the sometimes poorly understood development and trading of derivative securities. Clearly, however, mortgage markets are much different than at the time of passage of the original RESPA. Tremendous communications and other technological improvements over the decades has dramatically altered the market possibilities for purchase and sale of receivables, servicing, and risk.

The resulting economic incentives for unbundling in the mortgage production process suggest that there will also be an accompanying incentive for participants to pass fees among themselves, to encourage each of the diverse entities in the intermediation process to participate. Importantly, the lenders that ultimately fund and hold the loans will have an incentive to pay fees to mortgage brokers as the originators of the assets. This is, in fact, often what happens.

The Payment of Fees and Yield Spread Premiums

Lurking within any question of how fees are paid and split among institutional participants in the mortgage process is the underlying question of how consumers advance the fees in the first place. Mortgage loans, as large credit contracts, are expensive for consumers, and they involve a fair amount of paperwork processing and necessary initial expenses, which frequently generate fees.[40] There also may be initial fees paid in exchange for lower subsequent interest rates and monthly payments. Fees for the latter purpose typically are referred to as *points* because they usually are calculated as a certain number of percentage points of the initial loan balance to buy down the interest rate. All of this means that large amounts of money change hands for the typical mortgage loan, often with a significant lump at the outset and smaller lumps each month until repaid (or refinanced). Since the initial fees can be sizeable for a number of reasons, lenders and other market participants have looked for ways to make the patterns of mortgage cash flows more palatable to consumers. These approaches include financing the fees and points as part of the loan advance. This approach tends not to be too controversial, at least if the fees and points are not too large, because it is easy enough for most people to understand. Another method is the indirect payment of the initial amounts by the consumer with direct payment undertaken by the lender through a mechanism known as a *yield spread premium (YSP)*. This method of paying fees tends to be somewhat more controversial because YSPs generally are harder for consumers to understand and appear to be more likely subject to abuses. For this reason, HUD's 2008 RESPA rule revisions also contains provisions for the more extensive disclosure of the mechanics and implications of YSPs.

Actually, neither points nor YSPs are especially difficult to understand. Simplified mathematics of buy-down points was alluded to briefly above in Chapter 5, "The Outlay and Unknown Future Events Issues; Closed-End Credit," notably with some examples in Table 5.2, "Some Additional Examples of APR Calculations." The examples focused only on the APR impact of points (upward, other things equal), and not upon how payment of points might be used to buy down the underlying contract rate. Building upon that earlier discussion, the following discussion reproduces Example 2 from Table 5.2 and illustrates how such a buy-down would work.

Assume for illustration the same basic loan of that transaction, even if unrealistic compared to a real consumer mortgage loan:

With a point paid by consumer in cash at closing:

Simplified, generic, transaction terms:	
Cost of house:	$100,000
Down payment:	$20,000
Contract amount of loan, therefore:	$80,000
Contract simple interest rate:	10%
Maturity of loan:	1 year
Repayment:	Single payment at maturity
Interest on loan, therefore:	$8,000
Other closing costs:	$1,000

$$100{,}000 + 80{,}000 + 1{,}000$$

$$= 20{,}000 + 80{,}000 + 1{,}000 + 800 + (80{,}000 + 8{,}000)*(1+r)^{-1}$$

$$79{,}200 = (88{,}000)*(1+r)^{-1}$$

$$r = (8{,}800/79{,}200) = 11.11 \; percent = APR$$

Notes:
Finance charge: $8,800; Amount financed: $79,200
Consumer's cash out of pocket at closing: $21,800 (down payment, closing costs, and point).

Now suppose that the consumer has available a choice of paying a point now to buy down the interest rate to 9 percent and, therefore, lower the size of future payments. Under these circumstances, the APR calculation would be as follows:

$$100{,}000 + 80{,}000 + 1{,}000$$

$$= 20{,}000 + 80{,}000 + 1{,}000 + 800 + (80{,}000 + 7{,}200)*(1+r)^{-1}$$

$$79{,}200 + (87{,}200)*(1+r)^{-1}$$

$$r = (8{,}000/79{,}200) = 10.1 \; percent = APR$$

Notes:
Finance charge: $8,000; Amount financed: $79,200
Consumer's cash out of pocket at closing: $21,800 (down payment, closing costs, and point).

Thus, through the payment of a point ($800) at the outset, the consumer could lower the contract rate and the future payment. Importantly, by also financing the point into the loan advance, as in Example 3 in Table 5.2 above but not reproduced here, the consumer could also reduce the out-of pocket outlay now, albeit for the repayment of a larger amount later, while only increasing the APR by a small amount (to 10.1 percent).

Besides financing fees into the loan balance, another common method of reducing initial out-of-pocket outlays for consumers arises from the payment of the fees by the lender, therefore making the consumer only indirectly responsible through some other aspect of the loan terms. Lenders might be induced to make the direct payments for the loan fees if they received a yield (APR) slightly higher than the otherwise available market rate. In particular, indirect payments of this sort by consumers can be made through YSPs. These YSPs are payments made by the lenders to services providers, including originators, and taken from the other charges on the loan. Within the legalistic and highly charged RESPA environment, these payments, not surprisingly, have become very controversial.

The YSP approach to paying fees can be attractive to many borrowers because it permits the borrowers, in effect, to pay the closing costs (fees for brokerage, appraisal, title insurance, etc.) over the life of the mortgage through the payment of a slightly higher interest rate rather than in cash at settlement. Thus, the YSP approach manages the fees through a higher rate, whereas financing the fees does the same thing through a larger loan. In either case, the result is a reduced initial cash obligation for the consumer (other things equal) by reducing the amount of cash needed at the settlement. Consequently, like the financing of fees, the YSP approach has been especially attractive to borrowers without sufficient additional cash to pay the fees (that is, in cases in which cash for a larger down payment is not available) and the loan-to-value ratio already approaches the underwriting limit of the lender. It has led to the concept of the no-fee loan in which the broker's compensation comes from the YSP, and therefore, indirectly from the borrower rather than directly. Without the clarification of Section 8 of RESPA, however, the YSP has also produced a lot of controversy and litigation.[41]

It is easy enough to explain how a yield spread premium comes about. A YSP on a mortgage loan is possible whenever the loan is made *above par*. Such a loan arises whenever the cash flow to the lender is greater than necessary to produce the yield the lender requires to make the loan, given current market conditions. Then, the larger cash flow makes the lender willing to pay extra to acquire the loan (in other words, the loan's price is above par). Under the circumstances, the amount of the excess is available for payment to someone else for delivering the loan (or to pay for something else, like other closing costs), while still retaining the lender's willingness to make the loan. Above-par lending is a well-known practice in bond markets, but it is newer in the consumer mortgage area. An example can show how it works.

Returning again to the now-familiar simplified mortgage example, assume again the existence of the lending conditions discussed here and the simple example described in Chapter 5, in the section entitled, "Mortgage Reform and the Annual Percentage Rate, Example 1, "A Plain-Vanilla Mortgage Transaction":

Cost of house: $100,000
Down payment: $20,000
Contract amount of loan, therefore: $80,000
Contract simple interest rate: 10%
Maturity of loan: 1 year
Repayment: Single payment at maturity
Interest, therefore: $8,000
Points: None
Closing costs: $1,000

For solving, again it is necessary to put on the left side everything the consumer receives, and on the right everything the consumer pays. As before, the APR is the rate that discounts the future payments to their present value. Following Example 1 in Chapter 5, the consumer here receives a house worth $100,000, a loan of $80,000, and $1,000 of loan closing services; these amounts go on the left side of the equation. The consumer pays a down payment of $20,000 plus the closing costs of $1,000 immediately in cash, the down payment and the cash from the loan go to the seller, and the consumer then repays the entire loan of $80,000 in one year with interest of $8,000 (that is, the $80,000 loan times the 10-percent contract interest rate). Since the APR unit period of Appendix J to Regulation Z is one year, in this example, the APR equation from Chapter 5 is as follows:

$$\begin{aligned} &\$100,000 + 80,000 + 1,000 \\ &= 20,000 + 80,000 + 1,000 + (80,000 + 8,000)*(1+r)^{-1} \end{aligned} \qquad (A1)$$

and solving this equation for r:

$$\$80,000 = (88,000)*(1+r)^{-1} \qquad (A2)$$

$$r = 8,000/80,000 = 10 \text{ percent} = \text{APR} \qquad (A3)$$

Notes:
Finance charge: $8,000; Amount financed: $80,000
Consumer's cash out of pocket at closing: $21,000 (the down payment and closing costs).

Now suppose that the yield on this loan just satisfies the lender who, therefore, will make this loan, but someone offers the lender an alternative loan that, for the same advance of $80,000 to the consumer today, provides an inflow to the lender in one year from now of $88,800 (that is, a contract rate of 11 percent) instead of $88,000 (10-percent contract rate).[42] The question is, How much additional would the lender be willing to pay out now (the amount of the loan payout now plus any amount paid to anyone else) for the second cash flow (in other words, the amount above par of $80,000)? This amount can be determined by solving the APR/yield equation that just satisfies the lender but in reverse; that is, starting with the yield required by the lender (0.1, or 10 percent) and the new cash flow, calculate the corresponding amount financed (the left side of Equation A2). From the example, this is done as follows:

$$\$X = (88,800)*(1+0.1)^{-1} \tag{A4}$$

$$\$80,727.27 = (88,800)*(1+.1)^{-1} \tag{A5}$$

The difference between $80,000 (the left side of equation A2) and the new left side ($80,727.27 in Equation A5) is the potential YSP, the amount over par available for possible payment to someone else. Subtracting, in the example, this amount is $727.27. An actual example with a real mortgage would look much more complicated because there would be multiple years for discounting, but the mathematical principles would be the same.

Importantly, in this simple example, from the lender's viewpoint, the yield actually received does not change, although the cash outflows and inflows are a bit larger for the above-par loan. For both loans, the lender's yield is 10 percent. From the consumer's standpoint, the transaction is different, however, in that the YSP generates the additional cash payable to someone arising from the consumer's willingness to accept a contract rate over par. The transaction reduces out-of-pocket cash flow now, in exchange for the willingness to generate somewhat larger consumer payments later. The smaller initial cash outflow may be seen in the now-familiar sort of equation given by adjusting Equation A1 above, as follows:

$$\begin{aligned} \$100,000 + 80,000 + 1,000 + 727.27 \\ = 20,000 + 80,000 + 1,000 + (80,000 + 8800)*(1+r)^{-1} \end{aligned} \tag{A1*}$$

and solving this equation for r:

$$\$80,727.27 = (88,800)*(1+r)^{-1} \tag{A2*}$$

$$r = 8072.73/80,727.27 + 10 \text{ percent} = \text{APR} \tag{A3*}$$

Notes:
Finance charge: $8,800; Amount financed: $80,727.27

Consumer's cash out of pocket at closing: $20,272.73 (the down payment and closing costs of $21,000, less yield spread premium paid to borrower for payment to someone else).

The difficulty with YSPs is that, although they may be used to direct compensation to the brokers and other service providers for services rendered, there also is the potential for consumers not to understand the intricacies of the transaction and simply end up paying more to loan originators. This would happen if the originators who receive the YSP do not use them to offset any direct payments received from the consumer, and simply use it to extract more money from customers. Consumers often pay closing costs directly, but they may also enter into an above-par loan to pay all or part of the fees, thereby permitting more fees to flow to third parties and less out of their own pockets for closing costs. YSPs may not pose difficulties in many transactions, especially in segments of the markets that are sufficiently competitive and borrowers are well informed, but they may prove expensive to consumers in other parts of mortgage markets in which the competition is less intense and consumers may not effectively resist the possibility of higher total expenditures.

It is not clear that disclosures focusing on the mechanics of YSPs will solve the problem; the significant study in this area suggests the contrary. In a large experimental study aimed specifically at the YSP disclosure issue, Lacko and Pappalardo (2004) gave consumer subjects sets of hypothetical disclosures of YSPs and found that requiring them may well make the quality of consumer decisions in this area worse rather than better.

The 2002 RESPA reform proposed by HUD would have required mortgage brokers to disclose YSPs, but not direct lenders. In an experimental study, Lacko and Papalardo investigated some likely effects of the proposal. They gave treatment and control groups cost disclosures for hypothetical mortgages of the sort that would be required by brokers and by lenders under the proposed YSP rule. In treatment groups, participants received cost disclosures with YSP information (*i.e.*, such as broker originations). The control groups received identical disclosures but without the YSP information (*i.e.*, such as lender originations under the proposal).

When then presented with loans that had different costs, participants receiving YSP information were significantly less likely to identify less expensive loans than participants in control groups not receiving the YSP information. When presented with loans that had the same costs, participants receiving YSP information were less likely than the control group participants to recognize that the cost was the same. Furthermore, by far, most participants receiving YSP information believed that the broker loans were more expensive than loans from the lender (which did not disclose a YSP). It appeared that, when given YSP information, the participants were more likely to focus on it rather than on total cost.

From these findings, Lacko and Papparlado concluded not only that the disclosure of YSPs may well make consumer decisions in this area worse rather than better, but also possibly inhibit competition between brokers and lenders. According to their summary (Lacko and Pappalardo 2004, p. ES-1):

> This study of over 500 recent mortgage customers in an experimental setting finds that the mortgage broker compensation disclosure proposed by the Department of Housing and Urban Development (HUD) is likely to confuse consumers, cause a significant proportion to choose loans that are more expensive than the available alternatives, and create a substantial consumer bias against broker loans, even when the broker loans cost the same or less than direct lender loans…. Other components of HUD's RESPA reform proposal are far more beneficial.

Disposition of the Reform Proposal of 2002

Despite all of these difficulties and controversies that have dogged RESPA and any potential changes for decades, HUD issued its remarkable reform document for public comment in July 2002. The proposal was very detailed in every aspect. Despite the length and complicated details, its essence was easy enough to digest. (An extended discussion of the details is available in US Department of Housing and Urban Development (2002a, 2002b.) As indicated, some parts of it survived in the 2008 rulemaking.

First of all, the proposal, as released for comment, would have required the disclosure of a new method of reporting the broker's compensation for the origination services undertaken. Specifically, the proposal required the reporting of any payment by a lender to a broker, including a YSP, as a credit to the borrower. This would make calculating the total of the broker's compensation easy, and it would have to appear in the RESPA documentation (GFE and settlement statement,

HUD-1), as the sum of the payments by the consumer for this purpose. In addition, any discount amounts (points) paid by the consumer to reduce the interest rate would have to appear in the necessary documentation as payments by the consumer dollar-for-dollar to the lender, and none of it could be kept by the broker without these disclosures. In this way, both the broker's total compensation and the source and dispersal of discounts and surpluses from amounts due or arising from the lender (points and YSPs) would be accounted for and transparent. No longer could the YSP somehow disappear into a broker or lender's pocket as a largely hidden charge, without any trace (at least without one disclosed to the consumer). These provisions survived in the rule implemented.

Second, the proposal would have replaced the old required GFE of closing costs due three days after a mortgage application with a choice for mortgage originators between two approaches to firmer and more complete sets of new requirements for disclosures. One choice for originators was disclosing a revised GFE with a scale of strict tolerances on the components of the estimates, ranging downward to zero tolerance on the most important components, such as the broker's or lender's origination charges. (A lengthier summary of the HUD proposal for revisions to the GFE is in Table B.6, "Some Elements of the HUD Proposal for Revisions to the Good Faith Estimate and Establishing a Guaranteed Mortgage Package Under RESPA, July 2002.") The stricter GFE also survived the final cut.

The other choice for mortgage originators would have allowed lenders and other loan originators (such as brokers) to package a loan and a set of settlement services together, and offer them to borrowers as a package, at a guaranteed price. The originators willing to provide a mortgage loan with both a guaranteed interest rate and a guaranteed cost for a complete package of settlement services would then have been able to take advantage of new safe-harbor immunity from the anti-fee-sharing (kickback) provisions of Section 8 of RESPA in building the package from affiliated and unaffiliated services providers. The availability of the package would have served in lieu of a GFE for those loan–settlement service packages that met the strict requirements for the safe harbor, but this part did not survive.

When issued, the proposal seemed like a large step forward in the history of RESPA. HUD argued its views of the potential benefits strongly (see United States Department of Housing and Urban Development 2002b): (1) improvements in the welfare of individual consumers able to reduce

Table B.6 Some Elements of the HUD Proposal for Revisions to the Good-Faith Estimate and Establishing a Guaranteed Mortgage Package Under RESPA, July 2002

I. Addressing mortgage broker compensation and lender payments to brokers:
 1. Inform the borrower that mortgage brokers and other loan originators do not offer loans from all funding sources and cannot guarantee the lowest price or best terms available in the market.
 2. Explain to the borrower the option of paying settlement costs through the use of lender payments based on higher interest rates, or reducing the interest rate by paying the lender additional amounts at settlement.
 3. Disclose the loan originator's fees, including the mortgage broker's and lender's total charges to the borrower.
 4. Require, in transactions originated by mortgage brokers, that all payments from a lender other than the par value of the loan (including yield spread premiums [YSPs], servicing release premiums, and all other payments from lenders), be reported on the good-faith estimate (GFE) and the Form HUD-1 settlement statement as a lender payment to the borrower, and any discount points charged to the borrower must equal the discount in the price of the loan paid by the lender and be reported on the GFE and the Form HUD-1 as borrower payments to the lender.
II. Improving the GFE:
 1. Include an interest-rate quote in the form of the mortgage loan's note rate and annual percentage rate (APR), and notification of any prepayment penalties.
 2. Disclose the subtotals of the major categories of settlement costs to borrowers to eliminate the proliferation of fees by individual settlement services providers, and allow the borrowers to focus on and compare major fees.
 3. Provide additional shopping information for borrowers that includes a breakdown of lender and broker origination charges, title insurance, and title agent charges; and inform the borrower of lender-required and selected services, and those third-party services that can be shopped for by the borrower.
III. New rules for providing the GFE:
 1. Clarify the information necessary to qualify as an application requiring a GFE.
 2. Limit the fees paid by borrowers for the GFE, if any, to the amounts necessary to provide the GFE itself and exclude amounts used to defray later appraisal or underwriting charges.
 3. Require that loan originators not exceed the amounts reported on the GFE regarding their total compensation, lender-required and selected services, and third-party services, and government charges through settlement (absent unforeseeable and extraordinary circumstances).
 4. Require that the loan originators set upper limits or tolerances for specified major settlement charges.
 5. Clarify that the loan originators can make arrangements with third-party settlement service providers to lower prices for their customers, provided these prices and any charges are reflected accurately on the GFE and are not marked up.

(continued)

Table B.6   Some Elements of the HUD Proposal for Revisions
to the Good-Faith Estimate and Establishing a Guaranteed Mortgage
Package Under RESPA, July 2002 *(cont'd)*

IV. Inclusions in a guaranteed mortgage package (GMP) that can qualify for a
safe harbor from Section 8 violation:

    1. A guaranteed package price for a comprehensive package of loan
origination and virtually all other settlement services required by the lender
to close the mortgage (including, without limitation, all application,
origination, and underwriting services except hazard insurance, per diem
interest, and escrow deposits);

    2. A mortgage loan with an interest-rate guarantee either when the GMP
agreement is given or varying prior to borrower lock-in, only pursuant to
verifiable market changes evident from an observable and verifiable index.

Source: Department of Housing and Urban Development (2002a), as published in *Federal
Register*, July 29, 2002, p. 49136.

their costs of mortgage-settlement services; (2) improved understanding of
YSPs and the process of fee payment to mitigate abuses; and (3) increased
market competitiveness and reduced chance of monopoly pricing due to
the shopping improvements allowed by packaging. Elements of this position also survived, although, as noted above, the study by Lacko and
Pappalardo (2004) raised some questions about the efficacy of the specific
form of the YSP approach. The 2008 reform does not resolve questions
about the relationship between RESPA and TILA, each with their anomalies in the mortgage area, raised by Congress and others in the 1990s.

Conclusion

So far, much of the discussion here of the debate over the need for
reform of RESPA, or how the law would be more effective if somehow
combined with TILA, skirts around the core question: To what extent
are TILA and RESPA useful or not to consumers? A lot of the discussion
has circled around the question of how to make more accurate disclosures available earlier without ever answering (or sometimes even
asking) the question of whether consumers even use the disclosures and
how. As a disclosure regime, RESPA is similar to TILA; it may have
many potential objectives, but these are rarely mentioned, beyond the
clear intent to be an aid to shopping. Consequently, there has been a
good deal of discussion over the years about why the complete TILA
and RESPA disclosures are not available until the final settlement of
the transaction, a situation that the 2002 proposal for RESPA reform

was intended to revise. As discussed more fully above in Chapter 7, "The Rubber Meets the Road: Evaluating the Effectiveness of the Truth in Lending Act," shopping is only one of the many potential goals of required disclosures. Other objectives include making markets more competitive, and adequately recording the minute details of the final agreement for tax preparation and other purposes. Even though some RESPA disclosures are needed for shopping, it does not follow that all RESPA disclosures need to be perfectly accurate at an early stage in order to satisfy the goals of disclosure.

Further, by itself, fee sharing among the participants in the mortgage-lending process is not necessarily sinister or more costly to the ultimate borrower. For that matter, the existence of a yield spread is not necessarily sinister. The premium can save the consumer some out-of-pocket cash which may be very beneficial and well worth the added interest expense, especially if the consumer expects to sell the property or refinance the loan rapidly and the cost is not be very high. An important issue is the usefulness of additional disclosures. Although, in the abstract, it is difficult to argue that more information is ever bad, in the context of shopping, information overload can be more harm than help to the consumer. One important study in this area suggests that new information about the mechanics of YSPs may well compromise the usefulness of disclosures overall. More information on unfamiliar concepts may well make decision-making worse.

Regarding the appropriateness of fee sharing, economic theory suggests that, in a competitive market with full information, passing indirect fees back and forth among participants in the lending process must be less costly; if it is not, the transaction would be structured differently. In other words, in a competitive market, if the market incentives do not favor unbundling the components of a mortgage transaction, we would not see the long-term trend toward the practice of passing fees. Thus, researchable questions include: Are mortgage markets for consumers competitive and what are the information conditions? A further, policy-oriented question involves mortgage production costs and whether fees are appropriate for services rendered, and are not unearned kickbacks. The issue here is to identify the circumstances under which YSPs (or some portion of them) are or are not kickbacks under RESPA.[43] A third question involves the costs, benefits, and, in general, the role of YSPs in consumer mortgage markets.

The contention that technology and a changing mortgage market has produced a greater incentive for the unbundling of the components of a mortgage loan leads, then, to the question whether Section 8 of RESPA has become archaic. If it is difficult to pass fees among participants in the process, Section 8 could be a barrier to the efficient operation of mortgage markets. Indeed, some observers have argued that this has already happened (see, for example, a discussion by Kosin 1995). Under these circumstances, the anti-kickback provisions of RESPA, in the past, though designed with the intent of protecting consumers, could well do the opposite by making markets less competitive and less efficient. Certainly, government should do what it can to promote competition, and exercise care that the policies do not present blockages to efficient processes.

In contrast, the argument to retain this prohibition is that, without Section 8, mortgage lenders would have little or no incentive to provide or find low-cost originators (brokers) or settlement service providers for customers if mortgage markets are not competitive or adequately informed. Instead, they could raise prices (interest rates and fees such as points), and compensate affiliates and others at will with the overages. Ultimately, this argument concerning information is based on the presumption of a lemons dynamic. (See Chapter 3, "Why Disclosures?") The claim is that, in the absence of perfect information, the value to buyers of products available in the marketplace will be lower than the price. This is the *reverse competition argument* also made for other areas of consumer financial services (for example, the sale of credit insurance without price controls). Essentially, it argues that the suppliers of a service to a reseller will compete to provide the highest price for resale.

As with other manifestations of the reverse competition hypothesis, its existence in the market for settlement services depends on either the absence of competition in the provision of the services directly to ultimate users of the services (consumers) or the unavailability of information about alternatives. Either the providers must be able to coerce customers to accept unfavorable arrangements (because of insufficient competition and the absence of real alternatives for consumers) or the customers accept a less than best arrangement because they do not know any better. Of the two possibilities for mortgage markets, the latter seems the more realistic possibility. But, with TILA and RESPA in place, it is certainly also difficult to argue that prices are unknowable without undertaking extensive search efforts. More often, the contention is that so much information is readily available to consumers that they pay too little attention because they suffer from information overload. If so, it argues that some reasonable simplification of the whole process would aid shopping.

Truth in Savings

Like many other consumer protections in the financial area, the Truth in Savings Act is primarily a disclosure statute. It mandates that financial institutions provide information about the interest rates and fees on deposit accounts in specific forms and at certain times. The act requires that each covered institution maintain a schedule of such rates and fees and that it disclose the rates and fees to the consumer before the opening of an account. (An inventory of the required disclosures is in Table A.1).

The passage of the act was the culmination of decades of single-minded lobbying for additional disclosures on deposit accounts by a relatively small group of dedicated advocates. Although financial institutions already provided disclosures of deposit account terms at the time the act became law, most did not completely satisfy the specific requirements of the act as passed or its implementing regulation, Federal Reserve Board Regulation DD (12 CFR Part 230).[44] Consequently, when compliance became mandatory on June 21, 1993, the new Truth in Savings Act and the new regulation likely caused virtually every depository institution in the United States to change at least some of its practices for consumer deposit accounts. Although there is relatively little research on the impacts of truth in savings, some evidence is available on both the costs of implementation and the impact of the new law. Since the implementation of truth in savings, and unlike TILA, there have been relatively few changes to its regulatory regime.

The Costs of Implementation

In order to determine the effects of the new law on the practices and costs of affected institutions, the Federal Reserve Board surveyed thousands of institutions concerning their practices with respect to deposit accounts before the law and their costs of implementing the necessary changes after passage (see Elliehausen and Lowrey 1997). Although TISA is primarily a disclosure statute, it also contains an important substantive provision affecting the practices of some institutions: It requires that institutions calculate interest payments on the full balance of funds in a consumer's deposit account. With this provision, the new law outlawed the investable balances and low balances methods of paying interest, under which some institutions paid interest only on the portion in excess of the reserves on the account required by government policy, or the lowest amount in an account during the computation period.

Under the Truth in Savings Act, depository institutions must pay interest on the full balance in a consumer's account, using a daily balance method of calculation. Consequently, as part of their survey to gather cost information, the FRB also examined the frequency of various banking practices associated with deposit accounts, including balance computation methods.

The survey of banks found that before TISA, about 90 percent of the reporting banks were using the daily or average daily balance methods for the four main types of interest-bearing deposit accounts (interest-bearing checking, money market deposit, statement savings, and passbook savings accounts). Only about 10 percent of banks were found to be using the investable balances method at that time, and only a small fraction were using the low balance or other methods that became illegal. Although banks using the investable balances or low balances approaches had to change their practices in this area, most banks did not. Therefore, the biggest impact of the new law for most banks involved required changes in the methods of disclosures made to consumers.

In the survey on disclosure practices, banks were asked whether, before TISA, they had provided consumers with the disclosures that subsequently were required by the law and regulation. Survey findings revealed that before TISA, banks commonly had provided customers with written statements of the terms on new accounts. For interest-bearing checking accounts, more than 95 percent of all banks and 98 percent of large banks provided such statements (Elliehausen and Lowrey 1997, Table 3). Banks generally did not include in the statements all of the terms specified in the regulation, however. Well over 75 percent of the banks included most of the terms, but some terms were not commonly included. Fewer than 60 percent of banks included the rate of simple interest, for example, and only 22 percent included the effective yield in the precise form required by the new law. Only 16 percent of banks provided, in new account disclosures, all of the account terms subsequently required by the regulation.

Findings for savings accounts were very similar. Survey results indicated that most banks provided written disclosures for new savings accounts (especially large banks), but that only about 20 percent of banks provided written notice for all the terms subsequently required by truth in savings (Elliehausen and Lowrey 1997, Table 4). Findings for disclosures on new time deposits and on adverse changes on existing accounts were very similar. Thus, although most banks were already providing disclosures, they had to review their disclosure documents, and change their materials and practices to conform with the new regulatory requirements.

The survey evidence indicated these changes were costly. Even if the bank had been providing written disclosures that contained all of the information required by TISA, the institution undoubtedly incurred expenses because of requirements concerning the timing of disclosures, rules about advertising, formulas for computing yields, and require- ments for documentation, which the bank had to learn about and imple- ment. Managers had to review all documents for all varieties of all types of accounts and make changes as necessary. Products had to be altered, marketing programs reconsidered, and employees retrained, all of which were expensive.

Elliehausen and Lowrey (1997) reported that the average bank incurred $29,390 in start-up costs for truth in savings. Average start-up costs were $16,110 at small banks, $25,860 at medium-sized banks and $194,270 at large banks. Summing over all banks, they estimated start up costs of $337 million for banks and another $80 million for savings insti- tutions (not including credit unions that were regulated differently). The most expensive compliance activities, according to the survey, were data processing and information systems charges, which accounted for about 38 percent of the total. Management and in-house legal expenses for reviewing the regulation and existing products, changing account vari- eties and terms as necessary, and auditing compliance accounted for about 18 percent of costs. The next largest cost categories were training (14 percent of total costs) and redesign and replacement of disclosure forms (12 percent).

The statistical analysis of a cost function revealed that there were economies of scale in compliance related to truth in savings. A 10 percent higher number of consumer accounts was associated with the higher costs of implementing the regulation of 5.6 percent for small banks, 6.0 percent for medium-sized banks, and 6.5 percent for large banks. Thus, all banks accrued higher expenses associated with truth in savings if they had more accounts, but the increase was less than proportional, regardless of bank size. This is not especially surprising, given that much of the expense is related to managerial and legal expenses that are central overhead sorts of costs. It is also consistent with studies of consumer credit compliance costs (see Murphy 1980, Schroeder 1985, and Elliehausen 1998).

Analysis of the truth in savings cost survey data also produced the interesting finding that start-up costs for complying with the new disclosure law were insensitive to the extensiveness of the necessary changes. Banks incurred costs in implementing the regulation regardless of how extensively they had to change their practices. Again, this fact seems to arise from the nature of the problem at hand. Banks incurred legal, managerial, accounting, data processing, and printing costs, even if the changes they had to make were small. The finding of the insensitivity of costs incurred to the extent of the changes necessary suggests that a general regulatory requirement to alter an infrequent practice may impose costs on all institutions, not just those that must make major adjustments in practices. It also argues against a policy of making frequent minor revisions to regulations; historically, such changes have been an important feature of TILA, a law and regulatory regime that changes almost every year. An alternative policy is to delay minor regulatory adjustments until a number of them have accumulated. Thus, less frequent major revisions may reduce implementation costs by allowing the banks to exploit economies in changing their practices. Further study of implementation and adjustment costs would be useful to validate this conclusion.

Impacts on Consumers

Research on the impact of truth in savings on consumers is quite limited. Furthermore, it seems unlikely that the law has resulted in large changes in consumer knowledge or behavior, in light of findings of the survey of the banks, which showed that the banks were already disclosing much of the required information, albeit not necessarily in the required forms and formats. That survey found that most institutions already provided written disclosures of the account terms before passage of truth in savings, even though the law necessitated changes in form and content.

To record a benchmark, the FRB surveyed consumers about their experiences with deposit accounts before the effective date of TISA, much as it had done before TILA, more than twenty years before. Similarly, the FRB also undertook a second survey about a year after the effective date of the act. Unlike TILA, the truth in savings survey results have remained unpublished, however, largely because they do not report the sorts of substantial changes found 15 months after TILA (see Board of Governors of the Federal Reserve System 1970 and 1971 and Shay and Schober 1973 for the findings about TILA). This does not seem especially surprising, given that changes in institutional practices were also much less extreme following TISA.

In April 1993, the Board staff added questions to the *Survey of Consumer Attitudes* of the Survey Research Center, University of Michigan, to obtain information on consumer experiences with disclosure practices for deposit accounts before the mandatory date for compliance with Regulation DD, June 21, 1993. Consumers were questioned about changes in account terms, new account openings, and information problems with deposit accounts in the previous twelve months, as well as general attitudes toward the information provided on deposit accounts by financial institutions.

The survey responses suggest consumers knew that written disclosures were common, and that consumer satisfaction with deposit account disclosure practices was high in the year before enactment of TISA. About three of four respondents who experienced changes in deposit account terms in the previous twelve months recalled receiving a written notice of the change. Eighty percent or more respondents opening new deposit accounts in the previous twelve months reported receiving written information on account terms; even higher percentages of respondents were satisfied with both the quantity and clarity of the information received (written and oral) on these occasions. Fewer than two percent of respondents mentioned information problems on any of their family's own deposit accounts in the previous year; only about three percent reported cases of what they considered to be misleading advertising at institutions in which they did not have accounts. Finally, when asked about the information practices of financial institutions generally, about three of four respondents said that financial institutions generally provide enough information about interest rates and fees for deposit accounts, and nearly nine of ten respondents said that obtaining additional information on terms is relatively easy.

Respondents were also asked about the ease of comparing interest rates paid by different institutions. About 64 percent thought that such comparisons were relatively easy. Those who thought that comparing interest rates was difficult most frequently mentioned the number of choices as a reason for difficulty, but some noted different methods of calculating interest that they believed to be misleading. This sort of complaint was among the targets of the Truth in Savings Act and might reasonably be expected to decline upon implementation of the law. The new act contained restrictions on certain methods of calculating interest and requirements for the standardized disclosure of yield and fees.

The second set of consumer survey questions (fielded after TISA had been in effect for about a year) asked about respondents' experiences in the previous twelve months with several areas regulated by TISA. Specifically, respondents were asked about changes in the terms of any of their deposit accounts, openings of new deposit accounts, maturation of certificates of deposit, problems with disclosures for respondents' own deposit accounts, and problems with perceived inaccurate or misleading advertising for deposit accounts. This information was collected for each of three different types of accounts: checking accounts, money market deposit or savings accounts, and certificates of deposit. In addition, several questions in the surveys gathered respondents' opinions on the ease or difficulty of obtaining and using information on deposit account terms.

Responses to the two surveys provide some information on how truth in savings may have affected consumers' experiences with deposit account disclosures. Observed differences cannot be attributed conclusively to implementation of the disclosure law, however. Other events (such as changes in general economic conditions or competition in local markets) occurring between the dates of the two surveys might have altered institutions' policies for deposit accounts and affected consumers' experiences and attitudes.

Despite this qualification, a few conclusions on the effects of the law seem reasonable. Consumers reported noticing only small increases in the frequency of written disclosures and notices after the law. Satisfaction with the quantity and quality of information on deposit account terms, already very high before truth in savings, did not increase or increased by only a very small amount for most types of accounts. A notable exception was a moderate increase in the receipt of written and oral information on the renewals of certificates of deposit. This suggests that required TISA notices of upcoming maturity may also have stimulated owners of certificates of deposit to ask questions rather than merely passively allowing their certificates to renew. TISA may also have reduced complaints of misleading advertising, most likely because of the law's restrictions on the use of the term "free checking." Reports from consumers suggest that truth in savings did not, however, appear to make comparisons of interest rates any easier for many of them. The problems mentioned most frequently, both before and after the law, were the inherent complexity of the information and number of choices, not the availability of information.

Since its implementation, TISA has been relatively noncontroversial, probably because it has changed little and regulated institutions integrated the requirements into their systems so long ago that they have been the norm as long as many people can remember. There have been only a few amendment proposals during these years (apart from some minor changes in 1998 due to minor statutory amendments in 1996 and a regulatory revision to permit the electronic delivery of disclosures if the customer agrees).

The first of the more substantive amendments involved a fairly technical series of proposals concerning the mathematical calculation of the annual percentage yield (APY) for time deposit accounts that make periodic payments to holders rather than compounding the interest until paying it at maturity. This proposal went through a number of stages of proposal and public comment 1993–1998. The second substantive amendment (2004–2005) involved changes in the advertising provisions and periodic statement requirements for those institutions promoting to consumers the possibility of writing checks against insufficient funds, and then collecting fees from the consumers for any such checks that the institution clears. In promotions, banks offering this service typically refer to it as *courtesy overdraft protection* or *bounced check protection*, but it often is referred to more generically simply as *bounce protection*. The argument for amending Regulation DD was that some consumers might think of this service as a line of credit and not realize that fees were involved, or they might underestimate the cost of bounce protection. The initial proposal would have covered all institutions, but the adopted amendment covered only those institutions that promote the bounce protection service in some way. Amendments in 2008 tightened the requirements further and extended the disclosures.

Implementing both of these sets of amendments involved costs for the institutions affected, but neither of them affected so many accounts, at so many institutions, in such a serious way that they became very controversial. Since their scope was quite limited, they also likely did not influence consumer understanding or behavior very significantly either. Overall, TISA has not proven to be anywhere near as complicated or controversial as TILA. Generally declining interest rates on deposit accounts over most of the period following implementation of the regulation likely had much to do with this outcome.

Electronic Fund Transfer Act

Among the consumer protection laws designated in the first part of Table A.1 as information-based protections, the Electronic Fund Transfer Act (EFTA) is probably the one that relies least on its consumer disclosure provisions to address its protection goals.[45] The list of disclosure requirements in this act is actually fairly extensive, but over time its nondisclosure (or substantive) requirements have tended to become relatively more important than the disclosures. This leaves the EFTA, in effect, as only a borderline information-based protection.

The EFTA entered the corps of financial regulatory requirements in stages, beginning on February 8, 1979. This was the effective date for statutory restrictions on the issuance of unsolicited access devices, *i.e.,* debit and ATM (automated teller machine) cards and new federal limitations on consumers' liability for unauthorized electronic fund transfers (EFTs). The Federal Reserve Board's Regulation E that fully implemented the rest of the law (12 CFR Part 205) became effective May 10, 1980. The new act and regulation governed most electronic transfers of funds into or out of accounts intended for personal, family, or household purposes, including telephone-initiated transfers. It specifically excluded transfers originated with paper devices such as checks, and it did not cover transfers involving securities or commodities and regulated by the Securities and Exchange Commission (SEC) or the Commodity Futures Trading Commission (CFTC). It also did not encompass automatic transfers within a single institution (for example, internal automatic shifts of funds from a savings account to a checking account) or trust accounts.

As passed by Congress and implemented by the Federal Reserve Board, the EFTA addresses electronic transfer issues from a variety of directions. First, of course, it specifies disclosures, beginning with the requirements for the disclosure of the terms and conditions of the service. These disclosures are lengthy and of two basic types. The first involves notifying consumers about normal processing of EFT transactions: the types and limits of permissible EFTs, the rights to receive records of EFTs, the fees for EFT services, the conditions for giving information to third parties, and a requirement for advance notice of any adverse changes to account terms (unless the change concerns a matter of security of the EFT system). Requirements in this grouping also include information about the procedures for notifying consumers of arrivals at the depository of preauthorized credits to an account (the electronic delivery of pension benefits or dividends on corporate stocks, for example).

The second kind of disclosures concerns informing consumers about rights and procedures if something goes wrong with the account or an EFT. These disclosures included liability limits for unauthorized EFTs, the telephone number for reporting theft or loss of an access device, a description of error-resolution procedures, a description of stop-payment procedures, a description of the institution's business days, and a discussion of the institution's liability to a consumer for failing to make or to stop payment on an EFT.

Third, the act requires that institutions provide consumers with records of every electronic transaction, so that it is easy to understand their financial condition and reconcile the inflows and outflows. There are requirements for paper receipts for each transaction the consumer initiates electronically, (for example, ATM withdrawals), as well as for mandatory monthly account statements from the consumer's depository institution for any month in which there is an electronic transfer in an account. The paper transaction receipt is to have account, transaction, and location information on it. The periodic statements are to include listing of all EFTs, all payees, and all fees charged.

Turning to the substantive requirements, the act regulates distribution of unsolicited EFT access devices. Distinct from the outright prohibition of unsolicited credit cards by TILA, the EFTA permits the unsolicited distribution of ATM cards, but the card cannot be validated for actual use without the intended consumer's permission. This necessitates a separate step, including consumer identification.

The law also provides for error-resolution procedures. There were timing rules for depository institutions to respond to, investigate, and resolve allegations of errors concerning electronic funds transfers and to notify consumers of the outcome of the process. It has turned out that the disclosure of these procedures has been much less important in the scheme of consumer protection than the requirement that the institution maintain them in the first place.

The EFTA also specifies liability limitations for consumers experiencing an unauthorized transfer. A consumer's maximum liability for a loss associated with an unauthorized EFT depends upon how quickly the consumer notifies the institution of the possibility of an unauthorized transaction. In most cases, the loss would be limited to fifty dollars, although higher amounts are possible under some circumstances.

There is little available evidence specifically concerning the usefulness of the disclosures required under the EFTA and Regulation E. Limited survey evidence suggests, in fact, there is little awareness of so much as the existence of this federal law, which is not to say that it has been ineffective.

To examine these issues, the Federal Reserve Board commissioned some surveys of consumers on these topics in the first decade or so after the effective date of Regulation E. The surveys found that the prevalence and usage of EFT features on deposit accounts increased sharply over the years from 1981 to 1990, but not the frequency of reported account errors. In 1981, fewer than half of domestic families reported holding a deposit account with an EFT feature, but this proportion had risen to 69 percent by 1990 (Table B.7, line 2). Only a small proportion of consumers reported an error on their accounts, less than ten percent in each year (Table B.7, line 3).

When questioned concerning knowledge of notices of error resolution procedures, only about three-fifths of account holders with an EFT feature even recalled receiving such a notice, despite mandatory periodic distribution beginning in 1980 (Table B.7, line 4). An even smaller proportion claimed to know that a federal law concerning billing errors exists, which dropped to only about 10 percent or less in the later surveys (Table B.7, line 5). Both of these proportions also were low among those who claimewd to have experience an EFT error of some sort (Table B.7, lines 8 and 9).[46]

Table B.7   Consumers' Experience with Electronic Funds Transfer Features on Deposit Accounts 1981–1990 (Percent)

	1981	1983	1990
Respondents:			
1. With deposit accounts	87	90	92
2. With deposit accounts with an electronic funds transfer (EFT) feature	47	62	69
Respondents with deposit accounts: with an EFT Feature:			
3. Reporting an error	8	6	8
4. Aware of notice of error-resolution procedures	61	54	57
5. Aware of existence of a federal law concerning error resolution	20	10	4
Percent of error cases:			
6. Complaint made to institution	92	91	88
7. Did nothing	8	9	6
Percent of respondents reporting an EFT error:			
8. Aware of notice of error-resolution procedures	48	50	76
9. Aware of existence of a federal law concerning error resolution	28	15	4
Percent of error cases in which a complaint was made:			
10. Satisfied with outcome	85	82	77

Source: Surveys of Consumers, various years.

Consumers seem to have had considerable success in working out the problems associated with electronic transactions, a success that is probably more important than whether they understand federal laws and mandatory procedures. Among those reporting EFT errors, the most common response was to complain to the institution involved, with approximately 90 percent of error cases generating this not-surprising result (Table B.7, line 6). A few respondents reported not doing anything about the problem (Table B.7, line 7), which calls into question whether they really identified an account error as opposed to an error of their own. A few consumers reported other actions, such as closing their accounts.

Most important, of those who took action by complaining, most reported satisfaction with the outcome (Table B.7, line 10). This suggests that error-resolution procedures for EFTs worked pretty well, even if little of the credit for this outcome accrues to the required disclosures. Of the remaining unsatisfied consumers, undoubtedly some unknown portion learned that the error was their own, not that of the institution; these consumers were probably not destined to be any happier for having been given an explanation.

Over the years, the EFTA and its disclosure regulation have triggered little controversy. (A substantive amendment in 2010 concerning the pricing and electronic routing of debit card transactions is highly controversial.) In the disclosure area, neither the act nor regulation has needed much amendment, despite occasional updating for changed circumstances. Amendments to the regulation over recent decades have been mostly of three types: (1) clarification of the relationship of the regulation to needs-based electronic benefits transfers programs under the auspices of federal, state, and local governments (generally exempting these agencies); (2) the update and clarifications of certain exemptions in the regulation for small institutions and activities regulated by other agencies (such as the SEC and or CFTC); 3) some updates associated with new methods of electronic delivery of consumer disclosures. Included in the latter are changes to Regulation E in 2001, mandating the disclosure of fees for using an ATM, either on the ATM screen or on paper at the ATM, before the customer is committed to completing the transactions and, in 2009, concerning the fee implications of overdrafting deposit accounts using ATMs.

Notes

Chapter 1

1. One of the problems with the Truth in Lending Act (TILA), however, was that it established more than one way to calculate the finance charge underlying the APR. This issue is discussed in Chapter 4.

2. In Senate questioning that year, he said he had held this view for "over fifty years" (see US Senate 1967, p. 44). The economics department at the University of Chicago was also the academic home of the individual frequently receiving credit as the father of the economics of information, George J. Stigler (1911–1991). Stigler, however, was more of a kindred academic visionary, rather than political ally, of Douglas.

3. Strictly speaking, the term *usury law* in the United States applies only to rate ceilings on interest for the loan of money and not for the purchase of goods and services using credit. Rate ceilings on the latter kinds of consumer credit are contained in *retail installment sales laws*. Except in specialized legal usage, the distinction is not necessary and the term usury laws is used here for both. For an interesting discussion of the differences in the historical growth of lending and financing institutions under the two types of laws, see Calder (1999). For development of the law, see Curran (1965).

4. A pioneer in using the bank discount method for consumer lending was Arthur J. Morris who began his Morris Plan lending at the first of his chain of industrial banks in 1910 in Norfolk, Virginia. It appears that the bank discount method of charging interest goes back to at least the middle of the seventeenth century (see de Roover 1946).

5. At the time of passage of TILA, many observers considered the difficulties of the mathematical calculations involved to be formidable obstacles. Even if not especially complicated conceptually for someone versed in the field (like a financial analyst or an actuary), the computations necessary for calculating the

APR were considered complicated enough at the time that President Johnson went out of his way at the act's signing ceremony to single out and commend the Treasury Department actuary who did the TILA mathematical work, even contending the passage of the act depended upon this mathematical effort:

"I particularly want to single out one person in the executive department, one of our much overlooked individuals, the career public servant, Mr. Cedric W. Kroll of the Treasury Department. Mr. Kroll is the Government's actuary. He is a veteran of more than 25 years of Federal service.

He and his colleagues in the Treasury's Office of Public Debt Analysis had a tough job to do before we could even begin to get a truth-in-lending bill. The lenders had argued that any bill was unworkable because of the variety of credit transactions involved. They said the requirements were just too complicated to be calculated with accuracy. Well, Mr. Kroll and his associates didn't buy those arguments. They put their heads together and came up with a set of interest rate tables and schedules that make disclosure of the many varieties of credit transactions relatively simple. They cracked this tough, impossible, big, technical problem that had stalled a truth-in-lending bill for years.

These few men, these quiet, effective men, whom the Government is filled with — men and women like them — are called bureaucrats sometimes in the heat of debate in the Congress. I call them real patriots. They were working backstage and they proved that this bill could be made to work. These men, and thousands like them, are living proof of how our Government works for the people.

We owe this bill and other good bills to our career civil servants who are always working behind the scenes to better our lives and usually doing the things for which we take the credit.

I am proud today to speak for not only our consumers and for all of our people in recognizing our debt and paying our thanks to the public servants who go unheralded, unknown, and unsung, and who make our prosperity and our security better by their careers."

6. See Rubin (1991) for a review of the tone and experience of these hearings and of the hearings held in 1967 upon introduction of the law embodying TILA.

7. Creditors and other observers raised many difficult questions for Senator Proxmire and the committee members to consider right at the outset. In the later summarizing words of one knowledgeable observer (Rohner 1984, P. I-7):

As noted, the exclusive thrust of the early bills was to assure standardized, complete, and accurate disclosure of credit terms. On its face, the legislative goals seemed virtuous and straightforward. But there were in fact any number of stumbling block issues:

If a standardized rate computation was to be used, should it be a simple interest percentage or some other formula such as dollars per hundred? Should the finance charge be measured by creditor yield or consumer cost?

How could any accurate projection of finance charges be made in open-end credit where transaction patterns could vary the actual yield?

Should the same rules be applied to home mortgages (where abuses were fewer) as were imposed on small loans?

Which transactions were sufficiently "non consumer" in nature to justify their exclusion from coverage?

What items of credit information other than the basic finance charge and annualized rate were necessary to promote consumer understanding and intelligent credit shopping?

Each of these issues has plagued the underlying goals of the Truth in Lending Act since its inception.

8. There are difficulties even in counting the number of amendments to both TILA and Regulation Z. For example, is a single action of the Federal Reserve Board that amends two sections of the regulation one amendment or two? Relying on narrative discussions in the Board's *Annual Report on Truth in Lending* would produce a higher total than stated here, which is compiled from the more general *Annual Report of the Board of Governors of the Federal Reserve System*.

9. It appears, based upon its 1980 wording in *Ford Motor Credit Company versus Milhollin*, (444 US 555) that even the Supreme Court became frustrated with the situation and decided to clarify the role of staff opinions by making them extremely powerful. In that case the Court wrote: "Unless demonstrably irrational, Federal Reserve Board staff opinions construing the Act or Regulation should be dispositive... ." From this tone, it seems that the plausible, but unwritten, next line could well have been "And furthermore, we never want to see a case like this again." The *Milhollin* approach may in some sense be good public policy in a technical area, but it likely is bad law in that it apparently gives immense interpretive power to unelected, mid-level government officials. It also has not prevented the Supreme Court from needing to review subsequent TILA cases.

10. Rubin (1991, p. 237) stated the problem in a particularly pithy manner: "Regardless of the Act's intent, it is an admittedly imaginative enforcement strategy to facilitate the detection of violation by making violation unavoidable."

The present authors are not generally enthusiastic about reporting anecdotes, but two conversations years ago about TILA compliance have since haunted the understanding of one of them about the early days. In the first, a consumer-oriented lawyer bragged to him (this author has no idea about the correctness of the statement): "Because of the interaction of federal Truth in Lending and state law, you cannot write a mobile home [purchase/financing] contract in the state of Florida that I can't break." Second, a creditor, when asked about how he handled TILA compliance growled: "You get an expert. Truth in Lending is like corporate tax. You don't do it yourself. You get an expert. Only stupid people do Truth in Lending or tax themselves." Both of these examples are further telling commentaries on what happened to a simple idea. They certainly lead to the question of whether it is an appropriate function of law to raise such concerns among those operating businesses in good faith, even if they also occasionally trip up intentional wrongdoers.

11. Apparently, two additional decades did not change things very much. A Federal Deposit Insurance Corporation (FDIC) supervisory letter in 1997 indicated that more than 76 percent of FDIC-examined institutions in 1996 were

cited for one or more TILA compliance violations. See FDIC Financial Institution Letter FIL-87-97 (September 2, 1997), referenced in Keest, Meredith, and Yen (1998), p. 983.

12. For a concise review of issues and cases in the period before 1980 see, among other sources, Federal Reserve Bank of Atlanta (1978), Miller (1979), and Willenzik (1979).

13. Review and discussion of the specifics of the changes may be found in Climo (1980), O'Conner (1980), and Rohner (1981). See also United States Senate Committee on Banking, Housing, and Urban Affairs (1979). Some other changes altered the requirements for disclosure of components of the finance charge and the amount financed and changed a variety of other technical areas. In addition, there were clarifications concerning mathematical tolerances, rounding rules, and issues surrounding the right of rescission on credit secured by dwellings.

14. For discussion of continuing problems see, for example, Garwood, Hobbs, and Miller (1993), Griffith (1998, 2000), and the annual review of TILA in *The Business Lawyer*, usually in the May issue but more recently February.

15. The Board attached to the revision a separate rulemaking of specific practices of credit card issuers that would be outlawed. Although closely intertwined with the Regulation Z changes, the outlawed practices are part of the Federal Reserve Board's Regulation AA (Unfair or Deceptive Acts or Practices, 12 CFR Part 227). The barred practices do not specifically concern TILA or disclosures and so are not treated here.

The Regulation AA rules were issued in conjunction with substantially similar rules issued at the same time by the National Credit Union Administration, for credit unions; and by the Office of Thrift Institutions, for savings banks and savings and loan associations.

16. Appendix A, "Financial Disclosures in Federal Consumer Protection Statutes," ranks federal consumer finance disclosures according to the relative importance of the information they require. Lawyers may already be aware of much of this material, but unless they are disclosure specialists, they may be surprised by the sweep of the legal requirements.

17. Appendix B, "Discussion of Disclosures in Selected Federal Consumer Financial Protection Statutes Other than the Truth in Lending Act," looks briefly at experience with some other important financial information-based protections: the Consumer Leasing Act, the Real Estate Settlement Procedures Act, the Truth in Savings Act, and the Electronic Fund Transfer Act. Although these laws generally did not undergo as long a gestation period or present as much of a saga of birth and growth as TILA, they have their own anomalies and have raised their own sets of questions.

Chapter 2

1. Kinds of credit used by consumers and their sources, uses, and growth rates are discussed in a companion book to this one, by Durkin, Elliehausen, Staten, and Zywicki (2011, Chapters 1–2). This companion book examines many questions and issues about consumer credit that go well beyond disclosure matters discussed here. They include credit demand and supply, growth, institutions, general regulation, and other policy matters.

Chapter 3

1. The academic field of marketing, which has become largely an applied branch of psychology and behavioral science, was, in its earlier days a century ago, an offshoot of the branch of economics then known as *distribution*. (See the interesting discussion in Wilkie and Moore 2003.)

2. The exceptions would involve conditions in which a monopolist could engage in price discrimination. *Price discrimination* is the practice of charging different prices for the same product in different markets. Price discrimination is possible if there are differences in demand among consumers that a monopolist can exploit because the consumers are unable for some reason to arbitrage. Today, these conditions seem unlikely for financial products, given the assumption of perfect information and modern communications that easily overcome geographic barriers that otherwise might impact product delivery.

3. For discussion, see any standard text, for example, Stiglitz and Walsh (2006) or Katz and Rosen (1997).

4. The classic work of the founding father is Stigler (1961). For surveys, see Rothschild (1973), Stiglitz (1985), and Ippolito (1988). In part for his pioneering work in this area, Stigler received the Nobel Prize in Economic Sciences in 1982.

5. For a review of Stigler's work and some of the early economic models arising from Stigler's insights, see Rothschild (1973).

6. For a readable though highly technical discussion of a model of this sort with a specific discussion of some empirical implications of the model, see Carlson and McAfee (1983).

7. This begs the question what is *truthful* advertising and the proposed legal stance for what is *untruthful* advertising. For a discussion of this issue, see Beales, Craswell, and Salop (1981). A discussion of evolution in the Federal Trade Commission's (FTC's) view of advertising is found in Muris (1991). An FTC staff study of trends in the content of advertising and the relationship between advertising and changing regulatory conditions (focusing on food advertising) is found in Ippolito and Pappalardo (2002).

8. The Truth in Savings Act and its implementing rule, Federal Reserve Board Regulation DD, contain extensive disclosure requirements for deposit products.

9. On occasion, the argument is made that the low-income or so-called ghetto marketplace uncovered by Caplovitz (1967) and others, or the market for new, complex products among senior citizens who do not have advisers, shows characteristics of the lemons model. In these cases, potential purchasers have little information about product quality and little ability or inclination to obtain it. Sellers of higher quality products may be unable to crack the market because getting the attention of these buyers is difficult. If such conditions exist, a lemons-model dynamic might well ensue and only low-quality products are for sale. If these consumers are also unaware of prices offered in the marketplace and they end up dealing with monopolists in local markets, they may be subject to the worst possible conditions: Only low-quality goods or services are available, but at high prices.

10. For a discussion and summary of some of these models, see Stiglitz (1987).

11. Of the two, bonds would appear to be more efficient than reputations because bonds impose significant costs only on cheaters. Attaining a good

reputation can be costly both for those prone and not prone to cheat. Nonetheless, the difficulties of organizing bonding arrangements for many consumer products and services appear to have made other signaling methods, including reputations, more important.

12. For a discussion of this point, see Barzel (1977).

13. For some products, even advertising and market share may serve as signals under some circumstances. The arguments for advertising and market shares are similar. For advertising, the idea is that only producers of higher quality products or services will be able to recoup advertising expenses through multiple or repeat purchases. Thus, those who advertise heavily are producing good enough quality that customers will continue to buy their product. If the advertising takes the form of a refutable claim, then it becomes a stronger signal because cheating (if discoverable) can have an immediate and significant negative impact on the advertiser. For market share, the argument is that after obtaining a large market share, higher quality producers have a strong interest in defending their share by producing high-quality products or services that continue to sell. In some ways, the argument in this area is not as strong, in that sellers sometimes can trade on their positive reputations for a while without an immediate negative impact if quality slips a bit, unlike the advertising expenditure case in which the advertising cost is already expended.

14. *Inspection* characteristics or some other alternative word might have been a better word choice than *search* characteristics to avoid confusion with the activity of searching.

15. For discussions of some of the issues, see Wilde (1980) and Lancaster (1981). Some analyses introduce yet another level of information difficulty arising from *credence goods* for which quality is rarely learned, even after consumption or use (see Darby and Karni 1973). The economic study of market functioning and equilibrium is even more complicated with credence goods.

16. For a further discussion of difficulties with information on product characteristics beyond pricing, including some problems not mentioned here, see Salop (1978) and Beales, Craswell, and Salop (1981).

17. For a discussion of a model in which creditors use indirect (dealer) lending versus direct lending as a screening or sorting device, see Staten, Umbeck, and Gilley (1990).

18. For good risks, posting a bond may be even less costly than acquiring a good credit record, which may take years, and may never be free from the risks of changing circumstances. In effect, collateral enables good risks to acquire the same cachet more quickly. For discussion of how the willingness to enter into a home equity loan, even at a high loan-to-value ratio, may be a signal of creditworthiness, see Calomiris and Mason (1999).

19. Landers and Rohner (1979) note how Congress framed the Truth in Lending Act with the behavior of individuals in mind. They then give reasons why that statute was unlikely to have an effect on consumer behavior.

20. An exception is Board of Governors of the Federal Reserve System (1987), which examines the impact of experimental shoppers guides for consumer credit on the level and dispersion of prices for three types of consumer loans, as well as the apparent impact on individuals.

21. Compare the Board of Governors of the Federal Reserve System (1987) with Punj and Staelin (1983), for example. Using survey evidence, the former explores the impact of information on the functioning of markets,

while the latter explores the impact on individuals. Clearly, others have also noted this dichotomy. See, for example, Carlson and Gieseke (1983), which is an economic analysis but which focuses empirically on individual behavior and the effects of information on individuals. A notable exception is experimental economics, a branch of economics that uses experimental designs to investigate the functioning of markets and other exchange mechanisms (see Smith 1991).

22. For a more formal and complete discussion of some of these issues, see Wilde (1980).

23. For a summary of this work, see Katona (1975).

24. For economic theoretical discussion from the same period reconciling the lack of knowledge of interest rates with optimizing behavior, see Juster and Shay (1964). Juster and Shay argued that a large percentage of, but by no means all, consumers desired more credit than available at market rates, making their decisions to purchase durable goods more sensitive to the sacrifice in current consumption necessary to satisfy creditors' equity requirements (and, hence, to monthly payment size) than to the interest rate. That caused this group of consumers to be more aware of monthly payment size than of the interest rate, and others to be more sensitive to rates. For an extended discussion of this point, see Durkin, Elliehausen, Staten, and Zywicki (2011, Chapter 3).

25. See, for example, Bettman, Luce, and Payne (1998) and Reynolds and Olson (2001) for more recent derivatives of this important line of thought. Holbrook (2001, p. 337) well articulated the continuing importance of the buyer behavior approach: "Indeed, to this day, ICABS [Holbrook's acronym for the steps Professor John A. Howard designated as important in the model, Information, Cognition, Affect, Behavior, and Satisfaction] has continued to serve as the mainstream view of consumer choice—even when elaborated into information processing paradigms (the decision orientation), applied to advertising (the think-feel-do approach), loaded with qualifying conditions (the elaboration-likelihood model), or taken as a position against which to react (the experiential perspective). If we were to pick a watershed moment in the history of marketing thought, we would wisely consider the advent of John [Howard]'s model building approach, which would arguably qualify him as the Father of Buyer Behavior Theory."

26. For illustration, the discussion in the next few paragraphs draws upon ideas formulated by the Engel, Kollat, and Blackwell model as refined and updated by Blackwell, Miniard, and Engel 2006).

27. Olson and Reynolds (2001) argue that the purchase decision does not depend upon the characteristics of products, but rather upon fundamental behaviors to bring about outcomes, which sometimes involve buying products. Their approach concerns the fundamental objectives associated with purchasing and does not obviate the differences in the problem-solving effort necessary for complicated versus less complicated purchases.

28. Lowering search costs ultimately is the reason underlying the Federal Reserve Board's decision in recent years to have Truth in Lending disclosure forms improved through testing on real consumers in focus groups rather than having design depend solely on the opinions of lawyers. The discussion here suggests the usefulness of this effort but also that the multiplicity of influences

on search and buyer behavior hints that testing is not, by itself, going to be determinative of favorable policy outcomes.

29. Over the years, many observers have argued that consumers do not comprehend APRs in that they do not fully understand the mathematical relationship among the percentage rates disclosed, the contract or calculating rates, the finance charges in dollars, and creditors' yields. Actually, this is precisely the problem TILA was trying to obviate. Consumers do not need to know how to make these calculations, which adhere to rules and are given to consumers in specified format. With this (substantial) simplification of the problem in hand, it is hard to imagine that there are large numbers of consumers today who do not comprehend that lower rates are better for them than high rates, given that all other contract features are the same.

30. It is worth recalling again the view of the economists that the important factor is not the impact of information on any particular individual, but rather information's effect on the operation of markets, especially on competitive conditions and the pricing in markets. This clearly shows the difference between the concerns of the economists and the marketers. Marketers have much less interest in how their products and information disclosures (advertising) affect competitive conditions in markets. They, of course, are interested primarily in how the information they provide (advertising) affects the propensities of individuals to buy their products.

31. Satisficing does not work well in circumstances in which all outcomes sometimes fail. Because the heuristic is failure-driven (search if the outcome does not satisfy aspirations), it sometimes causes individuals to switch from a better to a worse alternative. Satisficing also creates problems if environments change and what works today does not work tomorrow. However, even under circumstances in which satisficing is ill-suited to inducing optimal long-run behavior, it may lead to changes in behavior that improve outcomes (see Bendor, Kumar, and Siegel 2009, pp. 24–25).

32. For example, Borges, Goldstein, Ortmann, and Gigerenzer (1999) found that stock portfolios chosen on the basis of firm name recognition (an availability heuristic) performed better than portfolios run by fund managers (and random portfolios). Also see Oaksford and Chater (1996), Gigerenzer and Goldstein (1999), and Griffiths and Tenenbaum (2006) for analyses and evidence suggesting that heuristics provide accurate predictions in many other areas.

33. Indeed, for the case in which the decision to use credit from some source has already been made, and under reasonable assumptions concerning identical choice of product across retail sources and identical down payment, this heuristic can also produce the best choice in the unrationed case. There is further discussion of this in Chapter 4, "What is Truth in Lending? Key Conceptual Problems Facing the Truth in Lending Act," in conjunction with the truth in lending outlay issue.

34. Loss aversion may also influence choices in situations that do not involve risk. Loss aversion may induce individuals' to consider sunk costs in decisions involving future actions. *Sunk costs* are costs that cannot be recovered once they have been incurred, but they can lead to wrong choices. For instance, managers considering the future funding of an unprofitable project, in the hope of avoiding a certain loss, might be tempted to continue funding the project. Loss aversion

may also explain some individuals' willingness to reject a credit card surcharge (a loss) but not accept an equivalent cash discount (a gain).

35. Expected values are for the first group (A) $7.50=0.25 \times 1.00 \times $30 and (B) $9.00 = 0.25 \times 0.80 \times $45 and for the second group (A) $30 = 1.00 \times $30 and (B) $36 = 0.80 \times $45.

36. Daniel Kahneman was awarded the Nobel Prize in Economic Science in 2002 for his work on prospect theory.

37. The prospects (1) $200 with probability 0.20, $100 with probability 0.50, and –$50 with probability 0.30 or (2) $200 with probability 0.20, $150 with probability 0.50, and –$100 with probability 0.30 provide another example of a possibility for discarding a common component. Eliminating the common component $200 with probability 0.20 reduces the prospects (3) and (4) to a choice between (1a) $100 with probability 0.50 and –$50 with probability 0.30 and (2a) $150 with probability 0.50 and –$100 with probability 0.30.

38. The value of a prospect is $V(x,p) = \Sigma\pi(p_i)v(x_i)$, where x_i is the monetary value of the outcome i, $v(x_i)$ is the utility of x_i, p_i is the probability of outcome i, and $\pi(p_i)$ is weight associated with p_i. The value of a two outcome prospect $600 with probability of 0.33 and $200 with probability of 0.67, for example, would be $V(x,p) = \pi(0.33)v(\$600) + \pi(0.67)v(\$200)$. This valuation differs from standard economic theory (expected utility theory), where the $v(x_i)$ are weighted by probabilities p_i, not the $\pi(p_i)$.

39. *Overweighting* is not the same as overestimating the probability of an event.

40. In the former case, net utility of consumption would be about equal to total utility of consumption because the imputed cost is essentially zero. In the latter case, the net cost would be about equal to the total cost because the imputed benefit is nearly zero.

41. For a brief description of this theory, see Samuels, Stich, and Faucher (2004).

42. That is, he substituted a frequency format: "There are 100 people who fit the description above. How many of them are (1)… bank tellers? (2)… bank tellers and active in the feminist movement?"

43. Several experimental studies used mugs to evaluate the existence of an endowment effect. Participants who were given mugs were offered the opportunity to receive cash in exchange for the mug. Other participants were offered opportunity to buy mugs. The researchers found that the mean and median exchange prices of the two groups differed.

44. Plott and Zeiler did not advance a comprehensive theory explaining participants' perceptions, but they speculated about the possible explanations for their findings. One potential explanation is that the valuations reflect motivations to announce a value other than the true value. Their experimental procedures sought to eliminate motivations based on strategic considerations or concern about how others might judge their valuations, but other such motivations might still exist. Other explanations include how participants might perceive that they were expected to remove any special value of ownership from their valuation or that a gap between the willingness to pay and the willingness to accept somehow involves a learning process. Plott and Zeiler's experimental results suggest that these other explanations do not play a role, but they provided no evidence regarding these latter explanations. (See their discussion on pp. 543–44.)

45. Evidence from equity markets supports the findings of studies in experimental economics. Reviewing studies of stock return anomalies attributed to behavioral biases, Malkiel (2003) noted that, although statistically significant, the anomalies are generally quite small. The anomalies sometimes persist for short periods but usually disappear quickly. Malkiel argued that, though market participants clearly do make mistakes and the actions of some market participants are demonstrably less than rational, the preponderance of evidence suggests that the market is remarkably efficient. Whatever evidence of anomalies in pricing of equities has been found, he concluded, does not persist and provides few opportunities for investors to obtain extraordinary returns. For a similar assessment of the evidence on behavioral anomalies in stock market returns, see Fama (1998).

46. See Frederick, Loewenstein, and O'Donoghue (2002) for a brief discussion of economists' views on the intertemporal choice before the development of the discounted utility model.

47. Hyperbolic discounting may have a biological basis. Hyperbolic discounting predicts animals' behavior in foraging and predation. Animals often choose a smaller reward if it is available sooner over a larger reward later, even though waiting for the larger reward would maximize their rate of energy intake. Some biologists have hypothesized that such discounting of the value of future rewards may be an adaptive response to the risks associated with waiting for delayed rewards. See Real and Caraco (1986), Green and Myerson (1996).

48. See Miller and Cohen (2001) or Camerer, Loewenstein, and Prelec (2005) for a neurobiological description of cognitive control structures.

49. All students submitted papers on time.

50. Smith (1991) noted that "...the subjective cost of exploring options and figuring out what to do must be part of the problem of rational choice as experienced by the decision maker. Decision cost is the cost of concentration, attention, information acquisition, thinking, monitoring, checking, deciding, and acting, all the things one does to realize a decision. When the benefits are small, the decision cost may not be worth it, or the decision cost incurred may be, rationally, correspondingly small so that the pain fits the pleasure, marginally speaking, although the typical subject will not consciously think about it in such terms (p. 888)."

51. Katona's (1975) view of rationality presented earlier in this chapter conforms to this concept.

52. See Durkin, Elliehausen, Staten, and Zywicki (2011) for further discussion, especially Chapters 3 and 4.

Chapter 4

1. Appendix J to FRB Regulation Z also outlines some much more complicated examples, such as the equation for loans involving multiple credit advances along with multiple payments. The mathematical principles are always the same; the more complicated examples just involve more terms.

2. As discussed further below, over the years, a number of financial experts have criticized this second equation, saying that instead of applying a simple rate of interest, it should reflect a compound rate: APR = $((1+r/n)^n-1)*100$. Congress legislated, in effect, that it should be a simple rate, however, and comparisons among APRs are possible with either simple or compound rates as long as all rates are calculated the same way.

3. For a review of many of the considerable complexities and discussion of the older cases that have interpreted many of them for TILA purposes, see Rohner (1984) and Rohner and Miller (1988), chapters 3, 4, and 7 in each. More recently, Rohner and Durkin (2005) extensively discuss the legal, economic, and historical elements of the outlay issue for open-end credit. For a year-by-year analysis of legal developments including litigation, see the annual TILA review in a spring issue of *The Business Lawyer*, usually May but more recently February.

4. It also has generated its share of finger-pointing about who is responsible for this situation. Industry personnel often accuse consumerists and their political supporters of making unreasonable demands for precision. Consumerists blame the financial industry for designing complicated products. *Post hoc* assigning of blame for complexity seems pointless in discussing the impact of the act on consumers. Regardless, there is enough blame for everyone. For a relatively recent short discussion of how we got where we are that raises and discusses some of these questions without the pretension of trying to answer them all definitively, see Rohner (1996).

5. For discussion of the significant outcomes and trends, see Rohner (1984) and Rohner and Miller (1988) and the annual reviews in a spring issue of *The Business Lawyer*.

6. In some ways, elements of this case, *Rodash v. AIB Mortgage Co.* 16F3d 1142 (11th Circuit, 1994), were similar to the parking lot fee example used here. This case is discussed further in Chapter 5.

7. Actually, it is possible for consumers, in effect, to intuit their own unit price index for a joint purchase by making some simplifying assumptions. Furthermore, this index would rank possible financed purchases in the same rank order as a joint purchase quasi APR, although it would not be possible actually to calculate such a rate because the underlying single equation would contain two unknowns. It seems unlikely that many consumers fully understand the mathematics of this simple approach, but it seems probable that many of them follow its basics, even if they do not fully comprehend the reasons, and the approach becomes a heuristic of the sort discussed in the previous chapter. Furthermore, the number that serves as the index is a required TILA disclosure.

The simplifying strategy for shopping for the best deal in a product–credit joint purchase is to make a few mental simplifying assumptions and then shop for the lowest monthly payment regardless of whether through one outlet (the dealer) or two (the dealer and the financial institution). This approach works as long as the number of payments is the same for each alternative under consideration, and all payments for each compared alternative are uniform in size after the down payment. The other assumptions are that the consumer makes a specific, constant handover to the dealer (that is a given trade in and a given cash down payment, either one or both of which can be zero) and receives a specific handover from the dealer (that is, the same product with the same features). Then, the best deal (the best joint purchase and credit price) in all cases is the one with the lowest monthly payment. Under the circumstances assumed, the monthly payment is perfectly correlated with the (unknown) underlying joint APR because it is the size of the cash flows in the monthly payment that determine the APR. (The other unknown in the equation is the present value of the credit package, the "amount financed" in TILA.)

Obviously, it may be difficult for consumers to squeeze all offerings of both the dealers and the joint dealer external credit sources into a single framework, but doing so makes direct comparisons possible. In fact, using this simplified approach to find the best deal makes it unnecessary to know the price of the car, the value of the trade-in, the finance charge, or the APR of the finance charge. The payment size summarizes all price components for the joint purchase of the vehicle and time payment. Using this approach, consumers do not have to evaluate tradeoffs between rebates and reduced finance charges, since the trade-off does not involve the consumer's out-of-pocket cash. Income taxes can complicate the analysis if finance charges are deductible for tax purposes; but under tax reform, finance charges are deductible only if home equity plans are used for financing.

Thus, the often-observed phenomenon that many consumers intending to use credit seem as or more interested in the monthly payment as in the APR does not by itself prove either ignorance or irrationality concerning financing costs and comparisons. Under reasonable assumptions, the monthly payment is strictly correlated with the APR, even if consumers cannot easily calculate the joint product and financing APR.

A residual difficulty with this approach is that since payments by themselves reveal only the ranking of the APR and not its numerical value, it is not possible to compare the financing arrangement with the alternative of liquidating other assets or paying cash. For consumers who decide they are going to use credit under any circumstances for whatever reason (including not having enough other assets or cash available), this would not seem to be important. For a theoretical discussion of this latter point see Juster and Shay (1964) and Durkin, Elliehausen, Staten, and Zywicki (2011, Chapter 3).

8. For discussion see National Commission on Consumer Finance (1972, Chapters 6 and 7).

9. For interesting historical discussions of pricing in the early days of consumer credit from domestic financial institutions, see Robinson and Nugent (1935), Tyree (1960), and Michelman (1966).

10. Closed-end credit actually is defined residually in Regulation Z as "credit other than open end credit" (Regulation Z 226.2(a)(10)), and open-end credit is specified in the regulation (Regulation Z 226.2(a)(20)) as:

> "Consumer credit extended under a plan in which
> (i) the creditor reasonably contemplates repeated transactions;
> (ii) the creditor may impose a finance charge from time to time on an outstanding unpaid balance; and
> (iii) the amount of credit that may be extended to the consumer during the term of the plan (up to any limit set by the creditor) is generally made available to the extent that the outstanding balance is repaid."

11. At one time, there were special requirements for multiple historical examples in certain variable-rate mortgage transactions. The required examples were not transaction-specific; rather, they were based upon a standard loan size and could be pre-printed. This requirement was repealed in 1996 as part of the Economic Growth and Regulatory Paperwork Reduction Act of that year (Public Law 104-208).

12. On the nature of this problem, see Linneman and Voith (1985).

13. Beginning in the late 1990s, the Congress considered a related approach for one aspect of credit card accounts under TILA, which finally passed in 2005. Congress amended this provision in 2009, however, before it even went into effect. The 2005 enactment required the FRB to "establish a detailed table" illustrating the number of months that it would have taken to repay an outstanding

credit card balance for consumers who make only the minimum required payment. Creditors would have had to make this information available to consumers who called a telephone number the card issuer (or in some cases, the government) would have had to set up for this purpose.

This requirement was the first instance of mandating an electronic medium for disclosures. In a true electronic environment, providing multiple disclosures potentially is simpler than on paper, because it may be possible to allow consumers to employ "what-if" scenarios based their own behavioral assumptions like different payment sizes. In 2005, however, the Congressional mandate stopped short of full multiple disclosures and was changed in 2009 to the old kind of monthly paper disclosures.

14. Rohner and Durkin (2005) discuss the rationale for this decision.

15. The insolubility of these mathematical expressions in open-end credit has not kept some observers from recommending otherwise. In one example pronouncement, an advocate who will remain nameless here because the authors merely find the suggestion humorous, opined: "The fundamental problem with Truth in Lending when it comes to credit cards will be solved only when the Fed realizes that open end credit needs the same kinds of disclosures as closed end credit, like mortgages and auto loans" (advocate quoted in Paletta 2004, p. 4). Actually, the FRB does not need to realize that disclosures on open-end credit differ from closed-end credit disclosures; it knows that. It just has not figured out how to require for open-end credit disclosing unknown and unpredictable amounts, and the solutions of insoluble equations.

16. This was a period of extremely high funding costs for banks as well as selective controls on consumer credit instituted by the federal government for macroeconomic stabilization purposes.

17. Regulation Z and its *Commentary* have long contemplated and designated, by examples, a list of charges that are not finance charges but must be disclosed and are subject to change in terms notices (see 12 *CFR* 226.7) for any alterations. In the structure of Regulation Z, they are known as "Other Charges." The official staff *Commentary* called them "significant" charges related to the open-end plan, but by definition they are not finance charges. Examples include late charges, over-the-limit fees, and certain fees for providing documentary evidence of transactions. Many of the disclosure requirements in this area changed substantially in 2008, as discussed in a later chapter.

18. The periodic rate might also be applied to balances calculated in different ways. For an extended discussion of different balance calculation methods, see Rohner (1984, chapter 7). For an empirical look at how different balance calculation methods actually impact consumer costs and card issuers' revenues, given their actual behavior in using card accounts, see McAlister and DeSpain (1975). Unfortunately, no one has updated their work to take into consideration more modern circumstances.

19. For an extended discussion and the interpreting cases, see Rohner (1984) and Rohner and Miller 1988), chapters 3 and 4 in each.

20. Definitions and usage of different interest-rate terms can quickly become inconsistent and complicated, even in basic textbooks, which is why much of the different uses of terminology is not mentioned here. For discussion, see Rich and Rose (1997) and the references there. For TILA purposes, the APR is defined more precisely in Appendix J to Regulation Z as just such a simple discount rate for a "unit period" times the number of unit periods in a year (the unit period is also defined in Appendix J, and for much of common consumer credit,

it is a month). In paragraph 226.22(a)(1), the Regulation Z *Commentary* calls the rate calculated according to the formula in Appendix J the "exact" APR.

21. Reasonable people may, of course, disagree about what constitutes a *dramatically altered* rate or what is a *major factor* in its calculation. And, it is possible that some consumers actually make decisions on the basis of very small differences in APRs, say to the second decimal point as in 11.21 percent versus 11.24 percent. No convincing evidence is currently available to show that many of them do so, however, and so, at this time, it is difficult to argue strongly that such minor differences are really important, except as an affront to those who demand mathematical truth at all costs (or who look for questions to litigate in the area). For a discussion of consumers' reactions to finance charges and APRs, see discussion in Chapter 7. For a fuller discussion of the entire range of tolerances and other simplifications associated with calculation of the APR and permitted under Regulation Z, see Rohner (1984) and Rohner and Miller (1988), chapter 7 in each.

22. Footnote from source omitted.

23. Footnote from source omitted.

Chapter 5

1. *Rodash v. AIB Mortgage Co.*, 16F3d 1142 (11th Circuit, 1994).

2. The case also involved clear violations of TILA in some other areas, and so there is no question that the lender was guilty of some TILA transgressions.

3. In the views of some observers, the court's view could simply be wrong in this important case. According to Cook and Meredith (1995), p. 1041:

> The court's decision (that the FedEx fee collected by the creditor is a finance charge) is arguably wrong. Regulation Z provides that any fee that would be paid in a cash transaction is not a finance charge simply because it is incurred in a credit transaction (Regulation Z 226.4(a)). Therefore, the FedEx fee incurred to deliver a payoff check to a previous creditor is not a finance charge if the borrower would have incurred the FedEx fee when paying off the loan in cash. It certainly would be reasonable for a borrower to elect to deliver a payoff check by FedEx in a cash transaction. A borrower could stop the running of additional odd-days interest on a mortgage loan by delivering the check by FedEx rather than by U.S. mail. On most loans, the interest that would accrue on an additional two or three odd days would far exceed a twenty-two-dollar FedEx charge.

Cook and Meredith also disagree with the court's conclusion concerning the intangibles tax (see page 1042). Since they are attorneys advising clients in this area and advocating reasonable positions, it is easy enough to see how clients could run afoul of situations in which courts simply go the other way.

4. The revisions are in Public Law 104-29, 109 *Stat.* 271. Further discussion of the context and outcome of this case, along with review of the legislative changes undertaken in response to it, may be found in Cook and Wisner (1996) and Lax (1996).

5. See National Commission on Consumer Finance (1972), especially Chapters 6 and 7 and references there for an extended discussion of usury laws and resulting market conditions.

6. Cynics dubbed it the FUD report. This second report actually was the result of a second congressional request, under Section 2101 of the Economic Growth and Regulatory Paperwork Reduction Act of 1996, Public Law 104-208.

7. Rohner and Durkin (2005) discuss at some length general principles for classifying fees as costs of credit or not and, therefore, finance charges or not. Their views are examined in the next chapter on open-end credit, in which the question also arises.

8. Nonetheless, the US Department of Housing and Urban Development decided to take on some of these questions on its own initiative with its July 2002 proposal for reform of the RESPA regulation (see United States Department of Housing and Urban Development 2002a). HUD withdrew the controversial proposal in 2003 for further consideration following significant congressional opposition, but it resurfaced later in the decade. More will be said about this proposal in Appendix B.

9. The use of a single-payment loan in this and subsequent examples allows the direct calculation of the APR without using a calculator, computer, or multiple steps with pencil and paper. APRs for multiperiod loans are calculated by reducing the equation to algebraic factors and proceeding iteratively using a trial-and-error method, the method actually used by calculators and computers. For a discussion of the mathematics, see Brealey and Myers (1991, Chapter 5). For discussion from a time before the ubiquitous presence of electronic devices to do the work, see Neifeld (1951).

10. Allowing for the possibility of multiple credit advances at different times on the same closed-end contract produces much of the complexity of the basic APR equation in section 8 of Appendix J to Regulation Z. In most transactions, the complexity of the left side of this equation in Appendix J does not apply.

11. In discussing the general equations in the previous chapter, it was necessary to include the annualizing equation from Section 7 of Appendix J to Regulation Z (designated herein as Equation 2), because payments were more frequent than annual. In the simplified examples here, there is only one discounting period in the year, and so Equation 2 is not needed.

12. Those who appreciate the more formal expression of the mathematical relationships exhibited in Appendix J to Regulation Z will note that the equations there do not normally contemplate including both the item purchased (the house) and the loan advance in the equation, because this would be double counting. The approach here includes everything for expository convenience, to account for every item contemplated in the transaction. As the algebraic cancellations take place, all the double counting is eliminated, and the equations quickly reduce to the conceptions in Appendix J.

Chapter 6

1. See the Board of Governors of the Federal Reserve System, Docket R-1136, November 26, 2002. The reasoning behind the distinction between the two sorts of fees was that the fees for expedited payment services, unlike delivery charges, typically are paid to avoid late charges that already were *other charges*.

2. The notice in the *Federal Register* requesting comments in 1995 on the Finance Charge Report to Congress initially tipped the hand of the FRB, or at least its staff, that these charges might sometimes be finance charges, by maintaining that the genesis of the charge as a credit cost or something else might make no difference. Speaking generally, but focusing on the concerns raised in the *Rodash* case, the notice asking for comments postulated that, "The finance

charge is defined as the cost of consumer credit expressed as a dollar amount. It includes any charge payable directly or indirectly as an incident to or a condition of the extension of credit. *The term imposed is interpreted broadly, to include any cost charged by the creditor (unless otherwise excluded), including charges for optional services paid by the consumer... ."* (emphasis added, see Board of Governors of the Federal Reserve System 1995, p. 66,179). Congress did not legislate such an outcome as part of its disposition of the *Rodash* matter, however, and, as of the end of 2010, this broad position has not been established in the regulation, despite continuous tinkering with it, such as in the 2008 open-end credit disclosure revisions discussed further later. Rohner and Durkin (2005) extensively discuss standards for finance charges on open-end credit.

3. These three steps are the authors' characterization of the process. There is nothing formally in the regulatory requirements specifically mentioning or mandating these steps.

4. Rohner and Durkin (2005) discuss the historical and economic background of what constitutes a finance charge and what does not at some length, focusing especially on open-end credit.

5. Courts can and do change these definitions. In a case generally referred to as the Pfennig case, (*Pfennig vs. Household Credit Services and MBNA America Bank,* 2002 FED App. 0123P (6th Cir.), April 11, 2002) the United States Court of Appeals for the 6th Circuit found that charges for exceeding the credit limit on a credit card are finance charges under some circumstances, despite clear wording in the Regulation Z official staff *Commentary* making them "other charges" (Commentary 226.6(b)-1(i)). In April, 2004 the Supreme Court reversed this decision.

6. In the most notable legislative action at the state level, in 2001, the legislature of the state of California passed a bill codified as section 1748.13 of the Civil Code of California that would have required an extensive new disclosure scheme for account duration for any card issuer that required a minimum monthly payment of less than 10 percent of the account balance outstanding, raising in that state all the questions about the reasonableness of the necessary calculating assumptions.

After much debate over these issues, the California legislature passed the bill, but it never went into effect. Unlike the federal bill, other aspects of the California plan caused the credit card industry to maintain that parts of the specific disclosure requirements of the state proposal were so difficult and onerous as to be unworkable or even impossible. As a result, the card industry contended, the California requirements were not really disclosure requirements but rather amounted to an attempt to regulate the business of banking of national banks by rendering a line of business infeasible due to disclosure requirements.

With this view in mind, in May 2002, some card issuing banks and their trade associations sued the state of California in federal court alleging that the action of the state was inconsistent with the supremacy and interstate Commerce Clause of the United States Constitution (*American Bankers Association,* et al. *vs. Bill Lockyer, et al.,* United States District Court, Eastern District of California Case No. CIV 5-02-1138). In the former claim. they were joined by the federal Office of the Comptroller of the Currency, the federal regulator of national banks, which secured from the federal district court the status of *amicus curiae* on the side of the banks. The judge granted a preliminary injunction in late June 2002, and summary judgment and a permanent injunction in December, in favor of the plaintiff banks. The court decided that the California statute indeed was inconsistent with the National Bank Act and other federal financial statutes and therefore overturned. Whether the state plans to resurrect this statute in a form that will withstand legal challenge remains to be seen.

7. Although he does not agree with this view, Zywicki (2000) discusses it at some length.

8. Durkin (2006b) examined details of the many other assumptions necessary for estimating time to payoff under the 2005 legislation and includes an extended discussion of the sensitivity of payoff time estimates to the various assumptions necessary.

9. See Durkin (2000, discussion on pp. 633–34).

10. For a fuller description of the data collection, see Barron and Staten (2004). As described there, the data set collected had three components representing accounts as part of the card issuers' college student marketing programs, accounts opened by other young adults, and accounts held by older individuals. For the analysis reported, these components were appropriately weighted so the weighted sample is representative of the age distribution of each issuer's overall portfolio.

Chapter 7

1. It does not, of course, tell individuals whether their wants and desires, for example, using credit rather than saving first and using cash, are *right* or *wrong* according to someone else's criteria or according to later hindsight. For an extended discussion of consumer choice in using credit, see Durkin, Elliehausen, Staten, and Zywicki (2011, Chapters 3-4).

2. In fact, many subprime lenders have failed financially in recent years. For discussion of rates and rate spreads in subprime mortgage lending versus prime lending, see Chomsisengphet and Pennington-Cross (2006).

3. Taking a considerably more limited view of TILA's goals based only on its own wording about its purpose, Rubin (1991) contended that truth in lending was largely a failure. His discussion of success or failure of the act is so brief, however (it is limited to three paragraphs referencing a very few old research papers), that it is more an assumption of failure for illustrative purposes than a real analysis of the act's effects. It seems his criterion was too strict, and he dismissed TILA too rapidly, but the purpose of his interesting paper was less to evaluate the success or failure of TILA than to use it as the motivation for a case study on developing good legislative methodology. He felt good developmental methodology was absent in the TILA case (he argues this case convincingly), and he argues for a better legislative approach.

In contrast, this chapter is a bit more optimistic in that it allows more room for TILA to be successful. It does not hold TILA to a handful of goals specified only within the body of a single paragraph in the act entitled "Purpose," though it acknowledges the importance of this congressional expression. Instead, it outlines the goals for TILA suggested by a variety of sources in a range of contexts, measures them against the available (albeit meager) data, and tries to review what are essentially empirical questions, whether and how TILA has "worked."

4. Even some behavioral scientists have expressly argued that goals of disclosure necessarily must go beyond their impact on individuals, because, in their view, it is so difficult either to understand or evaluate the likely impact of disclosures on behavior (Day and Brandt 1973, p. 21):

> The adoption of a new requirement is less likely to be influenced by arguments that the consumer will or will not use the information or

make better purchase decisions because so little is known about these questions. The uncertainty about possible effects typically persists after the policy has been implemented, in part because the impact of the policy is difficult to separate from other changes and influences in the marketplace.

5. A published transcript of a panel discussion at a meeting of the Committee on Consumer Financial Services, American Bar Association Section of Business Law, offers a useful illustration: Each of the panel members appeared to be frustrated with TILA and to contend that it was not working as well as possible, but each also seemed to base this contention on a different view of the purpose of TILA (see Golann, *et al.* 1998).

6. Juster and Shay (1964) evaluate the economics of this decision more fully. For extended discussion, see Durkin, Elliehausen, Staten, and Zywicki (2011, Chapters 3-4).

7. For a discussion of some of these methodological issues, see Phillips and Calder (1979, 1980).

8. The notable exception is the limited market populated by lower income, lesser educated, and/or elderly people, often in the inner city, where the lack of specific consumer skills or general sophistication can foster noncompetitive conditions and sometimes abuses. In discussing disclosures, the National Commission on Consumer Finance (NCCF) characterized this market as the high-risk market, as opposed to the general market, although low-income might have been a better word choice to characterize the market the commission was describing (see National Commission on Consumer Finance 1972, Chapter 11). Some observers before the Truth in Lending Act predicted, correctly it seems now, that the disclosures would have little impact on the consumer problems of the poor, especially the fraudulent practices of the unscrupulous (see, for example, Kripke 1969). Despite decades of hindsight on this issue, more disclosures are still sometimes proposed as solutions to the same problems (see, for example, the discussion in Board of Governors of the Federal Reserve System and Department of Housing and Urban Development 1998, pp. 17–19).

9. Again, the exception is the NCCF's high-risk market.

10. For a short review of some of the older studies of interinstitutional competition, see Durkin, Elliehausen, Staten, and Zywicki (2011, Chapter 11).

11. Holders of bank-type credit cards in 2001 were also asked for their views about the difficulties of other individuals in obtaining credit cost information. Fewer than half of respondents, in 2001, believed it was easy for others to obtain cost information compared to 65 percent for themselves, a difference dubbed by Durkin (2000, 2002) "the other guy effect."

12. Once again, it is worth noting that the NCCF's high-risk market may be an exception.

13. The later surveys did not use the same line of questioning as the 1971 effort, and the 1977 and 1984 surveys did not offer respondents exactly the same choices for ranking institutions by cost despite the same question. Consequently, the findings are not reproduced here in tabular form. Nonetheless, it is clear in all of the surveys that at least 75 percent of the respondents chose one of the depository institutions (typically credit unions) as the least costly source. In contrast, a similar proportion chose the nondepository sources as most costly. For a discussion of the 1971 survey, see Mandell (1973) and, for 1977, see Durkin and Elliehausen (1978, chapter 3, especially Table 3-4). The 1984 results, which look

much like the 1977 findings, are unpublished Federal Reserve survey results. For evidence of institutional awareness in the years before TILA, see Katona, Morgan, Schmiedeskamp, and Sonquist (1967, Table 7-13).

14. The hierarchy of effects model has a long tradition of usefulness in characterizing the impact of information disclosure and is now subsumed within the buyer behavior tradition. For further discussion of this research hypothesis, see Barry (1987).

15. These monographs present the basic data and analyses. See also Parker and Shay (1974), Day and Brandt (1974a), Day and Brandt (1974b), and Brandt, Day, and Deutscher (1975). The first reports of the data analyzed more fully by Shay and Schober and later by Parker and Shay are in the Federal Reserve Board's *Annual Reports on Truth in Lending* (Board of Governors of the Federal Reserve System 1970, 1971).

16. Surveys in 2001 and 2005 confirmed the long-term rise in the awareness level to year 2000, with awareness under the same definitions recorded in 2001 at 82 and 88 percent, within the normal range for statistical variation. The 2005 survey asked only those who said they frequently revolved their card accounts, but it produced among these consumers the highest aware percentage yet recorded: 96 percent using the broad definition.

17. Some other survey work in the 1970s using a somewhat different methodological approach and line of questioning reached the conclusion that truth in lending appeared to have a lesser effect. Some of this is due to questions in these other studies that do not appear to be as clear (see Mandell 1971) and to the drawing of conclusions from a population that included nonusers of credit as well as users (see Mandell 1973). Another aspect is a difference in the degree of optimism in drawing conclusions. All of the surveys found that substantial knowledge existed after TILA, but it was not perfect. The NCCF (1972), Shay and Schober (1973), and Durkin and Elliehausen (1978) concluded that TILA had apparently had a favorable impact. Even though their findings indicated that awareness and understanding were not perfect, they tended to conclude from the changed environment that the glass was half (or more) full and the level was rising. This seemed especially important, given that markets may not require complete understanding by everyone to function reasonably well. Others, in effect, tended to focus more on how the glass was (still) partly empty (see Mandell 1971, 1973 and Whitford 1972, p. 414–20, the latter interpreting the preliminary findings, later published, of Shay and Schober 1973 and others).

18. The original Day–Brandt questions concerned purchase of a color television set for $500. Researchers later adjusted the questions slightly to allow for the declining price of a typical purchase of a color television set and to simplify the math to its most basic form. Otherwise the question wording has remained the same over the years. The Day–Brandt questions, in turn, appear to be derived from a question asked by the Survey Research Center as early as 1959 concerning a $1,000 automobile loan for one year, an uncommon transaction even by 1970. Results of the earlier Survey Research Center questions are not reported in detail here because the question structure consisted only of the first part of the Day–Brandt questions, which Day and Brandt used to analyze understanding of credit amounts in dollars. The Survey Research Center effort apparently was looking for an answer in percentage rates, but permitted responses in rates or dollars, a deficiency Day and Brandt corrected by splitting the questioning into two parts. For a review of results of the Survey Research Center questions in 1959 and 1967,

see Katona, Morgan, Schmiedeskamp, and Sonquist (1967, Table 7-10 and discussion p. 138).

20. Comparison with the results of a similar question asked before TILA in 1959 and 1967 are much more dramatic, as might be expected, although the results are not directly comparable for the reasons outlined in the previous footnote. See Katona, Morgan, Schmiedeskamp, and Sonquist (1967, Table 7-10 and the discussion, p. 138).

20. Under the circumstances, the fact that consumers still use credit indicates that they also find it to be very useful. For discussion of this point, see Juster and Shay (1964) and Durkin, Elliehausen, Staten, and Zywicki (2011, Chapters 3-4).

21. Day and Brandt's (1973) finding in a 1970 survey that many consumers estimated about twice the actual charge may reflect their experience with add on rates before truth in lending. Multiplying an add-on rate times the original balance gives a reasonable estimate of the yearly finance charge. By the 1990s, few consumers had any experience with add-on rates, however. Whatever skills consumers may have had at converting rates to finance charges apparently were not helped by TILA's mandated APRs that do not easily permit such a conversion.

22. The full extent of the requirements and complications of TILA can only be appreciated by reviewing the legal literature on the subject. Some excellent summary sources already mentioned are Landers and Rohner (1979), Rohner (1984), Rohner and Miller (1988), and Rohner (1996).

23. The issue of information overload and consumer credit contracts is discussed extensively in Davis (1977).

24. As discussed in Chapter 3, to simplify decisions, consumers frequently use heuristics or rules of thumb, dividing up complex problems and focusing on specific elements.

25. The assumption that subprime borrowers as a group are less financially sophisticated than prime borrowers has not been satisfactorily documented empirically. Subprime borrowers generally have previous experience. As this experience often includes delinquencies and other credit problems, subprime borrowers may be more familiar with some credit terms than many prime borrowers.

26. Convincing consumers that credit is expensive and should be avoided has a long history among social critics. For historical discussion concerning the United States, see Calder (1999). For an even longer term view, see Rasor (1993), Homer and Sylla (1996), and Gelpi and Julien-Labruyere (2000).

27. The findings reported here are broadly consistent with those from other surveys. See, for example, Day and Brandt (1973), who reported on their 1970 California survey for the National Commission on Consumer Finance; Board of Governors of the Federal Reserve System (1987), which reported on an experiment concerning shoppers guides for credit; and Chang and Hanna (1991), who used data from the 1983 Survey of Consumer Finances. Brandt and Shay (1978) used a different shopping criterion, but results from their survey are consistent in that they found that shopping was fairly common but much less than universal.

28. The lines in the table do not add to the total proportion of all those who took some action because some individuals responded they had undertaken more than one action.

29. The lines in this section of the table also do not add to the percentage of respondents who took some action because individuals could answer they looked for more than one piece of information.

30. These were the proportions classified as *aware* in the NCCF's studies fifteen months after the effective date of TILA. The proportions classified as aware under the same definitions in 1977 were higher, as discussed above. See Durkin and Elliehausen (1978, Chapter 2).

31. See Punj and Staelin (1983) for a model of the consumer search process that attempts explicitly to include measures of the costs of external search as well as a variety of measures of benefits and modifying environmental variables.

32. This does not mean that this goal is entirely archaic today or by any means has vanished entirely. In fact, there is a view among some consumerists that TILA has become relatively more important in recent years for consumer defenses because of the relative decline in importance at the state level of interest rate ceilings known as *usury laws*. In this view, even if TILA is less important absolutely for institutional control, it still may be more important relatively. For discussion of this view see, for example, Keest (1997).

Chapter 8

1. See, for example, the Federal Reserve Board's press release accompanying its Advance Notice of Proposed Rulemaking (ANPR) on review and revisions to Regulation Z, Docket R-1217, December 3, 2004, and the 2007 proposal itself, discussed here in Chapter 6, "The Outlay and Unknown Future Events Issues: Open-End Credit."

Appendix A

1. The official name of this act when passed used the word *fund* in its title, not *funds* (see Public Law 95-630, November 10, 1978, Title XX).

2. For a review of HMDA and how the regulators use the information captured and disclosed, see Avery, Canner, and Cook (2005) and Avery, Brevoort, and Canner (2006).

3. A variety of substantive requirements affecting credit cards was implemented December 18, 2008, with an effective date of June 30, 2010, but these substantive requirements were included in Regulation AA (Unfair or Deceptive Acts or Practices), 12 CFR, Part 227, and not in Regulation Z. In 2009, Congress was also active in the credit card practices area and passed the Credit Card Accountability Responsibility and Disclosure Act of 2009 in May. This meant that the Federal Reserve undertook additional rulewriting including a reorganization that placed many of the Regulation AA revisions of 2008 into Regulation Z in 2010. The bulk of the implementing regulations for this act are also likely to end up in Regulation AA rather than Regulation Z, although Regulation Z will require some amendments too.

4. Although the HOEPA revisions to the Truth in Lending Act are commonly identified as the *high-cost mortgage* section, neither the HOEPA nor the implementing section of Regulation Z uses this term. For a review of the nondisclosure provisions of this 1994 amendment to TILA affecting high-cost mortgages, see Ornstein (1996).

5. See, for example, Federal Reserve Board Regulation P, 12 CFR Part 216, for state chartered banks that are members of the Federal Reserve System.

Appendix B

1. See Landers (1976), especially p. 629 and the following pages, for a discussion and references to the hearings.

2. The increase in consumer leasing over time is discussed in a variety of industry sources and publications. For earlier discussion of the frequency of leasing and a review of some data sources, see Aizcorbe and Starr-McCluer (1997). For a survey of some features of the leasing market such as approval rates, insurance sales, end of lease dispositions, delinquencies, see Staten and Johnson (1994).

3. There is only very limited academic literature on the criteria for a consumer's decision to lease an automobile (see Patrick 1984, Nunnally and Plath 1989, Miller 1995, and Giacotto, Goldberg, and Hegde 2007 for discussion). Instead, most studies of consumers and their automobiles focus more on the car-purchases decision (see, for example, studies referenced in Mannering, Winston, and Starkey 1999). For a more general discussion of leases and leasing (not specifically in the consumer context), see Schallheim (1994). For an extended discussion of the operating aspects of automobile leasing, see McCathren and Loshin (1991).

4. The alternative to an operating lease is a *full-payout* or *financial* lease, which finances the whole economic life of an asset by fully paying for (amortizing) the asset's capitalized cost, plus financing charges. Financial leases are not common in consumer leasing; they are more common in commercial leases and sale-leaseback transactions involving industrial buildings and equipment.

5. There may be a refundable security deposit to guarantee payment for damages. For automobiles, there may also be a relatively small disposition or drop-off charge specified in the contract. The typical automobile lease contract also specifies a yearly average mileage limit to avoid having charges for excessive usage.

6. Losses from this source can be substantial. (For discussion, see Gruber 1992.)

7. This difference is stated here in terms of the advantage of a lease for which there likely is a charge. Many consumers who regularly lease automobiles rather than purchase them probably analyze this decision in the reverse, but equivalent, form: There is a disadvantage to purchasing rather than leasing in the form of concern over the eventual trade-in value, as follows.

Suppose that a consumer likes driving new or recent cars and contemplates acquiring a new car every three years. This consumer could purchase the car and trade it in every third year, or lease a succession of vehicles. In the latter case, the consumer would know in advance the disposition terms for each car and, assuming reasonable care and good condition at turn-in time, this consumer would be free of haggling with the dealer over the trade-in value or running the risk that the value is low. Some consumers are probably willing to pay something for this freedom.

8. Although the discussion here concerns comparing a lease with a purchase, comparing two leases or two purchases would proceed in fundamentally the same way.

9. Because discounting the flows from a financed purchase at the APR paid for the credit equals the price of the asset, substituting the price of the asset for the discounted present value of the finance flows produces a standard net advantage of leasing (NAL) equation (see Myers, Dill, and Bautista 1976). For comparability to the lease, maturity purchase price must be adjusted to a net purchase price by subtracting the present value of the residual value, if any, after a comparable time period. Substituting into equation 1 produces the decision criterion:

If NAL = Net Purchase Price + PV (Option) - Sum PV (LP) > 0, then lease.

10. As a practical matter, the value of this option may not be very great to the extent that lessors are reasonably competent in predicting the values of used assets in the future, and set residual values and optional purchase prices at lease-end, accordingly. Still, if the absence of the haggle/hassle factor at lease-end is important to potential lessees/purchasers, then its value can be positive and potentially substantial. As indicated, Giacotto, Goldberg, and Hegde (2007) show that the value can be substantial, depending upon experience with used-car prices.

11. Services provided by the vehicle may also include psychological services, such as pride of ownership or the opportunity to drive a new or stylish automobile or truck. In the past, these psychological services may have varied depending on whether the transaction was a purchase with financing or a lease. For example, it is possible that at least some drivers felt better thinking they "owned" a vehicle rather than they merely leased its services. Leasing has recently become such a common financing alternative, however, that it seems reasonable to assume that these psychological services are similar for purchase financing and leasing today, and are of comparable value. Therefore, the psychological differences that may have existed formerly may be ignored today.

12. Transportation services may differ between the leasing and the purchase financing cases if the amount of yearly mileage permitted under a lease without an additional mileage charge (typically 12,000 or 15,000 miles per year, but with variations) constrains the potential purchaser. For illustrative purposes, this limitation is assumed not to be binding so that transportation services provided by the leased and financed vehicles are the same for this example. If the constraint were binding because the potential lessee intends to drive more than the yearly maximum, then another term for the present value of the expected deferred excess mileage charge due at lease end would be added to column 2 of the table.

13. Identifiable personal property taxes may be deductible from adjusted gross income for federal and state income tax purposes for some consumers, which also should be properly taken into account by those eligible for the deduction. There also may be sales taxes associated with both the credit purchase and the lease. For comparing a purchase to a lease, both must be accounted for properly to avoid erroneous conclusions. For example, for a purchase, sales taxes may be financed as part of the gross purchase price and paid for through the down payment and periodic payment flows. For a lease, they may be collected monthly as part of the monthly payment, either explicitly or not. Each of these possibilities would require an adjustment in the table to account properly for the facts of individual situations.

14. This purchase price may also be financed, in which case the price becomes another stream of outflows. The lessor and lessee may also agree to

another lease or to a continuation of the old lease agreement. The examples in the table do not reflect these possibilities.

15. The lessee still acquires the purchase option, even if the ultimate decision is to return the vehicle at lease-end, and so the present value of the option remains a term in Equation 1.

16. Even if there is a recognized prior probability of deferred gain or loss, there is no reason to expect a difference if the original acquisition is through a lease or purchase contract. If loss expectations are equal at the outset, they can be ignored in the calculations (and the table) when making comparisons.

17. For such a purchaser, who plans to sell, there is the real possibility of an unexpected loss upon disposition of the vehicle, but there may also be an unexpected gain. If the likelihood of the loss or gain is unknown at the outset of the lease arrangement, it might be argued that the expected value of the distribution of possibilities may well be zero, arguing for its dismissal from the calculations and the table. Because the risk of loss exists, however, an expected value of loss upon disposition is a potential outflow for a purchaser (column 4, line 11).

18. This is not an argument against required disclosure of the existence of such a risk, however.

19. The value of an option is a function of the value of the underlying asset, the variability in the asset's value, the price at which the option can be exercised, the length of time until the option can be exercised, and the rate of interest. Extended discussion and formulas can be found in textbooks of finance, for example Brealey and Myers (1991), Chapters 20 and 21. See Giacotto, Goldberg, and Hegde (2007) for further discussion about consumer automobile leasing.

20. This does not mean that compliance was automatically easy for lessors. Rather, as seems to be the case with any new regulation, Regulation M raised its own set of technical questions for interpretation and resolution. For a discussion of these issues, see Huber and Hudson (1998).

21. See Rohner (2003) for a discussion of the Uniform Consumer Leases Act and the Connecticut proposal.

22. The classic example is the *Rodash* case, discussed in Chapter 5.

23. The term for the present value of the expected loss from early termination, which appears in Table B.1, does not appear in Equation 4 because it is a contingency and not predictable. Therefore, it cannot be a part of the calculation for a disclosed percentage rate.

24. For illustrative simplicity, Table B.2 ignores the complicating factors of the security deposit, refund of the deposit, disposition charge, and value of the purchase option. All except the option value could easily be added to the table.

25. The backroom wonderland could even produce a negative percentage rate if depreciation is greater than the total of payments. This may be seen easily from the third column of Table B.4. If depreciation were raised further by continuing to raise the gross capitalized cost, it would exceed the total of payments and produce a negative ALR. It seems dealers likely would not attempt to advance such an outcome, because it probably would be a red flag to many consumers that there is something wrong with the transaction. But, raising depreciation one more dollar in the example of column 3 of Table B.4, and thereby producing this negative percentage rate outcome, is hardly different from column 3 itself that arrives at 0.0 percent. Consumers apparently seem to like 0.0 percent when they hear about it on purchase credit. Why not negative rates on leases?

26. The public comment process as a source of information is always interesting but frequently frustrating because, so often, comments merely illustrate the writer's anger, which is directed toward the various bureaucracies charged with implementing the enactments of the political branches of the government. Lists of problems from industry or other sources can be helpful, as can data on the origin and extent of problems or costs. Unsupported assertions from any commentator tend to be much less useful. Examples in the leasing area are much too numerous to cite.

27. This does not mean that lessors and their marketing firms have not undertaken proprietary research or that, on occasion, some findings may not be reported in trade sources. See, for example, CNW Marketing/Research (1995), which reports that a consumer focus group process found that consumers regard the monthly payment as the most important information on a lease.

28. As discussed in Chapter 5, there also are some legislative anomalies in TILA's mortgage-related requirements for calculating the disclosed finance charge and related APR that date all the way back to the original act in 1968. At that time, Congress legislatively excluded from the finance charge some cost items that otherwise would seem to be finance charges.

29. For further discussion of the home equity exclusion, see Bernstein (1994a and 1994b).

30. For a discussion of these matters, see Bernstein (1994b) and Board of Governors of the Federal Reserve System and Department of Housing and Urban Development (1998).

31. Interestingly, the original RESPA of 1974 integrated the RESPA disclosures with TILA requirements. They were separated by a RESPA amendment in 1975, largely in response to complaints, from both consumers and lenders, about the complexity of these disclosures.

32. For a discussion of this proposal, see US Department of Housing and Urban Development (2002a).

33. Congress passed a modified version of the simplification effort in 1980 as part of the Monetary Control Act that year. After extended hearings, discussion, and litigation, only part of the FTC effort was implemented.

34. As mentioned, both the timing provisions and the details of the various disclosures required under TILA and RESPA for mortgage-related credit are more complex than indicated here. For a discussion, see Board of Governors of the Federal Reserve System and Department of Housing and Urban Development (1998), Chapters 3 and 4.

35. For a discussion of HUD rulemaking in this area, see Buckley and Kolar (1997) and Jaworski (1998). For a HUD insider's view of the tortuous development of RESPA rulemaking, see Mitchell (1999). For review of recent HUD attempts to clarify Section 8 rules and an examination of related litigation, see US Department of Housing and Urban Development (2002a, pp. 49138–43).

36. It is interesting to note that guarantees of the initial estimate of closing costs were a feature of the original RESPA in 1974, but this provision (Section 6) was repealed in 1975 because of complaints that lenders were shading upward all estimates (and actual closing costs) to protect themselves from unwelcome negative surprises if some aspect of the closing process became unexpectedly costly.

37. The idea that consumers prefer a single price for settlement services and that providing a single price for closing costs benefits consumers is not new. Discussion from an earlier period is found in Wallace (1981, p. 185–88).

38. Section 8 and the implementing sections of Department of Housing and Urban Development Regulation X (24 CFR Part 3500) actually have not been static over the history of the act. For a summary of the evolution of the act and regulations in this area in earlier years, see Foote (1997a and 1997b).

39. The classic discussion of the role of financial intermediaries is found in Gurley and Shaw (1960). For a newer, textbook discussion, see Arshadi and Karels (1997).

40. The discussion in Chapter 5 briefly reviewed how some of the reason for separate fees derives historically from usury laws that sometimes provided an incentive to price components of the lending process separately.

41. For a discussion of the complicated and inconsistent court decisions in litigation over YSPs under RESPA, much of which concerns the conditions for certification of classes for class-action lawsuits, see Roos (1997), Jaworski (1998 and 1999), Schiff (1998), Byrd (1999), and Jackson and Berry (2002).

42. This amount, chosen for illustrative purposes, happens to correspond to a contract rate of 11 percent, but it does not have to be calculated from a contract rate, even if this is the common approach. Any amount could illustrate the YSP concept, no matter how it is chosen.

43. The Department of Housing and Urban Development attempted to do this in a rulemaking beginning in October 1997 known as the Broker Fee Proposal that includes, among other things, proposals for new disclosures. For a discussion, see Jaworski (1998).

44. Strictly speaking, Regulation DD applies only to depository institutions that are not credit unions, but Section 272 of the Truth in Savings Act requires that the National Credit Union Administration propose a "substantially similar" regulation for credit unions within 90 days, "taking into account the unique nature of credit unions and the limitations under which they may pay dividends on member accounts."

45. For whatever reason, Congress chose to title this act with the word *fund* rather than *funds*, that otherwise might seem appropriate. An earlier version of the bill that eventually became law, the Fair Fund Transfer Act, used the same word.

46. Low awareness of the specifics of provisions of the EFTA, despite frequent disclosures, is also visible in results of another question not reported in the table. The majority of respondents to a question about the liability on an unauthorized electronic transfer of $200 gave the response, "Nothing," rather than any of the amounts that would be given in their disclosures (correctly, $50 in the example in the survey question). The proportion answering $50, which is probably a reasonable guess, given that this amount is the liability for unauthorized use of a credit card (a Regulation Z required disclosure), was 14 percent in 1983 and 13 percent in 1990.

References

Agarwal, Sumit, Souphala Chomsisengphet, Chunlin Liu, and Nicholas S. Souleles. 2005. *Do Consumers Choose the Right Credit Contracts?* Working Paper, Federal Reserve Bank of Chicago (December 18).

Aizcorbe, Ana, and Martha Starr-McCluer. 1997. Vehicle Ownership, Purchases, and Leasing: Consumer Survey Data. *Monthly Labor Review* (June).

Akerlof, George. 1970. The Market for Lemons: Qualitative Uncertainty and the Market Mechanism. *Quarterly Journal of Economics* (August).

Ariely, Dan and Klaus Wertenbach. 2002. Procrastination, Deadlines, and Performance: Self-Control by Precommitment. *Psychological Science* (May).

Arshadi, Nasser, and Gordon V. Karels. 1997. *Modern Financial Intermediaries and Markets*. Upper Saddle River, New Jersey: Prentice Hall.

Ausubel, Lawrence M. 1991. The Failure of Competition in the Credit Card Market. *American Economic Review* (March).

Avery, Robert B., Glenn B. Canner, and Robert E. Cook. 2005. New Information Reported under HMDA and Its Application in Fair Lending Enforcement. *Federal Reserve Bulletin* (September).

Avery, Robert B., Kenneth P. Brevoort, and Glenn B. Canner. 2006. Higher-Priced Home Lending and the 2005 HMDA Data. *Federal Reserve Bulletin* (September).

Ayers, Milan V. 1946. *Installment Mathematics Handbook*. New York: The Ronald Press.

Barr, Michael S., Sendhil Mullainathan, and Eldar Shafir. 2009. Behaviorially Informed Home Mortgage Credit Regulation. In *Understand Consumer Credit*, Eric S. Belsky and Nicolas P. Retsinas, eds. Washington: Brookings Press.

Barron, John M., and Michael E. Staten. 2004. Usage of Credit Cards Received Through College Student Marketing Programs. *Journal of Student Financial Aid* (Vol. 34, No. 3).

Barry, Thomas E. 1987. The Development of the Hierarchy of Effects: An Historical Perspective. *Current Issues and Research in Advertising* (Volume 10, Issue 2).

Barzel, Yoram. 1977. Some Fallacies in the Interpretation of Information Costs. *Journal of Law and Economics* (October).

Beales, Howard, Richard Craswell, and Steven C. Salop. 1981. The Efficient Regulation of Consumer Information. *Journal of Law and Economics* (December).

Becker, Gary S. and Casey B. Mulligan. 1997. The Endogenous Determination of Time Preference. *Quarterly Journal of Economics* (August).

Bendor, Jonathan Brodie, Sunil Kumar, and David A. Siegel. 2009. Satisficing: A "Pretty Good" Heuristic. *The B.E. Journal of Theoretical Economics* (Issue 1).

Benhabib, Jess and Alberto Bisin. 2005. Modeling Internal Commitment Mechanisms and Self-Control: A Neuroeconomics Approach to Consumption-Saving Decisions. *Games and Economic Behavior* (August).

Bernstein, Leonard A. 1994a. Home Equity Lenders Need to Re-analyze Their Business Procedures to Meet the August 9 Deadline for Complying With the Real Estate Settlement Procedures Act. *National Law Journal* (May 23).

_____. 1994b. RESPA Invades Home Equity, Home Improvement, and Mobile Home Financing. *Consumer Finance Law Quarterly Report* (Spring).

Bettman, James R. 1979. *An Information Processing Theory of Consumer Choice.* Reading, Massachusetts: Addison-Wesley.

Bettman, James R., Mary Frances Luce, and John W. Payne. 1998. Constructive Consumer Choice Processes. *Journal of Consumer Research* (December).

Blackwell, Roger D., Paul W. Miniard, and James F. Engel. 2006. *Consumer Behavior,* 10th. ed. Stamford, Connecticut: Thomson South-Western.

Bloch, Peter H., Daniel L. Sherrell, and Nancy M. Ridgway. 1986. Consumer Search: An Extended Framework. *Journal of Consumer Research* (June).

Bloom, Paul N. 1989. A Decision Model for Prioritizing and Addressing Consumer Information Problems. *Journal of Public Policy and Marketing* (Volume 8).

Board of Governors of the Federal Reserve System. 1970. *Annual Report on Truth in Lending for the Year 1969.* Washington: Board of Governors of the Federal Reserve System.

_____. 1971. *Annual Report on Truth in Lending for the Year 1970.* Washington: Board of Governors of the Federal Reserve System.

_____. 1979. *Annual Report on Truth in Lending for the Year 1978.* Washington: Board of Governors of the Federal Reserve System.

_____. 1987. *Annual Percentage Rate Demonstration Project.* Washington: Board of Governors of the Federal Reserve System.

_____. 1995. Proposed Rules, Regulation Z, Docket R-0908. *Federal Register* (December 21).

_____. 1996. *Report to Congress on Finance charges for Consumer Credit Under the Truth in Lending Act.* Washington: Board of Governors of the Federal Reserve System.

Board of Governors of the Federal Reserve System and Department of Housing and Urban Development. 1998. *Joint Report to the Congress Concerning Reform to the Truth in Lending Act and the Real Estate Settlement Procedures Act.* Washington: Board of Governors of the Federal Reserve System and Department of Housing and Urban Development.

Borges, B., D.G. Goldstein, A. Ortmann, and G. Gigerenzer. 1999. Can Ignorance Beat the Stock Market? In *Simple Heuristics that Make Us Smart*, Gerd Gigerenzer and Peter M Todd, eds. New York: Oxford University Press, 1999.

Brandt, William K., George S. Day, and Terry Deutscher. 1975. The Effect of Disclosure on Consumer Knowledge of Credit Terms. *Journal of Consumer Affairs* (Summer).

Brandt, William K., and Robert P. Shay. 1978. Credit Shopping behavior and Consumer Protection Legislation. Paper presented at the Annual Meeting of the Midwest Finance Association (April).

Brealey, Richard A., and Stewart C. Myers. 1991. *Principles of Corporate Finance,* 4th ed. New York: McGraw-Hill.

Buckley, Jeremiah S. and Joseph M. Kolar. 1997. HUD Issues New RESPA Rules on Employer-Employee Payments, Controlled Business Arrangements, and Computerized Loan Origination Systems; Congress Passes RESPA Amendments in Banking Bill. *The Business Lawyer* (May).

Byrd, Chris, 1999. Comment and Note: The Rise and Fall of Consumer Protection Under RESPA. *University of Missouri at Kansas City Law Review* (Winter).

Calder, Lendol. 1999. *Financing the American Dream: A Cultural History of Consumer Credit.* Princeton, New Jersey: Princeton University Press.

Calomiris, W. and Joseph R. Mason. 1999. *High Loan-to-Value Mortgage Lending.* Washington: AEI Press.

Camerer, Colin, George Loewenstein, and Drazen Prelec. 2005. Neuroeconomics: How Neuroscience Can Inform Economics. *Journal of Economic Literature* (March).

Canner, Glenn B., Thomas A. Durkin, and Charles A. Luckett. 1994. Home Equity Lending: Evidence From Recent Surveys. *Federal Reserve Bulletin* (July).

_____. 1998. Recent Developments in Home Equity Lending. *Federal Reserve Bulletin* (April).

Caplovitz, David. 1967. *The Poor Pay More.* New York: The Free Press.

Carlson, John A. and Robert J. Gieseke. 1983. Price Search in a Product Market. *Journal of Consumer Research* (March).

Carlson, John A. and Preston R. McAfee. 1983. Discrete Equilibrium Price Dispersion. *Journal of Political Economy* (June).

Chang, Yu-Chun and Sherman Hanna. 1991. Consumer Credit: An Exploratory Study of Search Behavior. Paper presented at the Annual Conference of the American Council on Consumer Interests.

Chomsisengphet, Souphala and Anthony Pennington-Cross. 2006. The Evolution of the Subprime Mortgage Market. Federal Reserve Bank of St. Louis *Review* (January-February).

Climo, Beth L. 1980. Simplification and Reform of the Truth in Lending Act. *Journal of Retail Banking* (June).

CNW Marketing Research. 1995. Fuller Disclosure Likely to Increase Lease Share & Customer Satisfaction. *LTR/8+* (June).

Commission on Federal Paperwork. 1977. *Consumer Credit Protection: A Commission Report.* Washington: Government Printing Office.

Cook, Robert A. and Timothy P. Meredith. 1995. Truth in Lending Developments in 1994. *The Business Lawyer* (May).

Cook, Robert A. and Robert R. Wisner. 1996. Truth in Lending. *The Business Lawyer* (May).

Cosmides, Leda. and Tooby, J. 1996. Are Humans Good Intuitive Statisticians After All? Rethinking Some Conclusions from the Literature on Judgment under Uncertainty. *Cognition* (January).

Curran, Barbara A. 1965. *Trends in Consumer Credit Legislation.* Chicago: University of Chicago Press.

Darby, Michael R. and Edi Karni. 1973. Free Competition and the Optimal Amount of Fraud. *Journal of Law and Economics* (April).

Davis, Jeffrey. 1977. Protecting Consumers from Overdisclosure and Gobbledygook: An Empirical Look at the Simplification of Consumer Credit Contracts. *Virginia Law Review* (October).

Day, George S. 1976. Assessing the Effects of Information Disclosure Requirements. *Journal of Marketing* (April).

Day, George S., and William K. Brandt. 1973. *A Study of Consumer Credit Decisions: Implications for Present and Prospective Legislation.* In *Technical Studies of the National Commission on Consumer Finance,* Volume 1, Number 2. Washington: Government Printing Office, 1973.

_____. 1974a. Consumer Research and the Evaluation of Information Disclosure Requirements: The Case of Truth in Lending. *Journal of Consumer Research* (June).

_____. 1974b. Information Disclosure and Consumer Behavior: An Empirical Evaluation of Truth in Lending. *University of Michigan Journal of Law Reform* (Winter).

de Roover, Raymond. 1946. The Medici Bank Financial and Commercial Operations. *The Journal of Economic History* (November).

Deutscher, Terry. 1973. *Credit Legislation Two Years Out: Awareness Changes and Behavioral Effects of Differential Awareness Levels.* In *Technical Studies of the National Commission on Consumer Finance,* Volume 1, Number 4. Washington: Government Printing Office.

Durkin, Thomas A. 1993. An Economic Perspective on Interest Rate Limitations. *Georgia State University Law Review* (June).

_____. 2000. Credit Cards: Use and Consumer Attitudes, 1970-2000. *Federal Reserve Bulletin* (September).

_____. 2002. Consumers and Credit Disclosures: Credit Cards and Credit Insurance. *Federal Reserve Bulletin* (April).

_____. 2006a. Consumers and Disclosures: Results of Surveys About Credit Cards, Solicitations, and Privacy Notices. *Federal Reserve Bulletin* (Third Quarter).

_____. 2006b. Requirements and Prospects for a New Time to Payoff Disclosure for Open End Credit Under Truth in Lending Washington: Board of Governors of the federal Reserve System, Finance and Economics Discussion Series 2006-34.

_____. 2007. Should Consumer Disclosures Be Updated. Paper presented at Harvard University Symposium Understanding Consumer Credit (November 28–29).

Durkin, Thomas A. and Gregory E. Elliehausen. 1978. *The 1977 Consumer Credit Survey.* Washington: Board of Governors of the Federal Reserve System.

Durkin, Thomas A., Gregory Elliehausen, Michael E. Staten, and Todd J. Zywicki. 2011. *Consumer Credit and the American Economy.* Oxford and New York: Oxford University Press, forthcoming.

Edelman, Mark. S., Robert A. Aitken, and Raechelle C. Yballe. 2008. The Road Ahead: Emerging Trends in Personal Property Finance. *The Business Lawyer* (February).

Elliehausen, Gregory E. 1998. The Cost of Banking Regulation: A Review of the Evidence. Washington: Board of Governors of the Federal Reserve System Staff Study 171.

Elliehausen, Gregory E. and Barbara R. Lowrey. 1997. The Cost of Implementing Consumer Financial Regulations: An Analysis of Experience with the Truth in Savings Act. Washington: Board of Governors of the Federal Reserve System Staff Study 170.

Engel, James F., Roger D. Blackwell, and Paul W. Miniard. 1995. *Consumer Behavior,* 8th. ed. Fort Worth, Texas: The Dryden Press.

Engel, James F., David T. Kollat, and Roger D. Blackwell. 1968. *Consumer Behavior,* 1st. ed. New York: Holt, Rinehart and Winston.

Fama, Eugene F. 1998. Market Efficiency, Long-Term Returns, and Behavioral Finance. *Journal of Financial Economics* (September).

Federal Reserve Bank of Atlanta. 1978. Substantive Policy Issues in Truth in Lending: A Study Submitted to the Board of Governors of the Federal Reserve System as Phase I of the Board's Regulatory Improvement Project.

Federal Trade Commission Staff. 1979. *Consumer Information Remedies Policy Session.* Washington: Federal Trade Commission.

Fiedler, Klaus. 1988. The Dependence of the Conjunction Fallacy on Subtle Linguistic Factors. *Psychological Research* (September).

Fisher, Irving. 1930. *The Theory of Interest*. New York: The Macmillan Company.

Foote, Bruce E. 1997a. The Real Estate Settlement Procedures Act: Disclosure of Fees to Mortgage Brokers. Washington: Congressional Research Service, The Library of Congress.

_____. 1997b. The Real Estate Settlement Procedures Act: Implementing the Anti-Kickback Provisions. Congressional Research Service, The Library of Congress.

Frederick, Shane, George Loewenstein, and Ted O'Donoghue. 2002. Time Discounting and Time Preference: A Critical Review. *Journal of Economic Literature* (June).

Gabaix, Xavier and David Laibson. 2006. Shrouded Attributes, Consumer Myopia, and Information Suppression in Competitive Markets. *Quarterly Journal of Economics* (May).

Garwood, Griffith L., Robert J. Hobbs, and Fred H. Miller. 1993, Consumer Disclosure in the 1990s. *Georgia State University Law Review* (June).

Gelpi, Rosa-Maria and Francois Julien-Labruyere. 2000. *The History of Consumer Credit*. New York: St. Martin's Press.

Giacotto, Carmelo, Gerson M. Goldberg, and Shantaram P. Hegde. 2007. The Value of Embedded Real Options: Evidence from Consumer Automobile Lease Contracts. *Journal of Finance* (February).

Gigerenzer, Gerd. 1994. Why the Distinction between Single-Event Probabilities and Frequencies Is Important for Psychology (and Vice Versa). In *Subjective Probability*, G. Wright and P. Ayton, eds. New York: John Wiley.

Gigerenzer, Gerd and Daniel G. Goldstein. 1999. Betting on One Good Reason: The Take the Best Heuristic. In *Simple Heuristics that Make Us Smart*, Gerd Gigerenzer and Peter M Todd, eds. New York: Oxford University Press.

Gigerenzer, Gerd and Ulrich Hoffrage. 1995. How to Improve Baysian Reasoning Without Instruction: Frequency Formats. *Psychological Review* (October).

Golann, Dwight, et al. 1998. Re-examining Truth in Lending: Do Borrowers Actually Use Consumer Disclosures? *Personal Finance Law Quarterly Report* (Winter).

Green, Leonard and Joel Myerson. 1996. Exponential versus Hyperbolic Discounting of Delayed Outcomes: Risk and Waiting Time. *American Zoologist* (September).

Griffith, Elwin. 1998. Truth in Lending–The Right of Rescission, Disclosure of the Finance Charge, and Itemization of the Amount Financed in Closed end Transactions. *George Mason Law Review* (Winter).

_____. 2000. Searching for Truth in Lending: Identifying Some Problems in the Truth in Lending Act and Regulation Z. *Baylor Law Review* (Spring).

Griffiths, Thomas L and Joshua B. Tenenbaum. 2006. Optimal Predictions in Everyday Cognition. *Psychological Science* (September).

Gross, David B. and Nicholas S. Souleles. 2002. Do Liquidity Constraints and Interest Rates Matter for Consumer Behavior? Evidence from Credit Card Data. *Quarterly Journal of Economics* (February).

Grossman, Sanford J. and Joseph Stiglitz. 1976. Information and Competitive Price Systems. *American Economic Review* (May).

Gruber, Gerald H. 1992. Recovering Hidden Values in Retail Lease Portfolios. *Journal of Retail Banking* (Fall).

Gurley, John G., and Edward S. Shaw. 1960. *Money in a Theory of Finance.* Washington: The Brookings Institution.

Guttentag, Jack M. and E. Gerald Hurst. 1985. Truth in Lending a Applied to Mortgages: What Should Be Disclosed and When? *Housing Finance Review* (January).

Hertwig, Ralph and Gerd Gigerenzer. 1993. Frequency and Single Event Judgments. Unpublished paper, Max Planck Institute for Human Development, Berlin.

_____. 1999. The "Conjunction Fallacy" Revisited: How Intellegent Infererences Look Like Reasoning Errors. *Journal of Behavioral Decision Making* (Number 4).

Holbrook, Morris B. 2001. Remembrance: John A. Howard (1915-1999). *Journal of Consumer Research* (September).

Homer, Sidney, and Richard E. Sylla. 1996. *A History of Interest Rates*, 3rd. ed. New Brunswick, New Jersey: Rutgers University Press.

Howard, John A. and Jagdish N. Sheth. 1969. *The Theory of Buyer Behavior.* New York: John Wiley and Sons.

Huber, Elizabeth A. and Thomas B. Hudson. 1998. Road Testing the New Regulation M. *The Business Lawyer* (May).

Ippolito, Pauline M. 1984, Consumer Protection Economics: A Selective Survey. In *Consumer Protection Economics*, Pauline M. Ippolito and and David T. Scheffman, eds. Washington: Federal Trade Commission.

_____. 1988. The Economics of Information in Consumer Markets: What Do We Know? What Do We Need to Know? In *The Frontiers of Research in the Consumer Interest*, E. Scott Maynes, ed. Columbia, Missouri: American Council on Consumer Interests.

Ippolito, Pauline M. and Janis K. Pappalardo. 2002. Advertising *Nutrition and Health, Evidence from Food Advertising 1977-1997.* Washington: Federal Trade Commission Bureau of Economics Staff Report.

Jackson, Howell E. and Jeremy Berry. 2002. *Kickbacks or Compensation: The Case of Yield Spread Premiums.* Harvard Law School, incomplete manuscript provided to the United States Senate Committee on Banking, Housing, and Urban Affairs (January).

Jacobides, Michael G. 2001. Mortgage Banking Unbundling: Structure, Automation, and Profit. *Mortgage Banking* (January).

Jaworski, Robert M. 1998. The RESPA Soap Opera Continues for Another Year. *The Business Lawyer* (May).

_____. 1999. RESPA 1998: The Long and Winding Road. *The Business Lawyer* (May).

Johnson, Robert W. 1961. *Methods of Stating Consumer Finance Charges.* New York: Columbia University Graduate School of Business, Studies in Consumer Credit, Number 2.

Juster, F. Thomas and Robert P. Shay. 1964. *Consumer Sensitivity to Finance Rates*. New York: National Bureau of Economic Research.

Kahneman, Daniel, Jack L. Knetsch, and Richard H. Thaler. 1990. Experimental Tests of the Endowment Effect and the Coase Theorem. *Journal of Political Economy* (December).

_____. 1991. Anomalies: The Endowment Effect, Loss Aversion, and Status Quo Bias. *Journal of Economic Perspectives* (Winter).

Kahneman, Daniel and Amos Tversky. 1979. Prospect Theory: An Analysis of Decision Under Uncertainty. *Econometrica* (March).

Katona, George. 1975. *Psychological Economics*. New York: Elsevier Scientific Publishing Company.

Katona, George, James N. Morgan, Jay Schmiedeskamp, and John A. Sonquist. 1967. *1967 Survey of Consumer Finances*. Ann Arbor, Michigan: Survey Research Center.

Katz, Michael L. and Harvey S. Rosen. 1997. *Microeconomics*, 3rd. ed. Burr Ridge, Illinois: Irwin.

Keest, Kathleen E. Whither Now? 1997. Truth in Lending in Transition—Again. *Personal Finance Law Quarterly Report* (Fall).

Keest, Kathleen E., Timothy P. Meredith, and Elizabeth C. Yen. 1998. 1997 Truth in Lending Developments. *The Business Lawyer* (May).

Kosin, Gregory M. 1995. RESPA Information Snarl Demands Immediate Attention. *Title News* (May/June).

Kripke, Homer. 1969. Gesture and Reality in Consumer Credit Reform. *New York University Law Review* (March).

Krynski, Tevye R. and Joshua B. Tenenbaum. 2003. The Role of Causal Models in Reasoning under Uncertainty. In *Proceedings of the 25th Annual Conference of the Cognitive Science Society*, Richard Alterman and David Kirsh. eds. London: Psychology Press.

Lacko, James M. and Janis K. Pappalardo. 2004. *The Effect of Mortgage Broker Compensation Disclosures on Consumers and Competition: A Controlled Experiment*. Washington: Federal Trade Commission.

_____. 2007. *Improving Consumer Mortgage Disclosures: An Empirical Assessment of Current and Prototype Disclosure Forms*. Washington: Federal Trade Commission, Bureau of Economics Staff Report (June).

Laibson, David. 1997. Golden Eggs and Hyperbolic Discounting. *Quarterly Journal of Economics* (May).

Lancaster, Kelvin J. 1981. Information and Product Differentiation. In *The Economics of Information*, Malcom Galatin and Robert. D. Lister, eds. Amsterdam: Martins Nijhoff.

Landers, Jonathan M. 1976. The Scope of Coverage of the Truth in Lending Act. *American Bar Foundation Research Journal* (Volume 1, Number 2).

Landers, Jonathan M. and Ralph J. Rohner. 1979. A Functional Analysis of Truth in Lending. *UCLA Law Review* (April).

Lax, Howard A. 1996. The Truth in Lending Act Amendments of 1995. *Bankers Magazine* (September-October).

Linneman, Peter and Richard Voith. 1985. Would Mortgage Borrowers Benefit from the Provision of APR Schedules? *Housing Finance Review* (January).

Lynch, John G., Jr. and Gal Zauberman. 2006. When Do You Want It? Time, Decisions, and Public Policy. *Journal of Public Policy and Marketing* (Spring).

Malkiel, Burton G. 2003. The Efficient Market Hypothesis and Its Critics. *Journal of Economic Perspectives* (Winter).

Mandell, Lewis. 1971. Consumer Perception of Increased Interest Rates: An Empirical Test of the Efficacy of the Truth in Lending Law. *Journal of Finance* (December).

_____. 1973. Consumer Knowledge and Understanding of Consumer Credit. *Journal of Consumer Affairs* (Summer).

Mannering, Fred, Clifford Winston, and William Starkey. 1999. An Exploratory Analysis of Automobile Leasing in the United States. Working Paper, University of Washington.

Maynes, E. Scott. 1986. Towards Market Transparency. In *Price Information and Public Price Controls, Consumers and Market Performance: Proceedings of the Fourth European Workshop on Consumer Law*, M. Goyens, ed. Brussels: Bruylant.

McAlister, E. Ray, and Edward DeSpain. 1975. *An Empirical Analysis of Retail Revolving Credit*. West Lafayette, Indiana: Purdue University Credit Research Center, Monograph Number 1.

McCathren, Randall R., and Ronald S. Loshin. 1991. *Automobile Lending and Leasing Manual*. Boston: Warren, Gorham, and Lamont.

Michelman, Irving S. 1966. *Consumer Finance: A Case Study in American Business*. New York: Frederick Fell.

Miller, Fred H. 1979. Truth in Lending Act. *The Business Lawyer*. (April).

Miller, Stephen E. 1995. Economics of Automobile Leasing: The Call Option Value. *Journal of Consumer Affairs* (Summer).

Miller, Earl K. and Jonathan D. Cohen. 2001. An Integrative Theory of Prefrontal Cortex Function. *Annual Review of Neuroscience* (Volume 24).

Mitchell, Grant E. 1999. RESPA: The Inside Story. *Mortgage Banking* (November).

Moorthy, Sridhar, Brian T. Ratchford, and Debabrata Talukdar. 1997. Consumer Information Search Revisited: Theory and Empirical Analysis. *Journal of Consumer Research* (March).

Mors, Wallace P. 1965. *Consumer Credit Finance Charges*. New York: National Bureau of Economic Research.

Muris, Timothy J. 1991. Economics and Consumer Protection. *Antitrust Law Journal* (Spring).

Murphy, Neil B. 1980. Economies of Scale in the Cost of Compliance With Consumer Credit Protection Laws: The Case of Implementation of the Equal Credit Opportunity Act of 1974. *Journal of Bank Research* (Winter).

Murray, Keith B. 1991. A Test of Services Marketing Theory. *Journal of Marketing* (January).

Myers, Stewart C., David A. Dill, and Alberto J. Bautista. 1976. Valuation of Financial Lease Contracts. *Journal of Finance* (June).

National Commission on Consumer Finance. 1972. *Consumer Credit in the United States: The Report of the National Commission on Consumer Finance.* Washington: Government Printing Office.

National Conference of Commissioners on Uniform State Laws. 1999. *Uniform Consumer Leases Act. Draft for Discussion Only as prepared for the Committee on Style Meeting, April 15-18.* Chicago: National Conference of Commissioners on Uniform State Laws.

Neifeld, M. R. 1951. *Neifeld's Guide to Installment Calculations.* Easton, Pennsylvania: Mack Publishing Company.

Nelson, Philip. 1970. Information and Consumer Behavior. *Journal of Political Economy* (March-April).

Nicosia, Francesco M. 1966. *Consumer Decision Processes.* Engelwood Cliffs, New Jersey: Prentice Hall.

Nunnally, Bennie H., Jr., and D. Anthony Plath. 1989. Leasing Versus Borrowing: Evaluating Alternative Forms of Consumer Credit. *Journal of Consumer Affairs* (Winter).

Oaksford, Mike, and Nick Chater. 1996. Rational Explanation of the Selection Task. *Psychological Review* (April).

O'Connor, William J., Jr. 1980. Truth in Lending Simplification. *The Business Lawyer* (April).

O'Donoghue, Ted and Matthew Rabin. 1999. Doing It Now or Later. *American Economic Review* [March].

_____. 2000. The Economics of Immediate Gratification. *Journal of Behavioral Decision Making* (April/June Special Issue).

Olson, Jerry C. and Thomas J. Reynolds. 2001. The Means-End Approach to Understanding Consumer Decision Making. In *Understanding Consumer Decision Making: The Means-End Approach to Marketing and Advertising Strategy,* Thomas J. Reynolds and Jerry C. Olson eds. Mahwah, New Jersey: Lawrence Erlbaum Associates.

Ornstein, Stephen E. J. 1996. Examining the Effect of New Legislation on Consumer Protection for "High Cost" Mortgages. *Real Estate Law Journal* (Summer).

Paletta, Damian, 2004. Fed Seeks Card Disclosure Comments in Reg. Z Review. *American Banker* (December 28).

Parker, George G. C. and Robert P. Shay. 1974. Some Factors Affecting Awareness of Annual Percentage Rates in Consumer Installment Credit Transactions. *Journal of Finance* (March).

Patrick, Thomas M. 1984. A Proposed Procedure for Facilitating the Analysis of Lease-Purchase Decisions by Consumers. *Journal of Consumer Affairs* (Winter).

Phillips, Lynn W. and Bobby J. Calder. 1979. Evaluating Consumer Protection Programs: Part I, Weak But Commonly Used Research Designs. *Journal of Consumer Affairs* (Winter).

_____. 1980. Evaluating Consumer Protection Laws II: Promising Methods. *Journal of Consumer Affairs* (Summer).

Plott, Charles R. and Kathryn Zeiler. 2005. The Willingness to Pay-Willingness to Accept Gap, the "Endowment Effect," Subject Misconceptions, and Experimental Procedures for Eliciting Validations. *American Economic Review* (June).

Prelec, Drazen and George Loewenstein. 1998. The Red and the Black: Mental Accounting of Savings and Debt. *Marketing Science* (Number 1).

Proxmire, William. 1967. Introductory Remarks to Accompany S.5. *Congressional Record* (January 11).

Punj, Girish N., and Richard Staelin. 1983. A Model of Consumer Information Search Behavior for New Automobiles. *Journal of Consumer Research* (March).

Rasor, Paul B. 1993. Biblical Roots of Modern Consumer Credit Law. *Journal of Law and Religion* (Number 1).

Ratchford, Brian T. 1988. The Economics of Information: The Views of a Marketing Economist. In *The Frontiers of Research in the Consumer Interest*, E. Scott Maynes, ed. Columbia, Missouri: American Council on Consumer Interests.

_____. 2001. The Economics of Consumer Knowledge. *Journal of Consumer Research* (March).

Real, Leslie and Thomas Caraco. 1986. Risk and Foraging in Stochastic Environments. *Annual Review of Ecology and Systematics*. (Volume 17).

Reynolds, Thomas J. and Jerry C. Olson, eds. 2001. *Consumer Decision Making: A Means End Approach to Marketing and Advertising Strategy*. Mahwah, New Jersey: Lawrence Erlbaum Associates.

Rich, Steven P. and John T. Rose. 1997. Interest Rate Concepts and Terminology in Introductory Finance Textbooks. *Financial Practice and Education* (Spring/Summer).

Robinson, Lewis N. and Rolf Nugent. 1935. *Regulation of the Small Loan Business*. New York: Russell Sage Foundation.

Rohner, Ralph J. 1981. Truth in Lending "Simplified": Simplified? *New York University Law Review* (November-December).

_____. 1984. *The Law of Truth in Lending*. Boston: Warren, Gorham and Lamont.

_____. 1996. Whither Truth in Lending? *Personal Finance Law Quarterly Report* (Spring).

_____. 2003. Leasing Consumer Goods: The Spotlight Shifts to the Uniform Consumer Leases Act. *University of Connecticut Law Review* (Winter).

Rohner, Ralph J. and Thomas A. Durkin. 2005. TILA "Finance" and "Other" Charges in Open end Credit: The Cost of credit Principle Applied to Charges for Optional Products or Services. *Loyola Consumer Law Review* (Volume 17, Number 2).

Rohner, Ralph J. and Fred H. Miller. 1988. *The Law of Truth in Lending, 1988 Cumulative Supplement*. Boston: Warren Gorham, and Lamont.

Roos, Norman H. 1997. Issues in Litigation: Yield Spread Premiums. *Banking Law Journal* (October).

Rothschild, Michael. 1973. Models of Market Organization with Imperfect Information: A Survey. *Journal of Political Economy* (June).

Rubin, Edward L. 1991. Legislative Methodology: Some Lessons from the Truth in Lending Act. *Georgetown University Law Review* (December).

Russo, J. Edward. 1988. Information Processing from the Consumer's Perspective. In *The Frontiers of Research in the Consumer Interest*, E. Scott Maynes, ed. Columbia, Missouri: American Council on Consumer Interests.

Salop, Steven. 1976. Information and Monopolistic Competition. *American Economic Review* (May).

_____. 1978. Parables of Information Transmission in Markets. In *The Effects of Information on Consumer and Market Behavior*, Andrew W. Mitchell, ed. Chicago: American Marketing Association.

Samuels, Richard, Stephen Stich, and Luc Faucher. 2004. Reason and Rationality. In *Handbook of Epistemology*, Ilkka Niiniluoto, Matti Sintonen, and Jan Wolenski, eds. Dordrecht: Kluwer.

Samuelson, Paul A. 1937. A Note on Measurement of Utility. *Review of Economic Studies* (February).

Schallheim, James S., 1994. *Lease or Buy?* Boston: Harvard University Press, Financial Management Association Survey and Synthesis Series.

Schiff, Michael P. 1998. Consumer Law: Mortgage Brokers and Yield Spread Premiums: Legitimate Fees or Illegal Kickbacks? *The Florida Bar Journal* (December).

Schroeder, Frederick J. 1985. *Compliance Costs and Consumer Benefits of the Electronic Fund Transfer Act: Recent Survey Evidence*. Washington: Board of Governors of the Federal Reserve System Staff Study 143.

Schwartz, Alan and Louis L. Wilde. 1979. Intervening on Markets on the Basis of Imperfect Information. *University of Pennsylvania Law Review* (Vol. 127, p. 630).

Shay, Robert P. 1953. *Regulation W: Experiment in Credit Control*. Orono, ME: University of Maine Studies, Second Series, No. 67.

Shay, Robert P. and Milton P. Schober. 1973. *Consumer Awareness of Annual Percentage Rates of Charge in Consumer Installment Credit: Before and After Truth in Lending Became Effective*. In *Technical Studies of the National Commission on*

Consumer Finance, Volume 1, Number 1. Washington: Government Printing Office.

Simon, Herbert A. 1990. Invariants of Human Behavior. *Annual Review of Psychology* (Volume 41).

Smith, Vernon L. 1991. Rational Choice: The Contrast between Economics and Psychology. *Journal of Political Economy* (August).

_____. 2005. Behavioral Economics Research and the Foundations of Economics. *Journal of Socio-Economics* (March).

Spence, A. Michael. 1973. Job Market Signaling. *Quarterly Journal of Economics* (August).

_____. 1974. *Market Signaling: Informational Transferring in Hiring and Related Screening Processes*. Cambridge, Massachusetts: Harvard University Press.

Staten, Michael E., and Robert W. Johnson. 1994. *1994 Automobile Finance Study*. West Lafayette, Indiana: Purdue University Credit Research Center.

Staten, Michael E., John Umbeck, and Otis Gilley. 1990. Information Costs and the Organization of Credit Markets. *Economic Inquiry* (July).

Stigler, George J. 1961. The Economics of Information. *Journal of Political Economy* (June).

Stiglitz, Joseph E. 1979. Equilibrium in Product Markets With Imperfect Information. *American Economic Review* (May).

_____. 1985. Information and Economic Analysis. *Economic Journal.* (March).

_____. 1987. The Causes and Consequences of the Dependence of Quality on Price. *Journal of Economic Literature* (March).

Stiglitz, Joseph E., and Carl E. Walsh. 2006. *Economics*, 4th. ed. New York: W. W. Norton and Company.

Stiglitz, Joseph, E. and Andrew Weiss. 1981. Credit Rationing in Markets with Imperfect Information. *American Economic Review* (June).

Strotz, Robert H. 1955-1956. Myopia and Inconsistency in Dynamic Utility Maximization. *Review of Economic Studies* (Number 3).

Thaler, Richard H. 1980. Toward a Positive Theory of Consumer Choice. *Journal of Economic Behavior and Organization* (March).

_____. 1981. Some Empirical Evidence on Dynamic Inconsistency. *Economics Letters* (Issue 3).

_____. 1985. Mental Accounting and Consumer Choice. *Marketing Science* (Summer).

Thaler, Richard H. and Shlomo Benartzi. 2004. Save More Tomorrow: Using Behavioral Economics to Increase Employee Saving. *Journal of Political Economy* (February, Supplement).

Thaler, Richard H. and Eric J. Johnson. 1990. Gambling with House Money and Trying to Break Even: The Effects of Prior Outcomes on Risky Choice. *Management Science* (June).

Tversky, Amos and Daniel Kahneman. 1974. Judgment Under Uncertainty: Heuristics and Biases. *Science*, New Series (September 27).

_____. 1981. The Framing of Decisions and the Psychology of Choice. *Science* (January).

_____. 1983. Extensional Versus Intuitive Reasoning: The Conjunction Fallacy in Probability Judgment. *Psychological Review* (October).

Tyree, Donald A. 1960. *The Small Loan Industry in Texas.* Austin: Bureau of Business Research, University of Texas.

Urbany, Joel E. 1986. An Experimental Examination of the Economics of Information. *Journal of Consumer Research* (September).

US Courts Administrative Office. 1979. *Judicial Business of the United States Courts, Annual Report of the Director.* Washington: Administrative Office of the United States Courts.

US Department of Housing and Urban Development. 2002a. 24 *CFR* Part 3500: Real Estate Settlement Procedures Act (RESPA); Simplifying and Improving the Process of Obtaining Mortgages To Reduce Settlement Costs to Consumers; Proposed Rule. *Federal Register* (July 29).

_____. 2002b. *Economic Analysis and Initial Regulatory Flexibility Analysis for RESPA Proposed Rule to Simplify and Improve the Process of Obtaining Mortgages to Reduce Settlement Costs to Consumers.* Washington: Department of Housing and Urban Development, Office of Policy Development and Research.

US House of Representatives. 1998. *Reform of the Real Estate Settlement Procedures Act (RESPA) and the Truth in Lending Act (TILA), Hearings Before the Committee on Banking and Financial Institutions, Subcommittee on Financial Institutions and Consumer Credit July 22 and September 16, 1998.* Washington: Government Printing Office.

US Senate. 1967. *Hearings Before the Subcommittee on Financial Institutions of the Committee on Banking and Currency, Ninetieth Congress, First Session, on S.5.* Washington: Government Printing Office.

US Senate Committee on Banking and Currency. 1967. *Truth in Lending 1967, Report to Accompany S.5.* Washington: Government Printing Office.

US Senate Committee on Banking, Housing, and Urban Affairs. 1979. *Truth in Lending Simplification and Reform Act, Report to Accompany S. 108.* Washington: Government Printing Office.

US Senate Committee on Banking, Housing, and Urban Affairs, Subcommittee on Financial Institutions and Regulatory Relief. 1999. *The Joint Report from HUD and the Federal Reserve Regarding RESPA-TILA Reform, Hearings, July 17, 1998.* Washington: Government Printing Office.

Wallace, George J. 1981. "Explicit Pricing," Fraud, and Consumer Information: The Reform of RESPA. *Rutgers Law Journal* (Winter).

Whitford, William C. 1972. The Functions of Disclosure Regulation in Consumer Transactions. *Wisconsin Law Review* (Number 2, page 400).

Wilde, Louis L. 1980. The Economics of Consumer Information Acquisition. *Journal of Business* (July, Part 2).

Wilde, Louis L. and Alan Schwartz. 1979. Equilibrium Comparison Shopping. *Review of Economic Studies* (July).

Wilkie, William L. and Elizabeth S. Moore. 2003. Scholarly Research in Marketing: Exploring the "4 Eras" of Thought Development. *Journal of Public Policy and Marketing* (Fall).

Willenzik, David S. 1979. Truth in Lending Litigation, Specific Problem Areas. *Journal of Retail Banking* (June).

Williams, Julie L. 2005. Remarks Before Women in Housing and Finance and The Exchequer Club. Washington: Office of the Comptroller of the Currency (January 12). Available at www.occ.treas.gov/news-issuances/speeches/2005/pub-speech-2005-1.pdf

Zinman, Jonathan. 2007. Household Borrowing High and Lending Low Under No Arbitrage. Dartmouth College, Working Paper (April 19).

_____. 2009. Debit or Credit? *Journal of Banking and Finance* (February).

Zywicki, Todd J. 2000. The Economics of Credit Cards. *Chapman Law Review* (Spring).

Index